# Constructing an Eco-Balanced Copyright Regime for the Video Game Industry in China

Zhaoxia Deng

# Constructing an Eco-Balanced Copyright Regime for the Video Game Industry in China

Springer

Zhaoxia Deng
Guangdong University of Foreign Studies
Guangzhou, Guangdong, China

ISBN 978-981-96-6055-1 ISBN 978-981-96-6056-8 (eBook)
https://doi.org/10.1007/978-981-96-6056-8



This Springer imprint is published by the registered company Springer Nature Singapore Pte Ltd.
The registered company address is: 152 Beach Road, #21-01/04 Gateway East, Singapore 189721, Singapore

*Dedicated to my family*

# Foreword

In the rapidly evolving landscape of the digital entertainment industry, few sectors have experienced as much growth and transformation as the video game industry. With its blend of cutting-edge technology, creative storytelling, and interactive experiences, the booming of the video game industry has become a global phenomenon, captivating audiences worldwide and driving innovation across multiple platforms. China, with its vast market potential and burgeoning technological advancements, has emerged as a key player in this dynamic field, evidenced by the recent success of Black Myth: Wukong. However, with this rapid growth comes the critical challenge of balancing the protection of copyright with the promotion of creativity, innovation, and consumer engagement.

This challenge is at the heart of the book you are about to read, "*Constructing an Eco-Balanced Copyright Regime for the Video Game Industry in China*." As someone who has long been involved in the study and practice of intellectual property law, I am deeply aware of the complexities and nuances that arise when attempting to create a legal framework that is both robust and flexible. The video game industry, with its unique characteristics and rapidly changing dynamics, presents a particularly intricate puzzle for policymakers, legal scholars, and industry stakeholders.

The concept of an "eco-balanced" copyright regime is a novel and timely one. It recognizes that the protection of copyright is essential for fostering creativity and innovation, but it also acknowledges that an overly restrictive approach can stifle the very innovation it seeks to protect. Instead, an eco-balanced approach seeks to create a harmonious ecosystem where the rights of creators are respected, while also allowing for the free flow of ideas, the adaptation and modification of existing works, and the engagement of consumers in the creative process. This is particularly relevant in the context of the video game industry, where players often contribute significantly to the evolution and expansion of game worlds through modifications, fan creations, and live streaming.

The author of this book has undertaken a monumental task in exploring the legal and practical challenges of constructing such a regime in China. Through a detailed examination of the current state of copyright law, the unique attributes of video games, and the emerging issues related to game adaptations, game modding, live game streaming, and gaming addiction, the author provides a comprehensive and insightful analysis of the path forward. The book is not just a theoretical treatise; it is a practical guide for policymakers, industry leaders, and legal practitioners who are grappling with these complex issues on a daily basis.

What sets this book apart is its forward-looking vision. It does not simply critique the existing system; it offers concrete recommendations for how China can build a more sustainable and inclusive copyright regime. By advocating for a balanced approach that recognizes the rights of all stakeholders—developers, publishers, players, and society at large—the author presents a compelling case for a future where creativity and innovation can thrive without sacrificing the protection of intellectual property.

As you read through the chapters of this book, I encourage you to consider the broader implications of the arguments presented. The challenges faced by the video game industry in China are not unique; they are reflective of the broader issues confronting the global digital entertainment sector. The solutions proposed here offer valuable insights for anyone interested in the future of intellectual property law in the digital age.

In conclusion, I would like to commend the author for her dedication and expertise in tackling this complex and important topic. This book is a significant contribution to the field of intellectual property law and a must-read for anyone interested in the future of the video game industry. I am confident that this book will inspire further discussion, research, and action, ultimately leading to a more balanced and sustainable future not only for the video game industry but also for the academic discourse in this field.

Hong Kong, China
February, 2025

Yahong Li

# Preface

In the rapidly evolving digital age, the video game industry has emerged as one of the most dynamic and influential sectors of the global entertainment market. Its growth has been nothing short of meteoric, driven by technological advancements, increasing consumer demand, and the creative ingenuity of developers. However, with this rapid expansion comes the critical challenge of balancing innovation, commercial interests, and the protection of copyright within an ecological framework that ensures sustainability and fairness.

The idea for this book, "*Constructing an Eco-Balanced Copyright Regime for the Video Game Industry in China*," was born out of a recognition of the pressing need for a comprehensive and nuanced approach to copyright law in this specific context. As someone deeply immersed in the study of intellectual property and the intricacies of the video game industry, I have observed firsthand the complexities and contradictions that arise when trying to protect creative works while also fostering an environment that encourages innovation and competition.

This book aims to be a bridge between theory and practice, offering both a detailed analysis of the current state of copyright law in China as it pertains to video games and a forward-looking vision for how this legal framework can be adapted to meet the unique challenges of the digital age. It is my hope that by exploring the intersections of law, technology, and culture, we can develop a more ecologically balanced approach that benefits all stakeholders—developers, publishers, players, and society at large.

Chapter 1 sets the stage by examining the concept of copyright eco-balance within the video game industry. It explores the unique challenges posed by the digital nature of video games, including issues related to game adaptation infringement, game Mods, live game streaming, and the complex interplay between addictive potential of video games, creativity and commercial interests. This chapter also provides an overview of the copyright incentive mechanism and its application to the video game industry.

Chapter 2 delves into the legal attributes of video games, questioning whether they should be assessed as a single entity or broken down into their composite elements. This exploration is crucial for understanding how copyright law can effectively protect the diverse components of video games, from their code and graphics to their narrative and gameplay mechanics.

Chapter 3 focuses on the issue of copyright infringement in game adaptations. It proposes a more balanced approach that recognizes the rights of original creators while also allowing for creative reinterpretations and adaptations that can drive innovation within the industry. This chapter examines case studies and legal precedents to illustrate the complexities and potential solutions.

Chapter 4 shifts the focus to the players, exploring their contributions to the video game ecosystem through modifications and customizations. It reexamines the legal framework to determine how players' rights to their modified games can be better recognized and protected, fostering a more inclusive and participatory culture.

Live game streaming has become a significant part of the video game industry, raising new copyright issues. Chapter 5 discusses the potential of statutory licensing as a means to balance the interests of game developers and streamers. It examines the benefits and challenges of legalizing live game streaming through a more structured and regulated approach.

Chapter 6 presents a comprehensive regulatory framework aimed at balancing creative expression and societal well-being. It examines the interplay between copyright protection and administrative content censorship in China, and explores how China can build a robust copyright regime that not only protects intellectual property but also promotes innovation, cultural diversity, and social harmony. This chapter offers practical recommendations for policymakers, industry stakeholders, and legal practitioners.

In writing this book, I have been fortunate to engage with a wide range of experts, including legal scholars, industry professionals, game developers, and game players. Their insights and experiences have been invaluable in shaping the arguments and solutions presented here. I hope that this book will serve not only as a resource for scholars and practitioners in the field of intellectual property law but also as a catalyst for further discussion and action. The future of the video game industry in China, and indeed globally, depends on our ability to create a legal environment that is both robust and flexible, capable of adapting to the ever-changing landscape of digital entertainment. It is my sincere wish that this work will contribute to that ongoing dialogue and help pave the way for a more sustainable and equitable future for all.

Guangzhou, China

Zhaoxia Deng

# Acknowledgements

This book was revised from my Ph.D. thesis of the University of Hong Kong. In the journey of writing this book, I have been fortunate to receive invaluable support, guidance, and encouragement from numerous individuals and institutions. I would like to take this opportunity to express my sincere thanks to each of them.

First and foremost, I would like to give my deepest and heartfelt gratitude to my academic supervisors, Prof. Yahong Li and Prof. Shahla Ali of the University of Hong Kong, whose unwavering support, insightful advice, and critical feedback have been instrumental in shaping the ideas and arguments presented in this book. Their dedication to academic excellence has inspired me to strive for the highest standards in my research and writing.

I would also like to express my deep appreciation to my Thesis Examining Committee, Prof. Jyh-An Lee of the Chinese University of Hong Kong, Prof. Marcelo Thompson, Prof. Calvin Ho and Prof. Albert Chen of the University of Hong Kong for their thought-provoking questions and constructive and insightful comments, which helped me more deeply ponder legal issues and better refine my book.

My gratitude is also extended to the University of Hong Kong, the institution providing me with rich learning resources, generous scholarships and conference grants. I would also like to acknowledge the support and professional assistance of the administrative staff at the Faculty of Law. Moreover, I am also deeply indebted to the faculty and staff at the School of Law of the UCLA, where I have had the privilege of conducting much of the research for this book. Their expertise, resources, and collaborative spirit have been invaluable throughout this process and enable me to bring this project to fruition.

Taking this opportunity, I would like to show my special gratitude to Prof. Peng Wang from the Faculty of Social Science of the University of Hong Kong, who provided enlightening comments and suggestions on the empirical part of my book and helped my research project to be more feasible and reliable. Special thanks also go to the many industry professionals, legal experts, and game developers who generously shared their time and knowledge with me. Their firsthand experiences and perspectives have enriched the content of this book and provided a crucial grounding in the realities of the video game industry. I would also like to extend my appreciation to the school principals and teachers who supported my empirical study and helped distributed copies of the self-administered questionnaire, and those participants who spent time to accept my interviews.

Finally, I would like to take this opportunity to express my heartfelt thanks to my family and friends for their tremendous understanding, unwavering support and companionship. Without their selfless love and endless support in the past few years, it would be impossible for me to reach the destination of this journey. Taking this opportunity, I would also like to thank the editorial team at Springer for their professionalism, patience, and dedication. Their expertise in publishing has been invaluable in bringing this book to life.

This book is the result of a collective effort, and I am truly grateful to everyone who has contributed to its creation. I hope that this work will not only advance the discourse on copyright law in the video game industry but also inspire further research and collaboration in this exciting and dynamic field.

# Contents

# About the Author

**Dr. Zhaoxia Deng** is an Assistant Professor of the School of English for International Business, Guangdong University of Foreign Studies. She holds an LLM from the National University of Singapore and a Ph.D. from the University of Hong Kong. From September 2019, she has been accepted as a visiting scholar at the School of Law, UCLA, for one year. Her research interests mainly focus on international economic law, intellectual property law, and data privacy. Dr. Deng was awarded as the Outstanding Young Talents in Foreign related Rule of Law of Guangdong Special Support Plan, and she successfully received two ministerial level projects and participated in one National Social Science Fund Project. Her works appear in academic journals such as CLSR, JKE, GNLULR, JCIL, etc. She received the First Prize in the Competition for Early Career Scholar of the ATRIP 38th Annual Congress, the ISSN International Best Researcher Award 2023, the Outstanding Research Achievement Award of GDUFS, the First Prize for Excellent Undergraduate Teaching of GDUFS, and the Title of Excellent Undergraduate Supervisor. She is now an associate researcher of the South China Institute for International Intellectual Property, a member of the Creative Commons Hong Kong and a member of the International Association for the Advancement of Teaching and Research in Intellectual Property. She also serves as the editorial board or reviewer for some international journals.
e-mail: Angelina_dzx@163.com

# Abbreviations

| | |
|---|---|
| AO | Adults Only |
| BJTAP | Beijing Treaty on Audiovisual Performances |
| CC | Creative Commons |
| CEO | Chief Executive Officer |
| CERO | Computer Entertainment Rating Organization |
| CFAA | Computer Fraud and Abuse Act |
| CPC | The Communist Party of China |
| DMCA | Digital Millennium Copyright Act |
| DMP | Data Management Plan |
| DRM | Digital Rights Management |
| EOCS | Ethics Organization of Computer Software |
| ESRB | Entertainment Software Rating Board |
| EU | European Union |
| EULA | End User License Agreement |
| GRAC | Game Rating and Administration Committee |
| HKU | The University of Hong Kong |
| HREC | Human Research Ethics Committee |
| IARC | International Age Rating Coalition |
| ICD | International Classification of Diseases |
| IP | Intellectual Property |
| ISP | Internet Service Provider |
| JCRC | Japan Contents Review Center |
| JuSchG | German Youth Protection Act |
| KERI | Korea Economic Research Institute |
| KeSPA | Korean e-Sports Association |
| MC | Ministry of Culture |
| MCT | Ministry of Culture and Tourism |
| MPAA | Motion Picture Association of America |
| NVs | Network Videos |
| OECD | Organization for Economic Cooperation and Development |
| PC | Personal Computer |

| | |
|---|---|
| PCC | Player Contributed Content |
| PDCPCCC | Publicity Department of the CPC Central Committee |
| PEGI | Pan European Game Information |
| PRC | People's Republic of China |
| RPG | Role-Playing Game |
| SAPPRFT | State Administration of Press, Publication, Radio, Film and Television |
| SKSE | Skyrim Script Extender |
| ST | Skyrim Together |
| TOS | Terms of Service |
| TPM | Technical Protection Measure |
| TRIPS Agreement | Agreement on Trade-Related Aspects of Intellectual Property Rights |
| UCC | User Created Content |
| UGC | User Generated Content |
| UI | User Interface |
| UK | United Kingdom |
| US | United States |
| USK | Entertainment Software Self-Regulation |
| VG | Video Game |
| WCT | WIPO Copyright Treaty |
| WHO | World Health Organization |
| WIPO | World Intellectual Property Organization |
| WPPT | WIPO Performances and Phonograms Treaty |
| WTO | World Trade Organization |

# List of Figures

# List of Tables

# Chapter 1
# Introduction

## 1.1 Research Background

Historically, copyright law has played an important role in the development of copyright industries, and the video game (VG) industry is no exception. According to Kalvi (2005), copyright law provides the legal framework for market transactions involving the results of creative work and copyright protection forms the basis for copyright industries, because most of the economic activities in copyright industries are closely related to the use of authors' rights, and the conditions under which these rights can be exploited are prescribed by copyright law. The *WIPO Guide on Surveying the Economic Contribution of the Copyright Industries* (hereinafter referred to as "*WIPO Guide*") (2015) defined copyright industries as industries that "function under the protection of copyright and related rights." They are more or less the same as "cultural industries" or "creative industries" in which copyright plays an identifiable role. The *WIPO Guide* provided a figure illustrating the overlaps between core copyright, cultural and creative industries (Fig. 1.1).[1] Core copyright industries are "industries which are wholly engaged in the creation, production and manufacture, performance, broadcasting, communication and exhibition, or distribution and sale of works and other protected subject matter." The motion picture industry, the visual and graphic arts industry, and the computer game or VG industry are examples of core copyright industries.

Indisputably, VGs form the heart of a vital economic industry that relies on the creativity and innovation of game designers and companies to develop a consistently fresh supply of new games. Since the first VG, a tennis-themed game, was released in the 1970s (Hemnes, 1982), VGs have become one of the fastest growing and most lucrative entertainment industries in the world (Buckman, 2005). According to the market intelligence provider SuperData, "the COVID-19 pandemic reshaped the VG

[1] The notion of "industries" in these mapping exercises refers to clusters of activities which can be identified and are statistically measurable, as well as activities which have a certain scale and structure.

 
Z. Deng, *Constructing an Eco-Balanced Copyright Regime for the Video Game Industry in China*, https://doi.org/10.1007/978-981-96-6056-8_1

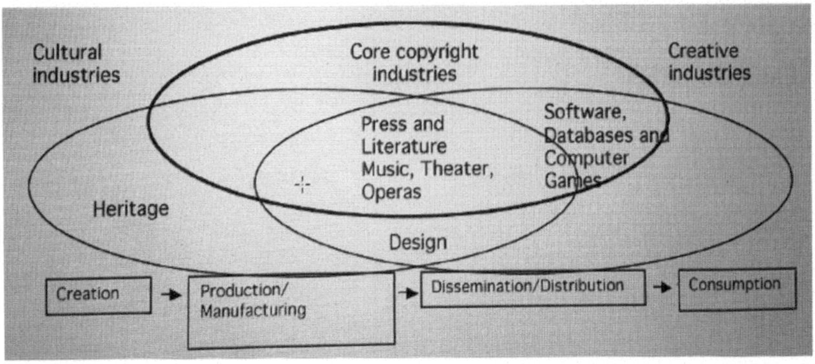


**Fig. 1.1** Venn diagram of the core copyright (WIPO), cultural (UNESCO 2009) and creative (DCMS 2011) industries[2]

market in 2020."[3] Specifically, "the game industry grew by 12% to $139.9 billion in 2020 from $120.1 billion in 2019." This massive growth occurred as people turned to games to combat boredom and to stay in touch with friends and family or to meet new people due to the unavailability of other forms of and venues for entertainment and socializing, such as professional sports and movie theaters. SuperData's report also revealed that during lockdown in 2020, people preferred to use mobile devices rather than PCs or consoles for video gaming. Accordingly, mobile earnings remained steady (10% growth) in 2020, continuing to generate the vast majority (58%) of the total income of the games market.[4]

VGs have quickly evolved in both hardware and software technology formats since their relatively recent introduction. Initially perceived as merely a leisure pastime, VGs today are an amalgam of traditional art forms, including music, narrative, sculpture, painting and storytelling. Unlike many other creative works, however, VGs fuse cutting-edge technology with imaginative artistic expression. The computer code underlying a game transforms ideas into a rich expression of visual art that comes alive on a range of devices: consoles, computers, tablets and smartphones. The imagined worlds they create offer richly textured, emotional and social experiences that cross the boundary from mere entertainment into culture and art. VGs are therefore increasingly recognized as the "ninth art," an artistic medium in their own right (Jewell, 2012). In 2011, the US Supreme Court put VGs on a par with other traditional artistic media, stating, "like the protected books, plays and movies that preceded them, VGs communicate ideas—and even social messages—through many familiar literary devices (such as characters, dialogue, plot and music) and

[2] See *WIPO Guide*, p. 44.

[3] Founded by veteran games industry researchers, SuperData is the world's leading provider of market intelligence, who offers quantitative and qualitative insights on free-to-play games, digital console, mobile, PC, streaming media, eSports, and virtual reality. See https://www.superdataresearch.com/reports/p/2020-year-in-review last visited December 30, 2024.

[4] Ibid.

through features distinctive to the medium (such as the player's interaction with the virtual world)" (Jewell, 2012). Copyright law influences the bases and conditions of the economic activities of the VG industry. It protects the economic value of VGs by ensuring that only the creator of a work has the right to duplicate, sell or produce related products from the game elements. Others cannot do so without the permission of the copyright owner. Without copyright, there is little incentive for game developers to create new games; "they naturally would be hesitant to create works that others could copy willy-nilly without any compensation" (Casillas, 2013). Thus, copyright law incentivizes the creation of VGs by helping to "overcome the free-rider problem with public goods" (Mcjohn, 2006). Due to its ease of use, power and versatility, copyright is the best tool to protect game property (Greenspan et al., 2014).

Nevertheless, "where there is profit, there is strife" (Yang, 2017). The booming VGs market has triggered an increasing number of lawsuits in recent years. Despite game developers' hope that the courts will protect their market penetration, VGs are in many ways unsuited to traditional forms of legal protection, particularly protection against copyright infringement (Nelson, 1996). There are two reasons for this. One is the multimedia nature of VGs, which makes their legal attribute difficult to be defined, either as a whole or as separate elements. The other is their interactivity, which creates a diverse group of stakeholders, such as game developers, players, live streaming platforms and game anchors. Balancing the rights of these parties is challenging. Besides, technological evolution has permitted VGs to be designed in more diversified forms, thereby expanding their market. This phenomenon has made copyright issues surrounding VGs more complex. Further complicating matters, compared with traditional forms of media, are that VGs display much stronger negative externalities. Although VGs can promote cognition, improve memory and increase capacity in relation to physical activity and education (Merino Campos & Del Castillo Fernández, 2016), they can also lead to the addiction, aggression or poorer school performance in minors (Jougleux, 2012), and these problems have increased as mobile games have flourished. On June 18, 2018, the World Health Organization (WHO) added "gaming disorder" to the International Classification of Diseases (ICD) (Scutti, 2018). Many parents and educators oppose the use of VGs, characterizing them as a great scourge. In such cases, whether copyright law should still extend its protection to VGs and how strong the protection should be are still unclear.

As Mezey (2001) stated, "the law is a social and cultural creation." Patry (2012) further noted that "law must be consistent with prevailing markets and technologies because technologies play a large role in creating consumer demand, and markets satisfy that demand. Although laws cannot create consumer demand, they can greatly interfere with the ability of market actors to satisfy that demand." This is especially true of copyright law. Changes in technological tools and the social norms that develop around copyrighted works make optimal copyright policy design a moving target. That is, copyright policy should always strive to achieve a normative equilibrium (Gervais, 2017). However, current copyright law is a "one-size-fits-all" regime—it provides a single set of rights and exceptions for rights holders, and the term of protection is typically the same for all works. This poses great challenges to the development of the VG industry. The lag in copyright legislation as pertaining to the VG industry has the potential to dampen the innovation and investment in game enterprises or to impede the public's passion for gaming and re-creation; either of these outcomes would hinder the sustainable development of this industry. Furthermore, the negative externalities of VGs (e.g., gaming addiction) may trigger prohibition policies that would be detrimental to this copyright industry, as "without consumer demand for your intellectual work, owning a copyright is meaningless" (Patry, 2012). As the foundational goal of copyright law has shifted from "incentivizing creation" to "incentivizing industrial development and technical innovation" (Kong, 2015), clarifying the copyright protection policy for VGs and the intensity of such protection is important for the sustainable development of this industry.

## 1.2 Brief Literature Review

Playing VGs has been a major leisure activity globally since the late of twentieth century (Greenspan et al., 2021), and the topic of digital gaming has consequently become the focus of legal academic interest. In the early twentieth century, it was a black letter law that "copyright does not protect games" (Affiliated Enterprises, Inc. v. Gruber, 1936; Chamberlin v. Uris Sales Corp., 1944). However, this principle of law was soon shown to be primarily based on board games and inapplicable to VGs (Data Cash Sys., Inc. v. JS&A Group, Inc., 1980; Stern Elecs., Inc. v. Kaulman, 1982; Cf. Williams Elecs., Inc. v. Artic Int'l, 1982). Some scholars, such as Hales (2012), have argued for the extension of copyright protection to board games. Indeed, it is generally acknowledged that copyright law extends to the protection of VGs. For example, copyright safeguards the creative and artistic expression that goes into the software (the code), the artwork and the sound (including the music) of a game. However, advances in technology have dramatically changed the games themselves, spawning a wide range of new formats, stories, and genres. Hence, despite the focus on copyright protection for VGs over the last few decades and the consequent achievements in scholarly research, some gaps remain in this protection, as discussed below.

First, the legal attribute of VGs has not been clearly defined and the copyright protection model for VGs remains ineffective. Romas et al. (2013) and Stein (2015b) explored the legal nature of VGs and identified four copyright protection models for VGs around the world: the computer program model, the audiovisual or cinematographic work model, the distributive protection model and the multimedia work model. However, these scholars' discussions were largely descriptive, without in-depth theoretical analysis; thus, questions remain regarding copyright protection for VGs, such as the pros and cons of each model, whether it is necessary to classify VGs as a new type of works due to their unprecedented technological advancements, and how to design a more effective copyright protection model for VGs in the Chinese context.

Second, although the VG industry has developing for over four decades, laws governing it lag behind in many jurisdictions, particularly China. This problem is exacerbated by rapid technological evolution. A typical example of the inadequate protection of VG copyright is the phenomenon of the "game clone," or "game re-skinning." Current copyright laws provide only thin barriers to copying, permitting competitors to "clone" or "re-skin" the fundamental mechanics, design and often story elements of a game to release a competing product (Dean, 2016). This activity discourages innovation and stifles creativity to the detriment of the public by taking advantage of a loophole in the current copyright regime. Another example is the rise of live game streaming, which refers to the simultaneous transmission of the players' gameplay process to the public through live streaming platforms or other online medias, enabling the public to learn about the gameplay strategies and skills used by the players and the state of play in real time. As the audiovisual images of a game are a main part of the game developer's creation and also a major component of live game streaming, this raises the question of whether live game streaming without authorization constitutes copyright infringement. This has been hotly debated; some have considered it an infringement (Feng, 2017; Li, 2017; Zhu, 2017), while others have argued that the defenses of fair use, transformative use or freedom of speech apply (Joo, 2011; Jungar, 2016; Puddington, 2015; Wang, 2016; Xie, 2017). Several prominent cases brought in recent years have resulted in fragmentary reasoning on the part of the courts that lacks theoretical focus and sometimes consistency. The uncertainty of laws not only threatens to mislead consumers and deters new developers from designing original game content but also burdens IP judges with an increasing number of disputes in this area.

Third, modern VGs provide game players with more open creative space, allowing them to make choices beyond the set of elements available (e.g., by creating their own modifications to the software) and to reproduce and redistribute the altered game contents. This phenomenon has drawn some scholars' attention to the rights of gamers. However, scholarly discussion of the topic has tended to focus on the users' right regarding their generated content in a broader remixed context, rather than in the specific gameplay environment (Beausoleil, 2017; Li & Huang, 2019; Reuveni, 2007). Besides, the literature has tended to justify for the rights of gamers with respect to their generated content from the perspective of user contribution, relying solely on legal theory (Goltz et al., 2015; Kennedy, 2008; Meng & Xu, 2016; Rosen, 2005); almost no studies have examined the issue from an industry-based or social perspective or provided empirical evidence to support their arguments. Due to the rise of game modifications (Mods) and the symbiotic relationship between the game industry and players, a more systematic review of this issue is necessary.

Fourth, VGs display stronger negative externalities than do traditional artistic works. While the problematic use of VGs is a complex issue comprising many different contributing factors, psychiatric research on gaming addiction has shown that video gaming has considerable potential to cause addiction, which may cause serious harm to minors (King et al., 2010, 2011). Supported by the addition of "gaming disorder" to the ICD by the WHO (Scutti, 2018), opponents represented by parents and educators considered VGs as "poison," fighting against playing them. Many Chinese scholars have attempted to provide solutions; however, their views have more or less coincided, discussing the problem from the perspectives of the family and school (Lin et al., 2021; Sun, 2020; Zhang et al., 2020; Zhou, 2020). Although some studies have focused on the legal aspects, they have merely called for stronger governmental supervision and improvements to legislation in their concluding remarks, without providing specific and feasible countermeasures to the problem of gaming addiction (Chang, 2019; Gong, 2020; Kang, 2019). Nowadays gaming addiction issue has become a great threat to the sustainable development of the VG (or core copyright) industry. Because VGs have become an influential form of narrative art, one common proposal from the public—prohibiting game playing outright, would undermine the societal goal of copyright law to promote cultural innovation and render copyright ownership of VG creations meaningless. Thus, it is urgently necessary to achieve the equilibrium between protecting the copyright of VGs and protecting users, particularly minors. Failure to do so would render the sustainable development of this industry an empty talk.

Fifth, scholars have tended to constrain their research to their own legal systems or countries, ignoring the variety of legal systems and national policies or traditions, which is a bit narrow. For example, Grosheide et al. (2014) explored the IP protection of VGs in the EU, and Stein (2015a) investigated the authorship and moral rights of VGs in the UK. Although a few professionals have conducted comparative studies, they have focused on common law jurisdictions, without taking China into consideration. For example, Nelson (1996) studied differences in copyright protection for VGs between the US and the UK, and Stamatoudi (2002) took VGs merely as a "test case" to justify the copyright protection of multimedia products in the US and the EU. Scholars who have taken a global perspective have focused narrowly on one or a few aspects of VGs. An example is Andy Romas' examination of the legal status of VGs, which listed the relevant laws and regulations of each country reviewed (Romas et al., 2013). Sun Lei's monograph—the first book on IP protection for online games in China—described the status of the game industry and the legal nature of VGs in Japan, South Korea, the US and France in its first chapter. The rest of the monograph, however, addressed different kinds of IP disputes involving online games and offered some solutions from a Chinese IP judge's standpoint, without making further comparisons or providing feasible suggestions for advancing the copyright regime to adequately protect rights with respect to VGs in this country (Sun & Cao, 2017).

In summary, the copyright laws currently in place in China to safeguard and encourage innovation and creativity are lagging behind the development of the VG industry, failing to provide adequate solutions to emerging and unforeseen problems. Furthermore, research on the copyright protection of VGs has been highly fragmented and limited in focus, rendering it unable to comprehensively inform and facilitate policymaking. In this book, I attempt to fill the identified gaps in the literature by constructing an "eco-balanced" copyright regime for the VG industry from an interdisciplinary perspective.

## 1.3 Research Questions

Based on the literature review and research gaps identified, I address the central interlocking questions of whether the current copyright regime for VGs is sufficiently balanced to promote the sustainable development of this industry and, if not, how such a balance can be achieved.

To answer the central questions, I address the following issues.

1. What is the legal attribute of VGs and how can a better copyright protection model for this type of products be designed?
2. To what extent do game developers have the right to control the derivations[5] of their VGs? This question concerns game developers' right to control the exploitation of their original games, and it involves three sub-questions:
   A. What difficulties are faced in addressing game adaptation infringement under the current rules and how can a more balanced approach be achieved?
   B. To what extent is game modding permissible and how can a new scheme be created that is more balanced for the stakeholders involved?
   C. To what extent is live game streaming legal and how can an equilibrium between stakeholders be achieved?
3. To what extent can copyright law restrict the negative externalities of VGs and how to balance creative expression with societal well-being from administrative regulatory perspective?

## 1.4 Research Objectives

The main objectives of this research are to address the copyright issues surrounding VGs and to balance the interests of the various stakeholders (in both legal and social contexts) to promote the sustainable development of the VG industry for social good. *Report of the World Commission on Environment and Development* (1987) defined the "sustainable development" as "development that meets the needs of the present without compromising the ability of future generations to meet their own needs." It is an approach to development that protects society in the long term, taking into account both present and future imperatives. In this book, "sustainable development" refers to the steady economic development of the VG industry without causing severe harm to social welfare. This can be achieved only by harmonizing three core processes: incentivizing innovation, promoting access to information, and reducing the negative externalities of VGs. To fill the research gaps identified in the literature review, I propose an "eco-balanced" copyright regime for the VG industry in the Chinese context.

---

[5] "Derivations" here refer to all kinds of derivative or non-derivative works created based on the pre-existing video games.

An analogy can be drawn between copyright and the biological phenomenon of the ecosystem. The term "ecosystem" refers to "a biological community composed of interacting organisms and their physical environment," and in its extended use, to "a complex network or interconnected system resembling this."[6] Copyright law can be viewed as subsisting within an ecosystem comprising institutions and actors that are ordered through various techniques (legal, economic, political, social, etc.) to create and sustain creative acts. However, the current copyright system propounds very general principles, acknowledging few significant differences between, for example, copyright industries that produce books and those that produce movies or VGs. It pays little heed to the concrete realities of different copyright industries. As one-size-fits-all copyright laws may not achieve the desired goals in all cases, there is an urgent need for "effective lawmaking based on the actual business practices of and evidence about the relevant industries" (Patry, 2012). As Breyer (1970) observed, "the desirability of copyright protection varies from one type of work to another, and one should know the facts about each particular industry before weighing the costs and benefits associated with copyright protection." Therefore, to ensure the homeostasis of the VG "ecosystem" as a virtuous cycle and to design a more balanced and systematic copyright regime for VGs, the book considers both internal and external aspects of the ecosystem, and includes empirical observations in the analysis of this copyright industry to ensure that the proposed copyright reform is not developed in an "evidence-free-zone" (Boyle, 2008).

Diverging from the existing literature, this book addresses copyright issues surrounding VGs from a global perspective and provide corresponding recommendations for copyright reform in China. As high-dimensional works with a cross-cutting nature, VGs are in many ways significantly unsuited to traditional forms of copyright protection. Cultural and legislative differences between countries contribute to the diversity of copyright protection models for VGs. Though the topic of copyright protection for VGs has been studied in other countries, it is not until recent years with the increasing number of lawsuits in this area that it has aroused the attention of Chinese scholars. Thus, China can draw lessons from other jurisdictions in formulating a copyright policy tailored to its unique cultural and political characteristics. Through comparative and critical analysis, this book identifies loopholes in the current copyright regime for VGs and proposes some new schemes to help resolve the problems posed by technological innovation and the negative externalities of VGs to facilitate the construction of an "eco-balanced" copyright regime.

While efforts to seek a balanced level of protection are not new in the copyright field, which can be traced back at least as far as the original text of the Berne Convention in 1886, translating this high-level balancing act into a structured approach and deriving actual policy objectives, levers and decisions are difficult tasks. Reform, or the "constructing" suggested in this book, is based on the public interest. But, unlike a number of commentators, I do not believe that the public interest is always best served by eliminating or attempting to reduce copyright (Determann, 2006).

[6] See "Ecosystem" in Oxford English Dictionary https://en.oxforddictionaries.com/definition/ecosystem last visited March 30, 2021.

The public interest is best served neither by over-protection nor by under-protection. Rather, "the level, mode and type of enforceability of copyright must all be balanced to achieve something as close to systemic protection at equilibrium" (Gervais, 2017), or the so-called "ecological balance." Additionally, the objective of copyright law has long been interpreted as incentivizing creation by granting authors a series of exclusive rights while promoting access to information by creating certain exceptions to and placing certain limitations on these rights (Hua, 2013). Following this vein, the "public interest" factor of copyright policy has generally been equated with the considerations of freedom of information and freedom of expression. However, different from most academics who adopt the above approach, I put the ultimate aim of copyright law to promote cultural innovation and social welfare as the utmost important place.[7] Whether "encourage learning" is defined as the goal or the means of copyright policy, it is an overwhelming reality that culture, information, and knowledge are among the most frequently consumed goods that contribute to the welfare of modern societies, and copyright laws are regulations created by governments to further such societal goal. Under this approach, the public interest factor requires consideration of any aspect of copyrighted works that is detrimental to social welfare, such as the high addictive potential of VGs to cause serious harm to minors both physically and psychologically and distract users from learning. This book, by treating a particular negative externality of VGs (gaming addiction) as a public interest consideration, explores how copyright law interacts with administrative regulations to better fulfill its societal goals. The proposed regime would mitigate gaming addiction while also be conducive to promoting the sustainable development of VG industry.

Copyright industries and copyright law are interactional, such that "the impact of copyright industries on copyright law means enactment of copyright rules that favor these industries or the non-enactment of such rules that do not favor them, and copyright industries may have a potential interest in influencing copyright law in a direction beneficial for copyright industries" (Kalvi, 2005). Therefore, an optimal copyright policy for the sustainable development of the VG industry should maximize cultural innovation while minimizing the negative externalities of VGs.

## 1.5 Research Methodology

This research is based on doctrinal, interdisciplinary, comparative and empirical approaches. These four approaches are described in detail below.

---

[7] More discussion about the ultimate aim of copyright law is in the following chapter.

### 1.5.1 Normative Analysis Approach

Normative analysis approach is "a two-part process involving both locating the sources of the law and then interpreting and analyzing the text" (Hutchinson, 2017). To conduct the research, I first accessed scholarly works such as monographs, journal articles and case reports on copyright issues surrounding VGs, and then critically analyzed these texts to ascertain "which legal areas or policies are still unclear or proving in some way problematic to practitioners, government or the public, and what type of research or information might be required to highlight any inadequacies" (Hutchinson, 2017). After identifying potential issues, I used theoretical analysis to explore the legal framework and principles of the subject in a comprehensive and accurate manner. I also examined some precedents and cases in detail to determine how courts have applied statutory rules in judicial practice. In summary, I used normative analysis method throughout the project.

### 1.5.2 Interdisciplinary Approach

Interdisciplinary approach is "a mode of method by teams or individuals that integrates information, data, techniques, tools, perspectives, concepts, and/or theories from two or more disciplines or bodies of specialized knowledge to advance fundamental understanding or to solve problems whose solutions are beyond the scope of a single discipline or area of research practice" (National Academy of Sciences, 2005). Research on constructing an eco-balanced copyright regime for VGs inevitably involves various areas of study, such as law, industry, economics, technology and policy. In view of this, I conducted extensive socio-legal research to examine the interplay between the development of the VG industry, copyright law, governmental policy, industrial policy and other social regulations, and to explore the inability of the current copyright system to attain its ultimate goal of promoting innovation and social welfare.

Furthermore, "carrying out research without assessing its economic implications and without incorporating the insights of economic theory is ultimately unsatisfactory" (Sanchez-Graells, 2017). This is especially true of research on copyright law, which is largely economic in nature (Chen, 2003). Economic analysis of law "examines the legal world from the standpoint of economic theory and, as a result of that examination, confirms, casts doubt upon, and often seeks reform of legal reality" (Calabresi, 2016). It can "offer valuable tools that help decision-makers reach a balance of interests that maximizes social welfare in the long run" (Sanchez-Graells, 2017). Thus, I combined value analysis and economic analysis of law to reveal the values manifested in copyright law regarding VG protection and highlight potential injustices arising from the current legal system. I also drew on the hypothesis of the "rational economic man" (Posner, 2003), and conducted transaction cost analysis and cost–benefit analysis (Posner, 2000) to propose a reform of copyright law that is "both effective in achieving its goals and efficient in doing so" (Sanchez-Graells, 2017).

### 1.5.3 Comparative Approach

As Bonazzi and Lipset (1997) put it, "to know only one country is to know no country." Comparative approach is "the study of the similarities and differences between the laws of two or more countries, or between two or more legal systems, with the aims to make a practical contribution to the local national system or to work out a common solution to a common problem" (Wilson, 2007). I conducted comparative analysis throughout the research. Specifically, I explored the copyright issues surrounding VGs from a global perspective and created a proposal for copyright reform in China. Hence some representative countries from both common law and civil law jurisdictions are selected for comparison during the research. Above all, although VGs have quickly became the most popular entertainment products in China, their copyright protection status of VGs has not developed accordingly. This feature, to some extents, allows China to be representative but also unique. Besides, research on the copyright protection of VGs in China has been highly fragmented and incapable of facilitating effective policymaking. Thus, the necessity for copyright reform in this country is axiomatic. In addition, the US, the EU, Japan and South Korea have a longer history of gameplay, and their legal systems in this regard are relatively mature. However, it should be noted that their legal systems are also distinct from each other, as their jurisdictions have unique cultures and customs. I compared the copyright systems in these countries and regions to assess their effectiveness and general applicability. I also considered the pioneering anti-gaming addiction measures taken in Japan and South Korea.

### 1.5.4 Empirical Approach

Copyright law has long been criticized on the grounds that it is based on rhetoric and faith rather than empirically sound evidence. To address this issue, I combined conventional legal methodologies such as archival research with empirical analysis. As observed by Bradney (2010), "quantitative and qualitative empirical research into law and legal processes provides not just more information about law, but information of a different character from that which can be obtained through other methods of research. It answers questions about law that cannot be answered in any other way." The knowledge obtained through the quantitative method was based on careful observation and measurement of the objective reality (Creswell, 2002), whereas the qualitative method involved field observations, open-ended interviews and analysis of public and private documents and audiovisual materials.

My empirical research had the following purposes:

1. to learn about game developers' and gamers' attitudes toward game Mods; and
2. to evaluate whether live game streaming constitutes transformative use of pre-existing games.

My application for ethical approval was approved by the Human Research Ethics Committee (HREC) on December 17, 2018 (Reference Number EA1810039). I submitted a data management plan (DMP) and dataset of research for long-term preservation in the HKU data repository.[8] The interview records, the questionnaire survey and their results were incorporated into this book as appendices.[9]

The methods I used were as follows.

1. In-depth Interviews:

There were primarily three categories of interviewees: game developers/designers, individual streamers, gamers who were also live game streaming viewers. I myself have created extensive local connections in the proposed research sites, and the existing connections helped me to identify and gain access to interviewees. There are no strict selection criteria for game developers/ designers, anyone who are willing to accept my interview can be selected. In order to make the interviewees more representative, the research tried to expand the interviewees' varieties and asked questions from both the defendants' and the viewers' perspectives. Therefore, some game developers/designers hosting their own streaming platforms and some individual streamers who didn't design VGs but live streaming VGs were selected. As for individual streamers and gamers/streaming viewers, they are all aged 20–30 because this age-range people are more familiar with VGs as well as live game streaming and their mental and cognitive abilities are relatively mature who can understand my research questions better. A snowballing approach, not a random sample but a defensible mode of selection, was used in this study. At last, five game developer/designers (of whom three had their own streaming platforms) and three individual streamers were selected to obtain their views on the expressive purposes of creating and using original game images, and five gamers who were familiar with playing games as well as watching live game streaming were interviewed to examine their views on the purposes of watching live game streaming and the function of the original game images. Moreover, additional questions were directed to the game developers/designers selected to identify their reasons for supporting or objecting to game Mods, and to the gamers selected to discover their main motivations for modding and their attitudes toward various kinds of game Mods. As I was visiting the University of California, Los Angeles, these interviews were conducted online via Wechat. As these interviewees are all Chinese, we used Chinese as our communication language. Each interview lasted from 30 min to 1 h.

2. Self-Administered Questionnaire:

I distributed copies of a self-administered questionnaire to game players aged 12–30 to explore the possible impact of watching live game streaming on the VG

[8] See Dataset Link https://figshare.com/s/3f182c49f59402fe7f5d.

[9] See Appendices 1 ~ 14.

market. To make the sample more representative and avoid error caused by too narrow a geographical or age range, the self-administered questionnaire was completed both offline and online. Approximately 950 hard copies of the questionnaire were distributed to teenagers aged 12–17 at primary schools, junior high schools and senior high schools in developed cities and rural areas. I obtained consent from the schools' principals and asked the subjects' teachers to distribute copies of the questionnaire to their students prior to field trips. Additionally, I distributed the questionnaire online to adult players, and at last collected 240 completed responses. Therefore, the total sample size was 1190. To protect the data better and facilitate data analysis, I imported the hard-copy questionnaire data into wjx.cn.[10] Ultimately, 1177 effective questionnaire responses were analyzed by using SPSS software. The possible impact of watching live game streaming on the VG market was explored from the perspective of the correlation between the behavior (purchasing, recommending, cognition, etc.) of the respondents and their act of watching live game streaming. The questionnaire also asked the respondents to evaluate the possibility of watching live game streaming as a substitute for playing VGs.

Apart from the above empirical methods, I also collected empirical data on the life cycle of VGs and cases related to game adaptation in China. Specifically, to learn about litigation related to game adaptation in China, I used the database LawinfoChina (also known as "Beida Fabao") as the instrument,[11] inputting "video game" and "adaptation right" as keywords to identify relevant cases. I then analyzed the cases within the time range selected for the study. Ultimately, I selected 309 cases related to game adaptation from 2011 to 2018 for further analysis. But these data were supplementary; their main purpose was to provide an overview of game adaptation litigation in China.

## References

Beausoleil, L. E. (2017). *Copyright Issues and Implications of Emerging Virtual Reality Technologies*. Boston College Intellectual Property and Technology forum. Available at: http://bciptf.org/2017/12/copyright-issues-and-implications-of-emerging-virtual-reality-technologies/. Accessed 7 July 2018.

Bonazzi, T., & Lipset, S. M. (1997). American Exceptionalism: A Double-Edged Sword. *The Journal of American History, 83*, 1365–1366.

Boyle, J. (2008). *The Public Domain* (Chapter 9). Yale University Press.

Bradney, A. (2010). The Place of Empirical Legal Research in the Law School Curriculum. In P. Cane & H. Kritzer (Eds.), *The Oxford Handbook of Empirical Legal Research* (p. 1033). Oxford University Press.

---

[10] Wenjuanxing [问卷星] is one of the most professional and popular questionnaire survey platform in China.

[11] LawinfoChina, also known as "Beida Fabao", was founded by the Department of Law of the Peking University in 1985. This database Includes Chinese laws, regulations and cases in Chinese (chinalawinfo.com) and in English/Chinese (lawinfochina.com), which is regarded as the most mature, professional and advanced omnibearing retrieval system of legal information in China.

Breyer, S. (1970). The Uneasy Case for Copyright: A Study of Copyright in Books, Photocopies, and Computer Programs. *Harvard Law Review, 84*, 281–351.

Buckman, D. F. (2005). Intellectual Property Rights in Video, Electronic, and Computer Games. *American Law Reports Fed. 2d, 7*, 269.

Calabresi, G. (2016). *The Future of Law and Economics: Essays in Reform and Recollection* (p. 2). Yale University Press.

Casillas, B. (2013). Attack of the Clones: Copyright Protection for Video Game Developers. *Loyola of Los Angeles Entertainment Law Review, 33*, 137.

Chang, Y. [苌雅洁]. (2019). Study on the Legal Protection Mechanism to Prevent Minors from Indulging in Online Games [防范未成年人沉迷网络游戏的法律保障机制研究]. *Changjiang Forum [长江论坛]*, 5.

Chen, C, [陈昌柏]. (2003). *Intellectual Property Economics [知识产权经济学]* (p. 191). Peking University Press [北京大学出版社].

Creswell, J. (2002). *Research Design: Qualitative, Quantitative, and Mixed Methods Approaches* (pp. 7, 17, 19). Sage.

Dean, D. S. (2016). Hitting Reset: Devising a New Video Game Copyright Regime. *University of Pennsylvania Law Review, 164*, 1239.

Determann, L. (2006). Dangerous Liaisons-Software Combinations as Derivative Works? Distribution, Installation, and Execution of Linked Programs Under Copyright Law, Commercial Licenses, and the Gpl. *Berkeley Technology Law Journal, 21*, 1421–1438.

Feng, X. [冯晓青]. (2017). Study on the Legal Attribute of Online Game Live Streaming Images and the Related Copyright Issues [网络游戏直播画面的作品属性及其相关著作权问题研究]. *Intellectual Property [知识产权]*, 1.

Gervais, D. J. (2017). *(Re)Structuring Copyright: A Comprehensive Path to International Copyright Reform* (pp. 2, 4). Edward Elgar.

Goltz, N., Franks, J., & Goltz, S. (2015). *Changing the Video Game: Innovation, User Satisfaction and Copyrights in Network Market Competition*. Available at: https://doi.org/10.2139/ssrn.2587507. Accessed 21 April 2019.

Gong, Y. [龚玉花]. (2020). Study on the Legal Mechanism of Correcting Minors' Gaming Addiction [未成年人网络游戏沉迷矫正法律机制浅析]. *Children's Study [少年儿童研究]*, 8.

Greenspan, D., Boyd, S. G., & Purewal, J. (2021). Video Games and IP: A Global Perspective. *WIPO*. Available at: http://www.wipo.int/wipo_magazine/en/2014/02/article_0002.html. Accessed 30 March 2021.

Greenspan, D., Boyd, S. G., Purewal, J., & Datum, M. (2014). *Mastering the Game: Business and Legal Issues for Video Game Developers* (p. 73). WIPO.

Grosheide, F. W., Roerdink, H., & Thomas, K. (2014). Intellectual Property Protection for Video Games: A View from the European Union. *Journal of International Commercial Law and Technology, 9*.

Hales, K. M. (2012). A Trivial Pursuit: Scrabbling for a Board Game Copyright Rationale. *Seton Hall Journal of Sports and Entertainment Law, 22*, 241.

Hemnes, T. M. S. (1982). The Adaptation of Copyright Law to Video Games. *University of Pennsylvania Law Review, 131*, 171.

Hua, J. (2013). *Toward A More Balanced Approach: Rethinking and Readjusting Copyright Systems in the Digital Network Era*. PhD thesis (p. 1). The University of Hong Kong.

Hutchinson, T. (2017). Doctrinal Research: Researching the Jury. In D. Watkins & M. Burton (Eds.), *Research Methods in Law* (2nd ed., pp. 10, 14, 18, 31). Taylor & Francis.

Jewell, C. (2012). Video Games: 21st Century Art. *WIPO Magazine*. Available at: http://www.wipo.int/wipo_magazine/en/2012/04/article_0003.html. Accessed 30 March 2021.

Joo, J. (2011). Public Video Gaming as Copyright Infringement. *American Intellectual Property Law Association Quarterly Journal*, 39.

Jougleux, P. (2012). *The Video Games and the Law*. Thessaloniki conference paper.

Jungar, E. (2016). Streaming Video Games: Copyright Infringement or Protected Speech. *Press Start, 3*(2), 23.

Kalvi, A. (2005). The Impact of Copyright Industries on Copyright Law. *Juridica International, X*, 97, 104.

Kang, Y. [康亚通]. (2019). The Governance of Teenagers' Internet Addiction [青少年网络沉迷问题的治理]. *Education and Protection [教育和保护]*, 5.

Kennedy, R. (2008). Virtual Rights: Property in Online Game Objects and Characters. *Information & Communications Technology Law, 17*, 95–106.

King, D. L., Delfabbro, P. H., & Griffiths, M. D. (2010). Video Game Structural Characteristics: A New Psychological Taxonomy. *International Journal of Mental Health and Addiction, 8*(1), 90–106.

King, D. L., Delfabbro, P. H., & Griffiths, M. D. (2011). The Role of Structural Characteristics in Problematic Video Game Play: An Empirical Study. *International Journal of Mental Health and Addiction, 9*(3), 320–333.

Kong, X. [孔祥俊]. (2015). *Judicial Philosophy and Legal Methods in Network Copyright Protection [网络著作权保护法律理念与裁判方法]* (p. 3). China Legal Publishing House [中国法制出版社].

Li, Y. [李扬]. (2017). Copyright Issues Surrounding Live Streaming of Online Games [网络游戏直播中的著作权问题]. *Intellectual Property [知识产权]*, 1.

Li, Y., & Huang, W. (2019). Taking Users' Rights Seriously: Proposed UGC Solutions for Spurring Creativity in the Internet Age. *Queen Mary Journal of Intellectual Property, 9*(1), 61.

Lin, Y. [林悦], Liu, Q. [刘勤学], et al. (2021). Study on the Relationship between Parental Neglection and Adolescents' Gaming Addiction: The Mediating Role of Hope and the Moderating Role of Gender [父母忽视与青少年网络游戏成瘾的关系: 希望的中介作用和性别的调节作用]. *Psychological Development and Education [心理发展与教育], 37*(01).

Mcjohn, S. M. (2006). *Copyright: Examples and Explanations* (p. 3). Aspen Publishers.

Meng, X., & Xu, K. [孟祥娟&徐坤宇]. (2016). Analysis of Copyright Protection and Authorization of Game MOD [游戏MOD著作权保护与授权探析]. *Intellectual Property [知识产权]*, 10.

Merino Campos, C., & Del Castillo Fernández, H. (2016). The Benefits of Active Video Games for Educational and Physical Activity Approaches: A Systematic Review. *Journal of New Approaches in Educational Research, 5*(2), 115–122.

Mezey, N. (2001). Law as Culture. *The Yale Journal of Law & the Humanities, 13*, 35–67.

National Academy of Sciences, National Academy of Engineering & Institute of Medicine of the National Academies. (2005). *Facilitating Interdisciplinary Research* (p. 26). The National Academies Press.

Nelson, G. J. (1996). The Sufficiency of Copyright Protection in the Video Electronic Entertainment Industry: Comparing the United States with the European Union. *Law & Policy in International Business, 27*, 805–824.

Patry, W. (2012). *How to Fix Copyright* (pp. 2, 74). Oxford University Press.

Posner, R. A. (2000). Cost-Benefit Analysis: Definition, Justification and Comment on Conference Papers. *Journal of Legal Studies, 29*, 1153.

Posner, R. A. (2003). *Economic Analysis of Law* (6th ed., pp 9–18). Aspen Publishers.

Puddington, J. (2015). Fair Play: Economic Justifications for Applying Fair Use to the Online Streaming of Video games. *Boston University Journal of Science & Technology Law, 21*.

Report of the World Commission on Environment and Development: Our Common Future. (1987). Available at: https://sustainabledevelopment.un.org/content/documents/5987our-common-future.pdf. Accessed 12 December 2024.

Reuveni, E. (2007). On Virtual Worlds: Copyright and Contract Law at the Dawn of the Virtual Age. *Indiana Law Journal, 82*, 261.

Romas, A., et al. (2013). The Legal Status of Video Games: Comparative Analysis in National Approaches. *WIPO*.

Rosen, Z. (2005). Mod, Man, and Law: A Reexamination of the Law of Computer Game Modifications. *Chi-Kent Journal of Intellectual Property, 4*, 196–215.

Sanchez-Graells, A. (2017). Economic Analysis of Law or Economically Informed Legal Research. In D. Watkins & M. Burton (Eds.), *Research Methods in Law* (2nd ed., pp. 172, 173, 176). Taylor & Francis.

Scutti, S. (2018). WHO Classifies "Gaming Disorder" as Mental Health Condition. CNN News. Available at: https://edition.cnn.com/2018/06/18/health/video-game-disorder-who/index.html. Accessed 30 March 2021.

Stamatoudi, I. A. (2002). *Copyright and Multimedia Products: A Comparative Analysis.* Cambridge University Press.

Stein, J. S. (2015a). Authorship and Moral Rights in Video Games. *Press Start, 2.*

Stein, J. S. (2015b). The Legal Nature of Video Games-Adapting Copyright Law to Multimedia. *Press Start, 2*, 43.

Sun, L., [孙磊] & Cao, L. [曹丽萍]. (2017). *Judicial Protection of Intellectual Property Rights of Online Games [网络游戏知识产权司法保护].* China Legal Publishing House [中国法制出版社].

Sun, Q. [孙秋梅]. (2020). Study on the Prevention of Gaming Addiction of Higher Vocational College Students by School Cooperation [学校联合构建预防高职大学生网络游戏成瘾屏障研究]. *Journal of Vocational College [职大学报]*, 3.

Wang, Q. [王迁]. (2016). Study on the Copyright Issues of Live Streaming of Video Game [电子游戏直播的著作权问题研究]. *Electronics Intellectual Property [电子知识产权]*, 2.

Wilson, G. (2007). Comparative Legal Scholarship. In M. McConville & W. H. Chui (Eds.), *Research Methods for Law* (p. 88). Edinburgh University Press.

*WIPO*. (2015). WIPO Guide on Surveying the Economic Contribution of the Copyright Industries, 30, 44, 45, 51, 53.

Xie, L. [谢琳]. (2017). Study on the Copyright Fair Use of Live Streaming of video Games [网络游戏直播的著作权合理使用研究]. *Intellectual Property [知识产权]*, 1.

Yang, Y. [杨延超]. (2017). *Copyright War [版权战争]* (p. 1). Intellectual Property Publishing House [知识产权出版社].

Zhang, Y. [张永欣], Zhang, H. [张惠雯], et al. (2020). Study on the Relationship Between Psychological Resistance, Parental Online Supervision and Junior High School Students' Gaming Addiction [心理阻抗、父母网络监管与初中生网络游戏成瘾的关系]. *China Journal of Clinical Psychology [中国临床心理学杂志], 28*(04).

Zhou, Y. [周瑛]. (2020). *Study on the Relationship Between Parentage Communication, School Belonging, Basic Psychological Needs and Adolescents' Gaming Addiction* [亲子沟通、学校归属感、基本心理需求与青少年网络游戏成瘾的关系]. Mphil These, Central China Normal University [中华中师范大学].

Zhu, J. [祝建军]. (2017). Study on the Copyright Issues Surrounding Live Streaming of Online Games [网络游戏直播的著作权问题研究]. *Intellectual Property [知识产权]*, 1.

## Cases

Affiliated Enterprises, Inc. v. Gruber, 86 F.2d 958 (1st Cir. 1936).

Cf. Williams Elecs., Inc. v. Artic Int'l, 685 F.2d 870, 872, 876–77 (3d Cir. 1982).

Chamberlin v. Uris Sales Corp., 56 F. Supp. 987 (S.D.N.Y. 1944), aff'd, 150 F.2d 512 (2d Cir. 1945).

Data Cash Sys., Inc. v. JS&A Group, Inc., 628 F.2d 1038 (7th Cir. 1980).

Stern Elecs., Inc. v. Kaulman, 669 F.2d 852, 855 (2d Cir. 1982).

# Chapter 2
# Copyright Eco-Balance in the Video Game Context and Practical Challenges

**Abstract** This chapter builds a theoretical foundation for the proposed eco-balanced approach to copyright protection for VGs. It first introduces basic information on VGs, such as their definition and classification. Next, it explains the purpose of describing copyright protection for VGs in the context of an "ecosystem" and examines interests balance theory and incentive theory in the VG context. The chapter then identifies the challenges posed by the current copyright regime for VGs: the ineffectiveness of the copyright protection models as applied to VGs, imprecise delimitation of copyright infringement in game adaptation, uncertainty regarding players' rights to their modified games, controversy regarding the legitimacy of live game streaming without authorization and the potentially addictive nature of VGs. Based on these challenges, the chapter emphasizes the need to construct an eco-balanced copyright regime for VGs to promote both economic efficiency and social welfare.

**Keywords** Copyright ecosystem · Balance of interests · Incentive theory · Ecological balance · Social welfare

## 2.1 VGs in a Nutshell

### *2.1.1 Definition of VGs*

Video games (VGs) have been defined in different ways depending on the jurisdiction. Generally speaking, a VG is defined as "an electronic or computerized game played by manipulating images on a video display or television screen" (European Commission, 2006). It is a subset of electronic games that notably utilizes "video display devices" to convey information and user feedback (Joo, 2011). From this angle, it can be seen that the broad definition of a VG covers both the simple electronic games which can be played in both the real world and the digital world, such as puzzle or table games, and the more complex games, such as Crossfire, which can only be played in the digital context. Nevertheless, it should be noted that this term has often been used synonymously with "electronic games," "digital games,"



Z. Deng, *Constructing an Eco-Balanced Copyright Regime for the Video Game Industry in China*, https://doi.org/10.1007/978-981-96-6056-8_2

"computer games," "entertainment software," and the broader category of "interactive media" (Herrera González, 2016). In China, VGs is commonly known as "online games," but as an up-concept, VGs essentially include both online games and console games.

During the past decade, VGs have evolved from their meek origins to become a more complex, realistic, indulgent fantasy world for gamers. Nowadays, VGs are no longer an expression of the author's creativity, but a playing field for the person controlling a character's actions (Turner, 2003). Based on the existing definitions of "game," "play," "interactivity," and "narrative," Esposito (2005) provided a short and simple definition of this kind of products, that "a VG is a game which we play thanks to an audiovisual apparatus and which can be based on a story." Unfortunately, this definition omitted the rules of games—a series of explicit or implied rules that provide some guidance or flexible challenges for players and affect their decision-making at each step.

As time has gone by, most scholars have realized the strong interactivity involved in gaming, and have emphasized the interactive component, noting that "a VG is the game which can read player inputs, and change its material substances as a result of the player's action according to some set rules" (Tavinor, 2008). The interactive feature was also stressed by Bergonse (2017), who defined a VG as "a mode of interaction between a player, a machine with an electronic visual display, and possibly other players, that is mediated by a meaningful fictional context, and sustained by an emotional attachment between the player and the outcomes of her actions within this fictional context." Given that it is the software or code of the game that allows for this interactivity, some emphasized the importance of the underlying computer program for a VG. A VG is therefore defined as "a game played by electronically manipulating images produced by a computer program on a monitor or other display,"[1] or "a computer game that you play by using controls or buttons to move images on a screen."[2] From this angle, it is understandable that most jurisdictions consider VGs to be computer programs (Jungar, 2016; Romas et al., 2013). However, these definitions also miss other essential features.

To provide a more precise and comprehensive definition, it is better to first reconsider the special characteristics of this kind of products. A VG must depend on computer program or game engine to drive. This is different from simple electronic games, such as bumper car games. A VG must have enough time to animate, which is different from the simple word games or data games. It consists of human–machine interaction and maneuverability, which is different from VG animation. Further, it contains a set of certain rules to guide gamers' actions. This is different from movies and general software. Combining the above features, this book defines a VG as "an electronic game based on computer program to drive and relied on video display devices to animate images and can read gamers' inputs, changing its material substances as a result of the gamer's action according to some set rules."

[1] Definition from Oxford Languages.

[2] Definition from Collins Dictionary, https://www.collinsdictionary.com/dictionary/english/video-game, last visited December 30, 2024.

**Table 2.1** Top grossing titles by category[4]

**Top Grossing Titles by category**
**Worldwide, ranked by June 2018 earnings**

| | PC | CONSOLE | MOBILE |
|---|---|---|---|
| 1 | League of Legends | Fortnite: Battle Royale | Honour of Kings |
| 2 | Dungeon Fighter Online | FIFA 18 | QQ Speed |
| 3 | PlayerUnknown's Battlegrounds | Call of Duty: WWII | Pokemon GO |
| 4 | Crossfire | The Crew 2 | Knives Out |
| 5 | Fantasy Westward Journey Online II | Grand Theft Auto V | Fantasy Westward Journey |
| 6 | Fortnite: Battle Royale | Tom Clancy's Rainbow Six: Siege | Clash Royale |
| 7 | World of Warcraft | NBA 2K18 | Monster Strike |
| 8 | World of Tanks | God of War | Fate/Grand Order |
| 9 | DOTA 2 | Far Cry 5 | Candy Crush Saga |
| 10 | Counter-Strike: Global Offensive | Overwatch | Clash of Clans |

Source: SuperData Arcade. Top selling games by total digital game sales, June 2018

SUPERDATA

### 2.1.2 *Classification of VGs*

In the VG field, there are multiple genres of games, including "action games, action-adventure games, adventure games, role-playing games, simulation games, strategy games, music games, e-sport games and trivia games."[3] While there is no precise standard to classify VGs, it is commonly to categorize them by platform, the electronic system used to play VGs. Today, modern VGs are generally played on three different platforms: consoles, PCs or Macintoshes, and mobile devices (Casillas, 2013). In recent years it has witnessed a rising number of VGs using applications downloaded to the smartphone or tablet and being played by connecting with webserver (Matsui, 2016) (Table 2.1).

[3] This list is provided by Wikipedia, https://en.wikipedia.org/wiki/List_of_video_game_genres, last visited December 30, 2024. While it is by no means exhaustive, it can provide a general information on the types of video games available on the market.

[4] Source from SuperData Arcade: https://www.superdataresearch.com/us-digital-games-market/, last visited December 30, 2024.

## 2.2 An "Ecological Balance" for VG Copyright

### *2.2.1 Copyright Ecosystem in the VG Context*

"Ecosystem" is a biological term describing "a biological community composed of interacting organisms and their physical environment." In its extended use, the term may also refer to "a complex network or interconnected system resembling this."[5] Introducing the concept of copyright to the ecosystem context, Song (2006) noted, "'copyright ecosystem' refers to the environmental factors in the process of copyright growth and their mutual constraints and promotive relations.... The changes of any factor or relationship will lead to the changes in the copyright system or institution, which will also affect the realization of the copyright value and the development of copyright industry." In 2012, Tussey (2012) expressed a similar view, arguing that it is important to understand copyrightable works as "being created and disseminated through networks of complex adaptive systems and to analyze those systems and the impact of copyright law on them." She further explained that "copyright law can be viewed as subsisting within an ecosystem comprising institutions and actors that are ordered through various techniques (legal, economic, political, social, etc.) to create and sustain creative acts." Consistent with Song's argument, Tussey (2012) stated that the copyright ecosystem, as "a nonlinear and dynamical system," shares the intricate architecture of most complex adaptive systems. In such cases, she noted, related policy prescriptions are often "reactive and unsustainable," as "unpredictability is an integral outcome of complex systems" (Savirimuthu, 2012). This is certainly true of the governance of copyright law, which—like all social systems—is constantly evolving.

However, the current copyright system is based on very general principles that recognize few significant differences between, for example, copyright industries that produce books and those that produce movies or VGs. These principles pay little heed to the complex realities of copyright regimes. As "one size fits all" copyright laws may not achieve the desired goals in all cases, there is an urgent need for "effective lawmaking based on the actual business practices of and evidence about the relevant industries" (Patry, 2012). As Patry (2012) remarked, "[s]aying we want to foster creativity without drilling down into the kind of creativity we want to foster and then figuring out how we can empirically foster that creativity is an empty gesture." Complexity models created for copyright systems should thus be specific and differentiated rather than mere reflections of the simple binary "private property versus commons" philosophical framework currently dominant in copyright analysis. Such models would "reflect the moderate-number contexts in which most economic, legal, social, and political interactions occur" (Ruhl, 2008).

Some scholars have acknowledged that copyright ecosystems are influenced by both internal and external factors, similar to biological ecosystems (Wang et al.,

[5] See Oxford English Dictionary, https://en.oxforddictionaries.com/definition/ecosystem, last visited December 30, 2024.

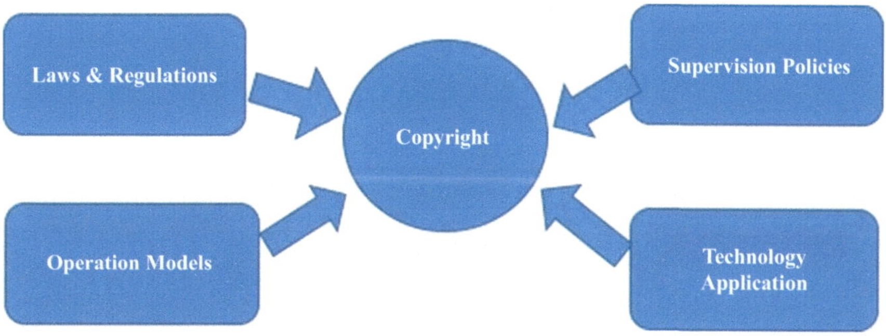


**Fig. 2.1** External factors influencing the copyright ecosystem

2015). In the mobile copyright ecological chain, the most influential external factors are "laws and regulations, supervision policy, technology application and operation model," and the most important internal factors include "digital content and its copyright, copyright owners, content operators, regulators and users" (Wang et al., 2015). Similarly, in the VG copyright ecosystem, important internal factors include game content and copyright, game designers, game service providers, gamers and live game streaming anchors. Relevant external factors include laws and regulations, public policies, technical protection measures (TPMs) and business operation models. Both internal and external factors must be considered when designing an eco-balanced copyright regime. Nonetheless, the existing copyright system for VGs generally focuses on certain factors, overlooking other important factors such as business operation models, technological advancement and some key stakeholders such as gamers and gamer anchors. Thus, constructing an optimal copyright system for VGs requires analysis of the functions of the typical copyright industry and recognition of the broader context, including relevant aspects of the political, social, economic and technological landscape (Tussey, 2012) (Figs. 2.1, 2.2 and 2.3).

### 2.2.2 *Objectives of Copyright Law and Balance of Interests in the VG Context*

All legal nexuses can be attributed to a relationship of interests. "Interest is deemed to be a substantial factor behind the law" (Feng, 2006). In the field of copyright in particular, great emphasis is placed on achieving a balance of interests. The basic spirit of copyright law is a balancing of interests or pursuit of harmony among various conflicting factors, including the rights and obligations of copyright owners; the relationships between creators, disseminators and users; the public interest and private interest; the short-term gratification of immediate consumption and the long-term goal of providing economic incentives that reward creativity and foster a dynamic culture (Fitzgerald & Gilchrist, 2015; Wu, 2005b). Language referencing such a

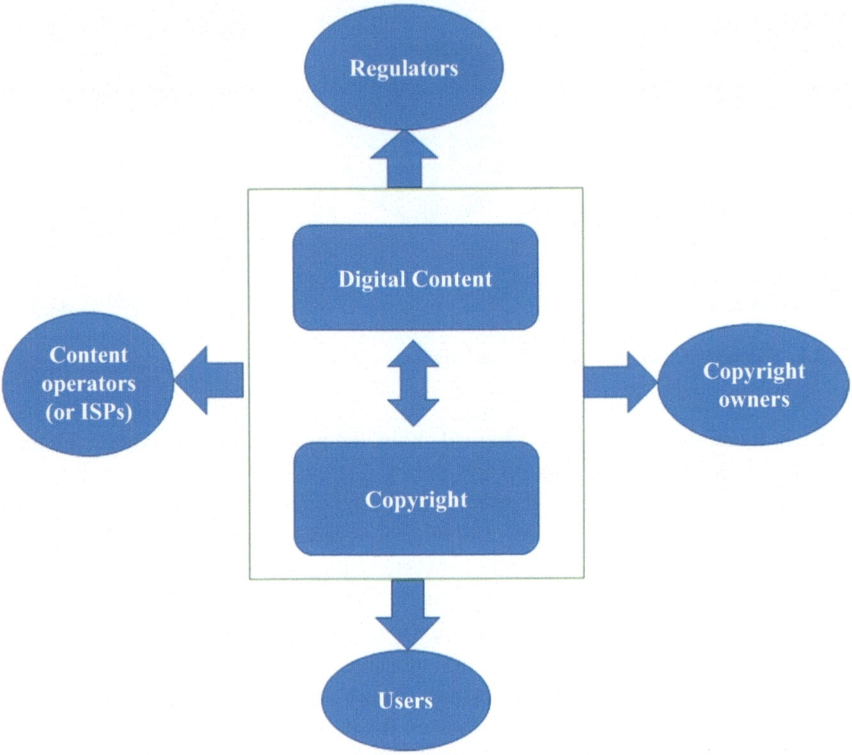


**Fig. 2.2** Internal factors influencing the copyright ecosystem

balance of interests can be found in international conventions relating to copyright. For example, the preamble to the 1996 WIPO Copyright Treaty (WCT) states that the signatories recognize "the need to maintain a balance between the rights of authors and the larger public interest, particularly education, research and access to information, as reflected in the Berne Convention." The preamble to the 1996 WIPO Performances and Phonograms Treaty (WPPT) contains an almost identical statement. Furthermore, one of the express aims of the TRIPS Agreement is to ensure that "the protection and enforcement of intellectual property rights should contribute to … a balance of rights and obligations" (Article 7, TRIPS Agreement).

Copyright law adopts this balance of interests theory to achieve its ultimate aim of promoting cultural innovation and the public welfare. The 1710 Statute of Anne, entitled "An Act for the Encouragement of Learning, by vesting the Copies of Printed Books in the Authors or Purchasers of such Copies, during the Times therein mentioned," stated that its primary goal was to encourage learning and that its instrument for achieving this goal was copyright. In recent years, certain scholars, responding to many copyright policy disputes, have focused on the policy objective of encouraging learning. For example, Cronin (2012) argued that "individual learning can enhance the quality and quantity of human knowledge as a whole, as well as

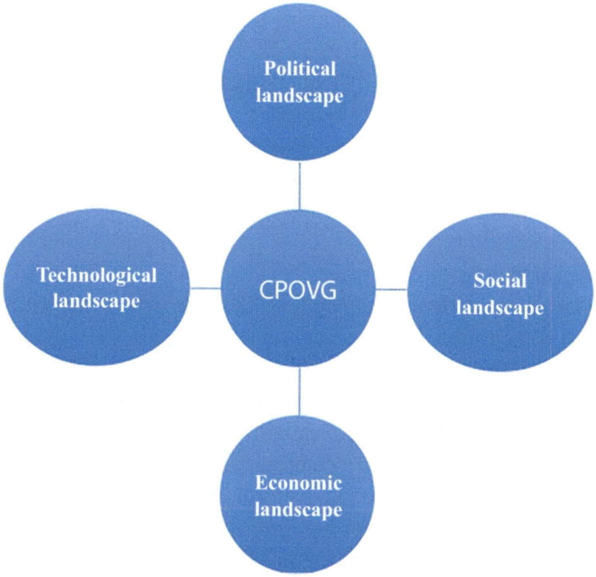


**Fig. 2.3** Copyright protection of VGs in context

promoting the flow and dissemination of information, hence encouraging learning is an important means for copyright law to achieve its goal to promote cultural innovation." Similarly, Patterson (1987) asserted that "the ultimate objective of copyright law is to promote and encourage learning, and some exceptions to copyright such as fair use are meant to facilitate this objective. Hence courts and policymakers should also take this into account when weighing the interests between copyright owners and users." Additionally, Patry (2012) argued that "apart from authorized uses, learning should also be encouraged through unauthorized uses that were not mere efforts to supplant sales of the original." Indeed, whether the encouragement of learning is defined as the goal or the instrument of copyright policy, it is an overwhelming reality that culture, information and knowledge are among the most consumed goods that enhance the welfare of modern societies, and copyright laws are created to further such broad societal outcomes.

To maximize societal welfare, copyright law provides certain exclusive rights to creators vis-à-vis their works while also restricting individual rights by means of certain corollary doctrines or rules to avoid excessive protection or unduly inhibiting the dissemination of works. Such rules include those governing formalities; those that set the scope and duration of copyrights; those relating to the idea/expression dichotomy; the fair use or fair dealing doctrine; the compulsory licensing for musical compositions, cable television and webcasts; and the first sale doctrine. The objective of copyright law is contradictory in the sense that "without legal monopoly, there will not be enough information, but the monopoly of law will lead to too little information being use" (Goldstein, 1994). This contradiction reflects the tension between the copyright system and the public domain; this tension is unavoidable, as it originates from "the dual functionality of knowledge as both a commodity and a driving social force" (De Rosnay & De Martin, 2012). Nevertheless, interest balance theory serves as both a philosophy and a guiding principle to achieve a reasonable compromise between these two contradictory goals. Within the VG copyright ecosystem, the doctrine of merger or scènes à faire, the doctrine of fair use or fair dealing and the safe harbor rules are all intended to balance interests. This research aids understanding of how those rules should be applied to solve practical issues under the guidance of the interest balance theory.

Compared with the traditional copyright system, the cyberspace copyright system has an additional stakeholder, the Internet service provider (ISP), which is central to the transmission of information. This reflects the impact of technological advancement on copyright's responsibility mechanism. The VG copyright ecosystem is more complex than the traditional system; it must balance the rights and obligations of game designers/developers, game service providers, live game operators, gamers and live game streaming anchors. Game service providers and live game operators have an interest in the development of Internet industries, while gamers' and live game streaming anchors' interests are related to public interests, such as the public use of network resources, public innovation space, freedom of expression and the negative impacts of copyrighted works on minors. These interests directly influence the level of copyright protection, the development of Internet industries and the protection of the public interest.

The objective of copyright law has long been interpreted as incentivizing creation by granting authors a series of exclusive rights while promoting access to information by creating certain exceptions to and placing limitations on these rights (Hua, 2013). Following this vein, the public interest factor of copyright policy has always been equated with considerations of freedom of information and freedom of expression. However, different from most researchers who adopt the above approach, I put the ultimate aim of copyright law to promote cultural innovation and social welfare as the utmost important place. Under this approach, the public interest factor requires consideration of any aspect of copyrighted works that is detrimental to social welfare, such as the highly addictive nature of VGs and their potential to bring serious harm to minors and to distract users from learning. Given the complex relationships between stakeholders, a legal framework clearly defining the boundaries of copyrights is necessary to ensure the certainty of legal adjustments. Such a framework would grant copyright owners a reasonable expectation of their rights, apportion appropriate responsibility to ISPs, allow the free enjoyment of public information resources and protect underage gamers from the negative externalities of cultural works, thereby promoting the sustainable development of the VG industry.

Maria A. Pallant, Director of the US Copyright Office, stated in the preface to the *Five-Year Plan 2016–2020* that "when the ways of creating, distributing and consuming copyright works are growing exponentially, the copyright office and copyright law cannot remain immutable" (Li, 2016). Thus, it is important to determine how the copyright system should be altered to deal with the newly emerging and

**Fig. 2.4** Various stakeholders' interests in VGs

complex issues surrounding VGs, what roles the various parties play in this copyright ecosystem and whether they deserve to be awarded special rights or to bear additional obligations. In this book, I attempt to design an eco-balanced copyright regime for the VG industry, with reference to the new demands arising from technical and economic development (Fig. 2.4).

## *2.2.3 Objectives of Copyright Law and Incentive Mechanism in the VG Context*

### 2.2.3.1 Incentive Theory and an Incentive Mechanism in the Copyright System

The key objective of copyright law is to promote "the progress of science and useful arts" (Article I, Section 8, Clause 8 of the U.S. C.) by rewarding copyright owners for their "unique creative efforts" (Midway Mfg. Co. v. Artic Int'l, Inc., 1981) and making their "ideas freely accessible to the public so as to the intellectual advancement of mankind" (Seltzer, 2006). Incentive theory offers important insights into how to achieve this objective.

Incentive theory posits that copyright law is an institutional instrument that motivates information generation and dissemination through rights allocation (Merges et al., 2006). The copyright system safeguards the profits that can motivate copyright owners to make investments prior to the publication of their original works. Incentive theory was developed via an economic methodology, and its legitimacy stems from the hypothesis of *homo economicus*, the "rational economic man," and the principle of externalities in economics (Posner, 2003). Legal rules constitute one of the constraints influencing rational people to make favorable choices when conducting their affairs, as individuals tend to measure the legal consequences of their behaviour to make decisions advantageous to profit generation. This natural instinct to gravitate toward profit and avoid negative consequences enables laws to distribute resources through the conferral of exclusive rights on those who can maximize the utility of those resources (Posner, 2003). Furthermore, the principle of externalities holds that individuals' behavior influences the welfare of others in society. Such externalities are of two types: personal behavior either creates benefits to others (positive externalities) or imposes additional costs on others (negative externalities) (Demsetz, 1967). These two types of externalities are borne by persons other than the actor. Externalities thus involve a break between the actor and his behavioural consequences; that is, the actor does not fully bear the costs and benefits of his own behavior. Legal regulations, by specifying rights and obligations, aim to force actors to bear all of the costs and reap all of the benefits of their own behavior; that is, they compel rational people to be fully responsible for the consequences of their actions. This transforms behavioral externalities into the actors' personal costs and benefits, thereby motivating actors to achieve the maximum benefits at the lowest cost to society while acting in their own self-interest.

Jeremy Bentham first formally linked the copyright system with incentives. In his words, "he who has no hope that he shall reap, will not take the trouble to sow" (Goldstein, 2002). Article I Section 8 Clause 8 of the US Constitution clearly states that "Congress shall have power…to promote the progress of science and the useful arts, by securing for limited times to authors and inventors the exclusive right to their respective writings and discoveries." The logic of the legislators is that the creation of works by the copyright owner can be regarded as an act of "disseminating knowledge and information for the general public good" (Mtima & Jamar, 2010). As a reward, the creator is granted a series of exclusive rights to his or her original works, bringing certain economic benefits, including both financial income and reputation or market share (Darling, 2015). The ultimate purpose of copyright law in providing incentives for creative efforts is to promote social utility; that is, to enhance culture and knowledge by increasing the supply of existing intellectual works (Fisher III, 1988). This was emphasized by the US Supreme Court when it explained the economic philosophy behind the constitutional provision for copyright protection, stating that the "encouragement of individual effort by personal gain is the best way to advance the public welfare through the talents of authors and inventors in science and the useful arts" (Lin, 1989). According to legislative reports on the US Copyright Act of 1909, Congress should focus on two issues during the implementation of the Act. First, it should determine to what extent the Act would inspire creators to benefit the public. Second, it should limit the scope of exclusive rights, as any exclusive rights affect the public interest (Mtima & Jamar, 2010). In this sense, copyright protection was created not primarily as an incentive but rather to represent the public interest and to promote societal development.

Nonetheless, it should be clear that this incentive mechanism has, throughout the evolution of copyright industries, gradually become the basis of the copyright system. Reforms to the copyright system are constantly the results generated from the game between competing interest groups in terms of copyright attribution. Parties such as creators, investors and consumers play different roles in the copyright ecosystem, each with their own interests. The theory of induced institutional change states that institutional change originates from rules created in response to new profitable opportunities in society. When newly created rules bring more benefits to society, the existing institution is likely to be improved or replaced (Lin, 1989). Under this theory, there is an interactive relationship between an organization and an institution. An institution is constructed to serve an organisation (the promoter) and organisations design institutions according to their own interests. Once an institution is able to produce mutual benefits, it will gradually be applied to society as a whole (North, 1990). Likewise, the current copyright system (the "institution" under the induced institutional change theory) was established through legislation by an interest group comprising investors in copyright industries (the "organization") and thus reflects the demands of these investors. The organization of investors is the leading promotor of copyright legislation and encouraging creativity has long been a cover-up of the investor-led legislation. The real purpose of the incentive mechanism is to establish the dominant position of property rights in copyright law and to realize investment utility maximization through the propertilization of information and the allocation of copyrights (Qi, 2011). Although investors and other stakeholders have reached compromises in copyright legislation by adding legislative objectives such as "promoting science and useful arts" and "reconciling social and public interests," the approach of guaranteeing benefits by granting exclusive rights has not changed (North, 1990). Therefore, the essence of copyright law is to facilitate investment in information production and dissemination through rights allocation rather than stimulating production and dissemination themselves. A noticeable result of copyright expansion under the market economy is the copyright owner's increase in revenue. Earning additional profits, as the incentive of additional investment, not only stimulates the development of copyright industries but also helps to realize the legislative purpose of achieving cultural and scientific prosperity through copyright law (Qi, 2011). This implies that the incentive mechanism, once established by investors to achieve personal goals, has been transformed into an institution conducive to social benefits.

#### 2.2.3.2 Constructing Models of Incentive Mechanism in the Copyright System

Incentive mechanism concretizes inventive theory at the legislative level; it is used to establish legal systems from the perspectives of cost–benefit tradeoff and incentive–access tradeoff. The cost–benefit tradeoff aims to solve the problem of negative externalities, whereas the incentive–access tradeoff aims to deal with positive externalities (Posner, 2003). In other words, the incentive mechanism of copyright focuses on granting copyrights to individuals who can maximize their utility. Above all, the cost–benefit tradeoff paradigm aims to affect individuals' decisions by setting the scope of copyrights to improve the efficiency of resource use. Copyright law acts as an institutional instrument to avoid market failure. In a market economy, creators and investors are regarded as "rational economic men" who instinctively seek benefits and avoid losses. Based on the hypothesis of *homo economicus*, individuals bounded by given regulations are expected to behave in a specific way (Posner, 2003). These regulations thus form a legal institution that increases overall social welfare. According to the cost–benefit tradeoff paradigm, information is produced and disseminated only when the benefits are expected to exceed the costs. The mechanism of granting exclusive rights to information producers or investors can motivate the right holders to use information resources efficiently and minimize transaction costs associated with the resources (Posner, 2003). However, approaches to and channels for information production and dissemination change with technological advancement. This changes the cost–benefit ratio, specifically generating new externalities. Therefore, the scope of copyrights should be revised in line with technological advancement to appropriately address newly generated externalities.

As for the incentive–access tradeoff paradigm, it aims to design an effective rights allocation regime that can influence individual choices based on the incentive-produced benefits and the costs associated with promoting public access to information (Posner, 2003). By creating "compulsory scarcity," exclusive rights reduce private costs (guaranteeing private benefits) at the expense of increased social costs (i.e. increasing the cost to users of accessing information). As any form of creation involves information use, legislators must ensure that right holders, after being granted exclusive rights, would not impede the public or subsequent creators from using the information as inspiration or reference. To achieve this goal, the incentive–access tradeoff paradigm requires that (a) when copyright expansion conflicts with access to necessary information, such expansion must be limited and (b) in the absence of such conflict, the expansion of rights must create additional incentives that are conducive to information production and dissemination (Qi, 2011). Therefore, on the premise of ensuring sufficient incentives, an incentive mechanism must take into account the control of social costs apart from considerations of social benefits, to ensure an incentive–access balance following the allocation of rights.

In establishing a copyright incentive mechanism, the initial allocation of rights is as important as the reallocation of rights. The initial allocation of rights should acknowledge the fact that creators and investors spend effort and capital in creating, processing and disseminating copyright works; thus, these parties have a proven

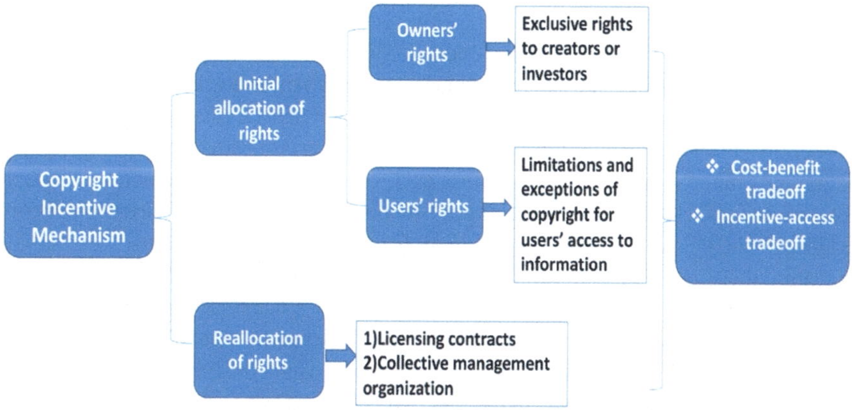


**Fig. 2.5** Copyright incentive mechanism

ability to use rights effectively. Accordingly, copyright law grants a series of exclusive rights to them. However, to increase public access to copyrighted works and thus not undermine new creators' incentives, copyright law also grants passive rights to users (Gordon, 1989). These come in the forms of exceptions to and limitations on copyrights, including the principle of *numerus clausus*, the idea/expression dichotomy, the limitation on the duration of rights and the fair use doctrine as well as statutory licensing and compulsory licensing. Therefore, the adjustment of initial rights allocation requires consideration of issues such as creation and limitation of rights. As for the reallocation of rights, its purpose is to reduce transaction costs associated with the rights, thereby realizing the private creation of resource allocation rules (Gordon, 1989). Licensing contracts should be facilitated as one way to effectively reallocate rights. Specifically, private contracts should supplement and transcend statutory rights, enabling parties to adjust the allocation of rights according to actual transaction costs under specific conditions. Indeed, common concerns of legislation include whether the generated private rules help achieve the goals of the incentive mechanism and how to link up with the existing limitation system of copyright law (Fig. 2.5).

#### 2.2.3.3 Limitations of Incentive Mechanism and Diverse Attributes of Copyright

The propertilization of information advocated by the copyright incentive mechanism has been criticized based on theories, including labor theory and personhood or "moral rights" theory (Hughes, 1988) as well as the emerging theories of democracy and human rights (Netanel, 1998; Torremans, 2004). Some scholars have argued that the utilitarianism inherent in such propertilization of information focuses on economic incentives and assumes a linear relationship between copyright incentives and creative production that should be testable, yet fails to acknowledge that copyright cannot provide the necessary initial economic conditions that most authors and artists need (Tussey, 2012). The incentive mechanism of copyright law also obscures other values inherent in copyright, such as the importance of artistic diversity and semiotic democracy. Further, it does not take into account certain values involving moral judgements that cannot be precisely measured, such as personal satisfaction, respect and esteem, and "first mover advantages" (Calandrillo, 1998). The artist Heilbrun and Gray (2001) said that "art is just a way for artists to express themselves. Apart from this, there is no other reason for creation". Similarly, Patry (2012) stated that "for most of us, the instinct to create arises out of our essence as human beings: we want to make things that are meaningful to ourselves and to others."

The actual role of copyright is admittedly limited; it is not the basis for creativity, as it does not cause people to create in the first place. Nor does it cause people to achieve economic or critical success. However, copyright law does serve a function. Although creators might not stop creating without copyright protection and the incentives it provides for creation, they certainly would not be stimulated to create as much as they do with such protection, and this would ultimately reduce the number of works available to society (Leite, 2014). Thus, we should acknowledge the valuable purposes served by copyright law: it ensures that those who wish to protect their creations from free riding and to benefit economically from them are able to do so (Patry, 2012). It allows creators to recoup their investment of time and effort in creating their works and thereby indirectly promotes creativity.

Copyright law applies to specific information that is valuable in various ways, whether as a tradable product producing economic benefits, as an element necessary in the public sphere to enable free expression, or as a key to creating a democratic institution of information disclosure. As such, the value of copyright law has been the topic of great controversy since the drafting of its initial legislation. No matter how well investors in copyright industries guide and promote copyright legislation or how well the value of copyright law fulfills the predictions of incentive theory, scholars have suggested improvements to the copyright system by borrowing legislative values from other legal fields (e.g., democracy and human rights) (Wong, 2009). Patterson and Birch Jr. (2009) believed that human rights such as the freedom of speech codified in the First Amendment of the US Constitution should be the guiding principle of copyright legislation. The fundamental goal of copyright is to stimulate learning, and it is understood that the allocation of rights must not hinder information dissemination and use. In the US, freedom of speech is a fundamental right that includes information access and free expression. Thus, to ensure public access to information, under this theory, the legislative goal of copyright law should be to enhance the public stock of knowledge and ensure that the public can access to copyrighted works. Similarly, Netanel (1996) regarded copyright law as an institutional instrument for promoting democracy in civil society, holding that copyright should be used not to maximize profits but rather to stimulate originality and diversity of speech, thereby facilitating the democratic mechanism in civil society.

In this book, I persist that copyright has diverse attributes. First of all, copyright is a type of private right. Copyright, like tangible property, can be the subject of exchange. Copyright is an inherent spiritual thing, but it can be presented through certain forms of expression. As a type of property right, copyright aims to reduce transaction costs by specifying rights allocation in a market. In addition, excludability and alienability are the basic attributes of copyright (Smith, 2007), with the limitations designed to prevent certain externalities arising from the exclusive right itself (i.e., to reduce transaction costs resulting from endowing creators and investors with exclusive rights). Therefore, as a type of private law, copyright law adopts the rights-based approach (Wu, 2011). Within the copyright law, sharing information and releasing rights must be considered inferior to stimulating investment and innovation.

In addition, copyright is a special type of human right. Given that protecting creators' rights is a fundamental prerequisite for the public to achieve cultural freedom and benefit from scientific progress, the IP provisions were ultimately incorporated by international human rights conventions such as the Universal Declaration of Human Rights and the International Covenant on Economic, Social and Cultural Rights (Liu, 2001). Some scholars argued that the ultimate goal of the IP system is "development"—personal development, social development, national development, and the common development of all human society (Wu, 2005a). From the perspective of moral right, protecting the rights of creators itself demonstrates the respect for human dignity and wisdom; Again, the protection mode and level of copyright should contribute to the realization of other human rights. Pursuant to the requirements of human rights conventions, the rights of creators should be consistent with the rights "to participate in cultural life" and "to enjoy the benefits of scientific progress," and this human rights factor is higher than "simple economic operations that manipulate copyright laws." Therefore, in the context of human rights, copyright emphasizes providing opportunities for the public to access knowledge for social development. For the purpose of public interest and respect for basic human rights, some restrictions should be imposed on copyright in certain circumstances. Specifically, the fair use doctrine and other limitations or exceptions of copyright represent the consideration of human rights, a viewpoint that advocates universal sharing (Wu, 2011).

Furthermore, copyright is a social policy instrument. Decisions regarding whether to protect a work's copyright, which types of knowledge are granted private property right, and what standards should be adopted to protect copyright are all public policy choices and arrangements made by a country based on its current development situation and future needs. Therefore, although copyright, like property rights and creditor's rights, is a type of private right, it also possesses a public policy attribute that transcends the private sector. In the formulation and implementation of copyright policies, the state emphasizes both the protection of the interests of specific entities and the balance of interests among different stakeholders. That is, when designing copyright systems, costs and benefits should be taken into account to ultimately achieve net benefits in the growth of knowledge wealth (Wu, 2011). Notably, in the public policy system, the goal of promoting the growth of knowledge wealth and economic and social development is not solely undertaken by IP policies; this goal orientation is also reflected in other public policies. At the same time, the achievement of IP policy goals also depends on the coordination of other public policies. Therefore, from an external perspective of copyright law, the realization of

**Fig. 2.6** Diverse attributes of copyright

pluralistic legislative values is undertaken by different laws with various regulatory objects and hierarchical levels. The incentive mechanism of copyright law should be reconciled with human rights and democracy as proposed by other departmental laws (Qi, 2011).

Given the limitations of incentive mechanism and the diverse attributes of copyright, this book emphasizes the importance to deal with the relationship between the value attribute and tool attribute of the copyright system, as well as the relationship between the principle of private protection of copyright and the principle of public interest in knowledge dissemination. To achieve this, copyright law should adhere to an efficient and fair-oriented incentive approach. From an internal perspective of copyright law, as a private law, copyright law should employ an incentive mechanism to stimulate investment and innovation with utility maximization as its priority, with the limitations or exceptions of copyright as auxiliary measures for the sake of human rights and democracy (the public interest to disseminate knowledge and free expression). From an external perspective of copyright law, as a social policy instrument, copyright policies complement other public policies to jointly promote the growth of knowledge wealth and economic and social development. When the economic value pursued by copyright law conflicts with the legal values, such as democracy and human rights, advocated by other laws, restriction of copyright should be considered according to the hierarchy of rights (Fig. 2.6).

#### 2.2.3.4 Applying the Incentive Mechanism to the VG Context

When applying the copyright incentive mechanism to the VG context, the focus should be on promoting the sustainable development of the VG industry. "Sustainable development" is widely understood as "development that meets the needs of the present without compromising the ability of future generations to meet their own needs."[6] It is an approach to development that protects society in the long term, taking into account both present imperatives and those of the future. In the context of VGs, "sustainable development" refers to the steady economic development of the

[6] See Report of the World Commission on Environment and Development: Our Common Future (1987).

VG industry without causing severe harm to social welfare. This can be achieved only by harmonizing three core processes: incentivizing innovation, promoting access to information and reducing the negative externalities of VGs.

Creation represents only one link in the copyright industry chain. Industry investors make constant adjustments to the decisions to create, organize and distribute works according to consumer demand. These adjustments are necessary, as both creating works and disseminating information involve significant costs, which must be kept in line with the supply and demand of the market to secure returns on investments and other incentive benefits. More often than not, a VG copyright is held not by one individual creator but by a company that hires many people to collaborate on a complex game. In most cases, game designers are paid by their employers (game companies or developers), and this relationship is regulated by contracts. Thus, to a certain extent, designing a VG is a matter of a company's strategy rather than an individual's creativity. The philosophers Horkheimer and Adorno (2002) were convinced that popular culture is being transformed into an endless stream of factory-produced, standardized entertainment goods and that the new creators of culture are not individuals but rather industrialists. Therefore, when constructing an eco-balanced copyright regime for VGs, the unique status of investors should be given priority; allocating rights to them would be an effective way to realize the inventive mechanism.

However, the costs arising from information propertilization are diverse, and an incentive mechanism can only generate positive impacts to a certain extent. From the internal perspective of incentive–access tradeoff, information propertilization without restriction would increase the cost of the public's access to information and bring a deadweight loss to consumers, thereby increasing the cost of creating new works. This means an optimal copyright system for VGs should not only provide copyrights to incentivize game developers but also consider the rights and interests of gamers and other subsequent users. Thus, within the copyright system, some negative rights for users such as fair use doctrine and merger or scènes à faire doctrine are necessary apart from the exclusive rights for game developers. Nevertheless, the book argues that these negative rights merely sever as defenses, which are hard to protect the rights of users in some circumstances. Hence some positive rights or instruments are proposed in this book to safeguard the interests of users.

From the external perspective of incentive–access tradeoff, excessive propertilization would unilaterally increase the profits of copyright owners and funnel the capital that should be applied in other fields to the copyright owners, thus reducing the overall benefits to society (Lunney Jr., 1996). Hence the degree of copyright propertilization should be based on the optimal use of resources, or to put it another way, the scope and allocation of copyrights should take into consideration the cost and benefit to society, not only the cost of copyright itself (Coase, 1996).In the context of an eco-balanced copyright regime for VGs, it should address considerations of the social costs of VGs' negative externalities (e.g., gaming addiction) in addition to the cost of denying subsequent game developers access to the original games, as the negative externalities of VGs would bring great burden for society and may also trigger prohibition policy that would render the copyright of this type of products meaningless. This has the added benefit of effectively avoiding conflicts between the economic value pursued by copyright law and other legal values, such as human rights (e.g., the protection of minors), advocated by other laws. Historically, administrative regulation mechanisms (e.g., the content censorship system) have been used to reduce the negative externalities of copyrighted works to facilitate the societal goals of copyright law. Whether this approach works well in the VG context and how to design a more balanced mechanism are issues of study in this book. In summary, to promote the sustainable development of the VG industry, an incentive mechanism should be used to stimulate game developers to design more cultural and educational based VGs while simultaneously encouraging them to proactively take anti-gaming addiction measures.

## 2.3 Challenges to the Current Copyright Regime in the VG Context

### *2.3.1 Ineffectiveness of Copyright Protection Models for VGs*

Modern VGs can be divided into two main parts: audiovisual elements (including images, sounds, texts and video recordings) and software, which consists of instruction sequences in computer code that manage audiovisual elements and control the operation of the whole game (Grosheide et al., 2014). This dichotomy has triggered debate on whether a VG should be classified as "a multimedia work, an audiovisual work or, primarily, a computer program" (Romas et al., 2013). Although every jurisdiction faces this classification problem, the approaches taken by legal systems to solve the problem vary immensely (Zweigert & Kötz, 2003). According to Romas et al. (2013), in some countries, such as Canada and Singapore, VGs are predominantly protected as computer programs, whereas in a few countries, such as South Korea, VGs are essentially treated as audiovisual works. In other jurisdictions, including Japan, the US and France, VGs are considered to have a "distributive classification"; that is, "legal protection of the VG must be found separately, according to the specific nature of each work." The Supreme Court of Italy, in contrast, defined a VGs as a single complex multimedia work in a case involving the circumvention of technical protection measures (TPMs) by mod chips installed in VG consoles (Stein, 2015). Indonesia was the first country to classify VGs as a new type of works.[7]

In the early stages of VG copyright development in China, VGs were considered essentially computer programs (Romas et al., 2013), but this notion has changed and there are now divergent views on the matter. Most scholars have argued in favor of the distributive approach (Cui, 2016; Hao, 2016). Others have praised courts' classification of the audiovisual elements of VGs as cinematographic works (Bai, 2017; Wang & Yuan, 2016; Yuan, 2017), and a few have echoed the Italian Supreme

[7] See Article 40 of the Indonesian Copyright Law.

Court's proposal to classify a VG as a kind of single "multimedia work" (Li, 2005; Sun & Cao, 2017).

In most jurisdictions, VGs are regarded as multi-dimensional works containing distinct elements that "can each individually be copyrighted if they achieve a certain level of originality and creativity" (Romas et al., 2013). Basically, VGs contain the following creative elements: musical compositions, sound recordings, images, text, characters, plots, maps, architectural works, rules of play, source codes and object codes (Lipson & Brain, 2009). Legally, source and object codes, storylines or plotlines, in-game text and dialogue are generally protected as literary works, given sufficient originality (Kim, 2014; Stein, 2015). It is also generally accepted that "background music in VGs enjoy the same protection as it does in any other context" (Kim, 2014; Stein, 2015) and that "the characters, maps as well as the series of frames on the screen constitute artistic works when satisfying originality" (Bai, 2017). However, there is ongoing debate concerning whether and how to provide protection for the rules of a game. In European jurisprudences, rules of play do not merit copyright protection to prevent monopoly (Boyden, 2011). However, since the *Tetris* case in the US (Tetris Holding, LLC v. Xio Interactive, 2012), some scholars have insisted that game rules should be protected, depending on the circumstances, to reduce piracy (Dean, 2016; Meyer, 2010; Zeng & Guan, 2017). As "cloning" becomes more common, the evaluation and treatment of these issues will greatly affect the future of the VG industry.

### *2.3.2 Imprecise Delimitation of Game Adaptation Infringement*

As copyright protection extends only to "expression," not to "ideas, procedures, methods of operation or mathematical concepts as such,"[8] its scope has traditionally been measured in terms of an "idea/expression dichotomy" (Glasser, 1986). However, most digital works contain a combination of ideas and expression. This is particularly true of VGs, posing a great challenge for IP judges. In *Nichols v. Universal Pictures Corp.*, an "abstractions test" was created; "general statements and descriptions, being closer to ideas than expressions, were less protectable by copyright than specific statements and descriptions."[9] This test is still not entirely clear as applied to VGs. Furthermore, as in most countries VGs deserve double copyright protection—that is, distributive protection as both computer programs and audiovisual works—some scholars have asserted limiting their copyright protection by the merger doctrine and the scènes à faire doctrine (Buckman, 2005; Casillas, 2013; Dean, 2016). The lack of copyright protection for VGs' ideas, procedures and methods of operation has been

[8] See Article 9 (2) of TRIPS and Article 2 of WCT. See also Berne Convention art.2.1: "The expression 'literary and artistic works; shall include every production in the literary, scientific and artistic domain, whatever may be the mode or form of its expression, such as…".

[9] 45 F.2d 119 (2d Cir.1930), *cert. denied*, 282 U.S. 902 (1931).

exploited by competitors, who can take advantage of the fundamental mechanics, rules and often story elements of VGs to clone the games and release competing products (Dean, 2016) without facing copyright infringement liability.

The "access + substantial similarity" test has long been applied to identify copyright infringement in Chinese judicial practice (Ding, 2019). Using this test to establish copyright infringement, the copyright owner must show that the defendant had access to the copyrighted work and that the defendant's and plaintiff's works are substantially similar (Cole, 1995). To determine substantial similarity, courts usually apply the "three-step" ("abstraction–filtration–comparison") test, the "total concept and feeling" test, the "extrinsic and intrinsic analysis" test, and the "decomposition" test (Sun & Cao, 2017). However, courts' logic and processes vary widely, and there is no unified standard for substantive similarity. Moreover, in practice, courts generally conflate adaptation infringement with reproduction infringement. However, studies have shown that cognitively, the making of an adaptation is "a creative activity not qualitatively different from that of making an original work" (Landes & Posner, 2003; Nimmer & Nimmer, 2015; Rachum-Twaig, 2017; Samuelson, 2013). While the law distinguishes between an adaptation work and an original work, it makes almost no distinction between adaptations and mere reproductions. As VG adaptations are common, it is time to reconsider the scope of the right of adaptation and devise a more balanced test to determine game adaptation infringement.

### *2.3.3 Uncertainty Regarding Players' Rights to Their Modified Games*

A significant feature of VGs is their interactivity with players. This has drawn scholars' attention to the rights of players. Reuveni (2007) asserted that "where a developer's code does not excessively limit the scope of a player's artistic creations, copyright should attach where originality and fixation are satisfied." This view has been accepted by other scholars, such as Kennedy (2008), who argued that the rights of players to their avatars and in-game possessions must be acknowledged, given the three principal theoretical bases for online property rights: utilitarianism theory, Locke's labor theory and Hegel's personality theory. Similarly, Beausoleil (2017) and Feng (2017) argued that whether players merit copyright for their generated contents should depend on the types of games and the players' contributions. Beausoleil (2017) suggested that co-authorship may provide a means of dealing with this issue. Feng (2017) proposed that where originality is not satisfied, a player could be classified as either a derivative author or a performer. Clearly, the literature has tended to justify the rights of gamers to their generated contents by pointing to users' contributions, relying solely on legal theory. Almost no studies have examined the issue from an industrial or social perspective or provided empirical evidence to support their analyses.

While many studies have discussed players' rights to their generated content, one avenue of game creation known as game modifications (or "Mods") merit particular attention. Views on the legality of game Mods are diverse. Some research on game Mods has focused on the rights holder, considering only damage to the initial copyright owner (Donnelly, 2004; Gordon, 1992; Kretzschmar & Stanfill, 2018; Lipton, 2011; Wallace, 2014). According to this view, game Mods are derivative works that do not fall within the doctrine of fair use and may thus be forbidden within a strict moral rights system. Furthermore, game Mods may violate the Digital Millennium Copyright Act (DMCA) as well as the end-user license agreement or terms of service established between end users and developers. Other scholars have adopted a more moderate attitude, classifying game Mods by type: minor alterations and extensive changes, or "total conversion" Mods (Baldrica, 2007; Rosen, 2005). These scholars have proposed two levels of copyright protection, depending on the type of Mod. A Mod classified as "total conversion"—relying on the underlying engine of a game but producing a seemingly new game—might be considered not a derivative version of the original game but an independent work meriting its own copyright protection (Nardi & Kallinikos, 2007; Rosen, 2005). In contrast, Meng and Xu (2016) considered game Mods to be derivative works requiring approval from the original copyright owners, pointing out that game manufacturers could apply the parallel creation model to solve the authorization problem by implied license. Due to the rise of game Mods and the symbiotic relationship between the game industry and players, creating a more balanced copyright scheme for stakeholders is vital.

### *2.3.4 Legitimacy of Live Game Streaming Without Authorization*

Gaming development has been accelerated by advancements in technology. One of the most significant features of gaming development is the generation of new types of game play, such as the live game streaming. Live game streaming involves the real-time transmission of players' gameplay process to the public via live streaming platforms or other online medias. Game copyright holders may also claim a violation of their exclusive right to public performance when a game is used at a competitive or communal gaming event. Joo (2011) argued that the fair use doctrine may be a defense for such uses, and that "copyright holders need to openly express an intent to profit from public gaming events in order to have any chance of attacking a fair use defense." This view was shared by Puddington (2015), who explored the economic justifications for applying fair use to the online streaming of VGs. Matsui (2016) noted that in Japan, live game streaming is "tolerated infringement," and proposed either denying such infringement or legalizing it. Jungar (2016) reported that in the EU, "streaming VGs infringes the game developer's right to communicate their works to the public, but freedom of expression can and should be used to rein in their rights in certain cases."

Live game streaming is fairly new in China, where it has also become a subject of debate. Wang (2016) asserted that unlike films, which are "passively appreciated" for their audio-visual elements, "VGs are highly dependent on each player's personalized and interactive participation, hence live game streaming constitutes transformative use." Xie (2017), drawing on utilitarian theory, also recognized live game broadcasting as fair use, arguing that the law "only needs to ensure that copyright owners have enough incentives to make games," that the benefits that are derived from live broadcasting "should not belong to the original copyright owners," and that this approach would be "more conducive to the development of the live broadcast industry." However, according to Li (2017), "live game streaming without consent constitutes the act of communicating to the public, which infringes the game copyright owners' 'other rights' stipulated in Article 10 (17) of the PRC Copyright Law." IP Judge Zhu (2017) expressed a similar view, stating that "live game broadcasting is a reasonable potential market of the game copyright owners, and doing it without authorization constitutes infringement, but economic interests generated from it should be allocated among different stakeholders in order to balance interests." Taking a somewhat stricter stance, Feng (2017) explained that "whatever the legal status of players are, they constitute joint infringement with the live streaming platforms when live game streaming without authorization." Cui (2016) suggested that "to eliminate the uncertainty of the court's decision, game developers can restrict the user's public transmission of the audiovisual display of the games by licensing contract." As live game streaming has become a booming market, an appropriate balance between game developers', streamers' and streaming platform operators' rights must be found.

### *2.3.5 Challenges Posed by the Addictive Potential of VGs*

As an interactive artistic medium, VGs are increasingly popular but also increasingly controversial in today's interconnected world. Research has examined the links between VGs and addiction, aggression, violence, social development, and a variety of stereotyping and sexual morality issues. It appears that the development of problematic use of VGs is a complex process with many different contributing factors (Kuss & Griffiths, 2012). Despite debate concerning how problematic VGs truly are, psychiatric research on gaming addiction has revealed that video gaming has high addictive potential, and such addictive potential may cause serious harm to minors. For example, Griffiths (2000) argued that "game playing can in some cases be addictive, especially online game playing where the game never ends and has the potential to be a 24/7 activity." He distinguished between healthy excessive enthusiasm and addiction, stating that the former can "add to life whereas addictions take away from it" (Griffiths, 2008). According to another study, "computer game addicts or gamblers may show reduced dopamine response to stimuli associated with their addiction, presumably due to sensitization" (Weinstein, 2010). In addition, loneliness has been identified as "a consequence of pathological gaming" (Lemmens et al., 2011). Studies examining "problematic gaming behavior and depressive tendencies among people who play different types of online-games" (Stetina et al., 2011) have provided "empirical data-driven identification of a group of addicted online gamers" (Van Rooiji et al, 2010).

In response to the WHO's addition of "gaming disorder" to the ICD (Scutti, 2018), parents and educators opposing VGs have described them as "poison" and waged a battle against their use. Many Chinese scholars have attempted to provide solutions; however, their views have more or less coincided, discussing the problem from the perspectives of the family and school (Lin et al, 2021; Sun, 2020; Zhang et al, 2020; Zhou, 2020). Notwithstanding that some studies have focused on the legal aspect of VGs, they merely called for stronger governmental supervision and improvements to legislation in their concluding remarks, without providing specific and feasible countermeasures (Chang, 2019; Gong, 2020; Kang, 2019). Although the ultimate goal of copyright law is to promote cultural innovation and social welfare, the current copyright system was established through legislation by interest groups comprising investors in copyright industries and therefore reflects the interests of these investors. This raises the question of how the copyright system should be reconstructed to achieve an eco-balance between stakeholders to promote innovation and investment in game enterprises while also reducing the negative externalities of VGs in the public interest, particularly with regard to minors. Such reconstruction should be based on the optimal utilization of resources, ensuring that the financial gains of this copyright industry are proportional to societal gains.

Violent content is another serious issue. Mac Sithigh (2010) discussed the regulation of violent VGs in the EU, and Garon (2010) and Tsesis (2015) explored the contradiction between constitutional regulations for violent games and free speech in the US. In China, the administrative regulation mechanism (e.g., content censorship system) has historically been used to reduce the negative externalities (e.g., violent and sexual content) of copyrighted works to facilitate the societal goals of copyright law. Whether this approach works well in the VG context and to what extent the theory underlying the regulation of violent and sexual games can be applied to gaming addiction are issues worth exploring.

## 2.4 An "Ecological Balance" Emphasizing Economic Efficiency and Social Welfare

"Law is a tool which cannot provide the answers for all situations in advance, but it can provide the means to find those answers as copyright evolves" (Frankel & Gervais, 2014). Copyright law has not yet provided this level of guidance in the VG context. The copyright "ecosystem" as a whole is complex and adaptive. Due to its nonlinear behavior, the proposition that greater copyright protection must produce more creativity cannot be taken for granted, as there are many factors at play. Frankel and Gervais (2014) argued that "to achieve a balance of interests is not enough for copyright system." They reasoned that "equilibrium captures more than a simple balance between two opponents; it is about balancing multiple competing interests from multiple players." This is certainly true of the VG copyright ecosystem, which should maintain an "ecological balance" (or "eco-balance") between the various elements of the system and between the system and its external environment. Such an eco-balance would ensure a sustainable and effective supply of energy and optimize the system's structure and function to maintain homeostasis and foster a virtuous cycle.

More specifically, the main grounds upon which the concept of "eco-balance" is built can be addressed as follows. First of all, the common copyright notion of a "balance of interests" may give the incorrect impression that "the interests of copyright owners and users should always be seen in oppositional terms" or that "the interests of one group constantly have to be set off against those of another" (Burrell & Coleman, 2005). My proposed concept of eco-balance corrects this misunderstanding, emphasizing the complexity of both the relationships between different interests in the copyright field and the cultural creations involved. This is particularly important for VGs. VGs are notorious in the legal context for their complexity, which arises from both their interactivity and multimedia features and the emergence of new business models driven by technological advancement, such as game adaptations and live game streaming. Furthermore, the potentially addictive nature of VGs raises questions about the wisdom of promoting the industry—and thereby putting minors at risk—by providing copyright incentives. The negative externalities of VGs, such as gaming addiction, may trigger prohibition policies that would be detrimental to this copyright industry, as "without consumer demand for your intellectual work, owning a copyright is meaningless" (Patry, 2012). Copyright legislation for VGs lags behind the rapid advancement of the VG industry, which may reduce innovation and investment in game enterprises and/or dampen the public's passion for gaming and re-creation. To avoid these outcomes and ensure the sustainable development of the industry, it is vital to develop an eco-balanced copyright regime for VGs that not only maximizes game enterprises' cultural innovation but also minimizes the negative externalities of VGs.

However, the notion of balance in the copyright context has been criticized for limited utility; "it tells us very little about how to proceed in practice" (Burrell & Coleman, 2005). To address this shortcoming, I propose an incentive mechanism based on economic efficiency and social welfare. The ultimate goal of the law is to achieve distributive justice, promoting the distribution of wealth while harmonizing relations between people by governing their behavior as members of society (Martinez, 1995). This goal can only be achieved by considering multiple factors relating to both the law's creation and its interpretation. Economic utilitarianism sets a standard for justice in legislation, i.e. the goal of maximizing society's overall welfare by ensuring the greatest average well-being of its citizens (Miceli, 2017). Economic efficiency involves the most just distribution of resources with the fewest possible resources sacrificed; the law can only be economically efficient if it is structured to minimize resource waste. Although legal interpretations are not made consciously to promote economic efficiency, they are forces inherent in the decision-making process that propel judgements in the direction of efficiency as a means of achieving societal well-being (Miceli, 2017).

Kaplow and Shavell (2002) argued that social welfare should be the sole basis for evaluating legal policy and that the notion of fairness should not influence policy except to the extent that it enhances social well-being. They also asserted that narrow concepts of efficiency, such as wealth maximization, are inappropriate because they exclude factors that may affect the distribution of wealth. Copyright laws are welfare-based, created to realize certain societal goals and improve social welfare by stimulating the creation and dissemination of intellectual works. These goals are pragmatic rather than ideological, providing certain privileges to both copyright owners and the public. There are no standards by which to measure the importance of these privileges, as they all work toward the common good. Intellectual works arise from society at large, and everyone has a stake in the resolution of issues involving their creation and use. From this perspective, individuals' rights are less important than their obligations to each other and to society (Patry, 2012).

Promoting intellectual and cultural diversity relies on economic efficiency in the balance between the granting of exclusive rights and the limitations that those exclusive rights imposed. Economic efficiency takes two forms: static efficiency and dynamic efficiency. Static efficiency is the effective use of resources at the lowest possible cost (Kaplow & Shavell, 2002; Liebenstein, 1966) and dynamic efficiency describes a balance between short-term concerns (e.g. ensuring static efficiency) and long-term concerns (e.g. encouraging research and development) (Liebenstein, 1966). The economic rationale for copyright suggests that systems must be adjusted to provide static efficiency and dynamic efficiency simultaneously. This is based on the notion that information and knowledge are both inputs and outputs of their production process and offer balanced policy options regarding protection, limitations and exceptions, in addition to promoting the public interest. A well-designed copyright system can maximize static efficiency without negatively affecting dynamic efficiency, and in certain cases, the limitations imposed on copyrights can promote both static efficiency and dynamic efficiency (Landes & Posner, 1989). VG copyright protection should take into account VGs' production and investment costs, their technical and non-technical operational models, the transactional costs of accessing the information required for innovation, and the social costs of their negative externalities. To achieve economic efficiency and promote social welfare, copyright protection must grant game developers the opportunity to reap the fruits of their work while also allowing the public to productively use game materials for innovation and reducing or eliminating the conflict between the granting of rights and the protection of minors. Thus, based on the principles of economic efficiency and social welfare, I propose an eco-balanced VG copyright regime to maximize the benefits of additional intellectual creations while minimizing the losses resulting from limited access and the social costs of copyrighting such works (Fig. 2.7).

**Fig. 2.7** Eco-balanced copyright protection for VGs

## References


Bai, F. [白帆]. (2017). Frame of Games: Ideographic or Showy Technique [游戏画面:表意还是炫技]. *Zhichanli [知产力]*.

Baldrica, J. (2007). Mod a Heck: Frameworks for Examining Ownership Rights in User-Contributed Content to Videogames, and a more Principled Evaluation of Expressive Appropriation in User-Modified Videogame Projects. *Minnesota Journal of Law, Science & Technology, 8*(2), 686–687.

Beausoleil, L. E. (2017). *Copyright Issues and Implications of Emerging Virtual Reality Technologies*. Boston College Intellectual Property and Technology forum. Available at: http://bciptf.org/2017/12/copyright-issues-and-implications-of-emerging-virtual-reality-technologies/. Accessed 7 July 2018.

Bergonse, R. (2017). Firty Years on, What Exactly Is a Videogame? An Essentialistic Definitional Approach. *The Computer Games Journal, 6*(4), 239, 253.

Boyden, B. E. (2011). Games and Other Uncopyrightable Systems. *George Mason Law Review, 18*, 479.

Buckman, D. F. (2005). Intellectual Property Rights in Video, Electronic, and Computer Games. *American Law Report Fed.2d* (7), 269.

Burrell, R., & Coleman, A. (2005). *Copyright Exceptions: The Digital Impact* (pp. 190, 191). Cambridge University Press.

Calandrillo, S. P. (1998). An Economic Analysis of Intellectual Property Rights: Justifications and Problems of Exclusive Rights, Incentives to Generate Information, and the Alternatives of a Government-Run Reward System. *Fordham Intellectual Property Media & Entertainment Journal, 9*, 301, 316–322.

Casillas, B. (2013). Attack of the Clones: Copyright Protection for Video Game Developers. *Loyola of Los Angeles Entertainment Law Review, 33*, 137.

Chang, Y. [苌雅洁]. (2019). Study on the Legal Protection Mechanism to Prevent Minors from Indulging in Online Games [防范未成年人沉迷网络游戏的法律保障机制研究]. *Changjiang Forum [长江论坛]* (5).

Coase, R. H. (1996). The Problem of Social Cost. *Journal of Law and Economics, 3*, 2, 15–16.

Cole, R. R. (1995). Substantial Similarity in the Ninth Circuit. *Santa Clara Computer & High Technology Law Journal, 11*, 417.

Cronin, P. (2012). The Historical Original of the Conflict between Copyright and First Amendment. *Columbia Journal of Law & the Arts, 35*, 231.

Cui, G. [崔国斌]. (2016). Taking the Copyright of Games Seriously [认真对待游戏著作权]. *Intellectual Property [知识产权]* (2).

Darling, K. (2015). Occupy Copyright: A Law & Economic Analysis of U.S. Author Termination Rights. *Buffalo Law Review, 63*, 147–148.

De Rosnay, M. D., & De Martin, J. C. (Eds.). (2012). *The Digital Public Domain: Foundations for an Open Culture* (p. 18). Open Book Publisher.

Dean, D. S. (2016). Hitting Reset: Devising a New Video Game Copyright Regime. *University of Pennsylvania Law Review, 164*, 1239.

Demsetz, H. (1967). Toward a Theory of Property Rights. *The American Economic Review, 57*, 348.

Ding, W. [丁文杰]. (2019). The Basic Connotation and Identification Rules of "Access" Element [接触要件的基本内涵及认定规则]. *Intellectual Property* (2), 24.

Donnelly, J. (2004). Video Games and Reverse Engineering: Before and After the Digital Millennium Copyright Act. *Journal of Telecommunication & High Technology Law, 3*, 209–229.

Esposito, N. (2005). *A Short and Simple Definition of What a Videogame Is*. University of Technology of Compiegne, Digital Games Research Conference, Changing Views: Worlds in Play, Vancouver, British Columbia, Canada. Available at: https://www.researchgate.net/publication/221217421_A_Short_and_Simple_Definition_of_What_a_Videogame_Is. Accessed 30 March 2021.

European Commission. (2006). *Study on the Economy of Culture in Europe. European Affairs*. Available at: http://ec.europa.eu/assets/eac/culture/library/studies/cultural-economy_en.pdf. Accessed 3 August 2018.

Feng, X. [冯晓青]. (2006). *The Theory of Interest Balance in Intellectual Property Law [知识产权利益平衡理论]* (p. 1). China University of Political Science and Law Press [中国政法大学出版社].

Feng, X. [冯晓青]. (2017). Study on the Legal Attribute of the Frame of Live Streaming of Online Games and Related Copyright Issues [网络游戏直播画面的作品属性及其相关著作权问题研究]. *Intellectual Property [知识产权]* (1).

Fisher, W. W., III. (1988). Reconstructing the Fair Use Doctrine. *Harvard Law Review, 101*, 1669.

Fitzgerald, B., & Gilchrist, J. (Eds.). (2015). *Copyright Perspectives: Past, Present and Prospect* (p. 6). Springer.

Frankel, S., & Gervais, D. (2014). *The Evolution and Equilibrium of Copyright in the Digital Age* (p. 3). Cambridge University Press.

Garon, J. M. (2010). Video Games, Virtual Worlds and Social Media. In *Entertainment Law & Practice*. Carolina Academic Press.

Glasser, A. R. (1986). Video Voodoo: Copyright in Video Game Computer Programs. *Federal Communications Law Journal, 38*, 103.

Goldstein, P. (1994). Comments on A Manifesto Concerning the Legal Protection of Computer Programs. *Columbia Law Review, 94*, 2573, 2574.

Goldstein, P. (2002). *Cases and Materials on the Law of Intellectual Property* (5th ed., p. 6). Foundation Press.

Gong, Y. [龚玉花]. (2020). Study on the Legal Mechanism of Correcting Minors' Gaming Addiction [未成年人网络游戏沉迷矫正法律机制浅析]. *Children's Study [少年儿童研究]* (8).

Gordon, W. J. (1989). Fair Use as Market Failure: A Structural and Economic Analysis of the Betamax Case and Its Predecessors. *Columbia Law Review, 82*, 1600, 1601, 1604.

Gordon, W. J. (1992). A Property Right in Self-Expression: Equality and Individualism in the Natural Law of Intellectual Property. *Yale Law Journal, 102*, 1533–1609.

Griffiths, M. D. (2000). Does Internet and Computer "Addiction" Exist? Some Case Study Evidence. *Cyber Psychology and Behavior, 3*, 211.

Griffiths, M. D. (2008). Videogame Addiction: Further Thoughts and Observations. *International Journal of Mental Health Addiction, 6*, 182.

Grosheide, F. W., Roerdink, H., & Thomas, K. (2014). Intellectual Property Protection for Video Games: A View from the European Union. *Journal of International Commercial Law and Technology* (9).

Hao, M. [郝敏]. (2016). Intellectual Property Protection of the Elements of Online Games [网络游戏要素的知识产权保护]. *Intellectual Property [知识产权]* (1).

Herrera González, H. C. (2016). *Protection of Video Game Mechanics Through the Patentability of Software* (p. 11). WIPO Academy, University of Turin and ITC-ILO, Research Papers Collection-2015–2016. Available at SSRN: https://ssrn.com/abstract=2922218

Heilbrun, J., & Gray, C. M. (2001). *The Economics of Art and Culture* (2nd ed., p. 174). Cambridge University Press.

Horkheimer, M., & Adorno, T. (2002). The Cultural Industry: Enlightenment as Mass Deception. In E. Jephcott (Trans.), *The Dialectic of Enlightenment*. Stanford University Press.

Hua, J. (2013). *Toward A More Balanced Approach: Rethinking and Readjusting Copyright Systems in the Digital Network Era* (p. 1). PhD thesis, The University of Hong Kong.

Hughes, J. (1988). The Philosophy of Intellectual Property. *Georgetown Law Journal, 77*, 287.

Joo, J. (2011). Public Video Gaming as Copyright Infringement. *American Intellectual Property Law Association Quarterly Journal, 39*.

Jungar, E. (2016). Streaming Video Games: Copyright Infringement or Protected Speech. *Press Start* (3).

Kang, Y. [康亚通]. (2019). The Governance of Teenagers' Internet Addiction [青少年网络沉迷问题的治理]. *Education and Protection [教育和保护]* (5).

Kaplow, L., & Shavell, S. (2002). *Fairness Versus Welfare*. Harvard University Press.

Kennedy, R. (2008). Virtual Rights: Property in Online Game Objects and Characters. *Information & Communications Technology Law, 17*, 95, 106.

Kim, S. J. (2014). Study of Copyright Issues Surrounding Online Gaming. *Yonsei Law Journal, 5*, 75, 85–86.

Kretzschmar, M., & Stanfill, M. (2018). Mods as Lightning Rods: A Typology of Video Game Mods, Intellectual Property, and Social Benefit/Harm. *Social & Legal Studies, 28*(4), 517, 519.

Kuss, D. J., & Griffiths, M. D. (2012). Internet Gaming Addiction: A Systematic Review of Empirical Research. *International Journal of Mental Health and Addiction, 10*(2), 278–296.

Landes, W., & Posner, R. A. (1989). An Economic Analysis of Copyright Law. *Journal of Legal Studies, 28*, 325.

Landes, W., & Posner, R. A. (2003). *The Economic Structure of Intellectual Property Law* (p. 109). Harvard University Press.

Leite, E. L. (2014). The Fair Use Doctrine as a Limitation to Copyright and a Comparative Analysis of the Three-Step Test in the Copyright Systems of Brazil and the United States (p. 70). PhD thesis, American University Washington, DC.

Lemmens, J. S., Valkenburg, P. M., & Peter, J. (2011). Psychosocial Causes and Consequences of Pathological Gaming. *Computers in Human Behavior, 27*, 144.

Li, Y. [李亚虹]. (2016). *Copyright, Network and Right Balance [版权、网络和权利平衡]*. Hong Kong University Press [香港大学出版社].

Li, Y. [李扬]. (2017). Copyright Issues Surrounding Live Streaming of Online Games [网络游戏直播中的著作权问题]. *Intellectual Property [知识产权]* (1).

Li, Z. [李宗勇]. (2005). Legal Protection of Online Games [网络游戏的法律保护]. *Cyber Law Review [网络法律评论]* (1).

Liebenstein, H. (1966). Allocative vs. X-Efficiency. *The American Economic Review, 56*, 392–415.

Lin, J. (1989). An Economic Theory of Institutional Change: Induced and Imposed Change. *Cato Journal, 9*(1), 3.

Lin, Y. [林悦], et al. (2021). Study on the Relationship Between Parental Neglection and Adolescents' Gaming Addiction: The Mediating Role of Hope and the Moderating Role of Gender [父母忽视与青少年网络游戏成瘾的关系: 希望的中介作用和性别的调节作用]. *Psychological Development and Education [心理发展与教育], 37*(01).

Lipson, A. S., & Brain, R. D. (2009). *Computer and Video Game Law—Cases, Statutes, Forms, Problems & Materials* (p. 54). Carolina Academic Press.

Lipton, J. (2011). Moral Rights and Supernatural Fiction: Authorial Dignity and the New Moral Rights Agendas. *Fordham Intellectual Property, Media & Entertainment Law Journal, 21*(3), 537–578.

Liu, Y. (Trans.). (2001). Treating Intellectual Property as a Human Right: Obligations Related to Article 15, Paragraph 1, Section 3 [将知识产权视为人权: 与第 15 条第 1 款地 3 项有关的义务]. *Copyright Bulletin [版权公报]* (3), 6.

Lunney, G. S., Jr. (1996). Reexamining Copyright's Incentive-Access Paradigm. *Vanderbilt Law Review, 49*, 488–489.

Mac Sithigh, D. (2010). The Regulation of Video Games: Past, Present and Future. *Entertainment Law Review, 21*(8), 298.

Martinez, P. S. (1995). *The Texts of Philosophy of Law* (p. 297). Almedina.

Matsui, S. (2016). Does It Have to Be a Copyright Infringement: Live Game Streaming and Copyright. *Texas Intellectual Property Law Journal, 24*, 215, 244.

Meng, X., & Xu, K. [孟祥娟 & 徐坤宇]. (2016). Analysis of Copyright Protection and Authorization of Game MOD [游戏 MOD 著作权保护与授权探析]. *Intellectual Property [知识产权]* (10).

Merges, R. P., Menell, P. S., & Lemly, M. A. (2006). *Intellectual Property in the New Technological Age* (4th ed., p. 13). Aspen Publishers.

Meyer, K. R. (2010). Doctrine of the Dead: How Capcom v. MKR Exposes the Decreasing Fit Between Modern Copyright Infringement Analysis and Modern Video Games. *Chicago-Kent Journal of Intellectual Property, 9*, 132.

Miceli, T. J. (2017). *The Economic Approach to Law* (3rd ed., pp. 2–4, 10). Stanford University Press.

Mtima, L., & Jamar, S. D. (2010). Fulfilling the Copyright Social Justice Promise: Digitizing Textual Information. *New York Law School Law Review, 55*, 77, 81–82, 83.

Nardi, B., & Kallinikos, J. (2007). *Opening the Black Box of Digital Technologies: Mods in World of Warcraft*. In 23rd EGOS Colloquium, Vienna, Australia, pp. 5–7.

Netanel, N. W. (1996). Copyright and a Democratic Civil Society. *Yale Law Journal, 106*, 283, 288.

Netanel, N. W. (1998). Asserting Copyright's Democratic Principles in the Global Arena. *Vanderbilt Law Review, 51*, 217.

Nimmer, M. B., & Nimmer, D. (2015). *Nimmer on Copyright*. Matttew Bender Elite Products, p s.8.09[A][1].

North, D. C. (1990). *Institutions, Institutional Change and Economic Performance* (pp. 6, 8). Cambridge University Press.

Patry, W. (2012). *How to Fix Copyright* (pp. 11, 14, 18, 74, 215, 228). Oxford University Press.

Patterson L. R. (1987). 'Free Speech, Copyright, and Fair Use'. *Vanderbilt Law Review, 40*, p 3.

Patterson, L. R., & Birch, S. F., Jr. (2009). A Unified Theory of Copyright. C. Joyce (Ed.), printed in *Houston Law Review, 46*, 215, 305, 355–356.

Posner, R. A. (2003). *Economic Analysis of Law* (6th ed., pp 9–18, 20–27). Aspen Publishers.

Puddington, J. (2015). Fair Play: Economic Justifications for Applying Fair Use to the Online Streaming of Video games. *Boston University Journal of Science & Technology Law, 21*.

Qi, X. [熊琦]. (2011). *Copyright's Incentive Structure [著作权激励机制的法律构造]* (pp. 22, 24–25, 35, 182, 184–187). China Renmin University Press [中国人民大学出版社].

Rachum-Twaig, O. (2017). Recreating Copyright: The Cognitive Process of Creation and Copyright Law. *Forham Intellectual Property, Media and Entertainment Law Journal, 27*, 346.

Report of the World Commission on Environment and Development: Our Common Future. (1987). Available at: https://sustainabledevelopment.un.org/content/documents/5987our-common-future.pdf. Accessed 12 December 2024.

Reuveni, E. (2007). On Virtual Worlds: Copyright and Contract Law at the Dawn of the Virtual Age. *Indiana Law Journal, 82*, 261–284.

Romas, A., et al. (2013). *The Legal Status of Video Games: Comparative Analysis in National Approaches* (pp. 10, 11, 27–28). WIPO.

Rosen, Z. (2005). Mod, Man, and Law: A Reexamination of the Law of Computer Game Modifications. *Chi-Kent Journal of Intellectual Property, 4*, 196–215.

Ruhl, J. B. (2008). Law's Complexity: A Primer. *Georgia State University Law Review, 24*, 885–889.

Samuelson, P. (2013). The Quest for a Sound Conception of Copyright's Derivative Work Right. *Georgetown Law Journal, 101*, 1505.

Savirimuthu, J. (2012). Review on Complex Copyright: Mapping the Information Ecosystem. *International Journal of Law and Information Technology, 20*, 382.

Scutti, S. (2018). *WHO Classifies "Gaming Disorder" as Mental Health Condition.* CNN News. Available at: https://edition.cnn.com/2018/06/18/health/video-game-disorder-who/index.html. Accessed 30 December 2024.

Seltzer, L. E. (2006). *Exemptions and Fair Use in Copyright: The Exclusive Rights Tensions in the 1976 Copyright Act*. Harvard University Press.

Smith, H. E. (2007). Intellectual Property as Property: Delineating Entitlements in Information. *Yale Law Journal, 116*, 1742.

Song, H. [宋慧献]. (2006). Preliminary Study on Copyright Ecology and Copyright Innovation [版权生态与版权创新初论]. *Intellectual Property [知识产权]* (6), 27, 66.

Stein, J. S. (2015). The Legal Nature of Video Games-Adapting Copyright Law to Multimedia. *Press Start* (2), 43–53.

Stetina, B. U., et al. (2011). Beyond the Fascination of Online-Games: Probing Addictive Behavior and Depression in the World of Online-Gaming. *Computers in Human Behavior, 27*, 473.

Sun, L., & Cao, L. [孙磊 & 曹丽萍]. (2017). *Judicial Protection of Intellectual Property Rights of Online Games [网络游戏知识产权司法保护]* (pp. 20–29, 273–284). China Legal Publishing House [中国法制出版社].

Sun, Q. [孙秋梅]. (2020). Study on the Prevention of Gaming Addiction of Higher Vocational College Students by School Cooperation [学校联合构建预防高职大学生网络游戏成瘾屏障研究]. *Journal of Vocational College [职大学报]* (3).

Tavinor, G. (2008). Definition of Video Games. *Contemporary Aesthetics, 1*(6). See also Leino, O. (2010). *Emotions in Play: On the Constitution of Emotion in Solitary Computer Game Play* (pp 127–128). PhD thesis, IT University of Copenhagen.

Torremans, P. L. C. (Ed.). (2004). *Copyright and Human Rights*. Kluwer Law International.

Tsesis, A. (2015). Balancing Free Speech. *Boston University Law Review, 96*.

Turner, G. (2003). *Tony Hawk's Pro Skater 4*. Inside Mac Games. Available at: http://www.insidemacgames.com/reviews/view.php?ID=420. Accessed 30 December 2024.

Tussey, D. (2012). *Complex Copyright: Mapping the Information Ecosystem* (pp. 2–3, 55, 57). Routledge.

Van Rooiji, A. J., et al. (2010). *Online Video Game Addiction: Identification of Addicted Adolescent Gamers*. Research Report.

Wallace, R. (2014). Modding: Amateur Authorship and How the Video Game Industry Is Actually Getting it Right. *BYU Law Review*, 219–255.

Wang, L. [王亮], Liu, Y. [刘阳], & Zhang, L. [张丽]. (2015). Construction of Copyright Chain Under the Environment of Mobile Internet [构建移动互联网环境下的版权生态链]. *Science-Technology & Publication [科技与出版]* (9), 67.

Wang, Q. [王迁]. (2016). Study on the Copyright Issues of Live Streaming of Video Game [电子游戏直播的著作权问题研究]. *Electronics Intellectual Property [电子知识产权]* (2).

Wang, Q., & Yuan, F. [王迁 & 袁锋]. (2016). Legal Nature of the Whole Audiovisual Display of Online Games [论网络游戏整体画面的作品定性]. *China Copyright [中国版权]* (4).

Weinstein, A. M. (2010). Computer and Video Game Addiction—A Comparison Between Game Users and Non-game Users. *The American Journal of Drug and Alcohol Abuse, 36*, 268.
Wong, M. W. S. (2009). Toward an Alternative Normative Framework for Copyright: From Private Property to Human Rights. *Cardozo Arts & Entertainment, 26*, 775.
Wu, F. [吴峰]. (2005a). Intellectual Property, Human Rights, and Development [知识产权、人权、发展]. *Journal of Shanghai University of Technology [上海理工大学学报]* (3).
Wu, H. [吴汉东]. (2005b). *Research on the Copyright Fair Use System [著作权合理使用制度研究]* (p. 13). China University of Political Science and Law Press [中国政法大学出版社].
Wu, H. [吴汉东]. (2011). The Diverse Attributes and Research Paradigms of Intellectual Property rights [知识产权的多元属性及研究范式]. *Social Sciences in China [中国社会科学]* (5).
Xie, L. [谢琳]. (2017). Study on the Copyright Fair Use of Live Streaming of video Games [网络游戏直播的著作权合理使用研究]. *Intellectual Property [知识产权]* (1).
Yuan, B. [袁博]. (2017). Can the Audiovisual Display of Games Be Protected as "Film Like Work"? [游戏画面可以作为"类电作品"保护吗?]. *Zhichanli [知产力]*.
Zeng, X., & Guan, Y. [曾晰 & 关永红]. (2017). Copyright Protection and Path Exploration of Online Game Rules [网络游戏规则的著作权保护及其路径探微]. *Intellectual Property [知识产权]* (6).
Zhang, Y. [张永欣], et al. (2020). Study on the Relationship Between Psychological Resistance, Parental Online Supervision and Junior High School Students' Gaming Addiction [心理阻抗、父母网络监管与初中生网络游戏成瘾的关系]. *China Journal of Clinical Psychology [中国临床心理学杂志], 28*(04).
Zhou, Y. [周瑛]. (2020). *Study on the Relationship Between Parentage Communication, School Belonging, Basic Psychological Needs and Adolescents' Gaming Addiction [亲子沟通、学校归属感、基本心理需求与青少年网络游戏成瘾的关系]*. Mphil These, Central China Normal University [华中师范大学].
Zhu, J. [祝建军]. (2017). Study on the Copyright Issues Surrounding Live Streaming of Online Games [网络游戏直播的著作权问题研究]. *Intellectual Property [知识产权]* (1).
Zweigert, K., & Kötz, H. (2003). *Einfuhrung in die Rechtsvergleichung [比较法总论]*. (P. Handian, Trans., p. 56) [潘汉典等译]. Law Press [法律出版社].

## Legislations

Berne Convention
The 1710 Statute of Anne
The 1996 WIPO Copyright Treaty (WCT)
The 1996 WIPO Performances and Phonograms Treaty (WPPT)
The Digital Millennium Copyright Act
The Indonesian Copyright Law
The TRIPS Agreement
The US Constitution
The US Copyright Act of 1909

## Cases

Mazer v. Stein, 347 U.S. 201, 219 (1954).
Midway Mfg. Co. v. Artic Int'l, Inc., Copyright L.REP. CCCH) 25, 337, at 16,890 (N.D. III. June 2, 1981).
Nichols v. Universal Pictures Corp. 45 F.2d 119 (2d Cir.1930), cert. denied, 282 U.S. 902 (1931).

See Lateef Mtima & Steven D. Jamar (n 50), p. 83.
Tetris Holding, LLC v. Xio Interactive, Inc. 863 F.Supp.2d 394 (D.N.J. 2012).

# Chapter 3
# Piercing the Veil: Video Games' Legal Attribute

**Abstract** This chapter examines the legal attribute of VGs. First, it discusses and compares the pros and cons of the four key copyright protection models for VGs on a global scale: the computer program model, the audiovisual or cinematographic work model, the distributive protection model and the multimedia work model. Next, it explores the current status and drawbacks of the copyright protection model for VGs in China. In-depth analysis reveals that categorizing VGs is not a prerequisite for copyrightability; however, it is a necessity in dispute resolution. The chapter also finds that the degree of interactivity between VGs and end users does not affect the legal attribute of VGs, although strong intervention may allow gamers to create new works. It concludes with a statement on the importance of distinguishing VGs from computer programs and audiovisual works and of protecting them as a new type of copyrightable works irrespective of whether they can be protected as "other intellectual creations" under the miscellaneous provisions of copyright laws. Besides, the chapter proposes a hybrid protection model for VGs, that is, an amalgamative regime for the protection of audiovisual works and computer programs. The significance of this model is also indicated by its protection of game mechanisms or the expression of game rules, as discussed in the following chapter.

**Keywords** Legal attribute · Copyright protection models · Interactivity · A hybrid protection model

## 3.1 Introduction

Legal attribute is the most fundamental issue concerning VG copyright protection, as it determines the boundary between the rights of the original game developers and the rights of subsequent game developers and players. However, the multimedia nature of VGs renders them inadequately protected by the laws governing the existing categories of copyrighted works. This gives rise to my first research question. What is the legal attribute of VGs and how can the copyright protection model for this type of product be improved? In this chapter, I provide a succinct overview of copyright



Z. Deng, *Constructing an Eco-Balanced Copyright Regime for the Video Game Industry in China*, https://doi.org/10.1007/978-981-96-6056-8_3

protection models for VGs across the globe, with a focus on their pros and cons. These comprise the computer program model, the audiovisual or cinematographic work model, the distributive protection model and the multimedia work model. I then discuss the current copyright protection model for VGs in China. After a critical and comparative analysis, I propose to categorize VGs as a new type of copyrighted work and design a hybrid protection model to protect both their audiovisual nature and the underlying computer programs.

## 3.2 Copyright Protection Models for VGs Across the Globe

### *3.2.1 Computer Program Model*

VG software, also known as the "game engine," is the main part of a VG. It is a technical instrument used both for the development of the VG and to drive its function on the console, smartphone or computer. Given that a VG is in essence akin to software, some countries consider a VG to be predominantly a computer program. For example, Point 4 (b) of Singapore's Copyright (Excluded Works) Order of 2008 excludes the application of the Singaporean Copyright Act provision regarding the circumvention of TPMs to "any computer program or video game… which is distributed in an obsolete format and…to which access may be gained only by means of the original medium or hardware in or with which it was designed to be used or operated." This exclusion of protection seems to address only the circumvention of VG TPMs; however, in some IP experts' opinions, it literally means that VGs should otherwise enjoy the same protection afforded to computer programs (Romas et al., 2013). The Singaporean Copyright Act further protects computer programs as literary works (Section 7A) and provides for copyright protection of both the source codes and object codes (Creative Technology Ltd. v. Aztech Systems pte Ltd, 1997). These copyright regulations for computer programs are consistent with the Berne Convention and similar to those in most other countries.

However, classifying VGs as computer programs offers them inadequate copyright protection. First of all, unlike traditional literary works, the expression of computer programs seems to warrant no protection, as it comprises only a sequence of instructions directed at the machine, which is immaterial to be simple or cumbersome; it lacks the rhetorical or lyrical value, genre and deep meaning found in the expression of traditional literary works. Besides, the popularity of VGs primarily depends on the creativity of their audio-visual outputs rather than their software programs. Indeed, most players are uninterested in the software underlying a VG except insofar as it determines the audio-visual effects (Small, 1983). A further problem with classifying VGs as merely computer programs is that computer program infringement is determined by comparing source codes or object codes, and these codes can be easily converted into different expressions to the same effect. For example, program codes can be translated into different programming languages and certain lines of code can be reordered without any impact on the overall program. Competitors can develop VG software with functionality identical to that of a popular VG using entirely different text codes or reverse engineering to circumvent copyright law that protects only expressions but not ideas (Samuelson et al., 1994). For example, in SAS Institute Inc. v. World Programming Ltd (WPL), the central argument was whether WPL had infringed copyrights on SAS Institute Products and Manuals and whether WPL used SAS Learning Edition to reverse engineer SAS system in violation with its term of usage. The EU Court of Justice confirmed that neither the functionality of a computer program nor the programming language and the format of data files used in a computer program in order to exploit certain of its functions constitute a form of expression of that program, and so they are not protected by copyright. The court then ruled that there is no copyright infringement when a company without accessing to the source code of a program studies, observes and tests that program to create another program with the same functionality (SAS Institute Inc. v. World Programming Ltd., 2012). It is understandable that if the law allowed copyright protection of functionality, ideas would be monopolized and this could stifle innovation. Goldstein (1986), among others, argued that legislation and courts should limit the copyright protection of computer programs to "verbatim copying" of the code or even at a lower level. Such kind of protection might offer no substantive protection for game developers. But notably, the court did admit that reproducing parts of a user manual in another program or in a manual for another program would infringe copyright if the parts copied are the author's own intellectual creation (SAS Institute Inc. v. World Programming Ltd., 2012).

Other legal systems are in place to protect computer programs, namely patent law and trade secret protection. However, these systems have shortcomings as well. In terms of patents, it is difficult to determine whether software meets the requirements of novelty, usefulness and non-obviousness. The cost of a patent application is relatively high. Furthermore, patents provide a monopoly, which impedes the development of innovative software. Trade secret protection is also insufficient, as it does not prevent the use of reverse engineering technology to crack software. Given these facts, most countries have abandoned the idea of protecting VGs solely as computer programs, instead relying on other forms of copyright protection. Even Singapore, the country regarding VGs primarily as computer programs, does not rule out the possibility of viewing them as audiovisual works in some circumstances.[1]

[1] According to Section 102 of the Singaporean Copyright Act, "audiovisual works" means "a sound recording, a cinematograph film, a sound broadcast, a television broadcast or a cable programme", and "cinematograph films" means "the aggregate of visual images embodied in an article or thing so as to be capable by the use of that article or thing (a) of being shown as a moving picture; or (b) of being embodied in another article or thing by the use of which it can be so shown, and includes the aggregate of the sounds embodied in a sound-track associated with such visual images."

### 3.2.2 Audiovisual or Cinematographic Work Model

In early VG copyright cases, some national courts did not favor the audiovisual work model for VGs, for two main reasons. First, these courts held that the screen output of a VG was not original enough to qualify as an audiovisual work, as the images and their sequences were essentially generated by the game's computer program. Second, they held that VGs did not meet the fixation requirement to qualify as films, due to the intervention of players in the gameplay (Stamatoudi, 2002). However, some countries, such as the US and Japan, have viewed many VGs as audiovisual works from the beginning. In *Stern Elecs., Inc v. Kaufman*, the court ruled that "a moment of originality did occur in the creation of the specific images and sounds present in the game and that the originality of these images was not completely dependent upon the underlying program, as many different underlying programs could have been written to generate the images and sounds the game creator had imagined." As for the fixation requirement, the court held that "the role of the players was not found to be creative or in any aspect capable of transforming the form and nature of the work. He only gives rise in a pre-established program to one or other situation, the number of which is by definition limited. The sufficient elements of the look and feel of the game remain fixed regardless of the individual player's actions" (Stern Elecs., Inc v. Kaufman, 1982). Moreover, the Japanese Supreme Court stated that "the VG in dispute was expressed through a process producing visual or audiovisual effects similar to those of cinematography, and such expression was fixed in an object" (Supreme Court Case No. H13-ju-952).

In South Korea, VGs have always been protected as computer programs. However, jurisprudence and doctrine today mainly recognize VGs as audiovisual or cinematographic works when they satisfy the prerequisites set forth in the Korean Copyright Act of 2009. Article 2 (13) of the Act states that a cinematographic work is a "creative production in which a series of images (regardless of whether or not accompanied by sound) are collected, and which can be played by mechanical or electronic devices and can be seen, or both seen and heard." When a VG qualifies for protection as both a computer program and a cinematographic work, the owner of the VG generally seeks to protect it as a cinematographic work, as this offers much stronger protection.

Although classification as audiovisual works affords VGs stronger protection than does classification as computer programs, some countries have no specific copyrights for audiovisual works, and some jurisdictions' copyright laws for cinematographic works do not apply to VGs. Taking the UK's practice as an example, due to the judicial practice that copyright protection does not extend to the software functionality, the programming language used and the format of the data files used by the program (SAS Institute Inc. v. World Programming Ltd., 2012), in Nova Productions Ltd. v. Mazooma Games Ltd., when the copyright holder needs to rely on film copyright to protect the audiovisual appearance of the work, the High Court stated that "[f]ilm copyright in the UK only protects against infringement by frame-for-frame reproduction. For VGs this means the game must be copied as a whole, so there is no protection against close recreation of the game." In addition, VGs and films differ significantly: VGs are interactive, operational and rule-oriented, while films involve passive appreciation by consumers. This has produced strong opposition to the classification of VGs as cinematographic works.

### 3.2.3 *Distributive Protection Model*

Most countries adopt the distributive protection model for VGs. The Supreme Court of Japan, for example, affirmed that VGs could be classified as "cinematographic works" in accordance with Article 2(3) of the Japanese Copyright Act, which includes works "expressed by a process producing visual or audio-visual effects analogous to those of cinematography and fixed in some material form" (Supreme Court Case No. H13-ju-952). However, whereas the distribution rights of traditional cinematographic works may not be exhausted under the first-sale doctrine, the Supreme Court of Japan ruled that such rights for VGs may be exhausted (Romas et al., 2013). Additionally, the computer source code (and not the object code) is protectable as a literary work, provided that it is creative and original (Romas et al., 2013). Under the distributive protection model, if a VG meets all of the requirements for computer program classification and audiovisual work classification and is sufficiently original, then the protection for both types of works is afforded to the VG. Furthermore, if a VG fails to qualify for one form of protection (e.g. as a cinematographic work), third parties are permitted to copy only the corresponding part (e.g. the audiovisual output), not the entire VG.

In the US, there is no clear classification of VGs; thus, protection varies depending on the game and how it is classified. If it qualifies as a computer program, its source code is protected as a literary work. If its pictorial or graphic authorship is predominant, a VG may be classified and protected as a visual arts work. Alternatively, a VG may be protected as a motion picture or audiovisual work if the authorship of these elements is predominant (Romas et al., 2013).

France's distributive approach is also worth noting. In France, although no legislations provide a legal classification or a special regime for VGs, VGs can secure protection under the Intellectual Property Code of France as per Article L 112-1, which states that "the provisions of this Code shall protect the rights of authors in all works of the mind, whatever their kind, form of expression, merit or purpose." Case law has established that VGs are considered "works of mind" and protected under the general copyright law (Atari v. Valadon, 1986). A court recently held that "a VG is a complex work that cannot be reduced to its sole software dimension, however significant it may be, so that each of its components is governed by the legal framework applicable to it according to its nature" (Sarl Aakro Pure Tronic Inc., v. Societe Nintendo Co Ltd, 2011). Under this distributive approach, a VG is considered a complex creation which is impossible to categorize in one sole pre-existing category, and for which each component must be subject to the legal status applicable to it.

The distributive protection model is relatively flexible, providing judges with greater discretion in determining copyright protection. This is particularly helpful for VGs, as it is easiest to categorize them on case-by-case basis due to their wide variety. However, this model raises certain problems. For example, Section 201 (d) of the US Copyright Act provides that the copyrights in a given work may be transferred in whole or in part by means of an assignment or license. Such transfer of copyright ownership (as opposed to a license) requires a written, signed agreement, except that it is one type of statutorily defined "work made for hire" (Section 204 (a) of the US Copyright Act). Section 101 of the Act defines a "work made for hire" as

> (1) a work prepared by an employee within the scope of his or her employment; or (2) a work specially ordered or commissioned for use as a contribution to a collective work, as a part of a motion picture or other audiovisual work, as a translation, as a supplementary work, as a compilation, as an instructional text, as a test, as answer material for a test, or as an atlas, if the parties expressly agree in a written instrument signed by them that the work shall be considered a work made for hire.

In the case of a work made for hire, ownership of copyright belongs to the employer or the person for whom the work was prepared unless the parties have expressly agreed otherwise in a written, signed instrument (Section 201 (b) of the US Copyright Act). However, in scenarios where an enterprise contracts with a vendor to create deliverables, the vendor is generally an independent contractor but not an employee, and consequently the deliverables of the vendor will not qualify as a work prepared by an employee. In such a circumstance, the statutory work-for-hire rule applies only if the work falls into one of the nine classes and the parties enter into a written, signed contract. Because computer program or software is not explicitly listed in the statute, when VGs are defined as computer programs, the work-for-hire provision may not be applicable for use with contractors. What's more, the distributive method may lead to excessive decomposition, as in France, which may increase the complexity of comparing the elements of a VG with those of other types of works. It may also increase the cost of evidence collection and lead to a low level of indemnity.

### *3.2.4 Multimedia Work Model*

In the last few decades, most national courts have viewed VGs as a combination of various types of copyrighted work. The Supreme Court of Italy is a rare exception. This court defined a VG as a single, complex multimedia work and reasoned that "the computer program was only a necessary precondition to get to the crucial and central part of the video game, and the video game [had] more of an audiovisual character" (Romas et al., 2013). Italian doctrine thus created a definition for the multimedia work—"a product that combines simultaneously, in a digital form, text, graphic, sounds, images and software" (Romas et al., 2013). It is practical to consider VGs as a whole, particularly as case law has shown that copying even small parts of an entire work can constitute substantial infringement (Spelling Goldberg Productions Inc. v. P.P.C. Publishing Ltd, 1981). However, though the Italian court did provide a specific definition of the multimedia work, no copyright legislation since incorporated this interpretation.

Recently, Indonesian legislation has taken the lead in classifying VGs as a new type of work, based on both cinematographic works and computer programs. Article 40 of the Indonesian Copyright Lawstates that protection covers "work in the fields of science, art, and literature, [including]...cinematographic works; ... video games; and ...computer programs." The same approach has been proposed by academics, who have argued that VGs cannot qualify as audiovisual works due to their complexity and interactivity and proposed instead that a new type of copyrighted work, such as Italy's "multimedia works," be created to address the unique characteristics of this medium (Sun & Cao, 2017). There are, however, considerations that are not addressed by this approach, such as how to define the copyright ownership of a VG and whether the protection for VGs would be weakened by the extension of the "multimedia works" category to new types of works produced through advancements in technology.

## 3.3 Current Status of China's Copyright Protection Model for VGs

China has made enormous efforts to improve its legislation regarding copyright protection for VGs. In China's copyright legislation, the term closest to "video games" is "online games." Pursuant to Article 2 of the *Interim Measures for the Administration of Online Games*, enacted in 2010, "online games" refers to game products and services consisting of software programs and data that are provided via information networks such as the Internet and mobile communication networks. The *Regulations for the Protection of Computer Software* were formulated in 2002 to address the various interests emerging in the development, dissemination and use of computer software and to make any necessary adjustments thereto (Article 1). The PRC Copyright Law (Article 3 (8) & Article 53) also specifically provides for the protection of computer software. As VGs can be classified as computer software, they are protected under the *Regulations for the Protection of Computer Software* and the PRC Copyright Law.

Departing from this classification of VGs as strictly computer programs (Romas et al., 2013), China's People's Courts have gradually realized the importance of the audiovisual displays involved in VGs. As early as the *DOTA2* case, the court in question was reluctant to define the audiovisual aspects of a VG as copyrightable. The court reasoned that "because there is no script or other pre-design in the e-sport, the audiovisual displays of the e-sport are dynamic images generated by the players according to the rules of the game. It is an objective and intuitive form of expression of the contest situation in progress. The process of the contest is random and non-reproducible, and the result of the contest is uncertain. Therefore, the dynamic images of the e-sport do not belong to the 'work' stipulated by Copyright Law"

([2015] Civil Verdict No.191 (IP) People's Court of Pudong New Area of Shanghai; [2015] Shanghai (IP) Civil Verdict (Final) No. 641). It was not until the *Miracle MU* case that the displays of a VG were first recognized by a Chinese court as a "cinematographic work" ([2015] Civil Verdict No.529 (IP) People's Court of Pudong New Area of Shanghai). The Court of Appeal affirmed this judgement, holding that "the characteristic manifestation of a cinematographic work lies in the continuously dynamic images. The essence of such continuously dynamic images in VGs is produced by the choice of different operations, which does not exceed the pictures preset by game designers. Hence it is not the creation outside the preexisting game" ([2016] Civil Verdict Final No. 190 Shanghai 73). This view was later adopted by the Guangzhou IP Court in the *Fantasy Westward Journey* case ([2015] Civil Verdict No. 16 (IP) Guangdong). In April 2018, the Beijing High People's Court released the *Guidelines for the Trial of Copyright Infringement Cases.* According to Article 2.14 of the *Guidelines*, "[s]tatic game images can be protected as works of fine art; continuously dynamic game images can be protected as cinematographic works; and the whole game can also be protected as computer software." The *Guidelines* also acknowledge that "each element of an online game may constitute a work individually" (Article 2.15). Thus, the judiciary in China currently adopts a distributive approach to copyright protection for VGs.

In addition to the aforementioned shortcomings of the distributive approach, there are other disadvantages in the Chinese context. For example, in China, cinematographic works are defined as "works which are recorded on some material, consisting of a series of images, with or without accompanying sound, and which can be projected with the aid of suitable devices or communicated by other means" (Article 4 (11) of the *Regulation*). Some scholars argued that the continuous, dynamic images in games are not "recorded on some material" so that the cinematographic works classification seems a poor fit to protect the audiovisual displays of VGs (Wang, 2016). To address the above concerns, the latest PRC Copyright Law, which was passed on November 11, 2020 and came into effect on June 1, 2021, officially created the category of "audiovisual works" to replace that of "cinematographic works and works created by a process analogous to cinematography" (Article 3 (6) of the PRC Copyright Law (2021)). This revision eliminates some of the controversies surrounding the definition of cinematographic works and its application to VGs. However, other problems remain unsolved. Above all, if the continuous dynamic pictures can be defined as audiovisual works, then whether the specific dynamic pictures with unique audiovisual effects in a VG, such as blooming fireworks automatically popped up by the system after an excellent task, can also be defined as an independent audiovisual work? If so, then whether a VG contains several audiovisual works—the overall picture as an audiovisual work and the numerous short dynamic pictures as separate audiovisual works? Moreover, whether the dynamic images operated by different players can be recognized as multiple audiovisual works? If so, to what extent does the content addition, deletion and alteration can be identified as the new expression of an audiovisual work?

## 3.4 Concluding Remarks on VG Classification

### *3.4.1 Categorizing VGs: A Necessity in Dispute Resolution*

The above discussion seems to suggest that copyright protection for VGs can only be provided by properly identifying the category of copyrighted works to which they belong. However, this is not the case at all. The "*numerus clausus*" as a concept in property law states that "the categories of real rights and their contents shall be prescribed by law" (Article 116 of the PRC Civil Code (2021)). Adapting this concept to copyright law, I posit that "the categories and contents" of copyrights, not works, should be stipulated by law. To preserve freedom of creation, the creation of any new art form should be encouraged as long as it does not violate the prohibitive provisions of law, and the types of works defined by copyright law should not be permitted to constrain creativity and innovation (Li, 2018).

It can also be concluded from relevant international conventions and domestic laws that many provisions regarding the types of works under copyright law are enumerative rather than exhaustive. For instance, Article 2 (1) of the Berne Convention states that "the expression 'literary and artistic works' shall include every production in the literary, scientific and artistic domain, whatever may be the mode or form of its expression, *such as* books, pamphlets and other writings…." (emphasis added). Article 10 (1) of the Japanese Copyright Law similarly allows for an expansive interpretation of "works" in its definition of the term: "'works' shall *include*, in particular, the following…" (emphasis added). Additionally, Article L 112-2 of the Intellectual Property Code of France provides that "the following, *in particular*, shall be considered works of the mind within the meaning of this Code" (emphasis added). The use of the words and terms "such as," "include" and "in particular" indicate that the types of works listed are illustrative rather than an exhaustive list. This treatment allows for the possibility of diversification of works driven by technological advancement. As the legislative history of the US Copyright Act of 1976 suggests, "Congress probably wanted the courts to interpret the definitional provisions of the new act flexibly, so that it would cover new technologies as they appeared, rather than to interpret those provisions narrowly and so force Congress periodically to update the act" (Wgn Continental Broadcasting Co. v. U. Video, Inc., 1982).

Another indication that the classification clauses of these statutes are neither definitive provisions of works nor normative statements regarding copyrightability is that they only provide the denotation of "works" (with included categories), not the connotation or the requirements for copyrightability. Thus, there is no reason why copyright protection should not be extended to new forms of creative expression, provided that they are not explicitly excluded by legislation. In the context of VGs, as long as they meet the requirements set by national laws, including originality, they should be eligible for copyright protection, regardless of whether they belong to one or more of the conventional or listed categories of creative works.

The illustrative nature of the categorization of works, however, does not mean that VGs can be classified without careful consideration; they must be considered as a whole and provided with a relatively stable protection model. The first step in the mindful treatment of VGs should rely on their proper categorization, as such categorization makes it easier to find relevant rules and reduces the burden of interpretation. It is more intuitive and easier to judge a new form of expression such as VGs by comparing it with the existing types of works than by comparing it with the abstract concept of "works" (Li, 2018). The categorization of VGs would also facilitate the registration process. Although the enjoyment and the exercise of copyrights shall not be subject to any formality (Article 5(2) of the Berne Convention), copyright registration can help copyright owners determine and clarify the ownership of rights so as to facilitate the settlement of disputes. For example, in a copyright dispute where the copyright owner has to provide evidences to claim his rights, the registered items can be used as the preliminary proof of ownership of rights to protect his relevant economic interests. Moreover, copyright registration can serve as a channel to publicize your works. It is also conducive to copyright transactions and facilitate the signing of contracts, thereby promoting the dissemination of works and the realization of their economic value. By categorizing VGs, registration officers can have a clear idea about the category of a VG without worrying about whether it is a copyrightable work or what type of work it belongs to. Besides, some rules in copyright law are only applicable to certain types of work, which necessitates the classification of works to determine their eligibility. Examples are the special rule of ownership related to cinematographic works and the transferrable moral rights related to computer software.

Furthermore, determining the copyrightability (especially the originality) of a complex intellectual creation taken as a whole is consistent with semiotic principles. The semiotic theory proposed by the linguist de Saussure states (1980) that symbols comprise an indivisible "signifier" (the tangible, visible symbol) and a "signified (the abstract concept of that symbol in one's mind). As applied to copyright law, the physical work (the signifier) is the result of intellectual creation, or symbolic expression (the signified). Popper spilt the world into three categories: World One, which is the world of physical objects and events, including biological entities; World Two, which is the world of mental objects and events; and World Three, which comprises objective knowledge (Popper, 1972). According to Popper's three worlds theory, language, word, color and line may belong to the objective physical world (World One) as well as to the world comprising the products of the human mind (World Three). These elements initially belong to World One, when they are without order and free for all to use in the public domain. When an author or creator chooses and combines these elements, they then belong to World Three as original works protected by copyright law. The perceptible parts of a work, or the signifier of the work, contain the author's ideas, or the signified. Creation does not change the elements themselves; it merely changes the relationships among them (Xiong, 2016). The philosopher Goodman (1988) pointed out that "[i]f things are divided into small enough parts, they will be the same". A work is not equivalent to each of its elements; rather, it arises from the special permutation and combination of these elements and the proportional relationships among them. This abstract arrangement and these proportional relationships reflect the author's unique choice, design and creativity, which account for the originality of the work.

Therefore, when defining a relatively new type of work, such as VGs, we should consider not only the visible signifiers, such as the words, images, sounds, colors and actions within the work, but also the invisible signified, such as the arrangement of and proportional relationships among these elements and their connotations and implications. By considering both aspects of a VG as a whole, we can determine which elements or short expressions (such as the names of the characters, maps, game mechanisms or gameplay rules) carry the meaning of the entire work. This explains why judges in most jurisdictions have classified VGs in terms of existing types of protected works; it is not feasible to protect VGs in such an excessively distributive way as in France.

### 3.4.2 VGs' Interactive Nature: No Impacts on Their Legal Attribute

Realizing that protecting VGs as computer software is not an optimal strategy and acknowledging the significance of VG's audiovisual output, many countries have used the cinematographic or audiovisual work model when determining VG copyrights. However, there are significant differences between cinematographic works and VGs. Cinematographic works mainly rely on their plots to attract audiences, who passively enjoy them. In contrast, VGs allow gamers to enter and interact with virtual worlds. Many VGs, such as open world games, do not have preset storylines or plots. Hence it is a bit farfetched to classify VGs as cinematographic works. Another major difference between VGs and cinematographic works concerns the nature of their audiovisual elements. To address the fact that the continuous dynamic images in games cannot satisfy the requirement that films be recorded in some material form ("fixation") (Article 4(11) of the *Regulations*), the latest version of the PRC Copyright Law has replaced the category of "cinematographic works and works created by a process analogous to cinematography" with that of "audiovisual works" (Article 3 (6)). Given that the connotation and denotation of audiovisual works are broader than that of cinematographic works, it would be an attractive choice to regard the whole dynamic images in games as an audiovisual work when comparing for infringement.

VG design is advancing rapidly, generating more diverse forms and cultural content and offering more open space for gamers' interactivity. This may raise concerns that the originality and fixation requirements will again be tested. However, such concerns are uncalled-for. As to the requirement of originality, the continuous development of the games industry and its marketing has placed increased emphasis on the artistic and audiovisual components of VGs rather than their core computer programs. Competition between VG developers is also increasingly oriented toward creating aesthetically pleasing, distinctive and original game images to offer a more artistic game experience. Thus, the originality requirement is not a concern for VGs, although advanced technology may render cloning easier, which may require more attention from courts in the future.

As for the fixation requirement, some have suggested that the categorization of VGs as audiovisual works is no longer appropriate, as the increased interactivity of VGs puts the player in the role of creator, producing a new work through gameplay rather than choosing from preset elements resulting in screen output predefined by the VG program (Nichols, 2007). To examine this claim, we must first acknowledge the differences between early VGs and modern ones. Initially, most VGs were very simple, offering limited interactivity. Players could only temporarily arrange the sequence of a game's images; they could not alter these images. As a result, players could not exercise creativity for personal creation; their role was restricted by the choices available (Midway Mfg Co. v. Artic International, 1983). Sophisticated modern VGs, in contrast, allow for player intervention to the extent that players now have a creative role and can use their imagination to reconstruct existing works or construct entirely new works throughout gameplay.

This degree of interactivity does not affect VGs' legal attribute, however, as interactivity is not central to the nature of a modern VG. Central to the characterization of a VG is the combination of its various elements in one medium. Although different dynamic game images are visible to different players, "there is always a repetitive sequence of a substantial portion of the sights and sounds of the game, and many aspects of the display remain constant from game to game regardless of how the player operates the controls" (Williams Electronica, Inc. v. Arctic Intern, Inc., 1982). These invariable components are dominant and form a substantial part of the VGs. One US court pointed out that "no matter how the gamers operate, there are essentially unchanged parts between different gamer-operated images, and this is the core content of a VG that all gamers must experience" (Williams Electronica, Inc. v. Arctic Intern, Inc., 1982). Whether this content is original or not has nothing to do with the gamers' intervention, regardless of whether different gamer-operated images would make it difficult for courts to distinguish between the original content of a game and the contributions of a gamer (Lastowka, 2015). Thus, neither the content added by gamers nor the actions they invoke during gameplay would prevent the audiovisual images of a VG from being a distinct audiovisual work. Nevertheless, strong intervention may allow gamers to create new works. Accordingly, courts must take into account gamers' interaction when determining copyright ownership of gameplay (as discussed in Chapter 5).

Although the audiovisual displays of VGs can qualify as audiovisual works per se, the definition of "audiovisual work" varies among jurisdictions. Some countries, such as China, do not define this type of work at all.[2] The WIPO Performances and Phonograms Treaty (WPPT) merely provides a definition of "phonogram"[3] and Article 2(b)

[2] The latest PRC Copyright Law was passed on November 11, 2020 and will come into effect on June 1, 2021, but the corresponding *Regulations for the Implementation of the PRC Copyright Law* has not been amended to provide a definition for the "audiovisual works".

[3] According to Article 2(b) of the WPPT, "'phonogram' means the fixation of the sounds of a performance or of other sounds, or of a representation of sounds, other than in the form of a fixation

of the Beijing Treaty on Audiovisual Performances (BJTAP) only defines "audiovisual fixation" as "the embodiment of moving images, whether or not accompanied by sounds or by the representations thereof, from which they can be perceived, reproduced or communicated through a device." Neither of these regulations provides a definition of "audiovisual work." I suggest that it is time for countries to re-examine their definition of audiovisual works or to create such definitions, ensuring that they are broad enough to include both cinematographic works and the dynamic images of VGs.

The US has set a good example in this regard. Section 101 of the US Copyright Act defines "audiovisual works" as works that "consist of a series of related images which are intrinsically intended to be shown by the use of machines or devices such as projectors, viewers, or electronic equipment, together with accompanying sounds, if any, regardless of the nature of the material objects, such as films or tapes, in which the works are embodied." I suggest that China should similarly define "audiovisual work" under Chinese copyright law as "a work that consists of a series of related images that is intrinsically intended to be shown through the use of a machine or any other devices, regardless of whether it is accompanied by sound, including but not limited to films and NVs."[4] This would permit "audiovisual work" to describe "cinematographic works and works created by a process analogous to cinematography" and also include a variety of new digital forms of work, thus effectively anticipating the products of technological advancement.

### 3.4.3 Hybrid Protection Model for a New Type of Copyrighted Work

VGs are not the only recent innovation pushing the boundaries of copyright legislation. Diverse forms of literary and artistic expression that fall outside the established categories of copyrightable works have also resulted from innovations in communication technology and the vigorous development of the cultural industry. A legislative model that provides a closed enumeration of such work types cannot properly address these newly emerging works. Fortunately, Article 3 of the PRC Copyright Law (2021) has redefined "works" as "the intellectual creations with originality in the literary, artistic, or scientific domain, insofar as they can be reproduced in a tangible form," adding the word "including" to leave space in the classification clauses for new works. This is a practical solution, as it has the power to adapt to the continuous development of new technologies and thus accommodate new products. In cases in which the parties have no objection to the originality of a VG but are confused as

incorporated in a cinematographic or other audiovisual work". And according to Article 2(c) of the WPPT, "'fixation' means the embodiment of sounds, or of the representations thereof, from which they can be perceived, reproduced or communicated through a device".

[4] See U.S. Copyright Office, https://www.copyright.gov/eco/help-type.html last visited December 30, 2024.

to its copyrightability because it does not belong to a statutory category of works, the VG can be protected under "other intellectual creations." This approach not only echoes international conventions and other countries' laws[5] but has also been put into judicial practice in China, where courts have recently endeavored to break through the statutory type restriction to protect new types of works. For example, in the *Music Fountain* case, the court held that "although a music fountain is not a specific type of work stipulated by the Copyright Law, it is undisputedly original and should be protected by copyright law" ([2016] Civil Verdict No. 15322 Beijing 0108). Also, Article 2.1 of the *Guidelines for the Trial of Copyright Infringement Cases* provide that the object of copyright claimed by a plaintiff constitutes a work if it conforms to the general constitutive elements of a work, regardless of whether it belongs to one or more of the statutorily enumerated types of work. Specifically, the *Guidelines* state:

> [i]n investigating whether the object of copyright claimed by the plaintiff constitutes a work, the court shall generally take the following factors into consideration: (i) whether it is a creation made by a natural person in the field of literature, art and science; (ii) whether it possesses originality; (iii) whether it has certain form of expression; (iv) whether it is reproducible.

Notwithstanding VGs' implied copyright protection under the latest amendment of the PRC Copyright Law, I argue that a more solid statutory foundation for its copyright protection should be established by classifying VGs as a new type of copyrighted work. This proposal is motivated mainly by the extensive academic and practical controversy surrounding copyright protections afforded to VGs, including the WIPO's raising the topic for public consultation and debate.[6] Furthermore, VGs have become an increasingly popular form of mass entertainment, a powerful and exciting platform for innovative art and a multibillion-dollar industry.[7] This justifies their treatment as a unique category of work deserving of special treatment.

It is not a new practice to identify new copyrightable subject matter and incorporate it into copyright law. For instance, computer programs and compilations of data were added to the TRIPS Agreement (Article 10), when they were identified as distinct from other works and it was clear that their economic value deserved special protection (Li, 2020). Besides, the list of copyrighted works is critical, as "the rights an author has, the scope of protection for those rights, and the way the rights are protected, in practice, still depend in large part upon which type of listed work it is" (Mtima & Jamar, 2010). In view of this, I suggest that VGs should be listed as a new work category, distinct from computer programs and audiovisual works, and covered by a hybrid protection model.

[5] See Article 2 (1) of the Berne Convention. See also Article 10 (1) of the Japanese Copyright Law. See also Article L 112-2 of the Intellectual Property Code of France.

[6] See "Video Games", https://www.wipo.int/copyright/en/activities/video_games.html last visited December 30, 2024.

[7] See "Video Games: 21st Century Art", https://www.wipo.int/wipo_magazine/en/2012/04/article_0003.html last visited December 30, 2024.

I believe that VGs should initially be classified as a new type of copyrighted work in an international treaty or an amendment of an international convention; eventually, this principle will be incorporated into Chinese copyright law. Once such legislation is in place, copyright registration of VGs in China should be limited to the newly established category of VGs to eliminate the present dual registration problem, whereby VGs are registered either as audiovisual works or as literary works (to protect the computer program). As the transfer of moral rights differs between audiovisual works and computer programs under some domestic laws, including China's, it is advisable to establish a fixed term within which moral rights to VGs cannot be transferred, to eliminate uncertainty.

When comparing works to determine copyright infringement under the proposed law, both the test for audiovisual works and that for computer programs should be applied. Neither model alone is adequate to protect rights to VGs, due to the aforementioned complex nature of such games. As piracy is increasingly rampant in the games industry (Dean, 2016; Meyer, 2010), a hybrid protection model for VGs would be ideal to protect their audiovisual output and prevent reverse engineering of the underlying software. Under this model, the audiovisual images of a VG would receive a level of protection similar to that of an audiovisual work, and the underlying software would be protected as literary works are. The "total concept and feel" test would be used to determine game copyright infringement (Macatee, 1993),[8] emphasizing both the significance of the audiovisual output and the intrinsic interactive experience operated by the computer program.

The copyright ownership of VGs should be specified in legislation by jurisdiction. In the context of cinematographic works, the Berne Convention is silent regarding copyright ownership, leaving the matter to be resolved by national legislation (Article 14 bis (2)(b) & (3)). There are three primary approaches to cinematographic copyright ownership. One is the Hollywood model, whereby ownership of a film vests in the producer of the film, based on the work-for-hire doctrine. The other two models are compulsory assignment and presumption of assignment, which assign ownership to the producer as required by law and as a presumption, respectively (Song, 2015). One of the factors justifying the producer ownership of IP rights is the economic theory of incentives, which aims to maximize the public good by examining the transaction cost associated with the transfer of resources from one economic unit to another. Transaction cost theory requires us to consider "not only the cost of making things, but also the cost of transferring ownership from one economic agent to another" (Williamson, 1996). Heller (2009) put forward the anti-commons theory to explain the transaction cost associated with joint ownership. This theory states that "under-usage of the resources may occur as a result of the high cost of dealing with multiple, independent rights holders" (Heller, 2009). Merges (1999) identified four factors cited by courts when deciding IP ownership-related cases—"(1) bargaining

[8] The "total concept and feel" test relies on the subjective evaluation of observers who consider the question of whether the total concept and feel of one work is substantially similar to another. The test is subdivided into the "extrinsic test", wherein a complex analysis is conducted of the concepts underlying the work, and the "intrinsic test", wherein within the judgement of an ordinary person the expressions of the works are compared.

and transaction costs, particularly employee holdups; (2) the difficulties of monitoring and compensating the members of R&D groups; (3) principal-agent problems, in particular the danger that employee ownership would over-reward inventive tasks at the expense of other job requirements; and (4) a change in the implicit risk allocation between employer and employee", noting that the pre-assignment of IP ownership to one single party (the employer) can avoid both "the potential employee holdup problem" (i.e. increased transaction costs and delays in the dissemination of a work caused by multiple creators' claiming shares of the ownership of the work) and "the difficulty in determining and compensating actual contributors in a collective work," thus reducing transaction costs (Merges, 1999). Copyright ownership of VGs raises similar concerns. There are many contributors to the production of a VG, rendering it difficult if not impossible to determine the relative value of the contributions. Granting IP ownership of a VG to its creators is also likely to delay dissemination and increase transaction costs by allowing multiple individual creators to claim ownership. Besides, any additional transaction costs that game developers must bear ultimately pass to consumers. Thus, when determining copyright ownership, one must consider the incentives of contributing creators; the incentives of game developers, who initiate and oversee the production and distribution of VGs; and the interests of the general public, who embrace VGs as an indispensable part of modern culture. Given the complexity of the issue, it is best to avoid confusion by attributing copyright ownership of VGs to the investors—that is, the game developers—by law.

Finally, I suggest that Pamela Samuelson's proposal for a shorter protection term for computer software should be applied to VGs (Cohen et al., 2015). In general, VG development is driven and initiated by the market and industry, as game enterprises seek to recoup their investment in their creations. Due to rapid technological advancement and the quickly evolving market, a given VG becomes outdated very quickly, a phenomenon exacerbated by fierce competition in the games market. This is evident from the short life cycle of a modern VG. The life cycle of a VG covers the period from the launch of a game to its exit from the market, and comprises four stages, introduction, growth, maturity and recession, which vary in duration from game to game. A game's competitiveness and profitability depend on the duration of these stages of its life cycle.[9] With the exception of a few classic console games, the average life cycle of mobile and web games is relatively short. According to iResearch, the average life cycle of web games in China is 3–6 months and that of mobile games is 3–12 months.[10] Thus, these products are marketed immediately upon completion, and the investment is either recouped or lost within a short period. Copyright protection over the long term is thus of little concern to a VG's creators and exploiters; their main concern with copyright is only with respect to their ability to quickly recoup their investment. Long-term copyright protection is therefore an

[9] See 'A Brief Introduction to the Life Cycle of Online Games and the Characteristics of Each Stage' (Game Daily, 2017-04-05), http://www.youxiguancha.com/yanfazixun/36893.html last visited December 30, 2024.

[10] See iResearch Report http://report.iresearch.cn/content/2017/12/272357.shtml last visited December 30, 2024.

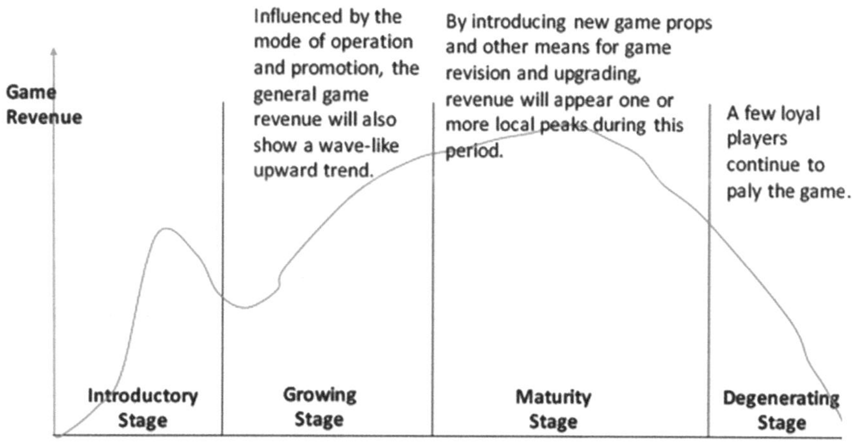


**Fig. 3.1** Life cycle stages of a VG and associated revenue

**Table 3.1** Average life cycle of VGs in China

| VG type | Average R&D cycle | Average life cycle |
|---|---|---|
| Web games | 3–6 months | 3–6 months |
| Mobile games | 3–12 months | 3–12 months |

unnecessary and unjustified restriction on competition (Bard & Kurlantzick, 1999). Empirical studies have shown that long-term copyright protection does not affect the market value of a work (Patry, 2012),[11] and the current copyright term has drawn criticism (Boyle, 2008; Rappaport, 1998). However, no legislative amendment has been proposed to shorten the duration of copyrights of VGs. Empirical evidence suggests that copyright terms should depend on the type of copyrighted work (Yuan, 2009). Thus, I suggest that a reasonable protection term should be set for VGs based on the empirical data and market observation so as to promote the creation of new works and the sustainable development of the VG industry (Fig. 3.1 and Table 3.1).

## 3.5 Conclusion

The legal attribute of VGs is the subject of some debate, owing to their multimedia nature, interactivity and rapid technical advancement. Samuelson (1997) noted that "technical advancement plays a considerable role for legal transformation, and copyright regime should be developed and designed in such a way that it can adapt to

[11] In November 2006, a study conducted by Andrew Gowers shows that extending the copyright term of a sound recording for 20 years will not necessarily increase the productivity and income of a performer. In 2009, a research conducted by Ivan Png and Qiu-hong Wang found no evidence that "longer term of copyright caused the creation of more works than the prior, shorter term."

the changes brought on by such advancement." I conclude from an in-depth analysis that it is essential to distinguish VGs from computer programs and audiovisual works and to protect VGs as a new type of copyrightable work rather than as "other intellectual creations" under miscellaneous provisions of copyright laws. This approach is consistent with the semiotic principle that the special arrangement and proportional relationships of a VG's elements reflect its designer's creativity and expression, which account for the originality of the work. Furthermore, I propose a hybrid protection model for VGs that combines the protections afforded to audiovisual works and computer programs. This model would also protect the rules of VGs. As discussed in the following chapter, the rules of a game (or the game mechanisms), especially its constitutive rules, can be copyrightable as an essential part of the gameplay. Moreover, the degree of a VG's interactivity would not affect its legal attribute, although strong intervention in the expression of a game by players may allow the players to create new works. Gamers' rights to their modified content are discussed in Chapter 5.

## References

A Brief Introduction to the Life Cycle of Online Games and the Characteristics of Each Stage. (2017). Game Daily. Available at: http://www.youxiguancha.com/yanfazixun/36893.html. Accessed 23 April 2021.

Bard, R., & Kurlantzick, L. (1999). *Copyright Duration: Duration, Term Extension, the European Union, and the Making of Copyright Policy* (p. 215). Austin & Winfield.

Boyle, J. (2008). *The Public Domain* (p. 9). Yale University Press.

Cohen, J. E., O'Rourke, M. A., et al. (2015). *Copyright in a Global Information Economy* (4th ed., p. 244). Aspen Publishers.

de Saussure, F. [Switzerland]. (1980). *General Linguistics [普通语言学教程]* (Gao, M. [高名凯], Trans., pp 101–102). Commercial Press.

Dean, D. S. (2016). Hitting Reset: Devising a New Video Game Copyright Regime. *University of Pennsylvania Law Review, 164*, 1239.

Goldstein, P. (1986). Infringement of Copyright in Computer Programs. *University of Pittsburgh Law Review, 47*, 119, 1124–1127.

Goodman, N. (1988). *Ways of World-Making* (5th ed., p. 74). Hackelt Publishing Company.

Heller, M. (2009). *Commons and Anticommons: Economic Approaches to Law*. Edward Elgar.

Lastowka, G. (2015). Copyright Law and Video Games: A Brief History of an Interactive Medium. In M. David & D. Halbert (Eds.), *The SAGE Handbook of Intellectual Property*. Sage.

Li, C. [李琛]. (2018). Legal Significance of Categorization of Works [论作品类型化的法律意义]. *Intellectual Property [知识产权]* (8).

Li, Y. (2020). The Age of Remix and Copyright Law Reform. *Law, Innovation and Technology, 12*(1), 30.

Macatee, S. B. (1993). Total Concept and Feel or Dissection: Approaches to the Misappropriation Test of Substantial Similarity. *Chi-Kent Law Review, 68*, 913, 935.

Merges, R. (1999). The Law and Economics of Employee Inventions. *Harvard Journal of Law & Technology, 13*, 1, 12.

Meyer, K. R. (2010). Doctrine of the Dead: How Capcom v. MKR Exposes the Decreasing Fit Between Modern Copyright Infringement Analysis and Modern Video Games. *Chicago-Kent Journal of Intellectual Property* (9), 132.

Mtima, L., & Jamar, S. D. (2010). Fulfilling the Copyright Social Justice Promise: Digitizing Textual Information. *New York Law School Law Review, 55*, 77, 96.

Nichols, W. J. (2007). Painting Through Pixels: The Case for a Copyright in Videogame Play. *Columbia Journal of Law & Arts, 30*, 101, 116.

Patry, W. (2012). *How to Fix Copyright* (p. 57). Oxford University Press.

Popper, K. (1972). *Objective Knowledge: An Evolutionary Approach.* Oxford University Press.

Rappaport, E. (1998). *Copyright Term Extension: Estimating Economic Value.* CRS Report to Congress.

Romas, A. et al. (2013). *The Legal Status of Video Games: Comparative Analysis in National Approaches* (pp. 27–28, 50, 54, 71, 89). WIPO.

Samuelson, P. (1997). The Digital Content Symposium. *Berkeley Technology Law Journal, 12*, 1, 145.

Samuelson, P., et al. (1994). Manifesto Concerning the Legal Protection of Computer Programs. *Columbia Law Review, 94*, 2308, 2317–2318.

Small, D. G. (1983). Stemming the Tide of Video Game Piracy: Copyright Protection for the Audiovisual Displays. *Brook Law Review, 49*, 889.

Song, S. H. (2015). China's Copyright Protection for Audio-Visual Works: A Comparison with Europe and the United States. *International Review of Intellectual Property and Competition Law, 46*(4), 410.

Stamatoudi, I. A. (2002). *Copyright and Multimedia Products: A Comparative Analysis* (pp. 174–175). Cambridge University Press.

Sun, L., & Cao, L. [孙磊&曹丽萍]. (2017). *Judicial Protection of Intellectual Property Rights of Online Games [网络游戏知识产权司法保护]* (p. 19). China Legal Publishing House [中国法制出版社].

Wang, Q. [王迁]. (2016). Study on the Copyright Issues of Live Streaming of Video Game [电子游戏直播的著作权问题研究]. *Electronics Intellectual Property [电子知识产权]* (2), 12.

Williamson, O. E. (1996). *The Mechanisms of Governance.* Oxford University Press.

Xiong, W. [熊文聪]. (2016). *Fact/Value Dichotomy: Logic and Rhetoric of Intellectual Property Law [事实与价值二分: 知识产权法的逻辑与修辞]* (p. 116). Huazhong University of Science and Technology Press [华中科技大学出版社].

Yuan, M. (2009). Should Different Information Economies Have the Same Duration of Copyright. *Review of Economic Research, 6*, 13.

## *Legislations*

Agreement on Trade-Related Aspects of Intellectual Property Rights (TRIPS Agreement 1994)

Beijing Treaty on Audiovisual Performances (BJTAP)

Berne Convention for the Protection of Literary and Artistic Works (1886)

Guidelines for the Trial of Copyright Infringement Cases (Beijing High People's Court)

Indonesian Copyright Law

Intellectual Property Code of France

Interim Measures for the Administration of Online Games

Japanese Copyright Law

Korean Copyright Act

PRC Civil Code (2021)

PRC Copyright Law (2021 version)

Regulations for the Implementation of the PRC Copyright Law

Regulations for the Protection of Computer Software (2002)

Singapore's Copyright (Excluded Works) Order of 2008

Singaporean Copyright Act

US Copyright Act

WIPO Performances and Phonograms Treaty (WPPT)

## Cases

Atari v. Valadon, Cour de cassation, 7 March 1986, 129 RIDA 130.
Beijing Zhongke Shuijing Technology Co. v. Beijing Zhongke Huanye Zhongzi Technology Co. & Xihu Administration [北京中科水景科技有限公司诉北京中科恒业中自技术有限公司、西湖管理] [2016] Civil Verdict No. 15322 Beijing 0108 [(2016) 京0108民初15322号民事判决书].
Creative Technology Ltd. v. Aztech Systems pte Ltd [1997] 1 SLR 621.
Midway Mfg Co. v. Artic International, Inc. 704 F 2d. 1009 (CA7 1983).
NetEase v. Guangzhuo Huaduo Ltd., [2015] Civil Verdict No. 16 (IP) Guangdong [(2015) 粤知法著民初字第 16 号民事判决书].
NetEase v. Guangzhou Huaduo Ltd., [2015] Shanghai (IP) Civil Verdict (Final) No. 641 [(2015) 沪知民终字第 641 号].
Nova Productions Ltd. v. Mazooma Games Ltd., [2007] EWCA Civ 219.
Sarl Aakro Pure Tronic Inc., v. Societe Nintendo Co Ltd, CA Paris, September 26, 2011.
SAS Institute Inc. v. World Programming Ltd., C-406/10 [2012] RPC 31.
Shanghai Yaoyu Culture Media Co. v. Guangzhou Douyu Network Technology Co., [2015] Civil Verdict No.191 (IP) People's Court of Pudong New Area of Shanghai [上海市浦东新区人民法院 (2015) 浦民三(知)初字第 191 号民事判决书].
Shanghai Zhuangyou Information Technology Co. v. Guangzhou Shuoxing Information Technology Co. and others, [2015] Civil Verdict No.529 (IP) People's Court of Pudong New Area of Shanghai [上海市浦东新区人民法院 (2015) 浦民三(知)初字第 529 号民事判决书]; [2016] Hu 73 Civil Final No.190 [(2016) 沪 73 民终190 号].
Spelling Goldberg Productions Inc. v. P.P.C. Publishing Ltd. [1981] R.P.C. 283.
Stern Elecs., Inc. v. Kaufman, 669 F. 2d 852 (2d Cir. 1982).
Supreme Court Case No. H13-ju-952.
Wgn Continental Broadcasting Co. v. U. Video, Inc., 693 F. 2d (7th Cir. 1982), at 627.
Williams Electronica, Inc. v. Arctic Intern, Inc., 685 F. 2d 870, 875 (3d Cir. 1982).

# Chapter 4
# Addressing Copyright Infringement in Video Game Adaptation: A More Balanced Approach

**Abstract** This chapter focuses on the issue of game adaptation infringement. It first provides an overview of game adaptation as a "bright spot" in cultural industries, followed by an explanation of the rise in "game re-skinning" cases caused by the current copyright regime's failure to properly define game adaptation infringement. The chapter reexamines the scope of the right of adaptation and its intersection with the right of reproduction from a normative perspective, and suggests that the normative target of the right of adaptation differs from that of the right of reproduction, in spite of their considerable overlap. This notion is further strengthened by an exploration of the game designing process. Drawing lessons from judicial practice in the US, the chapter proposes a more balanced testing scheme—a new three-step test—to address game adaptation infringement. Strictly compliance with the proposed three-step test would prevent courts from unduly restraining competition and follow-on innovation and interfering with the reasonable interests of the original creators.

**Keywords** Game adaptation infringement · Game re-skinning · Right of adaptation · Right of reproduction · A new three-step test

## 4.1 Introduction

With the rapid development of cultural industries, intellectual property (IP) has become an increasingly important concept. However, copyright law has struggled to adapt to the growing needs of cultural industries. The deluge of new works has stemmed from several sources. Derivative works, for example, have sprung up like bamboo shoots after a spring rain. The commercial value of a good novel, animation, film or even simple cartoon image is no longer limited to the work itself but extends to adaptations of that work. Both the commercial value and the influence of adaptations often outweigh those of the original works. Video game (VG) developers spare no effort to tap all manner of cultural products to develop new VGs, and most of them willingly cooperate with the copyright owners of original movies,

 
Z. Deng, *Constructing an Eco-Balanced Copyright Regime for the Video Game Industry in China*, https://doi.org/10.1007/978-981-96-6056-8_4

TV dramas, animations and novels to launch derivative games. Indeed, many best-selling works have been adapted as VGs, which in turn have formed the basis of other popular derivative works. While the game enterprises have taken advantage of this opportunity, developing swiftly and vigorously in the process, some have faced conflicts and lawsuits surrounding their adaptations of others' works. These conflicts have mainly concerned the phenomenon of "game cloning" or "game re-skinning." Because copyright protection for VGs is quite weak, VG competitors are able to copy the fundamental mechanics, rules and often story elements of a game to release a competing product without facing liability (Dean, 2016). This discourages innovation and stifles creativity to the detriment of the public. Game cloning takes advantage of a loophole in the current copyright regime that allows such game adaptation. In this chapter, I propose a more balanced test to determine game adaptation infringement to promote VG innovation and creativity. This test is created by examining the differences between the right of reproduction and the right of adaptation and by expanding the sphere of protectable expression in VGs.

## 4.2 Overview of the Game Adaptation Market

### *4.2.1 Understanding the Right of Adaptation and Game Adaptation*

A copyright holder's right of adaptation is an important economic right for creative works. The right of adaptation limits others' unauthorized derivative creations. Article 12 of the Berne Convention stipulates that "[a]uthors of literary or artistic works shall enjoy the exclusive right of authorizing adaptations, arrangements and other alterations of their works." The definition of the right of adaption varies by jurisdiction; however, legislative models generally belong to one of two types. Open models are used by the US and China, whereas a closed model is used by the UK.

In the US, a copyright owner has the exclusive rights "to prepare and to authorize others to prepare derivative works based upon the copyrighted work" (Section 106(2) of the US Copyright Act). The US Copyright Act defines a "derivative work" as "a work based upon one or more preexisting works, such as a translation, musical arrangement, dramatization, fictionalization, motion picture version, sound recording, art reproduction, abridgement, condensation, or any other form in which a work may be recast, transformed, or adapted" (Section 101). This broad definition does not distinguish between types of derivative works in terms of infringing the copyright holder's exclusive rights. Although adaptation is a form of derivative creation, no definition or scope of the right of adaptation is specified in the US legislation. In contrast with the US approach, the PRC Copyright Law does grant derivative rights according to the type of derivation, including the right of adaptation, the right of translation and the right of compilation (Article 10 of the PRC Copyright Law (2021)). Pursuant to Article 10 (14) of the PRC Copyright Law (2021), the right of adaptation is "the right to change a work into a new one with originality." This distinguishes the right of adaptation from other copyrights such as the right of reproduction or the right of translation. The specific scope of the right of adaptation, however, is undefined. There is no evidence that this right receives more attention in China than in the US.

The open legislative model allows the courts to incrementally advance the scope of the adaptation right. In contrast, the UK's closed model binds the courts' hands through clear statutory wording. Article 16 (e) of the UK Copyright, Designs and Patents Act 1988 provides, "[t]he owner of the copyright in a work has the exclusive right to make an adaptation of the work or do any of the above in relation to an adaptation." The term "adaptation" is narrowly defined, as follows:

> In this Act 'adaptation'—
>
> (a) in relation to a literary work [other than a computer program or a database], or in relation to a dramatic work, means—
>
> (i) a translation of the work;
> (ii) a version of a dramatic work in which it is converted into a non-dramatic work or, as the case may be, of a non-dramatic work in which it is converted into a dramatic work;
> (iii) a version of the work in which the story or action is conveyed wholly or mainly by means of pictures in a form suitable for reproduction in a book, or in a newspaper, magazine or similar periodical;
>
> [(ab) in relation to a computer program, means an arrangement or altered version of the program or a translation of it;]
>
> [(ac) in relation to a database, means an arrangement or altered version of the database or a translation of it;]
>
> (b) in relation to a musical work, means an arrangement or transcription of the work. (Article 21(3) of the UK Copyright, Designs and Patents Act 1988)

This rule-based approach to the right of adaptation provides a narrower scope of applicability. The UK's definition of "adaptation" is similar to the definition of "derivation" in the US statute in that they both include "translation" and "arrangement," whereas "adaptation" in the Chinese law is juxtaposed with the rights of translation and compilation (Article 10 of the PRC Copyright Law (2021)). Goold (2014) assessed the pros and cons of the two legislative approaches to derivative rights and argued in favor of the closed legislative model adopted by the UK. A similar comparison is unwarranted here. Instead, in this chapter I focus primarily on judicial practices in China as applied to game adaptation infringement, especially the "re-skinning" phenomenon, and draw lessons from the US to propose improvements to the current copyright regime in China.

China's law imposes two conditions on adapted works: first, the adapted work must contain the most basic content of the preexisting work; second, the adapted work must demonstrate original expressions, different from those of the preexisting work (Wang, 2016b). "Adaptation" has consistently been understood to include expanding or abridging, rewriting or changing the form of an original work (Wang, 2016). Accordingly, VG adaptations can be divided into three categories: (1) VGs adapted from other types of original works (e.g. novels, animations and films); (2) other types

**Table 4.1** VGs adapted from other types of original works

| Original works | | Adapted VGs | |
|---|---|---|---|
| Type | Name | Type | Name |
| Novel | *The Witcher* | Open-World Action Game (PC) | *The Witcher 3* |
| Novel | *Journey to the West* | Post-Apocalyptic Action Game (Xbox 360/ PlayStation 3) | *Enslaved: Odyssey to the West* |
| Film | *Friends* | Action RPG (mobile) | *Friends* |
| Novel/Film | *Harry Potter* | 3D Adventure Game (PC/ mobile) | *Harry Potter* |
| TV Series | *The Journey of Flower* | RPG (mobile) | *Action Man: Arctic Adventure* |
| Animation | *Beavis and Butt-head* | Action-Adventure Game (PC/PlayStation) | *Beavis and Butt-head in Virtual Stupidity* |

**Table 4.2** Other types of works adapted from original VGs

| Original VGs | | Adapted works other than VGs | |
|---|---|---|---|
| Type | Name | Type | Name |
| Genre-Defining Action RPG | *Diablo* | Novel | *Diablo* |
| MMORPG | *Warcraft* | Film | *Warcraft* |
| Action-Adventure Game | *Tomb Raider* | Film | *Tomb Raider* |
| MMORPG/Third-Person Shooters | *Final Fantasy* | Film | *Final Fantasy* |
| RPG/Third-Person Shooter/Action Game | *Danganronpa* | Animation | *Danganronpa* |
| Turn-Based Strategy Game | *Onmyoji* | Animation | *Onmyoji* |

of works adapted from original VGs and (3) VGs adapted from other forms of VGs (such as mobile games adapted from PC games). Tables 4.1, 4.2 and 4.3 list examples of some well-known VG adaptations.

### *4.2.2 Game Adaptations: A Bright Spot in the Cultural Industries*

The rapid development of digital cultural products and social media platforms has led to the unprecedented commercialization of copyright content. IP adaptations have both enriched people's cultural lives and greatly promoted the development of cultural industries and the cultural economy. The games industry has witnessed a rise in the cost of network flow. Adapted VGs have a clear advantage over original works in that they can rely on the original works' fan bases to reduce the cost of attracting consumers. The adaptation of works to other forms of entertainment products also

**Table 4.3** VGs adapted from other forms of VGs

| Original VGs | | Adapted VGs | |
|---|---|---|---|
| Type | Name | Type | Name |
| Strategy RPG (PC) | *Langrisser* | Mobile Game | *Langrisser* |
| Card Game (PC) | *Heartstone* | Mobile Game | *Heartstone* |
| Action RPG (PC) | *Fortnite* | Mobile Game | *Fortnite* |
| MMORPG (PC) | *Fantasy Westward Journey* | Mobile Game | *Fantasy Westward Journey* |
| Arcade Card Game | *Tetris* | Online Game | *Tetris* |
| Arcade Game | *Galaga, Puzz Bubble, Invader* | Mobile Game | *Galaga, Puzz Bubble, Invader* |

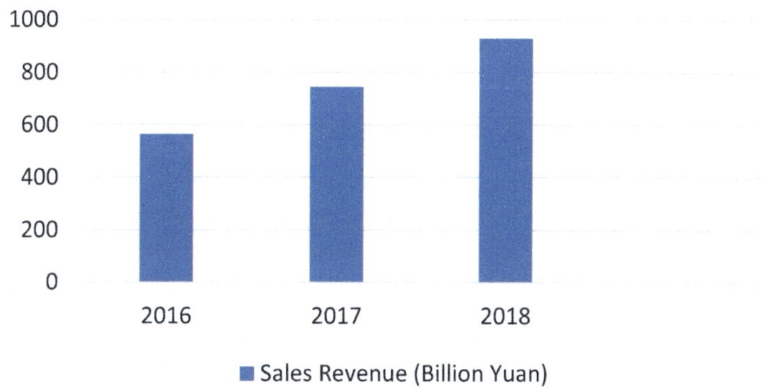


**Fig. 4.1** Sales revenue of adapted mobile games 2016–2018

provides diversified sources of revenue.[1] The 2017 China Game Industry Report found that Chinese netizens displayed a strong willingness to consume adapted mobile games, with over 52.4% and 83.5% of the respondents having played and expressed willingness to play adapted VGs, respectively, in the first half of the year.[2] Thus, adapted products have become a significant source of revenue in the Chinese games market. During 2016–2018, revenue from adapted games accounted for approximately 65% of all revenue in the mobile games market, and the market revenue of adapted mobile games was expected to exceed 1000 billion yuan in 2019[3] (Figs. 4.1 and 4.2).

[1] See 'Analysis on the Development Status and Prospect of China's Game Market in 2018' (January 31, 2018), http://www.chyxx.com/industry/201801/609609.html last visited December 30, 2024.

[2] See 'Analysis on the Development Status and Prospect of China's Game Market in 2018' (March 12, 2018), http://www.chyxx.com/industry/201803/617751.html last visited December 30, 2024.

[3] See '2019 Analysis Report on China's Game Market—Industry Competition Pattern and Future Trend Research' (April 29, 2019), http://market.chinabaogao.com/it/042941Q1H019.html last visited December 30, 2024.

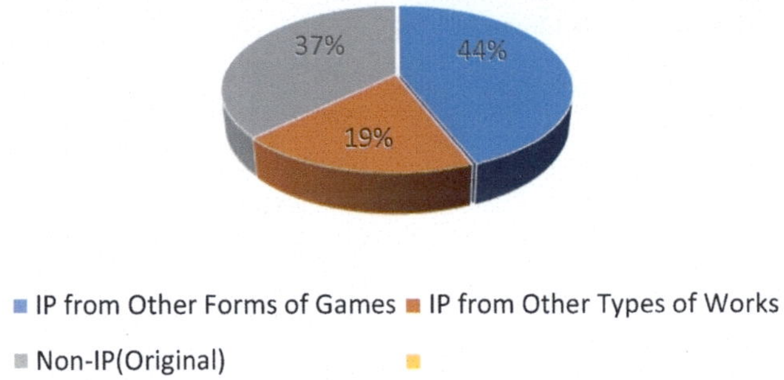


**Fig. 4.2** Proportion of adapted mobile games in the top 100 mobile games in 2018

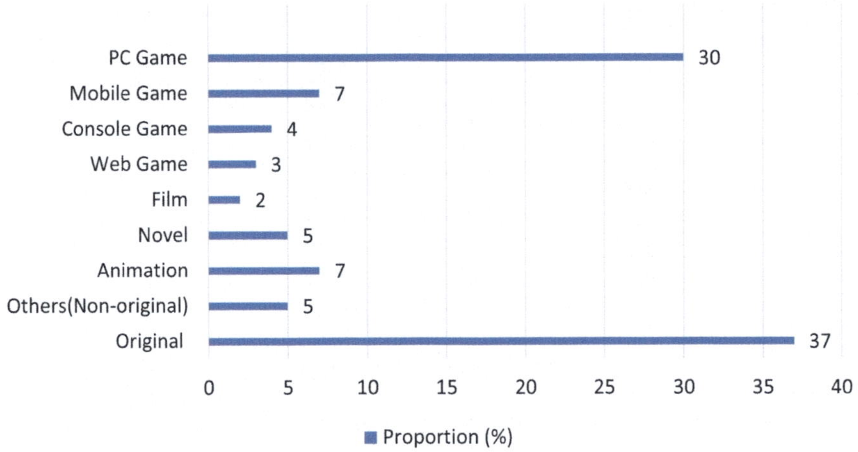


**Fig. 4.3** Proportions of top 100 mobile games by IP type in 2018[4]

To date, most popular PC games have been adapted to the mobile format, such as *Jade Dynasty*, *My Own Swordsman*, *Perfect World*, *Asktao* and *Chor Lauheung*. As the number of PC games available for adaptation has decreased, game developers who focus on adapting games to the mobile format have had to turn to other forms of games or other types of works to adapt. Figure 4.3 compares types of original works serving as source materials for mobile adapted games. The advantages offered by popular original IP products include their verification by the market and their users' network flows; these and other aspects can be built upon and improved in the adaptations. At present, the adaptation rights of most popular games are controlled by the original developers, safeguarding their rich IP resources.

[4] Ibid.

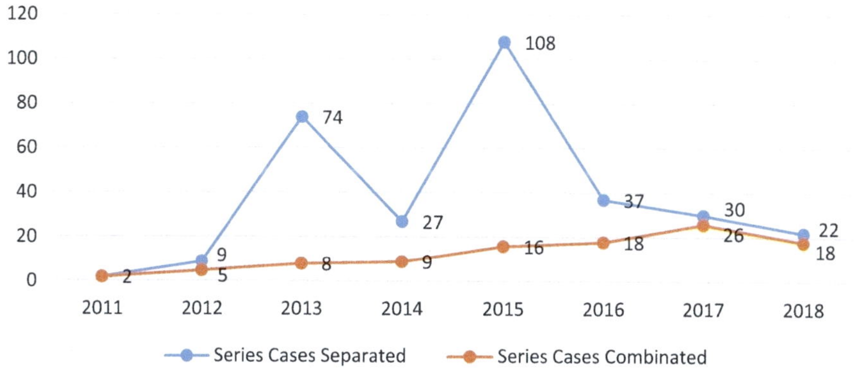


**Fig. 4.4** Disputes related to game adaptation infringement 2011–2018

## 4.3 Game Adaptation Infringement in Context

### *4.3.1 Game Adaptation Infringement: A Lion in the Way*

While game adaptation has created a thriving cultural market, it has also led to many disputes. To examine recent legal disputes involving game adaptations in China, I referred to the database LawinfoChina (also known as "Beida Fabao").[5] I inputted "video game" and "adaptation right" as keywords to identify relevant cases in the database, and then analyzed these cases by year. I selected and sorted cases involving game adaptation from 2011 to 2018. The results are shown in Fig. 4.4. The blue line indicates the number of cases with the series cases separated for calculation, and the orange line indicates the number of cases with the series cases combined for calculation.[6] During the period under study, there was a moderately upward trend in the number of cases related to game adaptation (orange line). Although I could not rule out either the possibility that some judgements had not been submitted to the database or the possibility of delayed submission of some judgements after 2018, the figure offers a useful overview of the development trend of game adaptation cases in recent years.

An in-depth analysis of the 309 cases revealed that the winning rate of the plaintiffs was 100% (see Fig. 4.5). However, the courts took an extremely cautious attitude toward the plaintiffs' claims for adaptation infringement; the rate of support for

[5] LawinfoChina, also known as "Beida Fabao", was founded by the Department of Law of the Peking University in 1985. This database Includes Chinese laws, regulations and cases in Chinese (chinalawinfo.com) and in English/Chinese (lawinfochina.com), which is regarded as the most mature, professional and advanced omnibearing retrieval system of legal information in China.

[6] The "series of cases" here refers to the cases in which the defendant infringes the plaintiff's multiple rights in multiple acts, and these cases have the similar litigation content and litigation claims. The two peaks in 2013 and 2015 are caused by the series of cases involving "character adaptation infringement".

adaptation infringement claims was only 15.5% (see Fig. 4.6). These cases generally involved a plaintiff's claim of infringement of the right of adaptation filed with other claims, such as unfair competition, infringement of the right of reproduction or infringement of the right of communication through information network. The strategy of casting a wide net with multiple claims, while improving plaintiffs' odds of winning their cases, undoubtedly increases judges' workload, reducing the efficiency of judicial proceedings. Further exploration of these cases revealed that the nature of the claims changed over time from predominantly "character adaptation" infringement claims to "plot adaptation" infringement claims and, ultimately, to claims of "re-skinning adaptation" infringement. This trend also indicates that the disputes became more complicated over time, and that the trial of these cases consequently became more difficult.

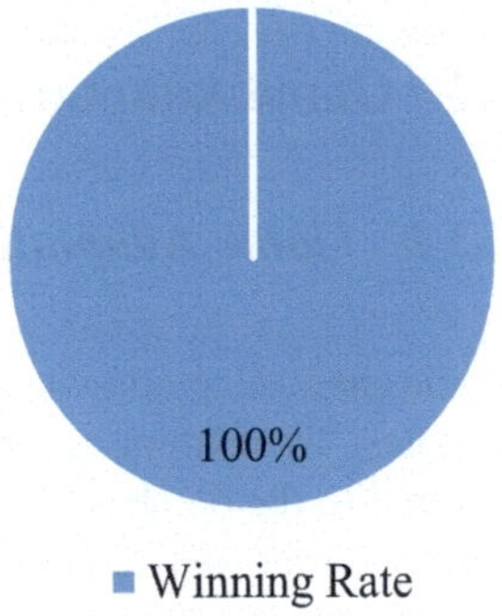


**Fig. 4.5** Winning rate of plaintiffs

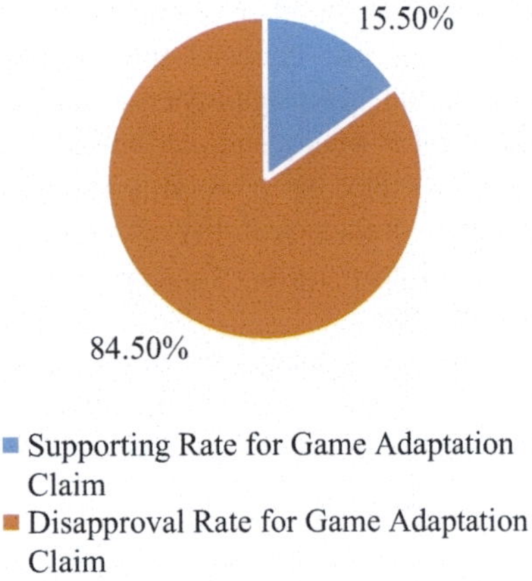


**Fig. 4.6** Supporting/disapproval rate for game adaptation claims

### 4.3.2 *Rise of the Game Re-skinning Phenomenon*

Game re-skinning is a process whereby, rather than creating a game from scratch, a game developer instead obtains the core resources (generally the source code) of an original game and changes the external expression to give the game a brand new look.[7] It is like placing new flesh onto an old skeleton: the architecture of the game remains the same, but the look and feel are fresh, unique and exciting. The main goal of game reskinning is to capture new audiences using time-tested, popular themes and designs. Examples abound in app stores, including the *Candy Crush Sagas*, *Deer Hunter*, and *Temple Run*, whose mechanics and physics are similar to those of other artworks bearing different "skins."

There are many advantages of game re-skinning, such as faster turnaround time, lower production cost, proven quality and a high level of audience engagement (Chong, 2018). Perhaps most importantly, re-skinning helps to greatly reduce game development time from months or years to days or weeks, thus permitting faster monetization. Making games completely from scratch is quite expensive and challenging. It requires a large team of developers to write code, design and combine various elements and involves extensive testing, editing and other post-production work.[8] Game re-skinning, however, retains the core elements and relies on content authors' and graphic designers' new stories to guide gamers throughout the gameplay. Developers can reallocate time that "would normally be reserved for brainstorming, design and development to thorough market research, detailed graphic refinement and the creation of a thoughtful mobile game marketing plan."[9] Furthermore, re-skinning lowers certain risks associated with developing a game from scratch, as "online source code marketplaces typically test code before it is approved to be sold"(Chong, 2018). Thus, using the source code of a game that has proved to be profitable and functional can minimize the risk of code development problems. This frees time and funds to explore new markets, specifically to understand and research potential consumers, the competition and effective marketing techniques to ensure an optimal user experience.

Re-skinning is a legitimate and viable business model for small studios committed to creating multiple quality games on a budget. However, some developers re-skin others' games instead of using their own source code to develop re-skinned games. These developers most often imitate or copy the salient aspects of others' games' mechanics, rules or plots, rewriting the source code and replacing the external artistic expressions to piggyback on the creators' financial success. For example, in 2013, while the game *Hearthstone* was still undergoing internal testing, its developers sued the developers of the mobile game *Wolongsb* for copyright infringement on the grounds that it closely imitated *Hearthstone*'s game rules, user interface (UI) and

[7] See 'What Is a "Game Reskin"?' https://www.marketjs.com/reskin last visited December 30, 2024.

[8] See 'Re-Skinning—Making Games Fresh' https://meliorgames.com/game-development/reskinning-making-games-fresh/ last visited December 30, 2024.

[9] See 'The Benefits of Reskinning a Mobile Game' https://www.chartboost.com/blog/the-benefits-of-reskinning-a-mobile-game/ last visited December 30, 2024.

card description ([2014] Hu Yi Zhong Civil Verdict Five (IP) No. 23). In 2015, the developers of *The Journey of Flower* were sued for completely copying the game rules, UI and design of *Tai Chi Panda* ([2015] Su Zhong IP Civil Verdict No. 00201). In 2017, the developers of *The Battle of Heroes* were sued for a re-skinning of the *Overwatch* game ([2017] Hu 0115 Civil Verdict No. 77945).

Although the term "re-skinning" is relatively new, flagrant copying is not a new phenomenon in the games industry, and copyright protection for VGs has been a matter of discussion since the introduction of the medium in the late 1970s (McArthur, 2013). If a re-skinning game can draw off even a small portion of a successful antecedent game's sales, "either by confusing customers or by offering a cheaper gaming experience, then the re-skinning game can turn a profit without the hassle of devising something new" (Glu Mobile Inc. v. Hothead Games Inc., 2014). Many re-skinning developers market their copied games as free versions of the original paid game, stealing the antecedent's customers while recouping their investment through in-game advertising revenue. Re-skinning poses a threat to innovative game developers and, by extension, to consumers. As the tools for programming new mobile games have become more widely disseminated and user friendly, and as mobile gaming has grown in popularity, game re-skinning has become easier, more widespread, and more lucrative for clone developers, becoming commensurately more harmful to innovative developers (Parkin, 2011).

### *4.3.3 Paradox of the Current Regime to Define Game Adaptation Infringement*

#### 4.3.3.1 Idea–Expression Dichotomy in the VG Context

VGs receive copyright protection under Chinese law. According to Article 2.14 of the *Guidelines for the Trial of Copyright Infringement Cases*, "[s]tatic game images can be protected as works of fine art; continuously dynamic game images can be protected as cinematographic works; and the whole game can also be protected as computer software." The *Guidelines* also state:

> [t]he following elements of an online game may constitute a work individually, including but not limited to: (i) characters, costumes, props, maps, and settings may constitute works of fine art; (ii) title, ending and interlude music, theme songs and interludes may constitute musical works; (iii) lines, asides, narrations and introduction to game may constitute literary works; and (iv) title, ending and interlude cartoons and videos may constitute works created in a manner similar to cinematographic production. (Article 2.15)

Thus, VGs invoke a complex amalgam of copyright principles; they are copyrightable as computer code and as audiovisual representations of this code on a screen. When a developer clones a VG by copying the underlying computer code verbatim or by rewriting distinct software code that closely mimics the audiovisual aspects and gameplay of an antecedent game, he has engaged in copyright infringement

(Nimmer & Nimmer, 2015). However, because game re-skinning involves neither verbatim copying of the existing code nor mimicking the audiovisual images of the original game, it presents a unique challenge for courts in terms of determining the appropriate scope of copyright protection.

The most basic tenet of copyright holds that "while one's expression of an idea is copyrightable, the underlying idea one uses is not" (Mazer v. Stein, 1954). This distinction is known as the idea–expression dichotomy, codified in the WIPO Copyright Treaty (WCT). Pursuant to Article 2 of the WCT, "[c]opyright protection extends to expressions and not to ideas, procedures, methods of operation or mathematical concepts as such." One development of the idea–expression dichotomy is the recognition that even when a shared idea causes works to appear similar on an abstract level, these similarities alone do not indicate copyright infringement (Nichols v. Universal Pictures Corp., 1931). This concept is commonly referred to as Judge Learned Hand's abstraction test. The struggle to identify which elements of a work are ideas and which constitute expression has defined copyright disputes for more than a century (Baker v. Selden, 1879). Historically, the mechanics or rules of a game have been considered as uncopyrightable subject matter, because courts have recognized them as ideas rather than forms of expression (Tetris Holding, LLC v. Xio Interactive, Inc., 2012). In the *Hearthstone* case cited above, the First Intermediate People's Court of Shanghai stated, "the rules of the game are abstract ideas and have practical functions, which thus cannot be protected by copyright law" ([2014] Hu Yi Zhong Civil Verdict Five (IP) No. 23). As the mechanics or rules of the game are not protected by copyright, clone developers can easily escape accusations of copyright infringement when using an existing game template and changing the audiovisual elements that are presented to a player.

Nevertheless, the Shanghai IP Court reasoned in the *Miracle MU* case, "because the overall picture of the game is original in its level setting, the map name, the pattern design of the map and the scene, the professional characters' setting and skill design, the modeling design of weapons and equipment, and the game images can be fixed in tangible form, it belongs to a 'work' in the sense of copyright law" ([2016] Hu 73 Civil final No. 190). From the Shanghai IP Court's perspective, the level setting, the professional characters' setting and the skill design are the embodiment of the rules of game, which can be protected by copyright law. But notably, the defendant had also used visual content identical to that in the plaintiff's original game, such as its digital map and some of its characters. Therefore, the defendant was ultimately found to have infringed the plaintiff's right of reproduction rather than the plaintiff's right of adaptation ([2016] Hu 73 Civil final No. 190). This case reveals that the expression of game rules can be protected by copyright law; however, it remains unclear to what extent the game rules are copyrightable when applying the idea/expression dichotomy.

#### 4.3.3.2 Limiting Doctrines in the VG Context

"There is no litmus paper test by which to apply the idea–expression distinction; the determination is necessarily subjective" (Atari, Inc. v. N. Am. Philips Consumer Elecs. Corp., 1982). However, courts have crafted a set of doctrines— namely the doctrines of merger and scènes à faire—to assist them in applying this distinction. The merger doctrine holds that "when one could not convey a given idea without a certain expressive technique, that means of expression merges into that un-copyrightable idea and does not receive protection" (Educ. Testing Servs. v. Katzman, 1986). The purpose of this doctrine is to avoid conferring a monopoly on an idea, thus helping copyright law "to promote the progress of science and useful arts" (U.S. Constitution, art.I, §8.). In *Morrissey v. Procter & Gamble Co.*, the court ruled against the plaintiff's claim, arguing that there were a limited number of ways to express the substance of the contest rules. As all types of VGs consist of abstract game mechanics and rules, their sphere of copyrightability is particularly vulnerable to limitation by the merger doctrine.

Overlapping in some respects with the merger doctrine, the scènes à faire doctrine holds that "certain elements of a creative work are not protected when they are mandated by or customary to the genre, or they are incidents, characters or settings which are as a practical matter indispensable, or at least standard, in the treatment of a given topic" (Atari, Inc. v. N. Am. Phillips Consumer Elecs Corp., 1982). This doctrine applies to the subject matter, style and genre of a game, ensuring that certain stereotypical or commonly associated elements of particular genres, such as stock characters and plot tropes, cannot be copyrightable (Lunsford, 2013). For example, in one case, the court stated, "[t]he characters and roles in [the game] *Bang!* are drawn from general alignment of stock characters in 'spaghetti Westerns,' which are not considered to have delineated personalities, or other features typical of characters in movies and books that can make those characters protected" (DaVinci Editrice S.R.L. v. Ziko Games LLC, 2016). Similarly, in *Capcom U.S.A., Inc. v. Data East Corp.*, the court found that even though the defendant's martial arts game possessed a number of characters that were graphically similar to and shared moves with characters in the plaintiff's game, the scènes à faire doctrine rendered many of these moves and character tropes incapable of protection. In *Data E. USA v. Epyx, Inc.*, the court identified certain scènes à faire ("scenes that must be done") specific to that genre by isolating features that "encompass the idea of karate," such as common moves and stances, and also identified "constraints created by the computer system and the limits of possible animation quality."

Because expression is protected only against "virtually identical copying" where the merger and scènes à faire doctrines apply (Apple Comput., Inc. v. Microsoft Corp., 1994), these doctrines limit courts' ability to find copyright infringement in re-skinned games, which mimic the mechanics and rules of original games, sometimes together with the style and genre and thus the common characters, moves and stances of those games. This approach fails to distinguish between the rules of a game and its general rules, thereby going against the original intention of copyright law to protect the interests of real copyright owners for promoting creativity and innovation. In light of the abstraction test put forward by Judge Learned Hand (Nichols v. Universal Pictures Corporation, 1930), some scholars have divided the rules of a game into three layers: constitutive rules, operational rules and implicit rules or unwritten rules (Salen & Zimmerman, 2004). Operational rules set out the basic rules for gameplay, which determine genre. For example, the basic rule for shooting games is "hitting the target accurately," while that for tower defense games is "guarding against any threats" (Salen & Zimmerman, 2004). General rules fall into this category; these rules are constrained by the merger and scènes à faire doctrines by the fact that they are (some of) the only means of expression of that gameplay. As for implicit or unwritten rules, they are generally the fruits of players' long-term actual combat and experience, derived from public wisdom without fixed forms of expression. For example, in the VG *League of Legends*, each party must choose five hero characters to form a team before gameplay. Most players do so by referring to the characteristics of the available hero characters and the winning/losing rules of the game, then selecting heroes based on optimal matches. This strategy has no fixed form and thus cannot be copyrightable.

In contrast, constitutive rules are the combination of a series of mechanisms affecting the players' decision-making at each step in the gameplay environment. They comprise a series of concrete and tangible forms of expression combined with the game's audiovisual elements, such as music, texts and characters. Such rules are key to the game designing process and reflect the subjective intention of the game developers as the products of their intellectual creation. Each constitutive rule in a game has been carefully conceived, calculated and repeatedly tested by the game developers and is thus highly original. Determining the structure and design of the constitutive rules is usually the most time-consuming and costliest part of game development. These game rules therefore merit no less protection as original creations than do other creative elements of a VG. Indeed, replacing traditional copyright elements such as artwork and music in a game while retaining its constitutive rules has little impact on the nature of the game and the core users experience (Corbett, 2016). If the constitutive rules were excluded from copyright protection, this would greatly increase the number of unauthorized "re-skinning" or "cloning" games, which would undermine the sustainable development of the games industry.

#### 4.3.3.3 Copyright Infringement Tests in the VG Context

The "access + substantial similarity" test has a long history in identifying the copyright infringement in Chinese judicial practice (Ding, 2019). To establish copyright infringement in China, a plaintiff must show that the defendant had access to the plaintiff's work and that the two works are substantially similar (Cole, 1995). To determine "substantial similarity," courts usually apply the "three-step" ("abstraction–filtration–comparison") test, the "total concept and feeling" test, the "extrinsic and intrinsic analysis" test and the "decomposition" test (Sun & Cao, 2017). However, the logic of and steps taken by courts vary; there is no unified standard for the substantive similarity comparison. Moreover, in practice, courts have generally conflated adaptation infringement and reproduction infringement. For example, in the *Dragon Nest* case, when making the "substantial similarity" comparison, the court found that two main characters (the heroine, Leah, and the master, Tie), some castle settings and some scenes in the defendant's film were substantially similar to those in the plaintiff's game. After evaluating the defendant's possible access to the plaintiff's work, the court held that the defendant's use of these characters, settings and scenes had violated the plaintiff's right of reproduction, right of adaptation and other rights relating to these elements, without clarifying whether the substantial similarity test had been applied to determine reproduction infringement or adaptation infringement ([2016] Hu 0115 Civil Verdict No. 82169). My analysis of the facts indicates that the defendant had not made the original contributions required to create new works from the infringed elements. Therefore, there was no infringement of the plaintiff's right of adaptation, although the defendant's film, as a whole, was indeed an adaptation of the plaintiff's game.

Although "character adaptation" infringement is relatively easy to judge, courts have sometimes confused reproduction infringement with adaptation infringement. In the *Calabash Brothers* case, for example, the court found reproduction infringement based on the substantial similarity between the allegedly infringing game and the original animation *Calabash Brothers.* However, it ruled against the adaptation infringement on the ground that "the two constitute substantial similarity" ([2018] Hu 73 Civil Final No. 300). In essence, the substantial similarity test is used to determine both reproduction and adaptation infringement, albeit with different focuses: the test as applied to reproduction infringement focuses on external expression, while it focuses on internal expression to determine adaptation infringement (Gervais, 2013). For example, in *Guangdong Original Power Culture Communication Co. v. Xiamen Shize Network Technology Co.*, the court found that the defendant had provided on his website three games that used certain character images "without the authorization of and no remuneration to the plaintiff." The court ruled that the defendant had infringed the plaintiff's right of adaptation and right of communication through information network ([2015] Si Civil Verdict No. 4252–4254). Despite the court's reasoning, from a theoretical perspective, the works had infringed the right of reproduction and not the right of adaptation, as these cartoon characters were identical to the plaintiff's ones.

This problem also appears in the judgement of "clone" games. In *Wemade Entertainment Co. v. Shanghai Xinshuo Network Technology Co.*, for instance, the defendant had developed and operated the game *Legend of King*, in which the characters' setting, images, attributes, skills, weapons, clothing, jewelry, monsters and other aspects were very similar or identical to those featured in the *Legend of Mir2.* The court therefore held that "the *Legend of King* is substantially similar with the *Legend of Mir2* in its genre, content, core elements, mechanics and other aspects, thus the defendant infringes the plaintiff's right of adaptation and other copyrights" ([2017] Hu 0107Civil Verdict No. 19813). In another litigation brought by the Wemade Entertainment Company, the court ruled in favor of the plaintiff's claim of adaptation infringement on the ground that there were no substantial differences between the *Legend of Hegemony* and the *Legend of Mir2* in terms of the appearance and names of their characters, parameter settings, or other core contents ([2016] Jing 73 Civil Verdict No. 229). As courts thus regard cloning—i.e. copying the external expression of the plaintiff's game—as adaptation infringement and not reproduction infringement, they are less likely to consider re-skinning to be copyright infringement, potentially leading to many unjust and incorrect judgements.

Furthermore, courts' ignorance regarding the difference between adaptation infringement and reproduction infringement has resulted in their neglect of an important step in determining copyright infringement, namely evaluating "probative similarity" to establish the possibility of "access." This was illustrated in the *Swords of Legend II* case, in which the court found that the defendant had had access to the original work, based on the fact that the plaintiff's infringed game had been released and made available to the public before the defendant's infringing TV series was released and that "the outline of the TV series draft had been provided to the defendant" ([2016] Hu 0115 Civil Verdict No. 62371). If access to the original work is established, this greatly reduces or eliminates the possibility of identical works having resulted from independent creation. Courts often omit this step in determining game adaptation infringement, advancing directly to the "substantial similarity" judgement (Ding, 2019). A case in point is that of *The Journey of Flower*, in which the court held that "*The Journey of Flower* made full use of the basic expression of *Tai Chi Panda* in terms of the specific presentation mode and the selection, arrangement and combination of the rules of the gameplay, and on this basis, it recreated certain visual contents such as arts, music, animation and texts. Hence it infringed the plaintiff's right of adaptation" ([2015] Su Zhong IP Civil Verdict No. 00201). The practice of only applying the single testing step of "substantial similarity," omitting the important step of "probative similarity" to determine the facts of copying, is not rigorous. It conflates fact determination with value judgement, ignoring the different functions of "similarity" in determining the source relationship of adaptation and the value judgement of infringement.

To clarify the double meaning of "similarity" in copyright law, Latman (1990) explained as follows:

> [t]wo distinct elements, 'copying' and 'unlawful appropriation,' are involved and should not be confused.... Copying may be proven directly (e.g., by defendant's admission), or by indirect evidence. The indirect evidence consists of 'similarities ... sufficient to prove copying,' which are usually accompanied by proof of 'access.' When there is the possibility of access, 'striking similarity' can effectively preclude the possibility of independent creation so as to justify the inference of copying. If copying is established, only then does there arise the second issue, that of illicit copying (unlawful appropriation).

In Latman's words, as a single "substantial similarity" prong only evaluates the value of unlawful appropriation, without proving the facts of copying, the term "probative similarity" is introduced to suggest that facts other than similarities may be probative of copying (Latman, 1990). This prong is extremely vital to determine game adaptation infringement. As adaptation appropriates the basic composition of the work, not the external form of expression, without the prong of "probative similarity" to establish the facts of copying, it is easy to misjudge some independent creations as unlawfully infringing works.

## 4.4 Right of Adaptation in Policy and Lessons from the US

### *4.4.1 Contextualizing the Right of Adaptation in Copyright Policy*

The right of adaptation is an important economic right, providing the copyright owner with the derivative interests arising from the subsequent use of his or her works. According to the *WIPO Guide to the Berne Convention* (2003), the right of adaptation "may find its origin in the right of reproduction." This is because an adaptation means "the combination of the pre-existing elements of the works concerned—the use of which in the adaptation, etc., may well be regarded as reproduction of those elements—with some new ones, as a result of which normally a new work emerges" (WIPO, 2003). While both rights are normatively motivated by a desire to protect legitimate market expectations, derivation is not a subset or *de minimis* adjunct of reproduction (Gervais, 2013). As observed by Samuelson (2013), "[t]he fact that derivative rights (including the right of adaptation) can be extracted from the right of reproduction and taken as independent copyright objects indicates that they have independent value.... The reason why the derivative works can be separated from reproductions is also due to the fact that the derivative work itself contains some extra originality, not simply 'copying.'"

Above all, the right of adaptation affects "the level of investment in copyrighted works by enabling the copyright owner to proportion its investment to the level of expected returns from all markets, not just the market in which the work first appears" (Goldstein, 1983). If a copyright owner realizes that he can charge licensing fees for abbreviations, integrations or derivations based on his novel, for example, he will probably invest more money and intellectual effort in creating and publicizing his work from the onset, as he expects to get returns from more potential markets, not merely from the single market of selling original novels. Besides, granting the right of adaptation gives authors time to decide "which derivative markets to enter, with whose assistance, on what terms, and when" (Abramowicz, 2005), which can improve the quantity and quality of the adaptations eventually produced. This supports the objective of the copyright system to stimulate the creation of intellectual works to increase the public welfare (Zybert, 2013), which can be achieved only by increasing both the quantity of the intellectual works and the quality of those works. The right of adaptation thus serves as tool for authors, allowing them to take enough time to make adaptations on the one hand, and to authorize well-qualified persons to prepare satisfactory adaptations on the other. This can prevent the rough production of adapted works and enable those adaptations to enter into the expected market.

Rachum-Twaig (2017) studied the relationship between the cognitive psychology of creativity and copyright law and noted that "the making of a derivative work is essentially a creative activity under cognitive approaches to creativity and is not qualitatively different than an original work." Stating that "the law makes almost no distinction between derivative works and mere reproductions," Rachum-Twaig (2017) noted that "the cognitive approaches to creativity view derivative works as part of creativity but not reproductions." Thus, in the following section, I reexamine the scope of the right of adaptation and its intersection with the right of reproduction and propose a system of determining game adaptation infringement that neither unduly restrains competition and follow-on innovation nor interferes with the free-expression interests of the subsequent creators.

### *4.4.2 Intersections and Distinctions: Right of Adaptation vs. Right of Reproduction*

Samuelson (2013) conducted an insightful study of the characteristics of the nine exemplary derivatives and discerned three principal features distinguishing the right of derivation (including the right of adaptation) from the right of reproduction:

> First, the derivative author contributes some original expression to the derivative work he or she creates; second, the second work's expression is intermingled with expression from the underlying work, either transforming or rendering the first work's expression so that the new work is distinguishable from the underlying work; third, although the second work will rarely supplant the whole or a substantial part of demand for the underlying work, it is generally likely to supplant demand for authorized derivatives.

Thus, the rights of derivation and of reproduction overlap but are distinguishable, and their respective spheres are defined by the expression of the original and infringing works. This is consistent with the notion that an "idea" cannot be protected by copyright law. To clarify the boundary between these two rights, it is first necessary to discuss from the meaning of "reproduction."

Reproduction can be defined either narrowly, by the strict provisions of the law, or more broadly. The right of reproduction is defined similarly across jurisdictions. The PRC Copyright Law defines it as "the right to produce one or more copies of a work by printing, photocopying, lithographing, making a sound recording or video recording, duplicating a recording, or duplicating a photographic work, or by other means" (Article 10(5)). It defines "copies" as "material objects, other than phonorecords, in which a work is fixed by any method now known or later developed, and from which the work can be perceived, reproduced, or otherwise communicated, either directly or with the aid of a machine or device."[10] The letter of the law requires that new copies of the original works be produced to constitute infringement of the right of reproduction. However, from a broader perspective as determined in judicial practice, "reproduction" or "copying" refers to producing a work "substantially similar" to the original work (Arnstein v. Porter, 1946). Works are substantially similar if an "ordinary, reasonable audience would find the works substantially similar in total concept and feel" (Cavalier v. Random House, Inc., 2002), regardless of minor modifications to, deletions from or rearrangements of the original work perceptible to

[10] See Section 101 of the U.S. Copyright Act. For more information, please also see Article 17 of the UK Copyright, Designs and Patents Act 1988, and Article L122-3 of the IP Code of France.

consumers. In this sense, the right of reproduction is infringed as long as the second work is so similar to the original one as to be considered a substitute for it.

When a second work is substantially similar to the original work, it may also infringe the right of adaptation. This is because an adaptation does not essentially change the protected elements or basic content of the original work, unlike a transformative use of the original work, which provides the work with different meanings. As one court observed, "if a modified work could exist independently from the basic content of the original work, why would the law bother to grant the previous copyright owner the right to exclude others from using the new work?" ([2012] Hu Yi Zhong Civil Five (IP) Final No. 112). Therefore, the right of adaptation regulates the unlawful appropriation of the basic content of the original work, just as the right of reproduction does. However, unlike reproductions involving verbatim or minorly modified copying, an adapted work incorporates a certain amount of creative effort on the part of the adaptor and thus contains a degree of originality. This implies that, to a significant extent, an adapted work is not a substitute for the original one.

This raises a question. To what extent is a work of unlawful appropriation controlled by the right of adaptation? Jozef Kohler described a work as "an abstract representation the author derived," and he further divided this representation into an "inner form" and an "outer form" (Gervais, 2013). The "inner form" refers to the general composition of the work, which exists in the internal structure of the work, such as the specific plot, the relationships of the main characters, the theme and rhythm of the music, and the artistic composition, whereas the "outer form" refers to the external expression regulated by the right of reproduction. When the "inner form" is appropriated and there is substantial similarity between the two works in terms of their general composition, this is deemed as "unlawful appropriation" and is therefore controlled by the right of adaptation. This approach is similar to that provided by Lu (2014), the dichotomy of "essence of expression" and "form of expression." In the VG context, the essence of expression comprises the constitutive rules of the game and the form of expression comprises the perceptible audiovisual contents such as words, images, colors, actions and sounds. When the most basic content (i.e., essence of expression) is illicitly appropriated, this infringes the right of adaptation. Only when the outer form of expression is copied does it constitute infringement of the right of reproduction (Fig. 4.7).

Courts sometimes make judgements against adaptation infringement based on the notion that "adaptation is to change a work from one genre to another," as stated by the court in the *Fantasy Westward Journey* case ([2016] Yue 0106 Civil Verdict No. 5333) and the *Wanjian Jianghu* case ([2017] Yue 0106 Civil Verdict No. 10491). However, in addition to modifying a work to another genre without changing the basic content, adaptation also includes altering a work into a new one without changing its genre (Hata, 1996). This was illustrated in the *The Journey of Flower* case; although both *The Journey of Flower* and *Tai Chi Panda* were online games, the former was an adaptation of the latter, as it had copied its constitutive rules and reskinned it as a new game ([2015] Su Zhong IP Civil Verdict No. 00201).

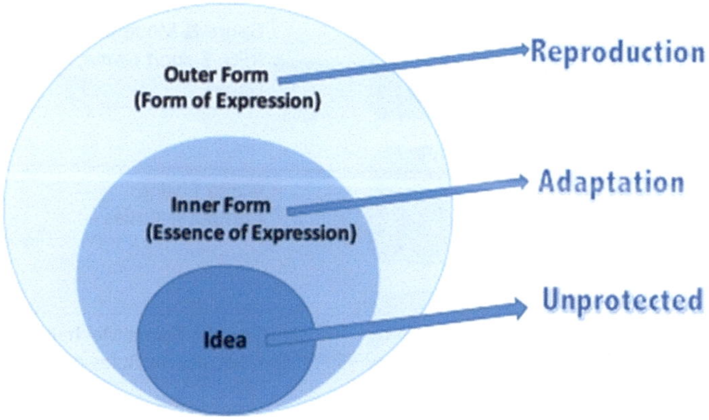


**Fig. 4.7** Scope of copyright protection by level of expression

### *4.4.3 Right of Adaptation from the Perspective of Game Design*

The above exploration reveals that the right of adaptation has its own normative footing and is distinct from the right of reproduction. To understand adaptations in the context of games better, I now examine it from the perspective of game design. Generally speaking, a VG design can be divided into four levels. The first level is the "soul," comprising the game's genre and mode. The second level is the "bone," that is, the game engine, expressed by computer code. The third level is the "muscle," referring to the specific game mechanics or the constitutive rules of the game, which includes specific rules and gameplay details. It acts as a connector between the characters, props, plots and other content based on the game engine. The fourth level is the "skin,' that is the game resources, including images, sounds, animation and text that can be perceived by the user's senses (Adams & Dormans, 2012) (Fig. 4.8).

From the perspective of copyright law, the soul level is the abstract idea that cannot be monopolized by game developers. The soul is necessarily in the public domain so that it can be developed and used by anyone. For example, the first role-playing game (RPG) developer could not prevent others from developing the same type of game, ultimately resulting in the availability of diverse RPGs. The other three levels—bone, muscle and skin—result from the intellectual effort of the game developer and are therefore protected by copyright law. The bone is copyright protected as computer software. The skin comprises the outer form of expression, while the muscle comprises the inner form of expression.

In terms of operational structure, the specific game mechanics or constitutive rules ("muscle") are generally composed of three core parts: a numerical system, a page layout and an operation design (Adams & Dormans, 2012). The rules of logic are contained in the numerical system, which is represented by complex digits

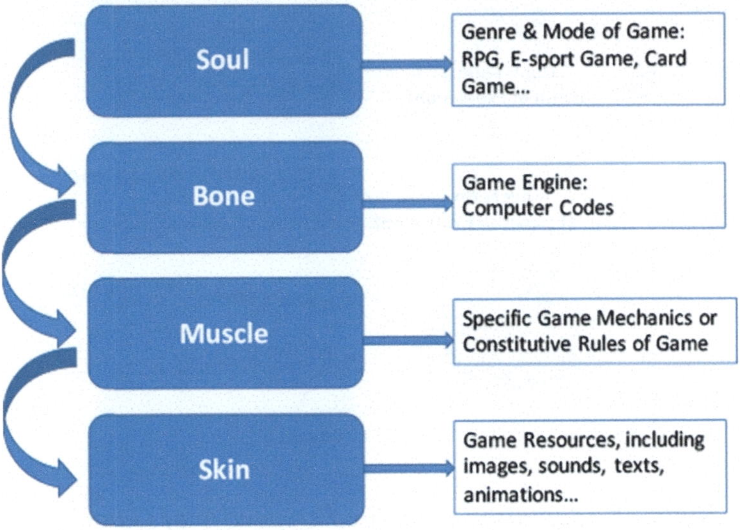


**Fig. 4.8** Four levels of VGs design

and computational formulas. The public generally does not have access to or understanding of the numerical system. It is highly technical in nature and well beyond the understanding of the layperson. Furthermore, the files of such a system are not published in isolation from the associated VGs. The function of the operational interface is to provide a better game experience for players. This element includes icons designed to guide and help players perform specific functions and achieve specific results in the gameplay. The contents of the operational interface are therefore functional as well as illustrative. Figure 4.9 illustrates the operational structure of gameplay. As shown, the specific game mechanics or the constitutive rules of game are a dynamic set of computation results appearing in the display devices through the data layer, and the final results of the rules presented to gamers are fixed contents, not isolated digits or functions (Adams & Dormans, 2012). Game mechanics are designed to drive the operation of preset contents according to certain logics to enable the predesigned plots to be expressed via dynamic media. Thus, when a game developer copies the specific game mechanics or the constitutive rules of a game by replacing the "skins"—the original sounds, images, text and other game resources—he cannot be excused from game adaptation infringement.

### *4.4.4 Lessons from US Case Law*

Over the past 30 years, excluding cases concerning identical copying in which the court ruled for the plaintiff (Manufacturing Mfg. Co. v. Dirkschneider, 1981; Stern Electronics, Inc. v. Kaufman, 1982), the predominant cases in the US cases have

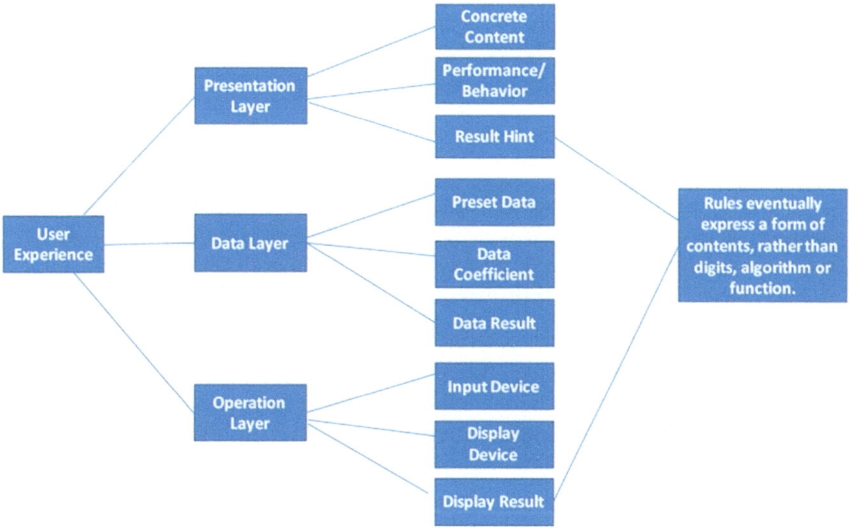


**Fig. 4.9** Operational structure of gameplay

predominantly provided thin copyright protection for VGs, allowing cloning practices to propagate (Atari, Inc. v. Amusement World, Inc., 1981; Capcom U.S.A v. Data East Corp., 1994; Data East USA v. Epyx, Inc., 1988). For example, in a case involving *Asteroids*, a VG in which players shoot their way through a barrage of asteroids, the court applied the "ordinary observer" test to determine substantial similarity and ruled that *Meteors* was not substantially similar to *Asteroids*, although it acknowledged some similarities between the two games (Atari, Inc. v. Amusement World, Inc., 1981). Applying the doctrines of merger and scènes à faire, the court reasoned that "most of these similarities are inevitable, given the requirements of the idea of a game involving a spaceship combating space rocks and given the technical demands of the medium of a VG." Similarly, in the *Street Fighter II* case, the court found similarities in the fighting styles, characters and special moves in both the plaintiff's and defendant's VGs; however, the court found no copyright infringement, arguing that "the vast majority of the moves are commonplace kicks and punches" and "the only three characters to be copied is insufficient to establish substantial similarity for the work as a whole" (Capcom U.S.A v. Data East Corp., 1994).

Due to the rise in cloning cases, US courts began to acknowledge the failure of copyright law to support the creation of original works as applied to VGs (Dean, 2016). Thus, a shift recently occurred in US VG cases whereby copyright protections for original game developers were expanded. In *Tetris Holding v. Xio Interactive*, for example, the defendant's game, *Mino*, had identical gameplay and game pieces featuring the same colors and shapes as those in the original VG *Tetris*. The court disagreed with the defendant's argument that *Tetris* was a puzzle game of abstract mechanics with little copyrightable expression due to the merger and scènes à faire doctrines. In the court's opinion, the scènes à faire doctrine is largely irrelevant to abstract puzzle games such as *Tetris*, which have no standard expressive elements. The court stated,

> [t]he principle that 'some functional aspect of a work cannot receive copyright protection' does not mean that any and all expression related to a game rule or game function is unprotectable. Such an exception to copyright would likely swallow any protection one could possibly have; almost all expressive elements of a game are related in some way to the rules and functions of gameplay. *Tetris* is as entitled to copyright protection for the way in which it chooses to express game rules or game play as one would be to the way in which one chooses to express an idea. (Tetris Holding, LLC v. Xio Interactive, Inc., 2012)

The court found that the merger doctrine was equally inapplicable, as "there were many novel ways Xio could have chosen to express the rules of *Tetris*. Xio's own expert admitted there were an almost unlimited number of ways to design the pieces and the board and the game would still function perfectly well" (Tetris Holding, LLC v. Xio Interactive, Inc., 2012).

The court in *Spry Fox v. Lolapps, Inc.* similarly restrained the application of the merger and scènes à faire doctrines. Although there were clear visual differences between the artwork and sound elements of the two games, the court nonetheless found substantial similarity indicative of infringement because the object hierarchy and field of play in *Yeti Town* comprised a setting and theme similar to *Triple Town*'s. This finding was cemented by evidence from numerous online bloggers (Spry Fox v. Lolapps, 2012). This case established an important guideline for game re-skinning cases. As the court put it,

> [t]he rules of the game are entitled to (at best) thin protection. Game rules are a hybrid of the concept of the game and functional considerations. A game designer could theoretically make expressive choices in presenting the rules of play. It could perhaps use creative language to express the rules. But that language, as an expression of game rules, would be only entitled to protection against nearly identical copying…. There are apparent differences between the games … but a court must focus on what is similar, not what is different, when comparing two works. (Spry Fox v. Lolapps, 2012)

In a recent US case concerning game re-skinning, the winning conditions, life points, action card functions and the rule of having unique character cards with special abilities in the defendant's game were identical to those in the plaintiff's game, *Bang!*. However, the defendant's game expressed these elements through the setting, artwork and general themes of ancient China instead of the Wild West (DaVinci Editrice S.R.L. v. Ziko Games LLC, 2014). This is a classic example of a game re-skinning case. When the defendant argued that "the identical or similar elements between the two games were systems, methods, or procedures that could not receive copyright protection," the court disagreed and found that the expression related to a game rule or game function may be protectable (DaVinci Editrice S.R.L. v. Ziko Games LLC, 2014). The court further noted that "the players' roles and their expression are not merely rules that prescribe what the player may do" but also "describe how the players may do it. The descriptions of the roles express the underlying creative idea that is the essence of *Bang!*, which are protectable expression here." The court further ruled that the merger doctrine did not preclude protection for player roles because "there were nearly infinite ways of expressing the concepts of player elimination or a contest between authorities and their opponents" (DaVinci Editrice S.R.L. v. Ziko Games LLC, 2014).

Fortunately, some Chinese courts have followed US courts' lead in expanding the realm of protectable expression in game re-skinning cases. In the *Hearthstone* case, the defendant had designed a game based on the plaintiff's game but had changed its theme from the "World of Warcraft" to the "History of Three Kingdoms" ([2014] Hu Yi Zhong Civil Verdict Five (IP) No. 23). Despite accepting the defense that the operation mode and the UI of a game were classified as uncopyrightable rules and procedures, the court argued that "the text description on the card is used to explain the skills or functions of the card in the game, and the combination of these descriptions can be regarded as a specification of the game, which can be protected as a written work." This approach was essentially adopted from the *Tetris* case, where the scènes à faire doctrine was deemed to play no role in an abstract puzzle game (Tetris Holding, LLC v. Xio Interactive, 2012). The court in the *The Journey of Flower* case also ruled in favor of the plaintiff, reasoning that

> copyright law only protects the specific expressions of ideas and not the abstract ideas and methods. To some extent, the original expression of the gameplay rules in online games can be protected by copyright law…. In this case, the specific rules of the game are expressed through the game operation interface, either by straightforward text form or by the continuous dynamic images, which can be clearly perceived by players and allow them to conduct interactive operation…. *The Journey of Flower* made full use of the basic expression of *Tai Chi Panda* in terms of the specific presentation mode, selection, arrangement and combination of the rules of gameplay, while recreating new contents such as artworks, music, animation and texts. Hence it infringed the right of adaptation enjoyed by the copyright owner. ([2015] Su Zhong IP Civil Verdict No. 00201)

In a recent case involving the VG *Overwatch*, the game developers of *Battle of Heroes* and *Gunplay Frontline* were sued for copying elements of game design from *Overwatch*, including but not limited to the gameplay rules, winning and losing conditions, character design, UI and battle map ([2017] Hu 0115 Civil Verdict No. 77945). The court found adaptation infringement, reasoning that,

> once players enter into the fast-paced first-person shooter game, the artistic images of heroes, the appearance and shape of the buildings, the colors and other aesthetic external presentations are diluted, whilst the elements of game design, such as the route on the map, the location of the entrance and exit, the location of shooting points and hidden points, the skills of characters, the selection and matching of teammates, and the placement of blood bags, are highlighted. These elements of game design are specific expressions of the rules of the game, which should be protected by copyright law. ([2017] Hu 0115 Civil Verdict No. 77945)

This was the first decision in China to explore the scope of copyrighted expression of online game from the perspective of game design, which is a possible solution to unauthorized game re-skinning.

## 4.5 A New Approach to Addressing Game Adaptation Infringement

VGs have become an indelible part of our culture, and their salience and complexity will continue to grow as the medium develops. The increased ease of VG development has resulted in the proliferation of re-skinned games, which may mislead consumers and deter new developers from developing original game content. To ensure that copyright fulfills its purpose of encouraging the creation of new works for the benefit of the public, I propose a restructured copyright regime that avoids rewarding clone developers at the expense of bona fide innovators. Based on the above analysis, I propose certain amendments to the existing rules for determining game adaptation infringement to create a new three-step test: determination of the facts of copying, interlayer analysis and infringement value judgement.

### *4.5.1 Determining the Facts of Copying*

The first step, determining the facts of copying, comprises a two-part inquiry: regarding "access" and "probative similarity." The plaintiff must prove that the defendant had access to the plaintiff's game and show that the two games are similar enough to support a reasonable inference of copying (Positive Black Talk Inc. v. Cash Money Records Inc., 2004). The possibility of access is proven by evidence and not by speculation (Li, 2014). For example, the public dissemination of the plaintiff's work proves public access to the work. In such cases, the court can presume, in the absence of contrary evidence, that the defendant had access to the plaintiff's game. "Probative similarity" refers to a "striking similarity" between the two works. This can also provide evidence of access (Arnstein v. Porter, 1946), as the courts follow the logic that "similarity that is so close as to be highly unlikely to have been an accident of independent creation is evidence of access" (Ty, Inc. v. GMA Accessories, 1997). To determine probative similarity, courts can hear from expert witnesses, technical investigators or other technical experts who are able to compare the similarities and differences between the two games. The court should take into consideration both the protected expression and the unprotected ideas or facts in this analysis. The plaintiff bears the burden of proving factual copying. The burden then shifts to the defendant to prove exclusion or independent creation.

### *4.5.2 Interlayer Analysis*

The second step is a key link in determining game adaptation infringement, constituting the "substantial similarity" investigation together with the third step of the "infringement value judgement". In this step, it is important to first isolate original elements of the plaintiff's and the defendant's works by identifying and eliminating ideas as distinguished from expression in the games. Next, the court must filter out unprotected habitual expression through the merger and scènes à faire doctrines. This can be complicated process, as "one cannot divide a visual work into neat layers of abstraction in precisely that same manner one could with a text" (Newman, 1999). "A story has a linear dimension: it begins, continues, and ends" (Warner Bros, Inc. v. Am. Broad. Cos., 1983); this is true of works such as novels and films as well as story-driven VGs, which are driven and distinguished by the characters they contain and the manner in which their plots unfold (Nichols v. Universal Pictures Corp., 1930). In contrast, some VGs, such as open-world games, lack a linear dimension and might be better perceived as compilations, just as "a graphic or three-dimensional work is created to be perceived as an entirety" (Warner Bros, Inc. v. Am. Broad. Cos., 1983). This is an important distinction, as even when a compilation consists of independently un-copyrightable elements, it gains protection through the author's creative selection, arrangement and coordination of the materials.[11] Therefore, the court should be especially careful not to filter out the inner expression of a game, such as its constitutive rules and elements of game mechanics. Moreover, it should restrict the application of the merger and scènes à faire doctrines and instead evaluate whether there are other ways to express the rules or concepts in the VG context, taking technological advancement into consideration.

Once the uncopyrightable elements have been set aside, the court must identify the homologous comprehensive expression (inner form of expression) of the two works. Most courts underemphasize this process, focusing instead on the outer form of expression. However, a claim of adaptation infringement requires the defendant to have unlawfully appropriated the basic internal expression of the plaintiff's work. To observe the similarities in the structure of comprehensive expression, the court must screen out the irrelevant expression elements resulting from the special characteristics of the two works, such as type or genre, and then extract the homologous comprehensive expression. For example, in the *Fights Break Sphere* case, the court asserted, "Feiyin Company adapted the novel into a web game that is an innovation in the form of expression.... It is because these two works have different forms of expression that, objectively speaking, the web game cannot provide a specific ... description of the story plots and relationships of characters ... like those of a novel. Hence we cannot deny the fact that the defendant has appropriated the basic expression of the novel" ([2015] Yuezhi Fazhu Civil Final No. 30). Thus, the type or genre of an allegedly infringing VG may affect its specific use of an original work of another type or genre. Regardless of such imposed limitations, game adaptation infringement may be found if there is homologous comprehensive expression between the two works. If it is difficult to identify a similar structure of comprehensive expression between the two works, then there is no comparative basis for the adaptation infringement value judgement. In such a case, even if there is factual

[11] 17 U.S.C. Section 101(2008) defines a compilation as "a work formed by the collection and assembling of preexisting materials or of data that are selected, coordinated, or arranged in such a way that the resulting work as a whole constitutes an original work of authorship."

copying between the two works, the plaintiff's work should be regarded as a source of the defendant's inspiration or material for reasonable reference, not an infringing adaptation.

### *4.5.3 Infringement Value Judgement*

As the third step, I propose that courts should apply the "decomposition" test or the "total concept and feeling" test to comprehensively examine the similarity of expression between the two works from qualitative and quantitative perspectives. These tests should be applied according to the results of the interlayer analysis. The decomposition test should be applied in cases involving derivative works with little originality, whereas the "total concept and feeling" test should be applied in cases involving works with significant originality (Macatee, 1993). Specifically, the decomposition test comprises an itemized comparison of the expressive elements of the works. In a case involving a story-driven VG's adaptation infringement of a novel, for example, the court should comprehensively itemize the specific forms of expression, such as the gist of the story, characters' personalities and relationships, the plot development and the interactions between characters and plots, for comparison. Due to the different forms of expression inherent in novels and games, differences such as less text used in the game do not serve as evidence to preclude the possibility of adaptation infringement. The copying of only the names and relationships of some characters from the novel in the game, accompanied by no other elements of the plot, does not constitute substantial similarity in expression. However, a game's use of the novel's plot or sentences expressing specific content is sufficient to establish infringement ([2016] Su 03 Civil Verdict No. 369). On the contrary, a case involving two nonlinear audiovisual works, such as open world games, merits the application of the "total concept and feeling" test, as excessively decomposing the expressive elements may evacuate the protected scope of the works. This approach emphasizes the similarities between the two works in terms of users' perceptions and appreciation, using the "ordinary, reasonable observer" standard. The "ordinary, reasonable observer" refers to the audience targeted by the original work (Litchfield v. Spielberg, 1984; Lyons P'ship, L.P. v. Morris Costumes, 2000). That means, when conducting the second prong of the substantial similarity inquiry, a district court must consider the nature of the intended audience of the plaintiff's work (Dawson v. Hinshaw Music, 1990). For example, in a case involving VGs targeted at teenage boys, the court specified that the similarities between the works that the plaintiff was required to show must be as perceived by 17.5-year-old boys (the average age of a consumer of the VG) (Data E. USA, Inc. v. Epyx Inc., 1988). In some cases, including those involving cloned games, courts must apply both of these tests to compare the external and internal expression of the works. In such cases, the "total concept and feeling" test can be used to determine the copying of internal expression (Meyer, 2010). If substantial similarity is found between the two works in terms of both external and internal expression, reproduction infringement is established. However, if substantial similarity is found only in terms of the internal expression, this constitutes adaptation infringement.

The "infringement value judgement" step evaluates not only the proportion of comprehensive expression in the defendant's work that is homologous to that in the plaintiff's work, but also the value of that expression in the defendant's work. As Manfred Rehbinder observed, "[t]he criterion of free utilization should be embodied in the significance of the new work to the cultural progress, and this kind of progress can only be judged by comparing the original features of both the old and the new works.... [I]t is not decisive in judging the free utilization or adaptation merely [to show] the quantity of original content [from] the old work, but [adaptation] depends more on the comparison of originality in both these two works from an overall impression" (Zhang, 2005). The adaptation is limited by the original content of the preexisting work. Thus, the homologous comprehensive expression must account for a significant proportion of the plaintiff's work. Furthermore, the adaptation does not directly affect the existing market of the preexisting work; rather, it indirectly affects its potential market (Deneau, 2013). Thus, it is important to examine the value of homologous comprehensive expression in the defendant's work to determine whether it constitutes an infringement or a transformative use. When the homologous comprehensive expression bears a new artistic value or achieves a different function from that in the original work, the defendant's work is considered as a transformative use rather than adaptation infringement (Fig. 4.10).

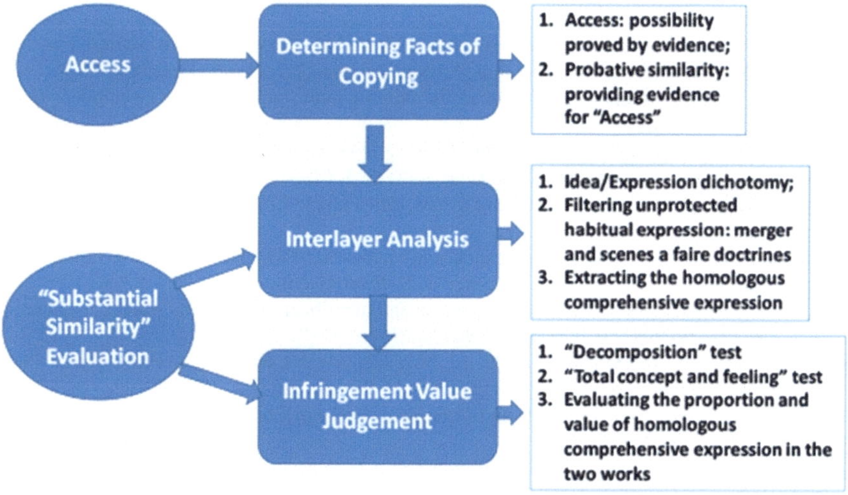


**Fig. 4.10** Proposed three-step test for addressing game adaptation infringement

## 4.6 Conclusion

With the development of digital cultural products and social media platforms, game adaptation has become a key part of today's social economy. Although they have enriched people's cultural lives, game adaptations have given rise to many legal disputes. The current copyright regime fails to acknowledge the core role of the right of adaptation in copyright theory and provides scant protection for VGs. This allows game developers to clone or re-skin games at the expense of the games' creators, thereby discouraging innovation. I suggest that the normative target of the right of adaptation differs from that of the right of reproduction, despite their considerable overlap. This notion is strengthened by the exploration from the perspective of game design. Drawing on US judicial practice, I propose a new three-step test to determine game adaptation infringement. If strictly implemented, this test would avoid unduly restraining competition and follow-on innovation and interfering with the reasonable interests of the original creators.

## References

Abramowicz, M. (2005). A Theory of Copyright's Derivative Right and Related Doctrine. *Minnesota Law Review, 90*, 317, 319, 320.

Adams, E., & Dormans, J. (2012). *Game Mechanics: Advanced Game Design* (pp. 156, 164, 165). New Riders.

Chong, B. (2018). *Game Reskin Advantages*. Available at: https://www.gamasutra.com/blogs/BenChong/20180604/318450/Game_Reskin_Advantages.php. Accessed 30 December 2024.

Cole, R. R. (1995). Substantial Similarity in the Ninth Circuit. *Santa Clara Computer & High Technology Law Journal, 11*, 417.

Corbett, S. (2016). Videogames and Their Clones: How Copyright Law Might Address the Problem. *Computer Law & Security Review, 32*(4), 615, 619.

Dean, D. S. (2016). Hitting Reset: Devising a New Video Game Copyright Regime. *University of Pennsylvania Law Review, 164*, 1239.

Deneau, K. (2013). The Historical Development and Misplaced Justification for the Derivative Work Right. *Boston University Journal of Science & Technology Law, 19*, 68, 77.

Ding, W. [丁文杰]. (2019). The Basic Connotation and Identification Rules of "Access" Element [接触要件的基本内涵及认定规则]. *Intellectual Property* (2), 24.

Gervais, D. (2013). The Derivative Right, or Why Copyright Law Protects Foxes Better than Hedgehogs. *Vanderbilt Journal of Entertainment & Technology Law, 15*, 785, 822, 825, 828.

Goldstein, P. (1983). Derivative Rights and Derivative Works in Copyright. *Journal of Copyright Society of USA, 30*, 209, 227.

Goold, P. R. (2014). Why the U.K. Adaptation Right Is Superior to the U.S. Derivative Work Right. *Nebraska Law Review, 92*(4), 843, 872.

Hata, M. [Japanese]. (1996). *An Overview of Copyright Law* (p. 148). Tokyo Ichigo.

Latman, A. (1990). "Probative Similarity" as Proof of copying: Toward Dispelling Some Myths in Copyright Infringement. *Columbia Law Review, 90*, 1187, 1193, 1206.

Li, M. [李明德]. (2014). *U.S. Intellectual Property Law [美国知识产权法]* (p. 358).

Lu, H. [卢海君]. (2014). *Copyright Object [版权客体论]* (p. 94). Intellectual Property Publishing House.

Lunsford, C. (2013). Drawing a Line Between Idea and Expression in Videogame Copyright: The Evolution of Substantial Similarity for Videogame Clones. *Intellectual Property Law Bulletin, 18*, 87, 105.

Macatee, S. B. (1993). Total Concept and Feel or Dissection: Approaches to the Misappropriation Test of Substantial Similarity. *Chi-Kent Law Review, 68*, 913, 935.

McArthur, S. C. (2013). *Clone Wars: The Five Most Important Cases Every Game Developer Should Know*. GAMASUTRA. Available at: https://www.gamasutra.com/view/feature/187385/clone_wars_the_five_most_.php. Accessed 30 December 2024.

Meyer, K. R. (2010). Doctrine of the Dead: How Capcom v. MKR Exposes the Decreasing Fit Between Modern Copyright Infringement Analysis and Modern Video Games. *Chi-Kent Journal of Intellectual Property* (9), 132, 141.

Newman, J. O. (1999). New Lyrics for an Old Melody: The Idea/Expression Dichotomy in the Computer Age. *Cardozo Arts & Entertainment Law Journal, 17*, 691, 698.

Nimmer, M. B., & Nimmer, D. (2015). *Nimmer on Copyright* §2.18 [H][3][b].

Parkin, S. (2011). Clone Wars: Is Plagiarism Killing Creativity in the Games Industry? *The Guardian*. Available at: https://www.theguardian.com/technology/gamesblog/2011/dec/21/clone-wars-games-industry-plagiarism. Accessed 30 December 2024.

Rachum-Twaig, O. (2017). Recreating Copyright: The Cognitive Process of Creation and Copyright Law. *Fordham Intellectual Property, Media and Entertainment Law Journal, 27*(2), 287, 346, 348.

Salen, K., & Zimmerman, E. (2004). *Rules of Play: Game Design Fundamentals* (pp. 13, 16). The MIT Press.

Samuelson, P. (2013). The Quest for a Sound Conception of Copyright's Derivative Work Right. *The Georgetown Law Journal, 101*, 1505, 1522, 1523, 1528.

Sun, L., & Cao, L. [孙磊 & 曹丽萍]. (2017). *Judicial Protection of Intellectual Property Rights of Online Games [网络游戏知识产权司法保护]* [pp. 273–284]. China Legal Publishing House [中国法制出版社].

Wang, Q. [王清]. (2016a). *Creating a Sequel Without Permission Infringes the Copyright of the Original Author?* [擅自创作续集会侵犯原作者著作权吗?]. State Copyright Administration [国家版权局]. Available at: http://www.ncac.gov.cn/chinacopyright/contents/4509/293330.html. Accessed 3 April 2021.

Wang, Q. [王迁]. (2016b). *Course of Intellectual Property Law* (5th ed., p. 222) [知识产权法教程(第五版)]. Beijing: China Renmin University Press [中国人民大学出版社].

WIPO. (2003). *WIPO Guide to the Berne Convention* (p. 81).

Zhang, Z. (Trans.). (2005). *Copyright Law* (p. 259). Law Press China.

Zybert, S. E. (2013). The Derivative Work Right: Incentive or Hindrance for New Literature. *Connecticut Law Review, 45*, 1083, 1089.

## *Legislations*

Berne Convention for the Protection of Literary and Artistic Works (1886)
Guidelines for the Trial of Copyright Infringement Cases (Beijing High People's Court 2018)
IP Code of France
PRC Copyright Law (2021)
U.S. Constitution
UK Copyright, Designs and Patents Act 1988
US Copyright Act
WIPO Copyright Treaty (WCT)

## Cases


Apple Comput., Inc. v. Microsoft Corp., 35 F.3d 1435, 1444(9th Cir. 1994).

Arnstein v. Porter, 154 F. 2d 464, 468 (2d Cir. 1946), *cert. denied*, 330 U.S. 851 (1947).

Atari, Inc. v. Amusement World, Inc., 547 F. Supp. 222, 229 (D. Md. 1981).

Atari, Inc. v. N. Am. Philips Consumer Elecs. Corp., 672 F.2d 607 (7th Cir. 1982).

Baker v. Selden, 101 U.S. 99, 104 (1879).

Beijing Wangyuan Shengtang Entertainment Technology Co., Ltd. v. Shanghai Xinlongmen Film & Television Co., Ltd., [2016] Hu 0115 Civil Verdict No. 62371 [(2016) 沪 0115 民初 62371 号].

Blizzard Entertainment Co., Ltd. & Shanghai NetEase Network Technology Co., Ltd. v. Shanghai Youyi Network Technology Co., Ltd., [2014] Hu Yi Zhong Civil Verdict Five (IP) No. 23 [沪一中民五(知)初字第 23 号].

Blizzard Entertainment Co., Ltd. & Shanghai NetEase Network Technology Co., Ltd. v. 4399 Network Co., Ltd., [2017] Hu 0115 Civil Verdict No. 77945 [(2017) 沪 0115 民初 77945 号].

Capcom U.S.A., Inc. v. Data East Corp., No. 93-3259, 1994 WL 1751482, at 12 (N.D.Cal. Mar. 16, 1994).

Cavalier v. Random House, Inc., 297 F. 3d 815, 822 (9th Cir. 2002).

Data East USA v. Epyx, Inc.,862 F. 2d 204, 209 (9th Cir. 1988).

Dawson v. Hinshaw Music, Inc., 905 F. 2d 731, 736 (4th Cir. 1990).

DaVinci Editrice S.R.L. v. Ziko Games LLC, 183 F. Supp. 3d. 820 (S.D. Tex. 2016).

DaVinci Editrice S.R.L. v. Ziko Games LLC, No. 13-3415, 2014 WL 3900139, at 3–4 (S. D. Tex. Aug. 8, 2014).

Educ. Testing Servs. v. Katzman, 793 F.2d 533, 539 (3d Cir. 1986).

Glu Mobile Inc. v. Hothead Games Inc., No. 14–04917, (N.D. Cal. Nov. 5, 2014)

Guangdong Original Power Culture Communication Co., Ltd. v. Xiamen Shize Network Technology co., Ltd., [2015] Si Civil Verdict No. 4252–4254 [(2015) 思民初字第 4252–4254 号].

Guangzhou Chuangyu Network Technology Co., Ltd. v. Shanghai Yishi Network Technology Co., Ltd. and others, [2017] Yue 0106 Civil Verdict No. 10491 [(2017) 粤 0106 民初 10491 号].

Hangzhou NetEase LEihuo Technology Co., Ltd v. Guangzhou Yuelang Network Technology Co. Ltd. and others, [2016] Yue 0106 Civil Verdict No. 5333 [(2016) 粤 0106 民初 5333 号].

Litchfield v. Spielberg, 736 F. 2d 1352, 1356 (9th Cir. 1984).

Lyons P'ship, L.P. v. Morris Costumes, Inc., 243 E. 3d 789, 801 (4th Cir. 2000).

Mazer v. Stein, 347 U.S. 201, 217 (1954).

Midway Manufacturing Mfg. Co. v. Dirkschneider, 543 F. Supp. 466 (D.Neb.1981).

Morrissey v. Procter & Gamble Co., 379 F. 2d 675 (1st Cir. 1967).

Nichols v. Universal Pictures Corp., 45 F.2d 119, 121 (2d Cir. 1930), *cert. denied*, 282 U.S. 902 (1931).

Nichols v. Universal Pictures Corporation, 45 F. 2d 119, at 121 (2nd Cir 1930).

Positive Black Talk Inc. v. Cash Money Records Inc., 394 F.3d 357, 368 (5th Cir. 2004).

Shanghai Jumping Network Technology Co., Ltd. and others v. Shanghai Fine Arts Film Studio Co., Ltd., [2018] Hu 73 Civil Final No. 300 [(2018) 沪 73 民终 300 号].

Shanghai Shulong Technology Co., Ltd. v. Suzhou Mili Film & Television Culture Communication Co., Ltd, [2016] Hu 0115 Civil Verdict No. 82169 [(2016) 沪 0115 民初 82169 号].

Shanghai Xuanting Entertainment Information Technology Co. v. Beijing Tianhang Huitong Information Technology Co., [2015] Yuezhi Fazhu Civil Final No. 30 [(2015) 粤知法著民终字第 30 号民事判决书].

Shanghai Xuanting Entertainment Information Technology Co. v. Chengdu Jiqian Technology Co. and others, [2016] Su 03 Civil Verdict No. 369[2016] 苏 03 民初 369 号].

Shanghai XX Culture and Art Co. v. Shanghai XX Theater & others, Shanghai No. 1 Intermedia People's Court (2012) Hu Yi Zhong Civil Five (IP) Final No. 112 (2012) [沪一中民五 (知) 终字第 112 号民事判决书].

Shanghai Zhuangyou Information Technology Co. v. Guangdong Shuoxing Information Technology Co. and others, [2016] Hu 73 Civil final No. 190 [(2016) 沪 73 民终 190 号].

Spry Fox v. Lolapps, Inc., Case No. C12-147RAJ (W.D. Wash. 2012).
Stern Electronics, Inc. v. Kaufman, 660 F. 2d 852 (2d Cir. 1982).
Suzhou Snail Digital Technology Co., Ltd. v. Chengdu Tianxiang Interactive Technology co., Ltd., [2015] Su Zhong IP Civil Verdict No. 00201 [(2015) 苏中知民初字第 00201 号].
Tetris Holding, LLC v. Xio Interactive, Inc., 863 F. Supp.2d (D.N.J. 2012).
Ty, Inc. v. GMA Accessories, Inc., 13 F. 3d 1167, 1170 (7th Cir. 1997).
Warner Bros, Inc. v. Am. Broad. Cos., 720 F.2d 231, 241 (2d Cir. 1983).
Wemade Entertainment Co., Ltd. v. 37 Interactive Entertainment (Shanghai) Technology Co., Ltd. and others, [2016] Jing 73 Civil Verdict No. 229 [(2016) 京 73 民初 229 号].
Wemade Entertainment Co., Ltd. v. Shanghai Xinshuo Network Technology Co., Ltd., [2017] Hu 0107Civil Verdict No. 19813 [(2017) 沪 0107 民初 19813].

# Chapter 5
# Beyond Player Contribution: Reexamining Players' Rights to Their Modified Games

**Abstract** This chapter proposes a more balanced scheme for regulating game Mods. It first traces the historical debate on the legality of game Mods, showing that existing law and terms of service cannot effectively address game Mods. Then it examines the rights of players regarding their modified games in terms of potential social benefit and harm, arguing that game Mods are shaped by not only legal but also economic and social factors, all of which should be taken into account when designing a new systematic framework to assess the issue. The chapter proposes a two-pronged solution—a modding right scheme and a community-based approach—to the modding problem, seeking to better balance the respective rights and obligations of game developers and players.

**Keywords** Game Mods · Rights of players · Social benefit and harm · A modding right scheme · A community-based approach

## 5.1 Introduction

A significant feature of Web 3.0 is that network users are no longer satisfied with being passive consumers; rather, they view culture as bidirectional and have a strong desire for self-expression and active participation. This is also true of the games industry, as the influx of new digital media technologies and platforms has made it easier for gamers to create and distribute their own works. Modern VGs also provide gamers with an open creative space in which they can make choices beyond a preset selection of elements as well as produce and distribute their own creations. In a departure from the traditional production of VGs by established professional creators, gamers can now act as creators and disseminators as well as consumers. It serves as evidence that digital technology breaks the distance between content creators and consumers, and the boundary between them is blurred gradually. This has triggered debate regarding whether and to what extent players can and should hold copyright ownership of their created content. In this chapter, I add to the literature by examining a distinct form of player-contributed content, namely game modifications

 
Z. Deng, *Constructing an Eco-Balanced Copyright Regime for the Video Game Industry in China*, https://doi.org/10.1007/978-981-96-6056-8_5

(or "Mods"), through the lens of social welfare rather than from the perspective of content creators or pure legal theory. I argue that game Mods are shaped by not only legal but also economic and social factors. Taking all of these factors into account, I design a new framework for systematically examining the copyright implications of game Mods. After presenting this four-quadrant framework for benefit/harm analysis, I propose a two-pronged solution—a modding right scheme and a community-based approach—to the modding copyright problem. Compared with the current copyright scheme, this system strikes a better balance between the rights and obligations of game developers and players.

## 5.2 Game Mods in Context

### *5.2.1 Locating Game Mods on the Spectrum of Player Contribution*

The term "player contributed content" (PCC) derives from the term "user generated content" (UGC) or "user created content" (UCC), defined by Wikipedia as "any form of content, such as image, video, text and audio, that has been posted by users on online platforms such as social media and wikis."[1] The OECD defined UCC as "content made publicly available over the Internet, which reflects a certain amount of creative effort, and which is created outside of professional routines and practices" (Vickery & Wunsch-Vincent, 2007).

The extent to which VG users can generate content depends on the gameplay environment, namely whether it is scripted or unscripted (Barker, 2012). A scripted environment is one in which a player has little or no freedom to create in-game items and is limited to the access of "closed" avatars, whose attributes, abilities and tools are predetermined solely by the developer. In contrast, players in an unscripted environment are free not only to roam and do as they please but also to script or create their own code and control "open" avatars, tailoring any or all aspects of an avatar's body, personality and abilities (Kromand, 2007). An unscripted environment also permits gamers to use game graphics or other elements to create non-game contents, such as virtual art projects.[2] The "spectrum of user contribution" proposed by Baldrica (2007) is helpful in distinguishing various forms of PCC. According to Baldrica (2007), content contribution is conceived of as falling within the spectrum of player contribution. Content with little input by the user lies at one end of this

---

[1] See "User-Generated Content", from Wikipedia, <https://en.wikipedia.org/wiki/User-generated_content> last visited December 30, 2024.

[2] See, e.g., "Velvet-Strike, a set of counter-military graffiti sprays for a spray-gun modification in the networked game Counter-Strike. Players could both download and spray images from the collection in-game and also create and contribute new spray paint graphics to the intervention." See <https://anthology.rhizome.org/velvet-strike≥ last visited December 30, 2024.

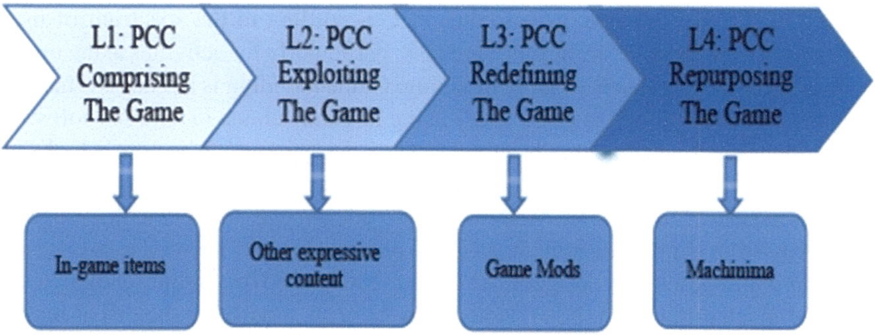


**Fig. 5.1** Levels of PCC on the spectrum of player contribution

spectrum, and content involving altering the game itself or using game assets to create completely independent expressive projects lies at the other end (see Fig. 5.1).

More specifically, PCC can be divided into four main levels according to its position on the spectrum of user contribution. At the simplest and lowest level is content generated strictly as a result of the investment of time while "playing" or "laboring" within the rules of the game, including but not limited to unique in-game items and virtual real estate. Such content can be understood as "PCC comprising the game." Content elements at this level are generally designed and dictated by the game developers and can only enter the game worlds through the contribution of shared labor of players. For instance, in a multiplayer online battle arena, gamers may assume specific roles, such as those of "carry," "support" and "tanker,"and implement their tactical strategies and methods of operation by controlling specific avatars (Gavrilova & Kenneth Tan, 2016). The second level of content, "PCC exploiting the game," is created when gamers "exploit the game environment or user tools as a forum to speak or create other expressive content" (Baldrica, 2007). For example, the sandbox game *Minecraft* offers unlimited opportunities to create; players are provided with various building materials to construct a world according to their own ideas and preferences, unrestricted by the rules of the game. Although the game resources, such as painting brushes and colors, are created by the game designers, the final audiovisual output is controlled by gamers rather than preset by the game designers (Baldrica, 2007). PCC at the third level is understood as "PCC redefining the game"; it is created by modifying, adding or enhancing the game engines or original codes that results in a different type of game or a new game extension. Game Mods generally fall within this category. Apart from the above three level of PCC, the last common one is "PCC repurposing the game," i.e., "using the game engine, graphics, or other elements to create a new expression which is no longer a game" (Baldrica, 2007). A case in point is the "machinima," players' creation of cinematic productions by adding narrative elements to the preexisting elements of VGs, including actors, props and stages (Bray, 2004).

Notably, this spectrum is not as clear as shown in the figure, because in essence, it is hard to say that the content of Level 4 must enjoy more contributions from players than that of Level 3. Hence categorizing PCC according to the spectrum of user contribution is often not a straightforward task, particularly for activities at the upper levels of the spectrum, such as game modding. Game modding is a process whereby players alter, add to or delete game codes using in-game editors or external software development kits to change one or more aspects of a game, such as how it looks or behaves, including but not limited to levels, characters, weapons, items, maps and mission scenarios.[3] Simply put, Mods are "fan-made changes to a VG with a range of complexity from simple adjustments in game play or variables to 'total conversions' where an entire game is redesigned" (Postigo, 2007a, 2007b). Some scholars have classified machinima as a type of Mods, as it involves modifying the visual replay of game usage sessions (Rosen, 2018; Scacchi, 2011). Within the realm of possible Mods, there are potential issues of IP infringement, with respect to the IP rights of both the original game developer and any third party whose IP the Mod too closely resembles. A Mod's position on the spectrum of user contribution helps to determine the level of copyright protection it merits under the current copyright law governing artistic appropriation and expression.

### 5.2.2 *Historical Primer: Legality of Game Mods*

Scholars have expressed various opinions on the legality of game Mods. Research on game Mods has tended to focus on the rights holder, considering only damage to the initial copyright owner (Gordon, 1992). Wallace (2014) stated that game Mods are derivative works, most of which do not fall within the doctrine of fair use, although the consent of game developers has allowed Mods to thrive despite this lack of legal protection. Disregarding economic rights, a strict moral rights system potentially forbids the creation of game Mods,[4] as modification of the original work risks creating "a false impression about the original author's intended meaning or message" (Lipton, 2011). In addition to potentially infringing copyright, Mods may violate the anti-circumvention provisions of the Digital Millennium Copyright Act (DMCA) by circumventing technological measures in source codes that protect games from being copied (Donnelly, 2004). Moreover, game Mods are "interpreted as presumptively illegal" (Kretzschmar & Stanfill, 2018) when they violate the end user license agreement (EULA) or the terms of service (TOS), as is prohibited by the Computer Fraud and Abuse Act.[5]

[3] See 'Mod (video gaming)', from Wikipedia <https://en.wikipedia.org/wiki/Mod_(video_gaming)> , last visited December 30, 2024.

[4] There are two moral rights for a copyright work: the right of attribution and the right of integrity. The right of attribution is the author's right to be recognized as the author of the work and the right of integrity is the author's power to prevent any tampering with the work as a whole. See Article 6 bis (1) of the Berne Convention.

[5] In Sandvig v. Sessions [315 F. Supp. 3d 1], the U.S. District Court of Columbia held that some violations of terms of service may be protected under the First Amendment; while the case focused

Some scholars have taken a more moderate approach, arguing for the legitimization of modding. Game Mods can be divided into two types: those involving minor alterations and those involving extensive alterations, or "total conversion" Mods (Rosen, 2005). According to Rosen (2005), among others, copyright protection depends on this classification, and a Mod rising to the level of total conversion—relying on the underlying engine of a game but producing a seemingly new game—is potentially not a derivative work of an original game but rather an independent work meriting its own copyright protection. Following this argument, total conversion Mods, "even those created for a commercial purpose, should qualify as non-derivative works, or alternatively, as fair use" (Spare the Mod, 2012). This is supported by the "convergence culture" view, which sees modding as a way for people to participate in culture (Nardi & Kallinikos, 2007). This view categorizes Mods as "transformative use," an exception to copyright protection carved out to serve free speech and the public good. Transformative uses of VGs differ from derivative works in that they build on the original games rather than simply copying them. Because "modders, as 'underground' creators using new media of art, are often the first to push the expressive goals of copyright ahead" (Baldrica, 2007), some scholars have suggested that digital rights management (DRM) should be made less restrictive to give gamers' more space for creative activity and self-expression, which in turn would contribute to the prosperity of the games industry (Landau et al., 2006). This is consistent with John Baldrica's and others' call for a compulsory licensing mechanism to grant these creators certain rights to unique expressions they created. However, compulsory licensing is limited to specific categories of use by specific institutions, and such licensing cannot be passed on to future users of the content (Li & Huang, 2019). All of these arguments in favor of granting rights to modders are based on the belief that increasing modders' rights "could shift the innovation paradigm of the enormous gaming industry, stimulate user creativity and broaden the digital canon" (Spare the Mod, 2012).

The above literature review shows that the relationship between game developers and modders can be either antagonistic or cooperative. From a purely legal perspective, game Mods qualify as derivative works in that they are "based upon one or more preexisting works"—the underlying original game engine— that "exists in any form in which a work may be recast, transformed, or adapted" (17 U.S.C. s101). The standards for copyrightability in derivative works are the same for that in non-derivative works: a derivative work must have "enough expressive variation from public domain or other existing works to enable the new work to be readily distinguished from its predecessors" (Schrock v. Learning Curve Int'l, 2009). Therefore, to be eligible for a derivative work, a game Mod must meet two conditions: first, it must contain the original expression of the pre-existing game; and second, its adapter must have imbued it with additional original expression. All Mods meet the first condition by virtue of being based on the original games. Furthermore, Mods are created to enhance the entertainment value of pre-existing games to satisfy the needs or desires

---

on scraping websites for academic research, the weakening of the Computer Fraud and Abuse Act would potentially also benefit modders.

of players, which entails intellectual input and creativity. If this additional creative effort reaches a certain level of originality, a Mod qualifies as a derivative work of a pre-existing game. In such a case, game modders own copyrights to their derivative work Mods as long as exercising such rights does not infringe upon the copyrights of the pre-existing game developers.[6] To avoid such infringement, a modder must obtain the consent of and authorization from the original game developer and remunerate the original game developer before commercializing the modded work (PRC Copyright Law art.13). Nevertheless, Mods falling further along the spectrum of player contribution—such as total conversion Mods—may have new graphics, new gameplay mechanics and new storylines, making them new, independent games. Such Mods may be transformative enough to escape liability for copyright infringement. It is therefore vital to clearly define the boundary between transformative Mods and those constituting infringement. However, copyright law fails to offer sufficient guidance regarding the complex issues surrounding game Mods created by technical innovation.

### 5.2.3 EULA/TOS: A Common but Unsatisfactory Regulatory Mechanism for Mods

Facing the dual dilemma from theory and reality, game developers generally rely on contracts for balancing their interests, which are commonly known as EULA or TOS (both hereinafter referred to as "TOS"). TOS provide a basis for the governance of online games and virtual worlds and work in tandem with copyright law to regulate online interactive spaces (Baker, 2012). TOS are adhesion, or boilerplate, nonnegotiable licensing contracts that can be issued to multiple parties simultaneously; a gamer must assent to a game's TOS by clicking "agree" to log in and use the software.[7] TOS are regarded today as an instrument for the secondary distribution of rights in the virtual world, and game developers use them to control how their copyright products and outputs are accessed, used and regulated. Some scholars such as Volanis (2007), favored TOS as a form of copyright distribution that helps promote innovation in the virtual world. Other scholars also argued that TOS allows game developers to protect their interests while giving modders express instructions for legal modding, which can meet the needs of both individual creators and the industry (Wallace, 2014). Indeed, TOS possess several advantages that make them popular in the gaming world. They are an effective means of informing gamers of the legalities involved in gameplay, particularly their rights and obligations (Gomulkiewicz &

[6] See Article 12 of the PRC Copyright Law, "Where a work is created by adaptation, translation, annotation or arrangement or a preexisting work, the copyright in the work thus created shall be enjoyed by the adapter, translator, annotator or arranger, provided that the exercise of such copyright does not prejudice the copyright in the preexisting work".

[7] See Terms of Use of League of Legends <http://na.leagueoflegends.com/legal/eula> last visited December 30, 2024; See also Terms of Use of Second Life <https://www.lindenlab.com/legal/second-life-terms-and-conditions> last visited December 30, 2024.

Williamson, 1996). As adhesion contracts, they reduce the transaction costs involved in negotiation and improve efficiency. Additionally, they are more effective than copyright law in protecting and even expanding copyright owners' rights, as they may address territory relatively uncharted in copyright law, including control of game derivatives and players' creations within and beyond the virtual world (Lastowka & Hunter, 2004a, 2004b).

Despite these advantages, TOS favor game developers, which has raised concerns regarding fairness (Balkin, 2004). A fundamental tenet of contract law is the freedom to contract (Printing and Numerical Registering Co. v. Sampson, 1875). The courts have viewed users' active assent to TOS as an indication of their voluntary agreement, which precludes investigation into bad faith (Richards, 2009). However, because TOS are usually presented on a "take it or leave it" basis, the user's freedom of contract is less than complete (Baker, 2012). Often, TOS provide that the game developer and game licensors to retain all rights to the IP-associated game works; they may also require a player to waive and sign over to the game developer any IP rights that he may obtain in his creations within the game.[8] Thus, gamers are often given only a license to use in-game items and wealth, not the absolute right to own them. For instance, the *Minecraft*'s Commercial Usage Guidelines state as follows: "by 'Mods', we mean something original that you created that doesn't contain a substantial part of our copyrightable code or content. We have the final say on what constitutes a Mod and what doesn't."[9] This statement places the game developer in the position of a "adjudicator." As parties are free to contract away their right to fair use of a work via contracts without being preempted by copyright law, a modder would probably lose the copyright to his created Mods under the TOS even if his Mod passed the test of originality or qualified for the fair use doctrine (Bowers v. Baystate Techs., 2003). In *Davidson & Associates Inc. v. Internet Gateway*, the court held that the TOS conserving the right to reverse engineering of the original game were enforceable due to contractual freedom, even though reverse engineering qualifies as fair use under US copyright law. Consequently, given the current validity of such clauses in relation to deferral copyright law, fair use defense would likely still fail to avoid publishers' control of modding market, even if otherwise viable on their merits.

Moreover, TOS are "click-wrap" agreements; they require only that a player click on a button to agree to the terms. Thus, there is no way to ensure that a player has either read or understood the content. Studies have shown that very few users ever read the contractual documents they sign (Bakos et al., 2009). Indeed, in a survey I conducted, only 3.14% of the players questioned fully understood the copyright terms of TOS; most of them had entered into the contracts without any knowledge of their contents or its potential implications (see Fig. 5.2). This does not conform to Article 496 of the Civil Code of the People's Republic of China (PRC), which states

[8] See Blizzard EULA <https://www.blizzard.com/en-us/legal/fba4d00f-c7e4-4883-b8b9-1b4500a402ea/blizzard-end-user-license-agreement> last visited December 30, 2024. See also League of Legends' TOS <http://na.leagueoflegends.com/legal/eula> last visited December 30, 2024.

[9] See 'Minecraft Commercial Usage Guidelines' <https://account.mojang.com/terms#commercial> last visited. December 30, 2024.

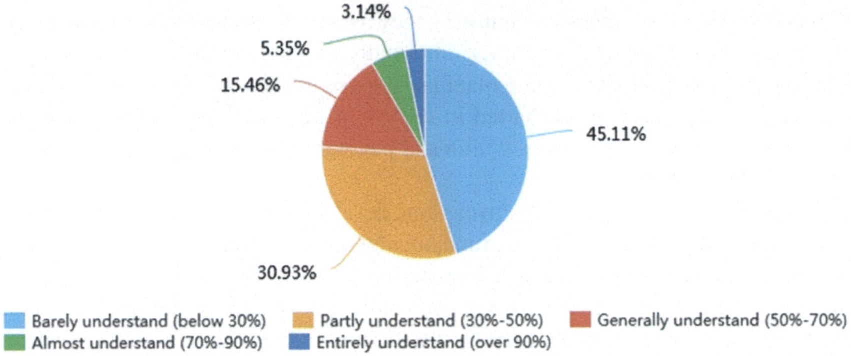


**Fig. 5.2** Players' understanding of copyright terms in TOS

that "the party supplying the contract terms shall inform the other party to note the exclusion or restriction of its liabilities in a reasonable way."[10] Pursuant to Article 497 of the PRC Civil Code, if "the party which supplies the standard terms exempts itself from its liabilities, increases the liabilities of the other party, and deprives the material rights of the other party, the terms shall be invalid." Some players believe that this law can be used as a defense against unreasonable TOS. This is similar to the practice in the US, where "unconscionable" contracts are unenforceable. Unconscionability is found in unfair results (substantive unconscionability) arising from an unfair negotiating procedure (procedural unconscionability) that cannot be implemented or enforced by the disadvantaged party from the perspective of equity (Sun, 2015). As unconscionability is a matter of equity, courts have considerable discretion to determine unconscionability according to the facts of each case.

Courts generally enforce click-wrap contracts irrespective of their inequity, because such contracts are made on the grounds that the parties have been given ample opportunity to read the terms of the agreement. Under contract law, TOS comprise an offer and clicking "agree" conveys acceptance; therefore, the argument that a party was not aware of the TOS is untenable. For example, in *Groff v. American Online Inc.*, the court held that the parties' contract, entered into online by clicking an "I agree" button, was enforceable. The court cited the general rule that a party who signs an instrument thereby manifests his assent to it and cannot later complain that he did not read the instrument or understand its contents (Groff v. American Online Inc., 1998). Articles 201 to 207 of China's Uniform Computer Information Transactions Act explicitly address click-wrap contracts, stating that these contracts satisfy

[10] See Article 496 of the PRC Civil Code (2021), "where standard terms are adopted in concluding a contract, the party supplying the standard terms shall observe the principle of fairness in defining the rights and obligations of the parties, and shall remind the other party in a reasonable way of the provisions that greatly affect the other party, such as those exclude or mitigate the other party's liabilities, and shall explain the standard terms at the request of the other party. If the party providing the standard terms fails to perform the obligation of presentation or explanation, causing the other party to fail to notice or understand the terms in which it has a material interest, the other party may claim that the terms do not form the contents of the contract".

the requirement that the offeree be given the opportunity to reject or to terminate the agreement. However, the legitimacy of click-wrap contracts is still questioned in China. Some scholars have expressed the belief that under competitive market conditions, rights holders ought to be allowed to use copyright licensing contracts to effectively enact "law" and that antimonopoly law should only intervene when the software constitutes a monopoly and the contract terms prevent other software from entering the market (Xiong, 2011).

Understandably, a developer's main licensing goals are to maximize its rights and to limit its obligations (Lastowka & Hunter, 2004a, 2004b). However, TOS drafted in support of these goals are not only legally controversial; they also undermine the sustainable development of the games industry. In recent years, some game developers, realizing the potential for disputes, have addressed ownership of PCC in their TOS, with some allowing users to retain ownership of their PCC, such as in the game *Second Life*.[11] Some scholars have also recommended that virtual worlds be viewed as architectural works to ensure that the products of machinima are "protected from copyright infringement by the pictorial representation exemption in the Architectural Works Copyright Protection Act" (Freedman, 2005). This trend reflects a recognition of the growing importance of PCC. However, most developers remain unwilling to relinquish their rights of control in the virtual world, and thus allow players to retain only limited copyright protection for their created content. In most cases, players are required to grant games' publishers and licensors wholesale licenses for game Mods.

Law is not the only factor affecting copyright owners' decision-making behavior; social and economic factors also play essential roles. These factors explain why game developers may tolerate or even encourage minor alterations to their work but prohibit total conversion Mods. As "rational men", game developers logically weigh the costs and benefits of the legal consequences of their behaviour to make decisions advantageous to profit generation (Posner, 2003). If exercising a legally established right is potentially harmful, they are more likely to waive that right. Likewise, if expanding their rights beyond what is established by copyright statutes has potential commercial value, as with Mods, they are likely to take advantage of this through their TOS. Thus, there is a very clear gap between the letter of the law and its practical application in the modding context (Rajan, 2011). This inconsistency suggests that the law is ripe for reform. Following the tenet that the "law is a social and cultural creation" (Mezey, 2001), in the following sections I explore how economic and social factors affect game developers' attitudes toward game Mods. This informs my proposed scheme for balancing the interests of stakeholders.

[11] See *Second Life* Terms of Service <https://www.lindenlab.com/tos> last visited December 30, 2024.

## 5.3 Beyond Good and Evil: Reexamining (Im)Permissible Game Mods

### *5.3.1 The Games Industry and Players/Modders: A Symbiotic Relationship*

Game Mods can be traced back to the early 1980s game *Castle Smurfenstein*, a total conversion of the game *Castle Wolfenstien*, a classic arcade-style shooter game designed for Apple II.[12] However, it was not until nearly a decade later that modding gained real momentum. In the early 1990s, *Doom* (developed by id Software) became one of the most prominent first-person shooter games of the decade. Although *Doom* was a successful game in its own right, its lifespan was greatly extended by a community of gamers generating new content and tools for the game. Eventually, the original game developers caught on to the potential benefits of modding and released their own modding tools. The line between game consumers and developers began to blur, especially as popular offerings were integrated as standard components of subsequent game releases. Apparently, at the very beginning, the relationship between game developers and modders was amicable. When the developers asked the modders to create content only for commercially released versions of games, not for freeware versions, most of the modders acquiesced, creating Mods that would only work with registered copies of the game. This self-policing became the foundation of modding culture, which contributed to software companies' commercial success and in support of which these companies provided modding tools. Gamers were happy to follow developers' rules in exchange for the freedom to "mix things up," which remains true today.[13] It quickly became apparent that modding was not only inevitable but would eventually also influence the very nature of gameplay. Much of today's multiplayer mayhem is the result of PCC. Some Mods have become far more popular than their "host" games. The growing significance of game Mods to the games industry has triggered ongoing disputes between modders and original game developers over ownership rights to Mods.

In response to these disputes, some game companies have encouraged modders by providing modding tools; others have granted permission only for noncommercial Mods or granted tacit permission by turning a blind eye to modding; and others have imposed strict legal and technological constraints on modding. However, these measures have thus far failed to establish effective regulations for modding, and some have made the situation even more complex. Given that the existing law and TOS cannot serve as "effective cure" for regulating game Mods, it is necessary to analyze Mods at the intersection of the games industry and users from a broader—economic and social—perspective. As Kow and Nardi (2010) noted, "it is imperative that we

---

[12] 'A (really) Brief History of Game Modding' <https://www.nag.co.za/2009/03/19/a-really-brief-history-of-game-modding/> last visited December 30, 2024.

[13] See 'History of Modding' <https://mediaindustries1.wordpress.com/modmoddermodding/history-of-modding/> last visited December 30, 2024.

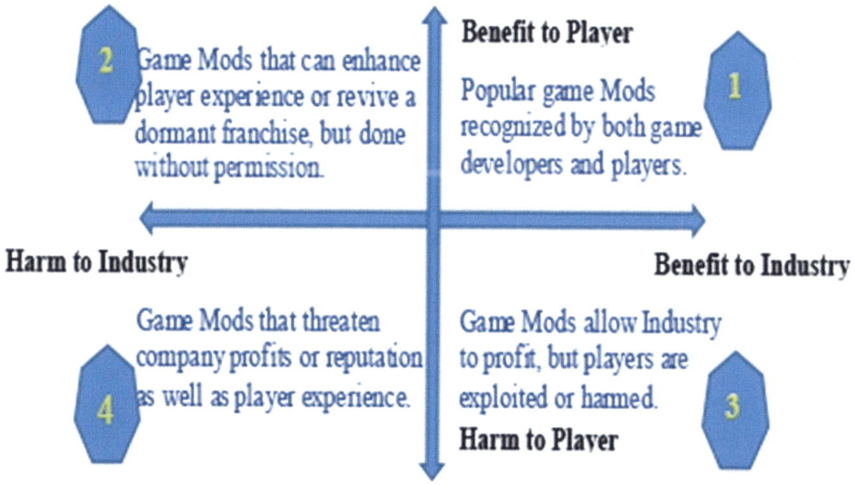


**Fig. 5.3** Quadrants of framework for game mod benefit–harm analysis

continue to examine intersecting ethical sets and to encourage actors with shared interests to probe beneath the surface of the products to the systems of production and their ethical sets". Thus, I propose a framework for analysis of the industry–player relationship that considers the potential benefits and harms of modding.[14] Figure 5.3 illustrates the proposed framework for benefit–harm analysis of game Mods. This analysis is detailed in the following sections to enhance understanding of when and how game developers should take legal actions and when they should waive their rights.

### 5.3.2 *Quadrant One: Mods as Mutually Beneficial to Industry and Players*

The incorporation of modding elements into professional, commercial products has long been a part of computer gaming culture.[15] Many game developers support modding culture, often authorizing software development kits used for modding, because Mods created by these amateurs can boost games' value (Kücklich, 2005). In particular, Mods can contribute to product branding without requiring additional investment from game developers. They can also prolong a game's shelf life and

[14] This benefits/harm analysis approach has been proposed by Mark Kretzschmar & Mel Stanfill. Different from their statements focusing on specific examples of Mods, my research mainly focuses on the motivations of game developers and gamers for supporting/engaging in modding, and their responses to different types of harmful Mods.

[15] For example, in *Skyrim* the *Dragonborn* expansion pack allowed users to fly on dragons, which was originally a mod that users had created for free.

increase its profitability through a "long-tail" sales effect, which occurs when players continue to purchase and play games for which a Mod community continues to generate new content (Moody, 2014). From a political economy perspective, game modders are "immaterial laborers," the strongest representation of free labor in gaming environment (Banks, 2007). Postigo (2003) calculated that supporting a 10-person development team costs approximately US$520,000 per year, and added that such a team takes 6–18 months to complete a large-scale Mod. Estimations I gleaned from experienced modders suggest that many small add-ons take about 20–40 h to complete, usually in the course of one month (Postigo, 2007a, 2007b). Thus, the labor contributed by game modders is valuable. Developers also benefit when modders serve as producers and testers of future games. For example, Mods provide opportunities for "risk-free" experimentation, allowing players to inject creativity into formulaic game genres, striking a balance between innovation and proven commercial success (Kücklich, 2005). In this manner, game companies avoid the initial costs of development as well as certain risks associated with the release of a new game. As modders often take more creative risks than game companies do, such as by incorporating a wider selection of genres and themes, players also benefit from this symbiotic relationship. Furthermore, modders may open up micro-markets to game companies by adding elements of interest to specific subsets of consumers (Postigo, 2007a, 2007b).

Yet, benefits are not unilateral, and modders also benefit from their own creative endeavors. This explains why they are willing to devote their time and energy to modding despite the lack of pay and strict company policies prohibiting them from using Mods for their own commercial gain. Postigo (2007a, 2007b) conducted interviews with modders to discover their motivations for modding. The responses revealed three central themes. First, the participating modders sought to contribute to their communities in a practical way by patching (updating, fixing or improving) games, not merely taking modding as "art for art's sake." Second, modding helped the modders to identify with the games and thus increased their enjoyment of gameplay. Finally, the modders benefited from the experience they gained and the skills they developed in the process of modding, which made them more attractive to potential employers in the lucrative digital games industry. Moody (2014) found that the participatory culture of modding placed modders in a unique position as both creators and users in the games industry. They willingly engaged in modding as a learning experience, as a social activity with fellow fans, and as a hobby. Similar to Postigo, Moody (2014) found that some gamers used skills sets they had acquired and products they had created during gaming to enter the games industry professionally. Renyi Hong's study further brings insight into the modders' motivation behind the voluntary free participation: creative self-expression (Hong, 2013), which is linked with the themes of pleasure and play. Good modding is both pleasurable and a means of self-improvement and is thus perceived as a superior leisure activity. Modders perceive their creative self-expression not only as an end in itself but also a means to attain utility in leisure and achieve a more satisfying and productive life (Heelas, 2002). Reputation—the desire to achieve a certain level of rank—is also a factor in such production (Moody, 2014). Driven by these motivations, most modders are

**Table 5.1** Motivations for supporting/engaging in modding and examples of mutually beneficial Mods

| Mutually beneficial mods: motivations and examples | | |
|---|---|---|
| Motivations to support mods (game developers) | Examples of mutually beneficial mods | Motivations to devote free labor (modders) |
| • Prolong the shelf life of a game | Aliens TC;<br>team fortress;<br>Chaos DM;<br>Counter-strike;<br>defense of the ancients;<br>red orchestra;<br>Garry's Mod;<br>Dear Esther;<br>CUBE experimental;<br>black mesa | • Contribute to communities as self-fulfillment |
| • Improve profitability through a "long-tail" sales effect | | • As a way for creative self-expression and enjoyment |
| • Reduce time and cost of development | | • Improve skills and accumulate experience for self-improvement and career development |
| • Provide opportunities for "risk-free" experimentation | | • Achieve a certain rank/gain a good reputation |
| • Increase game sales by attracting micro-markets and generating more fans | | |

willing to contribute high-quality labor without financial or other material compensation. Table 5.4 summarizes the main motivations of game developers for supporting modding and modders for undertaking game modification and lists some examples of mutually beneficial Mods (Table 5.1).

### 5.3.3 *Quadrant Two: Mods Only Benefiting Players*

Although modding represents a valuable source of low-risk innovation and experimentation within the games industry, Mods are not always profitable from the industry's perspective. Game modders sometimes create Mods for personal reasons, which may fail to benefit game companies or even harm them. Examples of such harm include IP rights violations (Postigo, 2008), industry backlash when modders uncover disguised game code (Bangeman, 2005) and the nullification of the possibility of for-profit expansions of game content by free, high-quality Mods (Meer, 2013). Mods falling into Quadrant Two of Fig. 5.3 generally reflect the tension between game developers' efforts to gain profit via control of their products and modders' culture of free creation and distribution (Jenkins, 2006; Postigo, 2010). In order to gain more forms of informational and economic power through this immaterial labor, game companies often seek to control modders via technological measures, TOS or other legal threats that modders are unable to defend.

TOS are the instrument most commonly used by game companies to prohibit modders from selling their Mods (Joseph, 2018). Game companies are particularly concerned about other companies' using their copyrighted materials in Mods (Coleman & Dyer-Witheford, 2007). The first known IP prosecution of modders occurred when Twentieth Century Fox shut down a *Quake Aliens vs. Predator* Mod. Fox became notorious as the first company to contact Mod teams to demand that they cease their production of Mods, take down their websites, surrender their files, destroy copies of their works and reveal the names and addresses of their members (Dyer-Witheford & de Peuter, 2009). However, other corporations soon followed suit. For instance, Midway brought a suit against Artic for producing a circuit board to speed up the play of Midway's games. The court justified extending protection for derivative works to the sped-up versions, focusing on the user experience and noting that a faster game is "more challenging and exciting" to play (Midway Mfg. Co v. Artic Int'l, 1983). Also, the *Micro Star* case involved a company, Formgen, that encouraged players to create new "add-on levels" or "map files" for *Duke Nukem 3D* (D/N-3D). Micro Star collected and packaged these user-generated levels and sold them commercially as *Nuke It*(N/I). The court identified the works created by the players as derivative works, ruling:

> [e]ven though N/I files only refer to the source art library, and do not contain any part of audiovisual displays, nevertheless they do infringe the underlined story in D/N-3D, as the stories told in the N/I files are surely sequels, telling new tales of Duke's fabulous adventures, which is a derivative work of the original game.... Besides, N/I cannot meet the four criteria of fair use, because N/I harmed the markets for the sequels of D/N-3D, and plaintiff generated financial gain through defendant's protected work, [and made] heavy use of defendant's work from both the quantity and importance perspective.... [T]he implicit license defendant passed on to its customers mandates that all user-created content must be free..... (Micro Star v. Formgen, 1998)

Apart from fearing that their copyrighted materials would be used by other companies for commercial gains, copyright infringement of a third party's IP right is another concern of game enterprises in the context of modding. For example, in *Marvel v. NCSoft*, Marvel, a publisher of superhero comic books and graphic novels, successfully sued NCSoft for copyright infringement. Marvel argued, "by creating a game in which the users could create heroes which resembled (and potentially infringed on) copyrighted/trademarked Marvel characters, NCSoft was liable for both direct and contributory infringement and should be enjoined from offering such user-customization options in their game [and held] liable for damages [associated with the loss of] Marvel's potential market for games…." (Marvel Enters. v. NCSoft Corp, 2005). Although this case concerned PCC other than game Mods, the principle is applicable to modding. Some game companies would also turn to TOS for regulating users' or third parties' behavior. For example, Article 4 §(2) of *Minecraft*'s TOS stipulates:

> 3) The user shall guarantee that any material/content produced or adapted should not infringe the legitimate rights and interests of any third party, or violate the agreement between the user and any other third party; 4) In respect of any unauthorized use of user materials and user adapted materials by any third party, the user grants and agrees NetEase to take any actions deemed appropriate by NetEase to stop it, and the relevant costs and benefits shall

**Table 5.2** Mods only benefiting players: threats to developers and their responses

| Mods only benefiting players | |
|---|---|
| Potential threats to game developers | Game developers' responses |
| • Free, high-quality Mods eliminate the demand for for-profit expansions of game content | • Prohibit game Mods or add-ons |
| • Mods sold by other companies for commercial gains | • Allow non-commercial add-ons and Mods but forbid commercial Mods |
| • Mods infringe a third-party's IP right | • Enforce TOS to regulate modders' behavior |
| • Mods damage the moral rights of the game manufacturer | • Use technical measures to protect the integrity of games and TOS to forbid reverse engineering |

be borne/enjoyed by NetEase. If NetEase deems it necessary, the user shall assist NetEase in providing relevant supporting materials.[16]

Some game manufacturers, including Ubisoft, resist any modifications to their games, trusting in the quality of their games to attract gamers without offering Mods or tools for modifying the games. The emergence of Mods of these games implies that the games have been "cracked," or pirated. These companies prefer to disappoint fans by failing to provide modding tools than to see their games pirated.[17] Mods also raise concerns regarding the maintenance of games' integrity. Arguably, modding would be forbidden in a strict moral rights system, as a Mod does not maintain the original work as a whole.[18] Game developers wishing to protect the integrity of their games may decide not to provide modding tools, but rather, to use technical measures to prevent modding or to use TOS to prohibit reverse engineering. These methods can be legally enforced; in *Blizzard v. Jung*, for example, the defendant was found to have violated both the TOS and the DMCA's anti-circumvention and anti-trafficking regulations by circumventing certain technological restrictions in the plaintiff's game. However, enforcement varies, and game companies' anti-modding strategies stifle creativity. Lawsuits have raised far-reaching questions about the scope of corporate control over networked software (Table 5.2).

[16] See *Minecraft's* End User License Agreement <https://mc.163.com/news/update/2017/10/20/25511_719812.html> last visited December 30, 2024.

[17] See 'Extension of Games from the Idea of Players: The Past and Present Life of Self-made Mod[按照玩家的想法扩充游戏 游戏自制MOD的前世今生]' (March 27, 2019) <https://baijiahao.baidu.com/s?id=1629146512429017772&wfr=spider&for=pc> last visited December 30, 2024.

[18] The right of integrity is the author's power to prevent any tampering with the work as a whole. See Article 6 bis (1) of the Berne Convention.

### 5.3.4 *Quadrant Three: Mods Benefiting Only the Industry*

As discussed above, Mods sometimes pose threats to game developers. However, more commonly, game developers benefit from these fan-created works at the expense of modders, and game developers may use TOS to regulate modders' behavior to avoid infringing a third party's IP rights. Nevertheless, in some cases, game developers may be blamed for the failure to police their fans' Mods. A case in point is the relationship between Bethesda's own modification community, bethesda.net, and the third-party modification site Nexus Mods. According to Nexus's policy, "the posting of any copyrighted material, unless the copyright is owned by you or you have consent from the owner of the copyrighted material, is strictly prohibited on any Nexus site."[19] Also, bethesda.net' s TOS state that users "may not contribute, provide, post, upload or otherwise submit any UGC that is copyrighted, protected by trade secret law or otherwise subject to third party IP rights," and that Bethesda's parent company, ZeniMax, "will terminate the Account of any user who is responsible for any or repeated acts of IP infringement."[20] Although these two sites agree that using extant IP is forbidden, Mods are often poorly protected. In 2016, Bethesda was publicly condemned for not doing enough to police Mods that had been stolen from Nexus and reposted on its official website, and was accused of operating like the illegal media index The Pirate Bay (DarkOne, 2016). This case indicates that modders do receive status and recognition for popular Mods even though they rarely commercialize their Mods, and their status is denied when someone else takes credit for their work.

A clear benefit of modding to game developers comes in the form of the aforementioned economic value of modders' volunteer contributions (Postigo, 2007a, 2007b). Modders must possess both technical and general knowledge and skills to make Mods, irrespective of the Mods' complexity. They must be familiar with the scripting languages, graphics programs and software development kits associated with games. If a game or Mod has a historical setting, modders must also have knowledge of the events, technology and architecture of the period in question. These skills and knowledge add to the richness of the modded content and thus to the continued success of the game in the market. However, the political economy of modding involves a form of neo-capitalist exploitation in which game companies do not pay laborers for creating new game content or fixing problems resulting from shoddy production (Downey, 2001; Hong & Chen, 2014; Zhang & Fung, 2014). As Terranova noted, digital labor involves work that is "simultaneously voluntarily given and unwaged, enjoyed and exploited" (Terranova, 2000). This contradiction has led to a series of debates. Some scholars have argued that modders are complicit in the exchange of free work for affective participation (Banks & Humphreys, 2008; Caraway, 2011). Incidents in which modders have accused game companies of exploitative treatment

---

[19] See 'The Nexus Forums: Terms of Service', available at: <https://forums.nexusmods.com/index.php?app=forums&module=extras&section=boardrules≥ last visited December 30, 2024.

[20] Bethesda's Terms of Service <https://bethesda.net/en/document/terms-of-service> last visited December 30, 2024.

suggest that they do at least have some awareness of the unequal terms of their relationship and can strike back when they sense that corporations are overstepping (Green & Jenkins, 2009; Ritzer & Jurgenson, 2010). For instance, many modders have complained about commercial copyrights not extending to modders and their works. One modder referred to those who pirate Mods as "rotten apples," and claimed that the presence of these people on the game distribution service Steam, combined with Steam's slow moderation of illegal content, discouraged modders from using the service. These "rotten apples" uploaded stolen content under their own names or uploaded Mods containing illegal content, and Steam allowed this content to remain on the site for weeks (Moody, 2014). One modder found that his Mods had been pirated by another player and removed from the site without his consent. Many modders, dissatisfied with the oversight of both Steam and the associated game developers, have chosen to remove their Mods from Steam rather than relinquish control over their works. In another case, some experienced modders received "annoying" requests for Mods from users unwilling to create their own. This behavior violated modding principles by both limiting the diversity of creations and attempting to turn experienced modders into volunteer developers for other community members (Moody, 2014).

Given the value contributed by modders and the considerable amount of time paid by them, some large game corporations, such as Value and Bethesda, have tried to implement a payment system for Mods as a way to give some rewards to modders; however, these efforts have failed. In April 2015, *The Elder Scrolls V: Skyrim* became the first game to sell Mods on Steam (Kamen, 2015). This move resulted in a swift backlash from the modding community, as many felt that Mods should be universally free, while others objected to the small proportion of the cost—25%—that went to the creators of the Mods (Chalk, 2015). Value ultimately removed the controversial paid Mods functionality and agreed to refund customers who had paid for Mods (Prescott, 2015). Another example involved Skyrim Script Extender (SKSE), a popular free Mod framework/loader on the Steam. In February 2019, the developers of SKSE discovered its code in another commercial project, Skyrim Together (ST), which had been banned from using the SKSE code. The ST team was thus sued for violation of the license both for using code without giving credit and for charging for access to a "closed beta" (Coldewey, 2019). These cases show that paid Mods are not always welcomed by modders despite that they act as a model to reward modders, for several reasons: they run counter to the traditional model of free Mods as a way to maximize pleasure; they may encourage the publication of content without creators' consent; they may be overpriced; modders are not paid in proportion to their contribution; and third-party copyrighted content may be infringed.[21] Although some game manufacturers nonetheless continue to sell Mods, the issue of modders' rights to their own Mods remains unresolved.

Another area of potential harm to users concerns sexualized Mods. For example, the most popular Mod in *The Sims 4* is a body modification tool for creating nude or

---

[21] See 'Mod (Video Game): Controversy Surrounding Paid Mods' from Wikipedia <https://en.wikipedia.org/wiki/Mod_(video_games)> last visited December 30, 2024.

**Table 5.3** Players'/modders' responses to harm posed by Mods benefiting only the industry

| Mods only benefiting the industry and exploiting or harming players | |
|---|---|
| Potential harm to players/modders | Responses of players/modders |
| • Mods poorly policed and modders uncredited by game developers | • Condemn game developers for operating like an illegal media index |
| • Mods pirated or removed by other players without permission | • Remove Mods from platforms |
| • Paid Mods overpriced and modders underpaid | • Complain as a community |
| • Sexualized Mods encouraging voyeurism with potential social consequences | • Welcomed by some gamers |

sexually explicit female characters. In this and similar games, players can use Mods to simulate and observe "adult" content in the gameplay, thereby indulging scopophilia, or the sexual pleasure derived from looking.[22] This type of Mods exacerbates the problems of VGs' portraying women mainly as sexual objects, particularly as gamers are invited to manipulate the individual physical attributes of the characters. Although such Mods are potentially socially harmful, game developers vary in their attitudes toward them, some enforcing strict rules against them[23] and others tolerating them.[24] However, game developers predominantly turn a blind eye to nude or sexualized Mods as long as their TOS are not violated, as the popularity of such Mods increases sales (except in cases of pirated games). The analysis of this quadrant of the model shown in Fig. 5.3 suggests that when game corporations benefit from Mods, they may be indifferent to the harm such Mods do to others and therefore refuse to use available legal remedies to prevent such modding (Table 5.3).

### 5.3.5 *Quadrant Four: Mods Without Benefit*

In contrast with the Mods discussed above, some Mods benefit neither game developers nor other players. Cheating Mods are a common example. A case in point was in 2014, Blizzard sued a *StarCraft II* modder for selling the "Valiant Chaos Map

[22] See 'What a Shame! Nude Mod in Sims4 Pays More Attention to Details <https://m.3dmgame.com/news/201410/3386915.html> last visited December 30, 2024.

[23] For example, the Bethesda.net Modding Guidelines for Skyrim Special Edition and Fallout 4 (October 27, 2016) stipulates that "Do not upload mods featuring nude or sexually explicit material." <https://bethesda.net/en/devnote/xxPlwl42Z2cseekMQwOUy/bethesda-net-modding-guidelines-for-skyrim-special-edition-and-fallout-4> last visited December 30, 2024.

[24] For example, Nexus's Terms of Service stipulate that "If your mod is not tagged as Adult then you may not use adult imagery or content either in your mod Description or in the Images section of your mod page, and you may not accept such images uploaded by users. If you intend to accept such images or use such content on your mod description page then you must retag your mod as Adult." <https://forums.nexusmods.com/index.php?app=forums&module=extras&section=boardrules> last visited December 30, 2024.

**Table 5.4** Mods without benefit and their potential harm

| Mods without benefit:<br>Mods that threaten industry profits or reputation as well as player experience | | |
|---|---|---|
| Examples | Potential harm to players | Potential harm to game developers |
| Cheating Mods | Giving some players an "unfair competitive advantage," thereby damaging the experience of legitimate players and discouraging them from playing | Damaging game companies' reputation and damage its business |
| Poor-quality Mods | Impairing gamers' playing experience and potentially deterring them from playing the game | Damaging game developers' reputation and potentially creating marketplace confusion |
| Malicious Mods enabling harassment, stalking or threatening of other players | Destroying players' enjoyment of the game and causing them distress | Harming game developers' goodwill and brand image |

Pack," a Mod that gave players an "unfair competitive advantage" in the game.[25] Blizzard argued that the defendants had "irreparably harmed the ability of …legitimate customers…to enjoy and participate in the competitive online experience of *StarCraft II*. That, in turn, caused users to grow dissatisfied with the game, lose interest in the game, and communicate that dissatisfaction."[26] Because the competitive aspect of this multiplayer game was a driving forces for its sales, Blizzard had an interest in preserving the core experience of the game, including its difficulty. A more recent case was brought by Blizzard against a Germany-based company, Bossland, for its development and sale of Mods offering hacks, bots and other tools to circumvent the intended gameplay of Blizzard's game *Overwatch* (Good, 2017). Blizzard argued that the creation and use of these Mods had not only violated its TOS and IP rights but also harmed its reputation and damaged its business by introducing unfair competition to the games, which had impaired the experience of legitimate players and discouraged them from playing. Bossland lost the suit and was prohibited from selling any of its cheat-enabling products applicable to Blizzard games within the US.[27]

Almost all game developers would provide terms and conditions that explicitly prohibit the use of hacks, Mods or any other unauthorized third-party software that gives players an unfair advantage, due to the harm caused to both game companies and their users. For example, Blizzard's TOS state, "[y]ou agree that you will not, in

[25] See 'Blizzard Suing StarCraft II Hackers' <https://www.gamesindustry.biz/articles/2014-05-22-blizzard-suing-starcraft-ii-hackers> last visited December 30, 2024.

[26] Ibid.

[27] Ibid.

whole or in part or under any circumstances ...[cheat]."[28] To cheat is defined in the TOS as to "create, use, offer, promote, advertise, make available and/or distribute the following or assist therein:

> Cheats; i.e. methods not expressly authorized by Blizzard, influencing and/or facilitating the gameplay, including exploits of any in-game bugs, and thereby granting you and/or any other user an advantage over other players not using such methods;
> bots; i.e. any code and/or software, not expressly authorized by Blizzard, that allows the automated control of a Game, or any other feature of the Platform, e.g. the automated control of a character in a Game;
> hacks; i.e. accessing or modifying the software of the Platform in any manner not expressly authorized by Blizzard; and/or
> any code and/or software, not expressly authorized by Blizzard, that can be used in connection with the Platform and/or any component or feature thereof which changes and/or facilitates the gameplay or other functionality."[29]

The consequences of cheating can be severe. In the case of the popular game *Blizzard*, players caught cheating may be "suspended or revoked from using the Platform, or parts, components and/or single features."[30]

In addition to using modding tools provided by game developers, reverse engineering is a common method of Mod production. Game developers' methods of defense against reverse engineering of their game code include using technological protection measures (TPMs), forbidding the circumvention of game code in TOS and enforcing copyrights in court. In *Blizzard Entertainment v. Jung*, the district court found that Blizzard's TOS prohibiting reverse engineering were enforceable contracts and that the defendants had violated these contracts in addition to the DMCA's anti-circumvention and anti-trafficking provisions.

Most modders have the desire and motivations to produce high quality Mods; however, games are also modified by players with poor technical skills. The results of their efforts may negatively affect gameplay, and if players mistakenly attribute this effect to the original game, this can damage the game developer's reputation. In competition between gaming companies, one company may use game Mods to purposely harm another company's reputation or to create marketplace confusion. Such Mods pose a threat to the games industry and may negatively impact gamers' playing experience to the point of deterring them from playing the modded games.

Arguably more harmful than poor-quality or cheating Mods are Mods that enable nefarious acts in gameplay. For instance, certain *Grand Theft Auto (GTA)* Mods allowed players to change their avatars (e.g., rendering them nude) and to manipulate other players' avatars' behavior (e.g., forcing them to strip or do push-ups)

---

[28] See Blizzard End User License Agreement (Last Revised June 1, 2018) <https://www.blizzard.com/en-us/legal/fba4d00f-c7e4-4883-b8b9-1b4500a402ea/blizzard-end-user-license-agreement> last visited December 30, 2024.

[29] Ibid.

[30] Ibid.

(Hernandez, 2014). Some players even reported nonconsensual virtual sex forced upon their avatars by unknown avatars. Such virtual assaults destroyed these players' enjoyment of the game and caused them distress. As these Mods were generally condemned by the game's community, they damaged the game developer's goodwill and brand images. In 2017, Take-Two Interactive, the parent company of Rockstar, which produced the *GTA Online* series, prohibited gamers from modding and shut down the modding tool OpenIV, which had been designed for the *GTA* game series (Livingston, 2017). OpenIV had enabled recent malicious Mods that allowed for the harassment of players, thus damaging all *GTA* players' experience. In this scenario, neither the games industry nor players benefited. Furthermore, Rockstar Game's TOS were violated, as they explicitly stated that a player "will not restrict or inhibit any other user from using or enjoying the Online Services (for example, by means of harassment, hacking, interfering, adversely affecting, or defacement)."[31] Other game developers, such as Riot Games, have imposed similar regulations, such as mandating that players "cannot harass, stalk or threaten other players while using the services," otherwise, their accounts would be banned (Table 5.4).[32]

## 5.4 Proposed Scheme for Regulating Game Mods

The above discussions show that game developers' responses to game Mods are diverse, ranging from outright banning of Mods or add-ons[33] to less stringent restrictions permitting user interface Mods and add-ons[34] and even general tolerance of modding and encouragement of free Mod distribution.[35] Wholesale restrictions on modding stem from extreme caution and suspicion related to both participatory media creation and fan manipulation of copyrighted IP. These restrictions create tension between game developers' desire for control and the traditional emphasis of modding culture on innovation and free distribution. A similar tension exists between gamers in the community as well (Moody, 2014). As Jenkins (2006) explained: "the media industry is increasingly dependent on active and committed consumers to spread the

[31] See 'Rockstar Game's Terms of Service' <https://www.rockstargames.com/legal> last visited December 30, 2024.

[32] See 'Riot Games' Terms of Service' <https://www.riotgames.com/en/terms-of-service> last visited December 30, 2024.

[33] For example, *Aion* is a massively multiplayer online game from South Korean game studio NCSoft, requiring that no user created Mods or user interface add-ons are allowed. Attempting to incorporate such changes would therefore conflict with its EULA and subsequently put such modders at risk of losing their access to networked *Aion* multiplayer game play.

[34] For example, the *World of Warcraft* allows for user interface customization mods and add-ons only, but no other game Mods, no reverse engineering game engine, and no activity intended to bypass WoW's encryption mechanisms.

[35] For games like *Unreal Tournament*, *Half-Life*, *NeverWinterNights*, *Civilization* and many others, the EULAs encourage modding and the free redistribution of Mods without fee to others who must have a licensed game copy, but no reverse engineering or redistribution of the game engine required to run the Mods.

word about valued properties in an overcrowded media marketplace, and in some cases they are seeking ways to channel the creative output of media fans to lower their production costs. At the same time, they are terrified of what happens if this consumer power gets out of control".

Game developers' responses to similar modding cases may vary widely, which is another indication that the current copyright regime is unsuited to modding. Game developers use a voluntary licensing mechanism, TOS, to address the failure of copyright law to adequately protect their works. Such licensing places game developers in the role of adjudicators with sole discretion to decide the fate of Mods, an arrangement that neglects the legitimate interests of modders. Some have stated that TOS should not deny modders' ownership of or dominion over their expressive or creative activities in a virtual environment when the same activities would be protected in the real world, even on private property (Castronova, 2004). Thus, voluntary licensing alone cannot effectively regulate modding. Furthermore, scholars have asserted that copyright law is destined to die in the digital and Internet era, given the unsuitability of copyright exceptions to game Mods and the prohibitive effects of exclusive rights (Lunney, 2001; Desai, 2011). Granted, the copyright regime is indeed outdated and fails to meet the massive challenges posed by new technologies, such as modding. However, I contend that copyright law remains important today because copyrights continue to play an essential role in connecting commercial interests and creativity and incentivizing creators to supply cultural goods in the digital era (Cohen, 2011). Thus, I propose an amendment to the copyright regime to strike a better balance between the interests of game developers, modders and other gamers.

Based on the four quadrants of my framework for benefit–harm analysis of modding, I propose a two-pronged solution to the modding problem. Specifically, the first prong concerns the social benefit of game Mods, aiming to change the copyright regime from being exclusive to becoming non-exclusive. The new regime would confer on gamers the legal right to modify VGs without permission but oblige them to remunerate the original developers for commercial use of those Mods. Under the proposed scheme, both the right to modify and the obligation to pay remuneration would pass to the future users of a given Mod. The second prong pertains to the social harm of game Mods and proposes a community-based approach. Under the new scheme, game operators are imposed a common law duty to monitor infringement and to ensure the fair implementation of game developers' TOS.

### *5.4.1 Prong One: Right of Modding for Modders*

My four-quadrant benefit–harm analysis of game Mods shows that game corporations and gamers/modders have a symbiotic relationship. Mods benefit game companies by extending games' shelf lives and enhancing consumer loyalty, and they benefit gamers/modders by increasing enjoyment of games and status in the gaming/modding community. These benefits are usually not dependent on the legality of any given Mod. Given that game developers are generally willing to provide modding tools, preferring to encourage and control modding through TOS rather than to prevent modification by enforcing their copyrights, and that Mods are cultural products incorporating the creative efforts of modders, which are situated in the grey area between derivative works and original copyrightable works/fair use, I propose to legalize game Mods by granting modders the right to modify games. My proposed scheme would give gamers more freedom to create without the need to navigate the uncertain boundary between transformative use and derivative use. It would also preserve and even increase game developers' benefits. Whereas the traditional exclusive copyright regime stifles the creation of excellent Mods by requiring modders to obtain permission and by offering ambiguous copyright exceptions, my proposed scheme would encourage modding. This would benefit both game developers and players, ultimately increasing the prosperity of the games industry.

The main features of the proposed modding right scheme are summarized as follows:

(i) in creating game Mods, players can modify a VG without asking for permission from the game developer, provided that (a) such use does not affect the normal exploitation of the work and does not unreasonably prejudice the legitimate interests of the game developer, and (b) the game developer has not used TPMs to prevent such modification;
(ii) a game Mod can be used for commercial or non-commercial purposes; in the case of commercial use, reasonable remuneration should be paid to the game developer. Remuneration, which may be made through e-payment, should be apportioned using a pre-determined method set by the game developer, with the modder taking no less than 50%; and
(iii) a game Mod can be used by subsequent modders without permission from either the original modder or the game developer of the underlying game; however, remuneration must be offered to both the original modder and the game developer under the remuneration scheme set forth in Clause (ii) in the case of commercial use, and such use must not undermine the reasonable exploitation of the Mod or the underlying game.

If implemented, the proposed modding right scheme would acknowledge users' right to modify games and offer more freedom and certainty for gamers wishing to create Mods than the current copyright regime provides. Under this new scheme, creating game Mods would be a user's right rather than a mere privilege or exemption. This would establish broader rights than does either the fair use doctrine, which is only available as a defense, or the Creative Commons (CC) license, which begs for copyright owners' mercy in surrendering some of their copyrights (Li, 2020).

My scheme is primarily based on the growing trend of recognizing users' value and granting them rights. As the musical artist Ben Folds pointed out, "amateurs are the people who are the more talented, more dangerous, more interesting, more creative" (Collins, 2013). In the creative industry economy, "origination" may come out of "production," "distribution" and "consumption" (Ghelfi, 2015). For example, free software and game companies are entirely dependent on the instantaneous feedback of users, not only due to their buying power but because they share information on a buyer-to-buyer basis. Allowing users to originate products thus establishes an effective and efficient supply chain. The rise in UGC (including Mods) in the creative industry economy has placed individual users at the forefront of creative materials (Elkin-Koren, 2015). In today's era of convergence, users or consumers have become authors and producers, giving them a key role in the creative process (Lessig, 2006). Game Mods are a product of this trend: modders act simultaneously as readers, writers, consumers and producers. It is therefore only natural and logical to provide modders with greater rights and protections to fulfill the copyright objectives of encouraging learning (Bently & Ginsburg, 2010) and promoting public access to creative works. Besides, this scheme also bears realistic foundation. The fact that many game developers are willing to waive part of their copyrights (generally the rights of derivation and integrity) to encourage game Mod creation signals their acknowledgement of the value that Mods contribute to the games industry, even in the absence of license fees. The substantial benefits of modding to the games industry and to society, as Loren (1997) noted, should be taken into account as a positive externality when determining whether modding should be considered as fair use and whether it deserves special protection. As discussed in previous sections, the main motivation for game developers to deviate from the industry's traditional rules by supporting modding is not simply generosity but the opportunity to obtain "invisible" profit by establishing good relations with fans (Lessig, 2008). Driven by this motivation, most game developers would be willing to accept such a properly designed modding right scheme.

The proposed scheme would allow both the commercial and the non-commercial use of game Mods, thereby promoting the sustainable development of modding culture. Some Mods have the potential to turn a profit: for example, the popular Mod *Counter-Strike* was sold by major retailers while the underlying game by Valve was still available online, after Valve entered into a contract with the Mod's creators (Postigo, 2007a, 2007b). However, very few Mods achieve *Counter-Strike*'s success, and many Mods are targeted at a few audiences. Furthermore, the modding community typically values the idea of "open sharing," and many modders consider their work to be "a labor of love" (Moody, 2014). Given the fact that it is players (also representing the part of modders) who would have to pay for Mods rather than game companies paying modders (Lahti, 2017), my scheme would allow modders to determine whether to commodify their Mods. In terms of non-commercial use, modders would be exempted from paying remuneration to the game developers, which is more tailor with the reality that most game developers encourage non-commercial modding creations without expecting any direct compensation for their distribution. As for commercial use, it bears some resemblance to compulsory licensing in that both follow an ex-post remuneration structure. The proposed remuneration rule would be more tailor-made to the modding context, as it follows the mode of a preset calculation of revenue sharing determined by the game developer, with a minimum contribution to modders of 50%. By providing game developers a right to determine the level of the commercialization of game Mods and at the same time, restricting such right by setting the minimum share of 50% for modders, these provisions would ensure the legitimacy of allocation proportion, prevent game corporations from receiving disproportionate benefits at the expense of players and avoid suppressing gamers' creativity. Thus, this dichotomous remuneration rule helps to facilitate the creation of game Mods and brings a win–win result in which gamers gain the freedom to modify games and developers would continue to receive economic benefits.

The proposed scheme includes two conditions for the modding right, one of which is that such use does not harm the reasonable exploitation of the game developer. This clause would address the potential harm done by Mods without any benefit (e.g., cheating Mods, poor-quality Mods, malicious Mods that can harass, stalk or threaten other players), as discussed in Sect. 5.3.5. To prevent such Mods from damaging the gaming experience and prejudicing the legitimate interests of game companies, game developers would have preemption to prevent their creation or stop their use. Traditional remedies would remain available for activities against which this scheme does not offer adequate protection. For example, for poor-quality Mods that may damage the reputations of game companies or Mods making minor changes that may create marketplace confusion, game developers could seek protection under the stricter requirements of trademark law and unfair competition laws (Baldrica, 2007). The repackaging and sale of game software with minor modifications (software piracy) should be addressed under the reproduction right of the game developer, as such uses are excluded from my proposed modding right scheme. Under my scheme, game developers could also continue to protect their games with TPMs. This leads to the second condition for exercising the modding right, namely that the game developer has not used TPMs to prevent such modification. This clause would enable game developers to opt out of the modding right scheme and retain exclusive control over their works. TPMs could also be used in a more limited fashion—to prevent only the creation of cheating Mods. This reflects gaming companies' common practice of providing modding tools to support modding but installing TPMs to prevent cheating Mods from being created. Where TPMs are used in this limited way, my modding right scheme would remain applicable to other, permitted game Mods.

Finally, the proposed scheme would incorporate the advantages of the CC licensing and compulsory licensing mechanisms into the copyright rules generally applicable to all modders. Unlike CC licensing and other public licensing mechanisms, which require restrictive attribution and are too complex for many to apply for (Li & Huang, 2019), the proposed modding right scheme would simplify, standardize and codify licensing conditions.[36] Furthermore, compared to the current voluntary licensing system, it would prevent game developers from abusing their discretion when choosing licenses and promotes collaboration between game developers and modders.

[36] E.g., Attribution requires the authors and any other parties designated by the licensor to be identified together with the web address of the licensed material and any modifications the licensee has made to the licensed material. This would be difficult to be achieved in the modding context. See 'Creative Commons: About the Licenses' <https://creativecommons.org/licenses/?lang=en> last visited December 30, 2024.

### 5.4.2 Prong Two: Community-Based Approach to Regulating Game Mods

Initially, the VG value chain comprised a number of actors: developers, publishers, distributors, retailers and consumers (Bellini et al., 2018). Recently, however, technological innovations have democratized VG production, both lowering the barrier to working in the industry and eliminating intermediaries such as publishers and retailers. Thus, today's VG value chain is relatively simple, comprising only game developers, game distributors and consumers. Game developers and distributors carry out the crucial tasks of organizing financing for game development, overseeing the entire production process and marketing. Developers and distributors usually cooperate and retain the copyrights to products, and thus make most of the profits (Bellini et al., 2018). In most cases, game developers may also establish their own online distribution platforms and game distributors may design games themselves, further shrinking the valve chain. This is especially true of large game corporations, such as Tencent, NetEase and Blizzard. I use the term "game operators" to refer to game developers or game distributors who provide online game services to the public.

The symbiotic relationship between game corporations and gamers/modders suggests that game operators have played a much greater role in the games industry than traditional Internet service providers (ISPs) do. However, game operators are not currently well suited to the task of regulating Mods, as they often ignore the harm that Mods cause to others when they themselves benefit from the Mods. Besides, their TOS regulating modding can be confusing or ineffectual. Given the negative externalities of some game Mods and the special role of game operators in the modding community, I propose a community-based approach to regulating game Mods. Specifically, I recommend that a common law duty to monitor IP infringement be imposed on game operators and that certain legal standards be established to secure the legitimacy of TOS.

It is important to acknowledge the special role of game operators in the games industry. Unlike traditional online intermediaries, game operators are not neutral platforms but invested in the industry as content adopters, distributers and retailers. They not only control the supply of content but also shape user demand by providing gamers with hardware equipment to download, retail content, editing tools and social networks in which to converse, negotiate and work together. Most likely they would cooperate with game developers to share the revenue generated from gaming, or sometimes they themselves are exactly the game developers who reap all of the profits. The deep engagement of game operators in the gaming environment suggests that they are ideally positioned to serve as moderators of the online gaming community as well as the modding community. Besides, game operators can also perform an educational function, informing gamers of copyright exceptions and proper Mod use, clarifying gamers' rights and obligations under TOS, offering suggestions regarding the mode and amount of remuneration, and perhaps offering private copyright enforcement mechanisms to efficiently settle disputes (Li & Huang, 2019). Game operators are different from traditional ISPs, which are normally exempted from infringement liability under the safe harbor rule. In most jurisdictions, if an online intermediary (i) is an ISP rather than an Internet content provider, (ii) lacks actual knowledge of an infringing activity or awareness of the facts or circumstances from which the infringing activity is apparent and (iii) does not receive a financial benefit directly attributable to the infringing activity that it has the right and ability to control, it can be exempted from liability by expeditiously removing or disabling the allegedly infringing material upon receiving sufficient notice (17 U.S.C.§ 512 (c)(A) and (B)). However, game operators cannot claim such a lack of knowledge, as game modding is considered part of the gameplay and editing tools are usually provided by game operators themselves. Nor can game operators claim not to profit from modding, as they share in the revenue generated by paid Mods. Furthermore, they are the major beneficiaries of free Mods, as such Mods increase the value of the original game platforms for other players. For these reasons, game operators should not enjoy the safe harbor exemption without assuming liability for game Mods' copyright infringement.

This raises the following question: what is the appropriate level of game operators' legal liability in the practice of modding? I argue that game operators should assume a common-law duty of *indirect* infringement on the basis of "cooperative operation/ direct financial benefit + know or should have known the infringing activity" for *presumption of fault* (emphasis added). My argument is based on the characteristics and business model of online games and the functions of game operators. First, VG itself is composing by many elements with complicated rights, and the emergence of PCC such as game Mods undoubtedly increases the complexity of rights. It is therefore objectively unrealistic to expect a platform operator that provides numerous online game services to review the IP issues raised by all game Mods uploaded or created by gamers and remove infringing materials in a timely and accurate manner. Even if this objective obstacle could be resolved by technology, the process would increase the operational costs of the games industry, rendering it difficult to meet the needs of players wishing to share free content and easily access the latest game Mods. Second, the condition of "direct financial benefit from the infringing game Mod" should not be used to identify the subjective fault of the game operator. For game Mods, whether free or paid ones, they all increase the value of the original game platforms. Moreover, other types of PCC also generate profits for game operators. It would be extremely difficult for game operators to identify specific game Mod infringements in a large gaming community. Therefore, it would be unfair to infer the *subjective fault* of game operators based on their direct financial benefit from a given Mod (emphasis added). Nevertheless, the fact that game operators are much more powerful than traditional ISPs cannot be denied. Due to economies of scale, network effects and users' lock-in costs, game operators hold monopolistic or oligopolistic power. Accordingly, I echo an earlier proposal to impose on online intermediaries (game operators) a more stringent duty to monitor (Elkin-Koren, 2012). Under the DMCA's "notice-and-takedown" rule in the US,[37] an ISP is liable for contributory infringement if it has "actual knowledge of infringing activities or awareness of facts

[37] This rule has been modelled by many jurisdictions as the safe harbor rules.

or circumstances from which the infringing activity is apparent" (17 U.S.C. § 512 (c)(A)(i)(ii)). This requirement is too stringent and difficult to satisfy. First, "actual knowledge" excludes mere possible inference from ambiguous circumstances or the availability of all relevant information to the game operator; the game operator must in fact have become aware of that information.[38] The element of "awareness of facts or circumstances" examines whether an infringement would have been apparent to a reasonable person with such knowledge (UMG Recordings Inc. v Veoh Networks Inc, 2011; Viacom Int'l, Inc. v YouTube, 2013). Only when the infringing activity is as blatant as a red flag waving in the game operator's face does his awareness meet this standard (Nimmer, 2013). On the contrary, China's safe harbor rule adopts a more objective standard, which requires that the alleged infringer "know and have justified reason to know" of infringing activity.[39] This standard is consistent with the common law criterion of "know or should have known" (Bohlen, 1908), both of which are much easier to meet than the subjective standard stipulated by copyright law. Given the aforementioned concerns, it is more reasonable to adopt the common law standard for game operators' liability. Specifically, if a game operator knows or should have known of an infringing activity in addition to gaining a direct financial benefit from this activity, it should be liable for copyright infringement. If the law were to impose on game operators such a duty to monitor rather than just passively obey takedown notices, game operators would no longer turn a blind eye to Mods that may infringe third parties' IP rights. This would better balance the rights and obligations of game operators and protect the interests of gamers.

Additionally, the function of TOS should not be neglected. I further propose that TOS should incorporate certain legal standards and principles and that they should be fairly implemented. As mentioned before, game operators provide online game services and facilitate collaborations with users through their own TOS. But the problem is that game operators are more exploitative than traditional distributors. Gamers' relatively weak bargaining power and legal uncertainties place them at a disadvantage with regard to TOS with game operators. To prevent game operators from abusing their powers, certain legal standards and principles should be applied to TOS. First, the copyright preemption principle should apply. In other words, TOS should not conflict with copyright law; any such conflict should invalidate the TOS (17 U.S.C.§301 (a); UCITA §105(a)). Under the scheme I propose, TOS that irrationally limit the modding right of gamers would be invalid. Second, unfairness would be prohibited; in other words, TOS would not be permitted to impose unreasonable duties on one party in terms of procedures or content (UCITA §111(a); PRC Civil Code art. 496&497). This principle would require TOS to be written clearly, especially those parts pertaining to users' rights and obligations, and it would prevent game operators from taking advantage of their position to exempt themselves from their main obligations, such as the common law duty to monitor infringement. Third,

[38] See 'The Supreme Court Defines Actual Knowledge' (February 26, 2020) <https://www.natlawreview.com/article/supreme-court-defines-actual-knowledge> last visited December 30, 2024.

[39] Article 22 (3) of the Regulation on the Protection of the Right to Communicate Works to the Public over Information Networks (2013 *Revision).*

the abuse of rights would be prohibited under the proposed scheme. This would prevent rights holders from illegally expanding their rights in violation of the basic objectives of copyright law (Lasercomb America, Inc. v. Reynolds, 1990). Game operators routinely overlook this principle; under the current regime, TOS normally allow a game's developer and licensors to retain all rights to the IP associated game works (including PCC and Mods) or require a player to waive any IP rights he may obtain in connection with his creations within the game and sign them over to the game's developer and its licensors instead. For instance, a widely adopted TOS clause states, "[b]y uploading the PCC, you hereby grant [the game developer] a perpetual, irrevocable, worldwide, fully paid up, non-exclusive, sub-licensable, right and license to copy, reproduce, fix, modify, adapt, publish, distribute, and publicly perform the Content in connection with the Service and [the game developer's] business."[40] This clause is overly broad and damages gamers' own appropriation mechanism. It may also affect other gamers' access to the PCC (Li & Huang, 2019). Finally, I propose that the public policy principle should apply. According to this principle, if the terms of a contract violate basic public policy, they are invalid (UCITA §105(b)). Applying this principle would make game operators responsible for policing socially problematic PCC such as overtly sexualized Mods. I argue that courts should rely on this principle when weighing the rights and obligations of game operators and gamers. The public policy principle could also be used by administrative bodies to supervise game operators, thus forming an interactive legal-administrative supervision mechanism. Game operators failing to monitor game Mods that violate social morals would be held both legally and administratively accountable.

## 5.5 Conclusion

In the VG context, there is a notable convergence between the users and producers of content. There is also a tension between control over created content and innovative uses of that content, which arises from the gap between copyright law and the emerging practices of online communities. Game Mods are typical products of this convergent culture. This chapter traces the history of the legality of game Mods and the diverse conclusions drawn by courts and game developers in their treatment of modding. Both copyright law and contract law factor into game developers' decision-making; however, both fall short of effectively regulating game Mods. Thus, I also explore the economic and social factors that impact how game corporations address modding, framing these factors in a four-quadrant model according to the relative benefits and harm of Mods to game developers and users/modders. An in-depth exploration of the model reveals inconsistent behavior on the part of game developers. This indicates that the current copyright regime is unsuited to modding and requires reform. Accordingly, I propose a two-pronged solution to the modding

[40] See Blizzard EULA (n 8). See also League of Legends' TOS (n 8). See also Minecraft's EULA (n 16).

problem. The first prong addresses the social benefit of game Mods, giving gamers the right to modify VGs without permission under certain conditions. The second prong pertains to the potential social harm of game Mods, involving a community-based approach under which game operators hold a common law duty to monitor infringement and ensure the fair implementation of TOS. I believe that if the proposed scheme were implemented, the business relationship between modders and game companies would remain mutually beneficial as long as the practices governing the game company–player relationship were to remain equitable.

## References


Baker, K. (2012). MMORPGing—The Legalities of Game Play. *European Journal for Law and Technology, 3*(1), 8.

Baldrica, J. (2007). Mod a Heck: Frameworks for Examining Ownership Rights in User-Contributed Content to Videogames, and a more Principled Evaluation of Expressive Appropriation in User-Modified Videogame Projects. *Minnesota Journal of Law, Science & Technology, 8*(2), 681, 686–687, 689, 691, 692, 711, 713.

Balkin, J. M. (2004). Virtual Liberty: Freedom to Design and Freedom to Play in Virtual Worlds. *Virginia Law Review, 90*(8), 2043.

Bangeman, E. (2005). Rockstar Breaks Silence on "Hot Coffee" GTA: San Andreas Mod. Ars Technica. Available at: https://arstechnica.com/uncategorized/2005/07/5088-2/. Accessed 30 December 2024.

Banks, J. A. L. (2007). Opening the Pipeline: Unruly Creators. In S. D. Castell & J. Jenson (Eds.), *Worlds in Play: International Perspectives on Digital Games Research* (pp. 143–150). Peter Lang.

Banks, J., & Humphreys, S. (2008). The Labour of User Co-Creators: Emergent Social Network Markets? *Convergence, 14*(4), 401–418.

Bakos, Y. N. Y. U., et al. (2009). Does Anyone Read the Fine Print? Testing a Law and Economics Approach to Standard Form Contracts. In *CELS 2009 4th Annual Conference on Empirical Legal Studies*. Available at: http://ssrn.com/abstract=1443256. Accessed 30 December 2024.

Barker, K. (2012). MMORPGing-The Legalities of Game Play. *European Journal for Law and Technology, 3*(1), 1, 3.

Bellini, A., et al. (2018). Industrial Relations and Creative Workers. Overall Report, IR-CREA for European Commission (pp. 35–36).

Bently, L., & Ginsburg, J. C. (2010). The Sole Right Shall Return to the Authors: Anglo-American Authors Reversion Rights from the Statute of Ann to Contemporary U.S. Copyright. *Berkeley Technology Law Journal, 25*, 1475, 1479.

Bohlen, F. H. (1908). Contributory Negligence. In *Harvard Law Review* (Vol. 21, pp. 233, 236).

Bray, H. (2004). Game On; Inspired Animation Tools from an Uninspired Sitcom. Boston Globe. Available at: http://archive.boston.com/news/globe/living/articles/2004/03/17/inspired_animation_tools_from_an_uninspired_sitcom/. Accessed 30 December 2024.

Caraway, B. (2011). Audience Labor in the New Media Environment: A Marxian Revisiting of the Audience Commodity. *Media, Culture & Society, 33*(5), 693–708.

Castronova, E. (2004). The Right to Play. In *New York Law School Law Review* (Vol. 49, pp. 185, 198).

Chalk, A. (2015). [Updated] Bethesda Responds to Outrage over Paid Skyrim Mods. Available at: https://www.pcgamer.com/bethesda-responds-to-outrage-over-paid-skyrim-mods/. Accessed 30 December 2024.

Cohen, J. (2011). Copyright as Property in the Post-Industrial Economy: A Research Agenda. *Wisconsin Law Review*, (2), 141, 147.

Coldewey, D. (2019). Skyrim Mod Drama Gets Ugly with Allegations of Stolen Code and Misappropriated Donations. Available at: https://techcrunch.com/2019/02/28/skyrim-mod-drama-gets-ugly-with-allegations-of-stolen-code-and-misappropriated-donations/. Accessed 30 December 2024.

Coleman, S., & Dyer-Witheford, N. (2007). Playing on the Digital Commons: Collectivities, Capital and Contestation in Videogame Culture. *Media, Culture & Society, 29*(6), 934–953.

Collins, J. E. (2013). User-Friendly Licensing for a User-Generated World: The Future of the Video-Content Market. *Vanderbilt Journal of Entertainment & Technology Law, 15*, 407, 440.

DarkOne. (2016). On Console Mods, Theft and Bethesda.net. Available at: https://www.nexusmods.com/skyrim/news/12815/? Accessed 30 December 2024.

Donnelly, J. (2004). Video Games and Reverse Engineering: Before and After the Digital Millennium Copyright Act. *Journal of Telecommunication & High Technology Law, 3*, 209, 229.

Downey, G. (2001). Virtual Webs, Physical Technologies, and Hidden Workers: The Spaces of Labor in Information Internetworks. *Technology and Culture, 42*(2), 209–235.

Dyer-Witheford, N., & de Peuter, G. (2009). *Game of Empire: Global Capitalism and Video Games* (p. 230). University of Minnesota Press.

Elkin-Kore, N. (2012). Governing Access to User-Generated Content: The Changing Nature of Private Ordering in Digital Networks. In E. Brousseau et al. (Eds.), *Governance, Regulations and Powers on the Internet* (p. 322). Cambridge University Press.

Elkin-Koren, N. (2015). Copyright in a Digital Ecosystem: A User-Rights Approach. Available at: https://papers.ssrn.com/sol3/papers.cfm?abstract_id=2637027. Accessed 4 February 2020.

Freedman, M. B. (2005). Machinima and Copyright Law. *Journal of Intellectual Property Law, 13*, 235, 253.

Gavrilova, M. L., & Kenneth Tan, C. J. (Eds.). (2016). *The Effects of Gameplay on Leadership Behaviors: An Empirical Study on Leadership Behaviors and Roles in Multiplayer Online Battle Arena Games* (p. 147). Transactions on Computational Science XXVI: Special Issue on Cyberworlds and Cybersecurity, Springer.

Ghelfi, D. (2015). Understanding the Engine of Creativity in a Creative Economy: An Interview with John Howkins. Available at: http://acpculturesplus.eu/sites/default/files/2015/03/25/wipo_creativeeconomyinterviewhowkins_0.pdf. Accessed 30 December 2024.

Gomulkiewicz, R. W., & Williamson, M. L. (1996). A Brief Defense of Mass Market Software License Agreements. *Rutgers Computer & Technology Law Journal, 22*, 335.

Good, O. S. (2017). Blizzard Wins $8 Million Judgement Against Overwatch Cheat Maker. Available at: https://www.polygon.com/2017/4/4/15177818/overwatch-cheat-maker-sued-loses-judgment. Accessed 30 December 2024.

Gordon, W. J. (1992). A Property Right in Self-Expression: Equality and Individualism in the Natural Law of Intellectual Property. *Yale Law Journal, 102*, 1533.

Green, J., & Jenkins, H. (2009). The Moral Economy of Web 2.0: Audience Research and Convergence Culture. In J. Holt & A. Perren (Eds.), *Media Industries: History, Theory, and method* (pp. 213–225). Blackwell Publishing.

Heelas, P. (2002). Work Ethics, Soft Capitalism and The "Turn to Life." In P. du Gay (Ed.), *Cultural Economy: Cultural Analysis and Commercial Life* (pp. 78–96). SAGE Publications.

Hernandez, P. (2014). GTA Online Mods Let People "Rape" Other Players. Available at: https://kotaku.com/gta-online-mods-let-people-rape-other-players-1618417938. Accessed 30 December 2024.

Hong, R. (2013). Game Modding, Prosumerism and Neoliberal Labor Practices. *International Journal of Communication, 7*, 984, 993–994.

Hong, R., & Chen, V. H. H. (2014). Becoming An Ideal Co-Creator: Web Materiality and Intensive Laboring Practices in Game Modding. *New Media & Society, 16*(2), 290–305.

Jenkins, H. (2006). *Convergence Culture: Where Old and New Media Collide*. New York University Press.

Joseph, D. J. (2018). The Discourse of Digital Dispossession: Paid Modifications and Community Crisis on Steam. *Games and Culture, 13*(7), 690–707.

Kamen, M. (2015). Skyrim is First Game to Allow Paid Game Mods on Steam. Available at: https://web.archive.org/web/20150505192753/http://www.wired.co.uk/news/archive/2015-04/24/steam-workshop-paid-mods. Accessed 30 December 2024.

Kow, Y. M., & Nardi, B. (2010). Who Owns the Mods? *First Monday, 15*(5). https://doi.org/10.5210/fm.v15i5.2971. Accessed 30 December 2024.

Kretzschmar, M., & Stanfill, M. (2018). Mods as Lightning Rods: A Typology of Video Game Mods, Intellectual Property, and Social Benefit/Harm. *Social & Legal Studies, 28*(4), 517, 519.

Kromand, D. (2007). Avatar Categorization. In *Suited Play, Proceedings of DiGRA 2007 Conference*. Available at: http://www.digra.org/digital-library/publications/avatar-categorization/. Accessed 30 December 2024.

Kücklich, J. (2005). Precarious Playbour: Modders and the Digital Game Industry. *The Fibreculture Journal*, (5). Available at: http://five.fibreculturejournal.org/fcj-025-precarious-playbour-modders-and-the-digital-games-industry/. Accessed 20 April 2020.

Lahti, E. (2017). Valve: Modders "Absolutely" Need to Be Paid. PC Gamer. Available at: https://www.pcgamer.com/valve-modders-absolutely-need-to-be-paid/. Accessed 30 December 2024.

Landau, S., Stratulate, R., & Twilleager, D. (2006). Consumers, Fans and Control: What the Games Industry Can Teach Tollywood about DRM. In *CCS'06 13th ACM Conference on Computer and Communications Security* (pp. 1–8).

Lastowka, F. G., & Hunter, D. (2004a). The Laws of Virtual Worlds. *California Law Review, 92*, 1, 20.

Lastowka, G., & Hunter, D. (2004b). The Laws of the Virtual Worlds. *California Law Review, 92*, 1, 45.

Lessig, L. (2006). Read Only Culture vs. Read & Write Culture. Available at: http://us.aving.net/news/view.php?articleId=17613. Accessed 20 March 2020.

Lessig, L. (2008). *Remix: Making Art and Commerce Thrive in the Hybrid Economy* (p. 259). Penguin.

Li, Y. (2020). The Age of Remix and Copyright Law Reform. *Law, Innovation and Technology, 12*(1), 113, 137.

Li, Y., & Huang, W. (2019). Taking Users' Rights Seriously: Proposed UGC Solutions for Spurring Creativity in the Internet Age. *Queen Mary Journal of Intellectual Property, 9*(1), 61, 74, 75, 84, 168.

Lipton, J. (2011). Moral Rights and Supernatural Fiction: Authorial Dignity and the New Moral Rights Agendas. *Fordham Intellectual Property, Media & Entertainment Law Journal, 21*(3), 537, 578–579.

Livingston, C. (2017). GTA Modding Tool OpenIV Shuts Down Due To Cease and Desist From Take-Two. Available at: https://www.pcgamer.com/gta-modding-tool-openiv-shuts-down-claiming-cease-and-desist-from-take-two/. Accessed 30 December 2024.

Lunney, G. (2001). The Death of Copyright: Digital Technology, Private Copying, and the Digital Millennium Copyright Act. *Virginia Law Review, 87*, 813. See also Desai, D. (2011). The Life and Death of Copyright. *Wisconsin Law Review*, (5), 219.

Loren, L. P. (1997). Redefining the Market Failure Approach to Fair Use in an Era of Copyright Permission Systems. *Journal of Intellectual Property Law, 5*(1), 1–58.

Meer, A. (2013). Tomorrowind's World: Skyrim-Dragonborn Out on PC. Rock, Paper, Shotgun. Available at: https://www.rockpapershotgun.com/tag/the-elder-scrolls-v-skyrim-dawnguard/. Accessed 30 December 2024.

Mezey, N. (2001). Law as Culture. *The Yale Journal of Law & the Humanities, 13*, 35–67.

Moody, K. A. (2014). *Modders: Changing the Game Through User-Generated Content and Online Communities* (pp. 21, 22, 34, 38, 90, 115–117). Theses & Dissertations of University of Lowa.

Nardi, B., & Kallinikos, J. (2007). Opening the Black Box of Digital Technologies: Mods in World of Warcraft. In *23rd EGOS Colloquium, Vienna, Australia* (pp. 5–7).
Nimmer, D. (2013). *Nimmer on Copyright*. LexisNexis, 12B.04[A][1] (pp. 12B-37).
Posner, R. A. (2003). *Economic Analysis of Law* (6th ed., pp. 9–18) Aspen Publishers.
Postigo, H. (2003). From Pong to Planet Quake: Post-industrial Transitions from Leisure to Work. *Information Communication and Society, 6*(4), 593.
Postigo, H. (2007a). Of Mods and Modders: Chasing Down the Value of Fan-based Digital Game Modifications. *Games and Culture, 2*(4), 300–313.
Postigo, H. (2007b). Of Mods and Modders: Chasing Down the Value of Fan-Based Digital Game Modifications. *Game and Culture, 2*(4), 300, 305, 307–308, 309, 310, 311.
Postigo, H. (2008). Video game Appropriation Through Modifications: Attitudes Concerning Intellectual Property among Modders and Fans. *Convergence: The International Journal of Research into New Media Technologies, 14*(1), 59–74, 134.
Postigo, H. (2010). Modding to The Big Leagues: Exploring The Space Between Modders and The Game Industry. *First Monday, 15*(5).
Prescott, S. (2015). Value has Removed Paid Mods Functionality from Steam Workshop. Available at: https://www.pcgamer.com/valve-has-removed-paid-mods-functionality-from-steam-workshop/. Accessed 30 December 2024.
Rajan, M. T. S. (2011). *Moral Rights: Principles, Practice and New Technology* (p. xix). Oxford University Press.
Richards, P. (2009). *Law of Contract* (3rd ed., p 389). Pearson Education Ltd.
Ritzer, G., & Jurgenson, N. (2010). Production, Consumption, Prosumption: The Nature of Capitalism in The Age of The Digital "Prosumer." *Journal of Consumer Culture, 10*(1), 13–36.
Rosen, Z. (2005). Mod, Man, and Law: A Reexamination of the Law of Computer Game Modifications. *Chi-Kent Journal of Intellectual Property, 4*, 196. See also John Baldrica (n 6).
Rosen, Z. S. (2018). Man, Mod, and Law: Revisiting the Law of Computer Game Modifications. *IDEA-The Law Review of the Franklin Pierce Center for Intellectual Property, 59*(1), 269, 286.
Scacchi, W. (2011). Modding as a Basis for Developing Game Systems. In *ICSE11: International Conference on Software Engineering* (p. 7). Waikiki.
Spare the Mod. (2012). In Support of Total-Conversion Modified Video Games. *Harvard Law Review, 125*, 789.
Sun, Y. [孙远钊]. (2015). Challenges to Intellectual Property Rights from Video Games and Virtual Environment[电子游戏与虚拟环境对知识产权的挑战]. *Zhichanli[知产力]*.
Terranova, T. (2000). Free Labor: Producing Culture for the Digital Economy. *Social Text, 18*(2), 33.
Volanis, N. (2007). Legal and Policy Issues of Virtual Property. *International Journal of Web Based Communities, 3*(3), 332.
Vickery, G., & Wunsch-Vincent, S. (2007). *Participative Web and User-Created Content: Web 2.0, Wikis and Social Networking*. Organization for Economic Cooperation and Development (OECD), Paris, France, p 9.
Wallace, R. (2014). Modding: Amateur Authorship and How the Video Game Industry Is Actually Getting It Right. *Brigham Young University Law Review*, 219–255.
Xiong, Q. [熊琦]. (2011). Study on the Validity of Software Copyright Licensing Contract[软件著作权许可合同的合法性研究]. *Studies in Law and Business[法商研究]*, Issue 6, p 25.
Zhang, L., & Fung, A. Y. H. (2014). Working as Playing? Consumer Labor, Guild and The Secondary Industry of Online Gaming in China. *New Media & Society, 16*(1), 38–54.

## *Legislations*

Architectural Works Copyright Protection Act

Berne Convention for the Protection of Literary and Artistic Works (1886)
Computer Fraud and Abuse Act
Digital Millennium Copyright Act (DMCA)
PRC Civil Code (2021)
PRC Copyright Law (2021)
Regulation on the Protection of the Right to Communicate Works to the Public over Information Networks (2013 Revision)
Uniform Computer Information Transactions Act (UCITA)
US Constitution

## Cases

Blizzard Entertainment, Inc. v. Jung, 422 F. 3d 630 (8th Cir. 2005).
Bowers v. Baystate Techs., Inc., 320 F. 3d 1317, 1337 (Fed. Cir. 2003).
Davidson & Associates Inc. v. Internet Gateway, 334 F. Supp. 2d The Eastern District of Missouri, 2004.
Groff v. American Online Inc., 1998 WL 307001 (R.I. Super.1998).
Lasercomb America, Inc. v. Reynolds, 911 F. 2d 970 (4th Cir. 1990).
Marvel Enters. v. NCSoft Corp, 74 U.S.P.Q.2d 1303 (C. D. Cal. 2005).
Micro Star v. Formgen, Inc., 154 F. 3d 1107 (9th Cir. 1998).
Midway Mfg. Co v. Artic Int'l, Inc., 704 F. 2d 1009 (1983).
Printing and Numerical Registering Co. v. Sampson (1875) LR 19 EQ 462 per Sir George Jessel.
Sandvig v. Sessions, 315 F. Supp. 3d 1(D.D.C.2018).
Schrock v. Learning Curve Int'l, Inc., 586 F. 3d 513 (7th Cir. 2009).
UMG Recordings Inc. v Veoh Networks Inc. (Case Nos. 09–56777, 10–55732) (9th Cir. December 20, 2011).
Viacom Int'l, Inc. v YouTube, Inc., 940 F. Supp. 2d 110, 121 (S.D.N.Y., April 18, 2013).

# Chapter 6
# Control or Promote? Legalizing Live Game Streaming Through Statutory License

**Abstract** This chapter considers the balance of interests in the live game streaming context. It first offers a brief introduction to the evolution and classification of live game streaming, and then examines the specific copyright infringement issues posed by this activity. As such streaming usually involves the unauthorized use of original game images, it may infringe the right of performance or the derivative right of game developers. Facing this challenge, most streamers seek to apply the fair use doctrine as a defense, especially from the transformative use perspective. The chapter explores this doctrine in depth and examines its application in the live game streaming context, finding a number of loopholes in the doctrine despite the fact that live game streaming slightly passes the "dual-standard" test to be considered "transformative use". Given the concerns of public interest, transaction costs and the significant potential profits of the live game streaming market, a proposal is made for a new statutory licensing mechanism for live game streaming. Implementing this new statutory licensing mechanism would not only protect the live game streaming industry, transforming it from an infringing business into a legitimate market, but also respect the rights of game developers and protect their economic interests, thereby achieving a dynamic balance between stakeholders.

**Keywords** Live game streaming · Unauthorized use · Fair use doctrine · Transformative use · A new statutory licensing mechanism

> Immature poets imitate; mature poets steal; bad poets deface what they take, and good poets make it into something better, or at least something different. –T.S. Eliot (1960)
> clearpage



Z. Deng, *Constructing an Eco-Balanced Copyright Regime for the Video Game Industry in China*, https://doi.org/10.1007/978-981-96-6056-8_6

**Table 6.1** Main live game streaming platforms in China

| Streaming platform | Date established | Operator |
|---|---|---|
| DouYu TV | 01/2014 | Wuhan Douyu Network Technology Co., Ltd |
| HuYa TV | 11/2014 | Guangzhou Huaduo Network Technology Co., Ltd |
| Penguin eSports | 07/2016 | Tencent Network Technology Co., Ltd |
| LongZhu TV | 02/2015 | Suzhou Youshi Network Technology Co., Ltd |
| ZhanQi TV | 01/2014 | Hangzhou Edge Network Technology Co., Ltd |
| Tentacle | 01/2011 | Hangzhou Kaixun Technology Co., Ltd |
| HuoMao TV | 10/2014 | Wuxi Qiaoxi Culture Media Co., Ltd |

## 6.1 Introduction

Due to their competitive and entertaining nature, video games (VGs) have won public favor in recent years, especially among young people. Live streaming has further enhanced their popularity. "Live streaming" refers to the simultaneous real-time recording and broadcasting of media content.[1] The practice of live game streaming, defined as the live online broadcasting of VGs' playing process, became popular in the mid-2010s on websites such as Twitch, where droves of people eagerly watched their favorite Internet personalities compete in live competitive games. Twitch spawned from Justin.tv, which it soon overshadowed; it was purchased by Amazon.com at the end of 2014 for US$970 million.[2] In 2015, YouTube Gaming was launched by YouTube to complete with Twitch.[3] Live game streaming has taken center stage on such sites; on Twitch alone, it attracts nearly 1.4 million daily viewers (Iqbal, 2020). Advancements in computer technology, high-speed Internet and the growing popularity of e-sports have further increased viewer numbers. In 2018, the revenue of China's live game streaming market reached 13.19 billion yuan, 60% higher than in 2017 (Table 6.1 and Fig. 6.1). In a 2019 report, this figure was expected to hit 25 billion yuan by 2020.[4]

On the downside, live game streaming poses certain copyright problems that must be mitigated to ensure that this new industry continues to flourish. Live game streaming depends on the use of audiovisual images of the games play, which raises questions regarding the rights of game developers to control this use of their games

[1] See 'Live Streaming' in <https://en.wikipedia.org/wiki/Live_streaming> last visited December 30, 2024.

[2] See 'Amazon to Buy Video Site Twitch for $970 Million' in The Wall Street Journal (August 25, 2014), <https://www.wsj.com/articles/amazon-to-buy-video-site-twitch-for-more-than-1-billion-1408988885?tesla=y&mg=reno64-wsj> last visited December 30, 2024.

[3] See 'Google Launches YouTube Gaming to Challenge Amazon-owned Twitch' in <https://www.theguardian.com/technology/2015/aug/26/youtube-gaming-live-website-apps> last visited December 30, 2024.

[4] See '2019 China's Game Live Streaming Industry Report' published by iResearch, p. 4, <http://www.iresearchchina.com/content/details8_57039.html> last visited December 30, 2024.

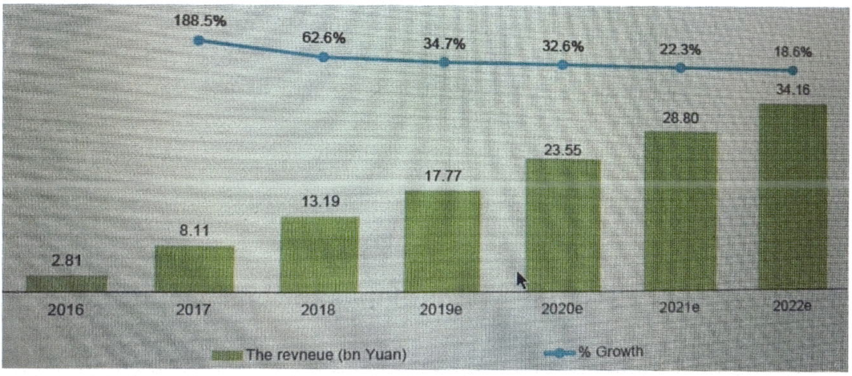


**Fig. 6.1** 2016–2022 revenue of live game streaming platforms in China[5]

or to share in the revenue generated by streamers. In the last few years, game developers and streamers have coexisted peacefully; most game developers have been willing to provide licenses to allow for the noncommercial streaming or uploading of videos of their games.[6] However, they reserve the right to forbid the streaming of their games at any time at their sole and absolute discretion and for any or no reason, and there are signs that such fragile relationship between developers and streamers is breaking down. In 2015, for example, Nintendo issued several takedown notices to a prominent video gaming YouTuber going by the name of Angry Joe, who had published videos showing materials copyrighted by Nintendo (Good, 2015). Later, the company launched the Nintendo Creators Program, which forced streamers using materials copyrighted by Nintendo to split the corresponding advertising revenue with the company. YouTube has barred its streamers outright from monetizing live game streaming (Gutelle, 2017). In the same year, the operator of the North American version of *League of Legends*, Riot, issued a strict copyright statement on the Azubu live streaming platform, asserting that rights related to the live broadcasting of gameplay content belonged exclusively to the game developer, not to the live streaming platform (Tryndamere, 2015). Also in 2015, the Guangzhou company Douyu was sued for copyright infringement for live broadcasting a *DOTA2* tournament without authorization ([2015] Civil Verdict No.191 (IP) People's Court of Pudong New Area of Shanghai; [2015] Shanghai (IP) Civil Verdict (Final) No. 641). Later, NetEase brought a lawsuit against the Guangzhou company Huaduo for setting up a live streaming window on its network platform, YY, and broadcasting gameplay ([2015] Yue Zhi Fa Zhu Civil Verdict No. 16; [2018] Yue Civil Final No. 137). This series of warnings, bans and lawsuits focused attention on the games

---

[5] Ibid.

[6] See e.g., Riot 'Legal Jibber Jabber' <https://www.riotgames.com/en/legal> last visited December 30, 2024; See also 'Blizzard Video Policy' <https://www.blizzard.com/zh-tw/legal/dd76b654-f2c4-4aaa-ba49-ca3122de2376/blizzard-video-policy> last visited December 30, 2024; See also 'Ubisoft Video Policy' <https://www.ubisoft.com/en-us/videopolicy.html> last visited December 30, 2024.

industry and the copyright consequences of live game streaming without authorization. However, it remains unclear whether live game streaming or rebroadcasts and transcriptions of streaming content constitute infringement and, if so, whether the fair use doctrine can be used as a defense. In this chapter, I address these matters and propose a more balanced scheme for stakeholders in the live game streaming context.

## 6.2 Live Game Streaming: Evolution and Classification

The VG industry has taken the world by storm. Over the last few decades, VGs have evolved from a hobby into a forum for e-sports, becoming a lucrative business worth over US$1 billion.[7] Tracking back to history, it was the popularity and emergence of live streaming service, the most common method of watching tournaments, that had driven the growth of e-sports industry. In the late twentieth century, a whirlwind of technology and innovation coming together to make it possible for all companies to use live streaming to build compelling brand images and attract consumers with the most up-to-date news on their products.[8] Increased Internet speed and video compression lowered barriers to using streaming technology for the average user. Websites such as Twitch, YouTube and Microsoft's Mixer have capitalized on live streaming by incorporating another form of popular media, VGs, and the VG industry has quickly become the champion of live streaming (Geeter, 2019). Twitch launched in 2011, focusing particularly on e-sports, also known as competitive video gaming. E-sports include competitive strategy games, first-person shooters, fighting games and other games requiring high-level skills and strategy. Competitive video gaming often takes the form of organized, multiplayer VG competitions, particularly between professional players participating individually or in teams.[9]

E-sports first became popular in Asia, specifically in South Korea and China. The Korean e-Sports Association (KeSPA) was founded in 2000, with the approval of the Ministry of Culture, Sports and Tourism, to promote and regulate e-sports in South Korea.[10] Following suit, in 2003, the State Sports General Administration approved e-sports as the 99th official sports event in China.[11] In the following year, China hosted a national e-sports league.[12] E-sports are also popular in Europe and the US,

[7] See 'Inside eSports: The Billion-Dollar Industry of Competitive Gaming' (July 19, 2019) <https://cs-agents.com/blog/esports/> last visited December 30, 2024.

[8] See 'A History of Live Streaming' <https://repertoireproductions.com/2017/02/18/a-history-of-live-streaming/> last visited December 30, 2024.

[9] See 'E-sports' <https://en.wikipedia.org/wiki/Esports> last visited December 30, 2024.

[10] See Korea e-Sports Association <https://en.wikipedia.org/wiki/Korea_e-Sports_Association> last visited December 30, 2024.

[11] See "E-sports was Recognized as the 99th Official Sports Events by the State Sports General Administration <http://www.seecn.net/html/job/30196.html> last visited December 30, 2024.

[12] See "China E-sports Games" <https://baike.baidu.com/item/全国电子竞技运动会/9939341?fr=aladdin> last visited December 30, 2024.

which host both regional and international events (Rapoza, 2019). By the 2010s, e-sports had come to represent a significant portion of the VG industry, with many game developers actively designing content for the professional e-sports subculture. According to GlobalData, the VGs market has the potential to become a US$300 billion industry by 2025, given the growth of streaming, cloud services and mobile e-sports.[13]

As the e-sports industry makes substantial contributions to economic growth and the development of e-sports depends heavily on the viewers attracted to live streamed events,[14] some have voiced the opinion that live game streaming should not be prohibited by copyright law. For instance, in a dispute with Blizzard, KeSPA stated that if game companies "assert their rights to maximize the pursuit of profits after their games become core e-sports titles," they may prevent e-sports from taking root as a "future-oriented entertainment industry."[15] Some commentators in the US have also believed that if a work has become the basis of an emerging industry and the original author expressed no intent to use the work in the same way, then the original author has no right to prohibit such use (Rogers, 2012). Consider the game *StarCraft*, which is regarded as a quasi-public good. Even if its developer, Blizzard, could obtain licensing fees from streamers, it should not be allowed to prevent the game *StarCraft* from being live streamed at will, as to do so would damage the public good and the interests of various stakeholders. However, I do not believe that the importance of live game streaming to the economy should be used as an excuse to deny the copyrights of game developers. The legitimacy of an industry that is either based on copyright infringement or otherwise functions only at the expense of another industry is questionable. Moreover, VGs other than competitive games can also be streamed, reflecting the diverse nature of today's streaming culture. If the live streaming of e-sports were to be exempted from copyright infringement while the live streaming of other types of VGs constituted to be deemed infringement, this discrepancy would cast doubt on the legality of the exemption. Thus, rather than merely focusing on matters of economics, it is essential to examine the rules of copyright law to determine game developers' rights regarding the unauthorized live streaming of their games (Fig. 6.2).

"Live game streaming" refers to the simultaneous transmission of gamers' state of play to the public via live streaming platforms or other online medias. Live game streaming enables the public to learn about talented players' gameplay strategies and

---

[13] See 'Video Games—Thematic Research' (April 2019) <https://www.globaldata.com/store/report/gdtmt-tr-s212--video-games-thematic-research/?utm_source=AffiliateFuture&utm_medium=affiliate&utm_campaign=skimlinks&affc=b7ef79ff-ce07-445d-9837-d41dac4896ba> last visited December 30, 2024.

[14] According to a new report from Newzoo, the global e-sports audience will grow to 453.8 million worldwide in 2019, with a year-on-year growth of + 15.0%. The average revenue per fan is anticipated to grow to $6.02 by 2022 and the e-sports market will reach $1.8 billion by that year. See <https://newzoo.com/insights/articles/newzoo-global-esports-economy-will-top-1-billion-for-the-first-time-in-2019/> last visited December 30, 2024.

[15] See Official KeSPA Statement (May 3, 2010) <http://www.teamliquid.net/forum/brood-war/123275-update-kespa-speaks-out-onintellectual-property-rights.> last visited December 30, 2024.

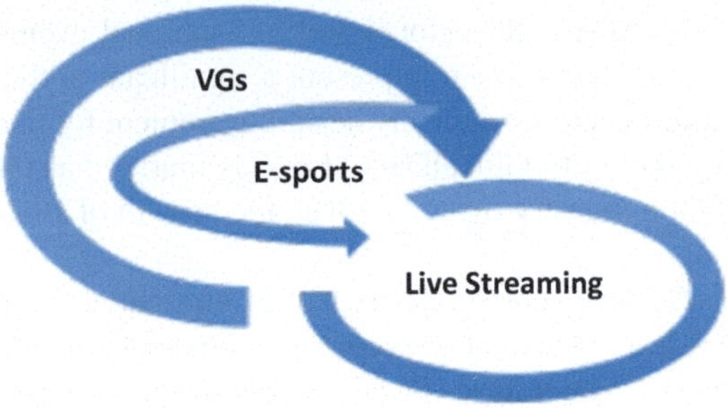


**Fig. 6.2** Asymmetric relationship between VGs, E-sports and live streaming

skills.[16] There are three primary types of game streaming: tournament streaming, streaming by professional players and variety streaming. Tournament streaming is the most popular type of game streaming.[17] Professional tournament organizers or professional streaming platform operators organize, host and commentate on tournaments broadcast on channels owned and managed by these entities. Tournament streaming broadcasts footage of the players, footage of the gameplay, images of lens selection and shifting, anchor commentary, footage of live audiences and sometimes added subtitles and music as well as slow motion playback of notable moments in the gameplay. While tournament streaming generates the largest number of viewers, the recent popularization of streaming services has allowed individuals to broadcast their own gameplay. The operator of a streaming platform profits from hits (views) and ads on individual streaming broadcasts, and the streamers share in some of this revenue. In professional player streaming, one of the most popular categories of individual streaming, both the gameplay and a webcam feed of the player are featured, and viewers interact with the professional through a chat function. These streamers often combine skilled gameplay with knowledgeable and entertaining commentary. However, charisma seems to be more important than skill, as the most popular streamers in this category are usually not the best players. Another popular type of individual streaming is variety streaming—the live broadcasting of a range of games. This type of streaming is highly interactive. Popular streamers entertain their viewers by, for example, exaggerating events in the gameplay, providing commentary, telling jokes or using moments in the game as inspiration to talk about other things (Jungar, 2016).

The above classification of live game streaming is primarily based on the professional level of players. From the perspective of the types of VGs, there are two main types of live game streaming: live streaming of competitive games and live streaming of creative games. Tournament streaming and streaming by professional players both involve competitive games. Regardless of VG type, however, every game streamed

[16] In this sense, the live game streaming images can be exactly the same with the original game images, but can also be the one with additional elements such as commentary, lens selection and shifting, interaction with viewers. The former is almost the "naked streaming", which is not common in live game streaming industry.

[17] See "Top 50 Twitch Users by Channel Views" <https://socialblade.com/twitch/top/50/channelviews> last visited December 30, 2024.

live adds audiovisual elements to the underlying game, such as the commentary of the game anchor, introductory text and viewers' interactive dialogues, in addition to the images automatically generated by the game software under the player's operation. This raises the question of whether a streamer should obtain the game developer's permission to use the original game images as the basis for live game streaming. The following sections explore the legal ramifications of this use of underlying games.

## 6.3 Live Game Streaming: An Innovative Endeavor Falling into the Copyright Hole

In Chinese cases involving live game streaming, courts have usually first determined whether the audiovisual elements of a VG, taken as a whole, constitute a copyrightable work. In the *DOTA2* case, the defendant had live broadcast a *DOTA2* tournament on its website without the game developer's authorization. The Shanghai People's Court ruled against the plaintiff's copyright infringement claim on the sole basis of the assertion that the audiovisual images of e-sports are not copyrightable works ([2015] Civil Verdict No. 191 (IP) People's Court of Pudong New Area of Shanghai; [2015] Shanghai (IP) Civil Verdict (Final) No. 641). Game images as a whole were first recognized as a copyrightable "cinematographic work" in the *Miracle MU* case ([2015] Civil Verdict No.529 (IP) People's Court of Pudong New Area of Shanghai). The same view was adopted in the *Fantasy Westward Journey* case, in which the Guangzhou IP Court held that the continuous dynamic images of the VG in question constituted a cinematographic work and that the defendant had infringed NetEase's copyright by setting up a live streaming window on its network platform, YY, and organizing a webcast exhibiting game images ([2015] Yue Zhi Fa Zhu Civil Verdict No. 16; [2018] Yue Civil Final No. 137). The courts' logic in these cases was simple; if game images are not copyrightable works, then there is no basis for copyright protection (PRC Copyright Law art. 1). However, this logic ignores the fact that a VG is a copyrightable work in itself. Even if game images are not considered a work independent of the game, they form a substantial and expressive part of the game and thus should be protected by copyright law in their own right.

On December 10, 2019, the Guangdong Higher People's Court made a final judgement on the *Fantasy Westward Journey* case, marking a milestone in the regulation of the live game streaming industry ([2018] Yue Civil Final No. 137). The court held that live streaming the images of a game as a whole constitutes public dissemination of the work, which may infringe the copyright owner's right of exhibition, right of presentation, right of performance, right of broadcasting and right of communication through information network under the PRC Copyright Law. Based on the characteristics of live game streaming, the court then ruled out violation of the rights of exhibition, presentation and performance. First, the court reasoned that live game streaming is not an act of "publicly displaying the original copy or reproductions of a work of the fine arts or of a photographic work" (PRC Copyright Law art. 10§1 (8)), and thus that the law governing the right of exhibition did not apply. Second, the court reasoned that the defendant's streaming was not an act of "publicly presenting a work by projector, slide projector or any other technology or instrument" (PRC Copyright Law art. 10§1 (10)) but rather an act of disseminating the content of a work through a network to members of the public who were not in the place where the communication first occurred. As such, the court concluded, the law governing the right of presentation did not apply. Third, the court stated that the right of performance stipulated by the PRC Copyright Law covers only "live performance" and "mechanical performance" with live audiences (PRC Copyright Law art. 10§1 (9)), excluding the act of disseminating the content of a work via a network to the members of the public not in the place where the communication first occurred. Thus, live game streaming, as an act of "online remote real-time transmission," was deemed not to violate the right of performance. Furthermore, "performance" as defined by the PRC Copyright Law does not cover cinematographic works or works created by a process analogous to cinematography, such as dynamic game images, because the presentation process of these works is not an act of "publicly communicating the performance of a work" ((PRC Copyright Law, 2021 art. 10§1 (9)) by voice, expression and actions. Based on this, the court held that live game streaming does not qualify as performance ([2018] Yue Civil Final No. 137). I agree with the court's reasoning as regards the rights of exhibition and presentation but not as regards the right of performance. The right of performance, the right of broadcasting, the right of communication through information network and "other rights to be enjoyed by copyright owners" have all been hotly debated by Chinese scholars. The following subsections explore these rights in detail.

### *6.3.1 Copyright Infringement: "Pigeon-Holing" for Live Game Streaming*

(1) Right of Communication through Information Network

The "right of communication through information network" in the PRC Copyright Law stems from the "right of communication to the public" specified by the WIPO Copyright Treaty (WCT). Pursuant to Article 8 of the WCT, "authors of literary and artistic works shall enjoy the exclusive right of authorizing any communication to the public of their works, by wire or wireless means, including the making available to the public of their works in such a way that members of the public may access these works from a place and at a time individually chosen by them." However, a bit different from the right of communication to the public, China's right of communication through information network is defined as "the right to make a work available to the public by wire or by wireless means, so that people may have access to the work from a place and at a time individually chosen by them" (PRC Copyright Law art. 10 §1(12)). This law emphasizes the right of the public to access a program without restriction by time or place.[18] As live streaming always restricts the time of access, it is not included in the scope of the right of communication through information network.

(2) Right of Broadcasting

Before the enactment of the latest version of the PRC Copyright Law (2021), the right of broadcasting was defined as "the right to broadcast a work or disseminate it to the public by any wireless means, to communicate the broadcast of a work to the public by wire or by rebroadcasting, and to publicly communicate the broadcast of a work by loudspeaker or any other analogous instrument transmitting signs, sounds or images" (PRC Copyright Law art. 10 §1 (11)). This definition implies that the right of broadcasting applies to the broadcasting or dissemination of a work by wireless means as well as to the subsequent transmission or rebroadcasting of such a wireless broadcast. Because live game streaming is an act of disseminating a work by wire, communicating a work directly to the public rather than broadcasting it through an information network after receiving it by wireless means, it does not fall within the scope of the right of broadcasting in the 2012 version of the PRC Copyright Law. However, the amended version of the PRC Copyright Law acknowledges the new means of communication in the network environment. It redefines the right of broadcasting as "the right to broadcast or rebroadcast a work to the public by any wire or wireless means, and to publicly communicate the broadcast of a work by loudspeaker or any other analogous instrument transmitting signs, sounds or images" (PRC Copyright Law art. 10 §1 (11)). This amendment brings the act of disseminating works by wire within the scope of the right of broadcasting; thus, live game streaming is regulated by the new right of broadcasting.

(3) Other Rights to Be Enjoyed by the Copyright Owners

"Other rights to be enjoyed by the copyright owners" is regarded as a miscellaneous catch-all clause designed to address new ways of using copyrighted works (PRC Copyright Law art. 10 §1(17)). Before the redefinition of the "right of broadcasting" and due to the failure of the rights of broadcasting and communication through information network to protect against live game streaming, most Chinese experts have attempted to apply the "other rights" clause to live game streaming (Li, 2017; Xie, 2017; Zhu, 2017). They have argued that the "right of communication to the public" in the WCT was created in response to the development of the Internet, equipping copyright owners with a broad right to control the communication of their works by any technical means. In these experts' opinion, to align with the rights given in the WCT, live game streaming should be regulated by this catch-all clause. Granted, the crux of the WCT's right of communication to the public lies in the dissemination of works to the public, whether they are disseminated in real time or stored on a server to allow public access at any time. However, there is no such right in the PRC Copyright Law, and, as discussed, live game streaming falls outside the

[18] The later part of the definition of the right of communication to the public that "the making available to the public of their works in such a way that members of the public may access these works from a place and at a time individually chosen by them" is regarded as "the right of making available to the public".

scope of both the right of communication through information network and the right of broadcasting as defined in the 2012 version of the law. Then whether it should be regulated by the miscellaneous provision— "other rights to be enjoyed by copyright owners"—is not a simple matter.

The miscellaneous provision was criticized by Liu (2019), who argued that it is both unnecessary and lacks a theoretical basis. The "*numerus clausus*" as a basic principle of property law refers to "the categories of real rights and their contents shall be prescribed by law" (PRC Civil Code art. 119). Applied to copyright law, it should be "the categories of copyrights and their contents shall be prescribed by law." This principle entails three meanings. Frist, the copyrights enjoyed by an author (including the type and scope of the rights and the standards for defining infringement) should be clearly defined by copyright law and not decided by judges at their discretion. Second, legislators should not arbitrarily change the scope of copyrights enjoyed by an author (including expanding or limiting their meaning at will); otherwise, they risk disrupting the balance of the copyright regime. Third, legislators should not leave matters that should be decided by themselves to judicial or administrative bodies for decision. This would risk contravening the principle of separation powers among these institutions, damaging the corresponding balance of rights or interests (Liu, 2019). Therefore, the introduction of the miscellaneous provision to the Copyright Law violates the *numerus clausus* principle and could lead to the inconsistent legal application or interpretation of the law and uncertainty of legal application standards. This is why no international conventions or copyright laws in other jurisdictions provide authors with such open-ended copyrights.

(4) Right of Performance

The right of performance is "the right to publicly perform a work, and to publicly communicate the performance of a work by any means or process" (PRC Copyright Law art. 10 §1(9)). In accordance with Article 37 of the PRC Copyright Law, "[a] performer (an individual performer or a performing group) who for a performance exploits a work created by another shall obtain permission from and pay remuneration to the copyright owner. A performance organizer who organizes a performance shall obtain permission from and pay remuneration to the copyright owner." It has been argued that "playing VGs can be regarded as performance, and displaying the audiovisual outputs of a VG through unauthorized streaming infringes the game developer's public performance right" (Ou et al., 2015; Qiu, 2017). However, some judges have disagreed, arguing that playing VGs is not "performance" in the sense of copyright law and that treating it as such would "destroy the unity of copyright law" (Feng, 2017). Other scholars have asserted that the identity of gamers is not recognized by the relevant legislations and thus that gamers cannot be regarded as "performers" in law (Jiang, 2019).

To determine whether a gamer can be considered a performer, I first refer to the definition of "performer" in relevant statutes. Article 3(a) of the Rome Convention defines "performers" as "actors, singers, musicians, dancers, and other persons who act, sing, deliver, declaim, play in, or otherwise perform literary or artistic works." Article 5 (6) of the *Regulations for the Implementation of the PRC Copyright Law* provides a similar definition of "performer": "an actor, or a performing group or any other person who performs literary or artistic works. Both the Article 2(a) of the WIPO Performances and Phonograms Treaty (WPPT) and the Article 2(a) of the Beijing Treaty on Audiovisual Performances (BJTAP) specify that "'performers' are actors, singers, musicians, dancers, and other persons who act, sing, deliver, declaim, play in, interpret, or otherwise perform literary or artistic works or expressions of folklore." Thus, compared with the Rome Convention, the WPPT and the BJTAP provide more comprehensive definitions of "performer," with a wider scope in terms of both the mode and the object of performance. In terms of the mode of performance, people who perform works by "interpreting" are included. An example is the conductor of a band or the director of a stage play who integrates his understanding or interpretation of a work into his performance, although he does not participate in the performance in person. In terms of the object of performance, literary or artistic works are complemented by "expressions of folklore;" thus, folk artists are included in the performers' list. The broad term "literary or artistic works" as objects of performance is also used in the Berne Convention and covers almost all forms of works, regardless of whether a given work's copyright protection has expired (WIPO, 1999). Nevertheless, the definition of "performer" under the Rome Convention is narrower than the concept of "performer" in daily life; for example, it does not include performers who do not performing literary or artistic works, such as magicians, circus artists or jugglers. However, Article 9 of the Rome Convention stipulates that "[a]ny Contracting State may, by its domestic laws and regulations, extend the protection provided for in this Convention to artists who do not perform literary or artistic works." The connotation of "performer" in national legislation has gradually expanded. For instance, Article L212-1 of the IP Code of France provides as follows: "[s]ave for ancillary performers, considered such by professional practice, performers shall be those persons who act, sing, deliver, declaim, play in or otherwise perform literary or artistic works, variety, circus or puppet acts." Also, in Brazil, football players are considered as performers (Feng, 2017). I suggest that Chinese copyright law should follow the lead of these countries in expanding its definition of "performer."

As to whether VG players qualify as performers, a US court answered in the affirmative, holding that "a video arcade owner's use of copyrighted circuit boards in coin-operated video machines available to the public for a fee constituted public performance of the copyrighted work under §106(4)" (Red Baron-Franklin Park v. Taito, 1989). However, in a later case, the court refused to treat playing VGs as "performance" in the sense of copyright law (Allen v. Academic Games League of Am., 1996). At issue in this case was whether the use of academic games in a tournament setting constituted public performance within the meaning of the Copyright Act (17 U.S.C.§106(4)). The court reasoned that "the interpretation of 'play,' as used to define 'perform' in §101 of the Copyright Act, has generally been limited to instances of playing music or records. The term 'play' has not been extended to the playing of games. To do so would mean interpreting the Copyright Act in a manner that would allow the owner of a copyright in a game to control when and where purchasers of games may play the games and this court will not place such an undue restraint on consumers" (Allen v. Academic Games League of Am., 1996). This reasoning, which is based entirely on policy considerations, is far from satisfactory. "To perform" is defined in the US Copyright Act as "to recite, render, play, dance, or act [a work], either directly or by means of any device or process or, in the case of a motion picture or other audiovisual work, to show its images in any sequence or to make the sounds accompanying it audible" (17 U.S.C. §101). "Publicly" is defined as "at a place open to the public or at any place where a substantial number of persons outside of a normal circle of a family and its social acquaintances is gathered" (17 U.S.C. §101). Applying these statutory definitions to the playing of games in a tournament setting, as gamers inevitably recite, play or display the scripts, music or pictures contained in the VGs in public, it is difficult to understand why live game streaming does not infringe the right of performance.

In terms of the effect of the performance of a work, there are two essential elements: the substantial presentation of the work and the personalized expression of the performer. The first element requires that the content or connotation of a work can be performed by the performer such that the author's personalized thoughts or expressions are substantially presented. The second element requires that the performer integrates his understanding of the content of the work into his performance to equip the performance with his personalized characteristics (Liu, 2020). These two elements permit a performance to reflect both the originality of the author's work and the creativity of the performer. The resulting performance serves to promote the work's dissemination and to facilitate the full realization of cultural or social values, thereby helping to achieve the basic legislative goal of copyright law: to promote social and cultural development. With the advent of new technologies, the "fixation" of works has expanded from traditional books or videotapes to digital carriers. In addition, the form of performance has expanded from a narrow form depending mainly on the performers' expressions, actions or voices to new digital forms, including various display effects achieved by operating the information input terminal of a software program. In the framework of copyright law, technology neutrality is an important principle that helps to maintain the fairness and efficiency of legal norms (Liu, 2020). This principle should also guide the definition of "performer" and "performance" in the digital era. That is, when defining the concept and scope of "performance," the essential elements of performance should be retained while the technical elements should be ignored, enabling the law to capture new forms made possible through technological development and continue to balance the rights of the copyright owner and other parties.

Thus, I believe that a person should be considered as a performer and enjoy a performer's rights in a lawful performance as long as he displays the substantial content of a work in a personalized way, regardless of whether the performance is displayed through the expression, action or voice of the performer (e.g. singer or dancer), through his interpretation of the work (e.g. conductor), or through the operation of the information input terminal of a software program (e.g. VG player). VGs are widely regarded as the "ninth art," classified as artistic works under the Berne Convention (Jewell, 2012). In competitive VGs, the framework of idea and expression is preset by the game developer. When a gamer plays a game, he displays the substantial content of the game by operating the computer or other equipment, which is essentially the same as a musician's performing music by operating an electronic organ. Just as a musician cannot break through the content of a work when playing or singing it, a gamer cannot break through the internal framework of the underlying game when playing it. Based on their own understanding and interpretation of the game, players display the actions, sounds, expressions and other aspects of the characters in the underlying game through their playing skills, thus bringing audiovisual enjoyment to audiences. Even for creative games, such as open world games wherein gamers have more freedom to create, the playing process qualifies "performance" because gamers play based on their own understanding or imagination and their presentation remains within the framework of the underlying game, exploiting the underlying game materials to a certain extent. As players have unique personality characteristics and personal interpretations of games, the dynamic images displayed by each player differ. Therefore, playing VGs can reasonably be considered "performance" under copyright law.

Some scholars, having conceded that playing VGs may fit the definition of "performance," have asserted that streamers do not infringe game developers' performance right (Feng, 2017). This argument is based on the fact that game developers design VGs to be played and support streaming to promote sales. The argument further states that players have obtained an implied license from game developers, thus avoiding infringing the performance right. While I agree that game developers sell the "right to play games" to gamers, I hold that they do not sell the right of performance, as the first sale doctrine does not apply to the performance right (Red Baron-Franklin Park v. Taito, 1989). Because a performance does not infringe the right of performance unless it is done publicly, it is the act of live streaming that triggers infringement rather than the act of playing or performing a game. Therefore, in the context of tournament streaming, the tournament organizers (generally the professional live streaming platforms) should be liable for copyright infringement. Individual streaming involves contributory infringement by the streamers and live streaming platforms involved.

### *6.3.2 Live Game Streaming Images: New Copyrighted Works?*

In the *Fantasy Westward Journey* case, the defendant reasoned that live streaming players had invested considerable intellectual labor in the game playing process, creatively combining the game materials and displaying them in the form of dynamic images, and thus should enjoy copyrights to the live game streaming images ([2018] Yue Civil Final No. 137). The court disagreed, holding that most of the gamers' operations were based on the considerations of practicability and efficiency and what they showed during the gameplay process were playing strategies and skills or proficiency, which do not qualify as original expression under copyright law. However, it is possible to imagine a different outcome for cases in which gamers/

game anchors carefully prepare the explanatory content, control the live broadcasting rhythm and select camera or game screen angles to attract more viewers, who also make some original contributions to the live game streaming images. Furthermore, in games with a high level of creative freedom, players can add and integrate new original expressions to the underlying game images, rendering the live game broadcast quite different from a live broadcast of the underlying game images. This would be considered a derivative work on the basis of an existing work, which requires the permission of the original copyright owner and remuneration (PRC Copyright Law art. 13). Although the PRC Copyright Law does not explicitly provide a derivative right, it does provide a similar right: the right of adaptation. Given that Chinese courts recognize a game's images collectively as a cinematographic work ([2018] Yue Civil Final No. 137) and that the PRC Copyright Law has been revised to change "cinematographic work" to "audiovisual work" (PRC Copyright Law art. 3(6)), live game streaming images may infringe the game developer' right of adaptation even if the gameplay constitutes a new audiovisual work.

The performance of a work requires creativity from performers to ensure its quality and market value. Just as a dramatic works adheres to a script but also requires performers for its dynamic presentation onstage, VGs cannot generate dynamic game images without the performance of players. By operating a computer information terminal, players display the original static achievements of the game developer on the screen in the form of moving images, which requires the input of intelligence and emotion. A performance is generally understood as a performer's interpretation of a work, which emphasizes the creativity and value of the performer as reflected in his personalized performance. Thus, whether a player's contribution reaches the required level of originality to make live game streaming images a new work or constitutes merely a performance of the game work, the act of live streaming exploits the underlying game materials and presents them publicly. This may infringe the performance right or the derivative right of the game developer.

## 6.4 Fair Use Doctrine: A Safety Net with Too Many Holes

As live game streaming is to a large extent based on the unauthorized exploitation of the preexisting game images, it is considered copyright infringement unless justified by an applicable exception. Copyright exceptions are designed to moderate the restrictions on cultural communication imposed by a copyright monopoly. From an external perspective, monopolies hinder cultural circulation and societal recreation. From an internal perspective, the increased transaction costs and rights protection costs brought by monopolies sometimes fail to offset the propaganda benefit brought by piracy (Landes, 2003). Copyright exceptions are designed to facilitate the public's access to works for "special purposes" (e.g. education, public welfare, cultural heritage, commentary and parody) and to allow some works to be used without authorization when the high costs of negotiating individual licenses would overly restrict the dissemination of the works.

The PRC Copyright Law chapter entitled "Limitations on Rights" details the circumstances in which a work can be used without the copyright holder's permission (Chap. 4). Article 24 of this chapter includes a "fair use" clause and Article 25 includes a "statutory license" clause. A statutory license permits unauthorized use with appropriate remuneration to the copyright holder (PRC Copyright Law art.25). However, a statutory license must be explicitly defined by legislation, and to date, no such statute exists defining a licensing scheme for live game streaming. Thus, streamers facing claims of copyright infringement must rely on the fair use doctrine as a defense. The reasonableness of this tactic is the subject of some debate. While proponents have argued that live game streaming is transformative enough to be excused for copyright infringement (Wang, 2016; Xie, 2017), opponents have asserted that live game streaming is a reasonable potential market for the game developer and that streamers are guilty of copyright infringement when doing it without authorization (Li, 2017; Zhu, 2017). Referencing other jurisdictions, both Joo (2011) and Puddington (2015) attempted to justify the fair use doctrine as a defense from an economic perspective. In Japan, live game streaming is "tolerated infringement": it is technically and theoretically illegal copyright infringement but tolerated by copyright holders. Based on this practice, Matsui (2016) suggested either denying infringement in case of live game streaming or legalizing the activity; however, he did not suggest a workable regime as an alternative to the current regime. In line with the EU's practice, Jungar (2016) advocated for a "freedom of expression" exception to curb game developers' rights in certain cases of streaming. However, freedom of expression is not available as an independent legal defense in China.[19] Therefore, in this section I focus on the fair use defense.

### *6.4.1 Legislative and Judicial Treatment of the Fair Use Doctrine in China: From Closed Model to Open Model*

"Fair use" refers to "the circumstances in which a copyrighted work can be used without authorization from, or paying remuneration to, the copyright owner" (PRC Copyright Law art. 24). Before the enactment of the latest PRC Copyright Law (2021), Article 22 of the PRC Copyright Law (2021) provided an enumerative and exhaustive list of such exceptional circumstances, none of which applied to live game streaming. Chinese courts have realized the disadvantages of limiting fair use to enumerated circumstances and have thus referred to the "four factors" of the fair use doctrine and the "transformative use" standard developed in the US ([2011]1st Intermediate People's Court of Beijing Civil Verdict No. 1321; [2015] Shanghai IP Court Civil Final No. 730). Moreover, in response to the call for an open fair use model among industries, Article 24 §1 (13) of the amended PRC Copyright Law (2021) adds "other intellectual achievements in line with the characteristics of the work" to

[19] In China, freedom of expression is not considered as an independent legal defense but is immerged into the fair use doctrine.

the fair use clause in an attempt to turn the closed fair use model into an open one. Article 24 §1 of the Copyright Law further states that the use "may not prejudice the normal use of the work" and "may not unreasonably prejudice the lawful rights and interests of the copyright owner." These two requirements are also stipulated in the *Regulations for the Implementation of the PRC Copyright Law* (art. 21), and clearly stem from the "three-step" test of the Berne Convention. Pursuant to Article 9(2) of the Berne Convention, legislators have the duty to limit their copyright exceptions to "certain special cases" and to ensure that a permitted exception "does not conflict with a normal exploitation of the work and does not unreasonably prejudice the legitimate interests of the author."

Even though Chinese courts have borrowed US Courts' more flexible approach to finding fair use, their opinions on what constitutes transformative use vary, resulting in legal uncertainty. For instance, in the *Fantasy Westward Journey* case, the court declined to find fair use, pronouncing that "even if the game screen was utilized as a tool to demonstrate the players' skill, it is just a difference of perspective between players and viewers, and it will not surely obliterate the value of the game screen, hence the value was not transformed" ([2015] Yue Zhi Fa Zhu Civil Verdict No. 16). The court's reasoning indicates a very high standard for transformative use, as it is almost impossible for a secondary user to prove that the original work's value has been completely transformed in the new work. Furthermore, the court wavered between taking a strict doctrinal approach and taking a more flexible approach. In its decision, the court asserted that "from the perspective of doctrinal analysis, live game streaming was not covered by any listed exceptions in Article 22 of the PRC Copyright Law (2021), and thus should not be held to be fair use." This decision reflects Chinese courts' struggle to determine whether to adopt an open model for the fair use doctrine and how to interpret transformative use. Given the profound influence of the principles of US copyright law on Chinese law, the following subsections examine the possibility of exempting live game streaming from infringement by referring to the fair use doctrine as applied in the US.

### 6.4.2 Fair Use Doctrine in the US: The Four-Factor Test

Section 107 of the US Copyright Act enumerates certain copyright exceptions, including "criticism, comment, news reporting, teaching (including multiple copies for classroom use), scholarship, or research." It also provides four factors used to determine fair use: "(1) the purpose and character of the use, including whether such use is of a commercial nature or is for nonprofit educational purposes; (2) the nature of the copyrighted work; (3) the amount and substantiality of the portion used in relation to the copyrighted work as a whole; (4) the effect of the use upon the potential market for or value of the copyrighted work." The four factors and enumerated exceptions are "in no case definitive or determinative" (House Report Rep. No.1476, 94th Cong., 2d Sess. 65 (1976)), but rather serve as references to help courts render judgements. Hence the fair use doctrine emphasizes a dynamic relationship between legislation and judicature in the US.

Applying the four factors of the fair use doctrine to live game streaming shows that the second and the third factors work against streamers. The second factor—"the nature of the copyrighted work" concerns the nature of the work that is being copied; for example, whether it is informational or entertaining in nature. Generally, courts are more likely to find fair use if material has been copied from a factual work, such as a biography, than if it has been copied from a fictional work, such as a horror movie. As the Supreme Court stated in the *Sony* case, "copying a news broadcast may have a stronger claim to fair use than copying a motion picture, because copying from informational works such as scholarly, scientific, or news journals encourages the free spread of ideas and encourages the creation of new scientific or educational works, all of which benefit the public" (Sony Corp. of America v. Universal City Studios, 1984). Courts also consider whether the work copied was published or unpublished at the time of copying. The scope of fair use is narrower with respect to unpublished works because of the author's right to control the first public appearance of his or her expression (Salinger v. Random House, 1987). The infringed copyrighted materials in live game streaming, i.e., the underlying games, are intended for commercial and entertainment purposes. They are designed and published by game developers after considerable investment, and the virtual world displayed is totally fictional with strong entertaining elements to attract as many gamers as possible. Hence in terms of this factor, there appears to be no public interest in justifying the reproduction and public transmission of VGs.

As for the third factor—"the amount and substantiality of the portion used in relation to the copyrighted work as a whole," it considers whether the defendant took the most valuable part of the plaintiff's work. When considering the amount and "substantiality" of the portion taken, the court looks at both the quantity and the quality of the material(s) used. The copying of a small portion of a work may count against fair use if that portion is qualitatively significant to the copyrighted work (Harper & Row, Publishers, Inc. v. National Enterprises, 1985). In the context of VGs, the game resource materials (including text, pictures, music and video) displayed in a game form the core content of the work; in using these materials, live streaming clearly makes use of a substantial part of the original game. Even in the case of a single player's reproducing and publicly transmitting only part of a game, it can be argued that the aggregation of all such uses by multiple streamers constitutes substantial use under the third factor (Matsui, 2016). Generally, therefore, the third factor is not favorable to streamers. However, copying an entire work may be regarded as fair use if it is reasonable and necessary to meet the purpose of the use. For example, in the *Google* case, the court ruled that the scanning of entire books was a necessity to achieve a searching function and held that it qualified as fair use (Authors Guild Inc. v. Google Inc., 2013). In another case, the Supreme Court also excused the copying of complete television programs (Sony Corp. of America v. Universal City Studios, 1984). This factor, therefore, is not determinative in the finding of fair use. Thus, to determine whether fair use can be used as a defense for live game streaming lies in the first and fourth factors of the four-factor test.

Beebe (2008) empirically demonstrated that "the first and fourth factors are overwhelmingly the most important factors in fair use analysis," as measured by their correlation with outcomes of the overall fair use test. The first fair use factor mainly concerns the function of the copied material. As the principles of copyright law encourage scholarship, research, education and commentary, a fair use determination is most likely if the defendant's use is noncommercial, educational, scientific and/or historical. While a non-profit use does not necessarily excuse infringement, the *Sony* case suggested that "every commercial use of copyrighted material is presumptively an unfair exploitation of the monopoly privilege…and may pose harm to the potential market under the fourth factor" (Sony Corp. of America v. Universal City Studios, 1984). However, this notion was clarified by the Supreme Court to be contrary to the long-held common law tradition of fair use adjudication. The court further explained that this presumption does not apply to transformative uses; that is, uses that alter the original work "with new expression, meaning, or message" (Campbell v. Acuff-Rose Music, 1994). Because live streaming is meant for personal enjoyment, not for education, and because it is also a source of revenue for live streaming platforms and streamers, it is difficult to show fair use unless it can be classified as transformative use. In tournament streaming, players play a game while the game anchor provides commentary. Similarly, in individual streaming, the streamer himself is commentating while playing the game. The commentary is usually not on the game itself but on the playing skills of the gamers or on other topics inspired by events in the game. Whether the added commentary is sufficiently transformative requires deeper exploration.

The fourth factor in a fair-use determination is the effect of the use on the potential market for the original work. The Supreme Court once described the fourth factor as "undoubtedly the single most important element of fair use" (Harper & Row, Publishers, Inc. v. National Enterprises, 1985). Consideration of this factor is intended to strike a balance between the benefit to the public if the use is permitted and the copyright owner's personal gain if the use is denied (Stim, 2023). Determining the scope of a "potential market" is complicated; one US court defined it as "a traditional, reasonable or likely to be developed market" (Authors Guild Inc. v. Hathi Trust, 2012). An essential element of the market harm to the copyright owner is whether his incentives have been or could be substantially impaired. This inquiry examines both the actual harm caused to the copyright owner by the defendant's specific use and any harm that "has not yet occurred but is likely to occur" (Williams & Wilkins Co. v. United States, 1973). This would appear to include the potential licensing market of VGs; however, the effect of live game streaming on the market value of VGs is difficult to determine. First, it is difficult to compute the game developer's loss as a result of live webcasting. Second, even if live streaming boosts a game's subscriptions or sales, a game developer may still argue that it has deprived the company of some sort of potential licensing profit (Matsui, 2016). Given the "near-perfect correlation" between judicial findings regarding the fourth factor and fair use outcomes, Professor Beebe (2008) hypothesized that the fourth factor is not an independent variable but rather serves as the analytic space in which courts engage in a two-sided balancing test, weighing "the strength of the defendant's justification for its use, as that justification has been developed in the first three factors, against the impact of that use on the incentives of the plaintiff." This observation was echoed by Sag (2015), who humorously commented, "[f]inding a 99% correlation in an empirical study is a bit like finding that 99% of Iraqis voted for Saddam Hussein—it is a statistic so impressive that it engenders disbelief." However, whether the fourth factor plays an essential role in determining fair use or is simply a post hoc cloak used by judges to justify results, the effect of live game streaming on the potential market for or value of the VGs played is a critical consideration.

### 6.4.3 Shifting Paradigm of Fair Use from Market-Centered to Transformative Use

Netanel (2011), an IP expert in the US, outlined the history of the paradigms of fair use. He argued that a market-centered paradigm prevailed for some two decades following its adoption in the *Harper & Row* case, but that since 2005, the transformative use paradigm adopted in the *Campbell* case has overwhelmingly driven fair use analysis in US courts.

Under the market-centered paradigm, fair use is an anomalous exception to the copyright owner's exclusive rights, applicable only in cases of irremediable market failure. Proposing a theory of market failure, Gordon (1982) stated that the fair use exception should come into play only when "(1) defendant could not appropriately purchase the desired use through the market (or market failure is present); (2) transferring control over the use to defendant would serve the public interest; and (3) the copyright owner's incentives would not be substantially impaired by allowing the user to proceed." The first part of this three-part test determines whether market failure is present, i.e. whether "the desired transfer of resource use is unlikely to take place spontaneously" or "special circumstances such as market flaws impair the market's ordinary ability to serve as a measure of how resources should be allocated" (Gordon, 1982). Where transfers cannot occur due to market failure, the court must determine whether the use yields an identifiable public benefit that would outweigh any harm caused to the copyright owner by granting fair use. Considering the market harm caused to the copyright owner, one US court explained as follows: "[a]ctual present harm need not be shown. Nor is it necessary to show with certainty that future harm will result. What is necessary is a showing by a preponderance of the evidence that some meaningful likelihood of future harm exists" (Sony Corporation of America v. Universal City Studios, 1984). Therefore, market harm is not limited to the market for the original work but encompasses the potential market for derivative works as well as the potential licensing market for "any of the rights in the copyrighted work" (Harper & Row, Publishers, Inc. v. Nation Enters., 1985). When the court weighs the plaintiff's loss against the benefit of the defendant's use, "it is making a comparison similar to that made by the participants in market transactions" (Posner, 1977). As Professor Gordon (1982) put it, "fair use implies the consent of the copyright owner by looking to whether the owner would have consented under ideal market conditions." Therefore, under the market-centered paradigm, fair use is available only when the defendant has been unable to negotiate a copyright license due to high transaction costs and a reasonable copyright holder would consent to the defendant's use.

Because evaluating market harm is essentially equivalent to examining the fourth factor in the four-factor test ("the effect of the use upon the potential market for or value of the copyrighted work"), US courts once regarded the fourth factor as the single most important element of fair use analysis (Harper & Row, Publishers, Inc. v. Nation Enters.,1985). However, according to Professor Netanel's empirical account of the near-perfect correlation between judicial findings regarding the fourth factor and fair use outcomes, this factor is not "an independent variable" (Beebe, 2008; Sag, 2015). Generally, Netanel's empirical data regarding judicial treatment of the fourth factor support the conclusion that the market-centered paradigm no longer exerts a hold on fair use case law (Netanel, 2011). Nevertheless, some Chinese scholars have ignored this finding, continuing to use the market-centered paradigm to explore the market harm of live game streaming. Based on Gordon's argument that "if the market failure in a given case is likely to be cured (and substantial revenues generated) by the parties' own actions following a finding of infringement, fair use should be denied" (Gordon, 1982), these scholars have argued that fair use cannot be applied in the live game streaming context because the market failure involved could be remedied by the parties' own actions (Fu, 2017; Xiong, 2018; Zhu, 2017). In their opinion, as the cost of obtaining permission to use the game images may be prohibitively high for individual streamers, streaming platform operators should instead be allowed to seek licenses, as this would simplify the permission process and thus streamline the functioning of the market. As streaming platform operators benefit the most from live streaming, their substantial revenues can reasonably be used to offset licensing fees. A proponent of this argument pointed out that "[t]o award fair use without regard to the possibility of imminent change in the market structure might be to make permanent an otherwise curable market failure and thus potentially to insulate a new and valuable use from the stimulus of consumer demand" (Gordon, 1982). Scholars taking this view have further argued that live game streaming was not at first expected to be a market for game developers, as live game webcasting through cable TV channels has been ongoing for more than 10 years[20] (Bi, 2015) and only in recent years has this peaceful relationship broken down. Given the substantial commercial benefits of live game streaming, almost all game developers in China today consider promoting live game streaming an important task when releasing new games.[21] Because "the potential market of a work is changeable and will expand with the emergence of new business models," fair use is not an effective defense

[20] In 2004 or so, live game streaming and broadcasting was showed in a China's cable TV channel called "Game Stormrider", and this channel soon became the most influential game channel in China.

[21] See 'A Big Test for Live Game Streaming: Tencent Released the Live Game Streaming Code of Conduct[游戏直播迎来大考, 腾讯发布游戏直播行为规范] (February 2019) <http://m.sohu.com/a/296205188_120099897> last visited December 30, 2024.

for copyright infringement involving live game streaming (Fu, 2017; Zhu, 2017). Granted, under the market-centered paradigm, market failure can be remedied and the market structure is changeable. Thus, live game streaming without authorization infringes the game developers' exclusive rights.

The transformative use paradigm was established by Judge Pierre Leval and first adopted by the US Supreme Court in the *Campbell* case in 1994. In the court's opinion, the concept of transformative use is central to a proper analysis of fair use (Campbell v. Acuff-Rose Music, 1994). "Transformative use" refers to the use of a work by "adding something new, with a further purpose or different character, altering the first with new expression, meaning, or message" giving the work new value, insights or meaning rather than simply superseding the original work (Campbell v. Acuff-Rose Music, 1994). Although transformative use often occurs in criticism or commentary with new expression added, Reese (2008) argued that "the focus of the transformative use rule is not how much the content of a work has been changed but how much its purpose". His study found that transformative use has been consistently defined by the US appellate courts as a use that was for "a new, different purpose," not a use that entailed "new expressive contributions" per se. The courts' statements in the *Google* case and the *Cariou* case strengthened this argument, emphasizing that a work need not produce "new expression, meaning, or message" to be transformative; the verbatim copying of a work for "a different, non-expressive purpose" can be a transformative use as well (Authors Guild Inc. v. Google Inc., 2013; Cariou v. Prince, 2013). In essence, this paradigm views fair use as "integral to copyright's purpose of promoting the widespread dissemination of creative expression, not a disfavored exception to copyright holders' exclusive rights" (Netanel, 2011). This view was expressed by the court in the *Campbell* case: "The goal of copyright is generally furthered by the creation of transformative works….The more transformative the new work, the less will be the significance of other factors, like commercialism, that may weigh against a finding of fair use" (Campbell v. Acuff-Rose Music, 1994).

The transformative use paradigm has come to be the prevailing view in fair use case law. According to Professor Netanel (2011), "during 2006–2010, 85.5% of district court opinions and 93.75%, or all but one, of appellate opinions considered whether the defendant's use was transformative." Although some scholars have suggested that transformative use is a post hoc justification used by courts to avoid the presumption of market harm attaching to commercial uses (Butterfield, 2018; Sag, 2015), the empirical data show that "courts have, in fact, embraced the transformative use doctrine as they have largely abandoned the commercial use presumptions, not that courts perceive it necessary to find transformative-ness in order to avoid the presumption that the commercial uses cause market harm"(Netanel, 2011). Netanel (2011) also showed that a use that is unequivocally transformative causes no market harm. This result arises not because transformative uses generally do no harm to the plaintiff's desired licensing market, but rather because the first factor (the purpose and character of the use) effectively delimits the legally relevant market for the fourth factor (the effect of the use upon the potential market). The allegedly infringing use "may not prejudice *the normal use* of the work, and may not unreasonably prejudice the lawful rights and interests of the copyright owner" (emphasis added) (PRC

Copyright Law art. 24 §1; *Regulations for the Implementation of the PRC Copyright Law* art. 21). If a use is unequivocally transformative, then, by definition, it causes no market harm, as the copyright owners only have the right to exclude others from the market for "normal use," not for transformative use (Bill Grahem Archives v. Dorling Kindersley Ltd., 2006).

### *6.4.4 Live Game Streaming Under the Transformative Use Paradigm*

As previously mentioned, whether a use is transformative depends upon whether it has a different expressive purpose from that for which the copyrighted work was created. "It is the relational difference between the two purposes that renders the defendant's use transformative, not the purpose or character of the defendant's use in and of itself" (Netanel, 2011). However, there are no dispositive rules regarding how different the defendant's expressive purpose must be from that of the author to qualify as transformative use. Besides, courts have discretion in how to characterize the author's and defendant's expressive purposes. In *Blanch v. Koons*, the court relied entirely on the defendant's own description of his expressive purpose. This approach, namely relying heavily on the defendant's statement of motive as the evidentiary basis for determining the expressive purposes of his use, has also been adopted by other courts (Bourne Co. v. Twentieth Century Fox Film Corp., 2009; Calkins v. Playboy, 2008; Salinger v. Colting (Salinger II), 2010).

However, courts have been urged to focus on viewers' response instead of the defendant's intention, as anti-intentionalists have warned of the defendant's interest in exaggerating or fabricating his transformative purpose (Heymann, 2008). Yet, the Supreme Court criticized this argument on the grounds that "there are a thousand Hamlets in a thousand people's eyes" (Levith, 2006) and the time and environment of viewing also affect the meaning of a work and viewers' perceptions of it (Pleasant Grove City v. Summum, 2009). Acknowledging the concerns on both sides, Picozzi (2017) suggested a dual-standard strategy to ascertain "whether the defendant intended to transform the copyrighted work and whether the accused work was actually transformative." Given the remarkable advantages of this strategy that "recognizes the need to avoid interfering with the defendant's communicative aims by looking into the defendant's intentions, while at the same time providing the viewers with an opportunity to influence the outcome of the fair use analysis" (Picozzi, 2017), I therefore use this approach to analyze the live game streaming issue.

To determine a defendant's intent to transform a game through live streaming, it is necessary to examine both the expressive purpose for which the game's developers created the game images and that for which the defendant used the game images. Game design is a complex process that requires artistic and technical competence as well as writing skills (Adams & Rollings, 2003). A game's images are an essential part of the work, which composes a combination of audiovisual elements, such as characters, sounds and text, and the game's rules and mechanics.[22] In general, game images serve two purposes. First, they allow gamers to interact with the virtual world. The various themes and rules of games must be expressed through game images such as displayed information and instruments. These elements determine the degree to which a player can interact with a game, and this interaction gives gamers satisfaction as they manipulate characters and complete various tasks according to the game's rules. Second, game images have aesthetic value. Good game designers usually have a good understanding of traditional art techniques and VG aesthetics and can design high-quality game images to provide rich gaming experiences for gamers. Game design and game art have become significantly more sophisticated, such that a character's actions adhere to a game's rules while remaining aesthetically pleasing and varied (Gee et al., 2019). From a game developer's perspective, therefore, the purpose of game images is to give players a better gaming experiences which in turn promotes game sales.

To determine live game streamers' expressive purpose in using original game images, I first turn to the defendant's statement in the *Fantasy Westward Journey* case as a reference.

> During live game streaming, gamers (streamers) usually show some fragments of the game images, accompanied by a large number of their own views on the game, so as to promote the communication with audiences. Hence live game streaming is a means of personal learning, research and appreciation in the network environment and is also a method of displaying the game for the purpose of introduction and commentary. What attracts the audiences in the live streaming context is not the game itself. Live game streaming helps extend the game play time of existing players and attracts new players to participate in the game. Some game companies even ask and pay for live streaming of their games. This shows that live streaming does not affect the interests of game developers, but rather, promotes their game sales..... ([2015] Yue Zhi Fa Zhu Civil Verdict No. 16)

Thus, from the defendant's perspective, original game images are used as raw materials by streamers to display their playing skills and as a basis for commentary. Personal images, humorous speech and fans' comments are added during the streaming process, enabling the game images to convey different messages. The attraction of live game streaming lies not in the original game images but in the gamers' playing strategies, the competitive atmosphere among players and streamers' commentary and interactions with viewers. Without streamers' involvement, the static game images would be meaningless in the live game streaming context. Streamers' purpose in using a game's original images (to demonstrate gaming strategies and offer a basis for commentary) thus clearly differs from the purpose for which the game developer created them (to enhance the gaming experience and thereby promote sales).

To test the above reasoning, I interviewed five game designers/developers, of whom three had their own streaming platforms. As streamers/gamers can be regarded as contributory infringers alongside streaming platform operators, I also interviewed

[22] See 'Video Game Design' <https://en.wikipedia.org/wiki/Video_game_design#cite_note-3> last visited December 30, 2024.

three individual streamers. Furthermore, as "the interpretation of a work is contextual, depending on how, and among whom, the work is situated" (Heymann, 2008), whether a work is actually transformative depends in part on the responses of "ordinary, reasonable observers" representing the audience targeted by the work (Litchfield v. Spielberg, 1984; Lyons P'ship, L.P. v. Morris Costumes, 2000). Thus, I also interviewed five gamers aged 20–30 who were familiar with playing VGs as well as watching live game streaming. Table 6.2 shows the results. As shown, the streaming platform operators and streaming gamers emphasized the importance of streamers' contributions, such as game operation skills, commentary and interactions with viewers; however, they also acknowledged the aesthetic value of the original game images. The streaming viewers described a variety of motivations for watching live game streaming: to learn game operation skills from streamers, to enjoy and learn about the plots of games and to chat with streamers to kill time. However, their main purpose in watching live game streaming was the same as their purpose in playing VGs: entertainment. Both groups admitted that without the original static game images and other materials, streamers could not operate the games and viewers could not understand the meaning behind them. According to this argument, although the original static game images and other materials are used by streamers for various specific purposes, the aesthetic value and function of these materials are not substantively transformed during streaming.

As no guidance available on how distinct a defendant's "new aesthetics" must be to qualify as transformative fair use, I distributed a self-administered questionnaire to game players aged 12–30 to explore the possible impact of watching live game streaming on the preexisting games market. The sample size of the survey was 1,190. Ultimately, 1,177 effective responses were analyzed by using SPSS software. I examined the correlation between the subjects' act of watching live game streaming and their associated behavior (purchasing, recommending, cognition, etc.). First,

**Table 6.2** Expressive purposes of game images for game developers, streamers and viewers

<table>
<tr><th rowspan="2">Expressive purposes of game images for game developers</th><th colspan="2">Expressive purposes of game images for streamers</th><th rowspan="2">Expressive purposes of game images for viewers<br>(other gamers)</th></tr>
<tr><th>Streaming platform operators</th><th>Streamers/ gamers</th></tr>
<tr><td>1. Provide tools enabling gamers to interact in the virtual world<br>2. Attract more gamers through aesthetically pleasing game images</td><td colspan="2">1. As raw materials helping to display gaming skills and as a basis for commentary<br>2. Combine with streamers' humorous speech and fans' comments to express new messages<br>3. Attract viewers and thus increase profit</td><td>1. Good game images and plots provide more enjoyable playing experiences<br>2. Live game streaming images enable viewers to learn operation skills from streamers, enjoy/learn about the plots of games or chat with streamers to kill time</td></tr>
</table>

I used Pearson's chi-square test to measure the correlation between watching live game streaming and playing VGs. The correlation was significant, with a chi-square value of 362.577 ($p < 0.001$). Next, the data on watching live game streaming were recoded to explore the correlation between this variable and subsequent gaming-related feelings and behavior. Watching live game streaming showed the strongest correlation with increased enthusiasm for the streamed VG, followed by increased gaming time and felling more passionate, then the act of purchasing/downloading or recommending the game, and finally a higher frequency of playing. In addition, approximately 92% of the respondents stated that watching live game streaming is not a substitute for playing VGs (Figs. 6.3 and 6.4).

These empirical data suggest that live game streaming poses little threat to the preexisting games market. On the contrary, it may play a marketing role, driving up sales of the games streamed and promoting the development of the games market in general. The viewers I surveyed generally expressed most interest in streamers

| | Value | df | Asymp. Sig. (2-sided) | Exact Sig. (2-sided) | Exact Sig. (1-sided) |
|---|---|---|---|---|---|
| Pearson Chi-Square | 362.577[a] | 1 | .000 | | |
| Continuity Correction[b] | 359.194 | 1 | .000 | | |
| Likelihood Ratio | 320.659 | 1 | .000 | | |
| Fisher's Exact Test | | | | .000 | .000 |
| Linear-by-Linear Association | 362.269 | 1 | .000 | | |
| N of Valid Cases | 1177 | | | | |

**Fig. 6.3** Correlation between watching live game streaming and playing VGs

| | | | Watching Live Game Streaming (Recoded) |
|---|---|---|---|
| Kendall's Tau B | Enthusiasm | Correlation Coefficient | .555** |
| | | Sig. (2-tailed) | .000 |
| | | N | 1177 |
| | Purchasing/Downloading | Correlation Coefficient | .438** |
| | | Sig. (2-tailed) | .000 |
| | | N | 1177 |
| | Recommending | Correlation Coefficient | .428** |
| | | Sig. (2-tailed) | .000 |
| | | N | 1177 |
| | Increase in Gaming Time | Correlation Coefficient | .497** |
| | | Sig. (2-tailed) | .000 |
| | | N | 1177 |
| | Increase in Frequency of Playing Game | Correlation Coefficient | .357** |
| | | Sig. (2-tailed) | .000 |
| | | N | 1177 |
| | Feeling More Passionate | Correlation Coefficient | .458** |
| | | Sig. (2-tailed) | .000 |
| | | N | 1177 |
| | Having Watched Live Game Streaming (Recoded) | Correlation Coefficient | 1.000 |
| | | Sig. (2-tailed) | . |
| | | N | 1177 |

**Fig. 6.4** Correlation between watching live game streaming and subsequent performance

who both play well and offer good entertainment value, such as by making jokes and commenting on pop culture and current events. They were less interested in watching live streaming of repetitive gameplay (Graziano, 2014). The results of the questionnaire indicate that after watching live streaming, most of the gamers were more enthusiastic about playing the streamed game, spent more time on gameplay or were more willing to buy or download the game. This explains why some game developers allow and even encourage players to stream their games. For example, when the *Fantasy Westward Journey* case had been settled ([2015] Civil Verdict No. 16 (IP) Guangdong), the CEO of the NetEase expressed a positive attitude toward live game streaming and revealed that the prosecution had been motivated by the large number of advertisements that the defendant had inserted into the streaming, diverting its viewers to another game.[23] The advertised game was of poor quality, and NetEase had been concerned that viewers might form a poor impression of the streamed game, thereby reducing its economic value. Nintendo has since scrapped the controversial Creators Program, making streaming easier for YouTubers. Under Nintendo's new guidelines, streamers are permitted to use gameplay footage and/or screenshots captured from its games as long as they add their own creative input and commentary.[24] Streamers can also monetize their channels using methods specified by Nintendo.

The above exploration is more inclined to support the argument that live game streaming successfully passes the dual-standard test to be considered transformative use. Under the transformative use paradigm, the third factor in the fair use four-factor test (the amount of the copyrighted work used by the defendant) becomes "a question not of whether the defendant took what is the most valuable part of the plaintiff's work, but rather whether the defendant used more than what was reasonable in light of the expressive purpose driving the transformative use" (Netanel, 2011). In most cases it is necessary for streamers to display the whole process of the game images to show their playing strategies and the competitive atmosphere. Thus, streaming counts as fair use under this factor. Likewise, the fourth factor (the effect of the use upon the potential market for or value of the copyrighted work) asks "not whether the use falls within a conceivable licensing market for the copyright owner as under the 'market centered' approach, but whether the copyright owner should be entitled to prevent others from entering the market for the use in question" (Netanel, 2011). Because live game streaming is transformative use and playing VGs cannot be substituted for by watching live game streaming from a reasonable audience's perspective, game developers should not be entitled to prevent others from entering the live game streaming market.

Yet, it may be argued that some game developers have already developed a licensing market for live game streaming and thus they should be entitled to prevent

[23] See 'The CEO of NetEase Company Interprets Financial Statement: Expressing Welcoming and Open Attitudes towards Live Game Streaming' (November 16, 2017), <http://bj-jysh.com/6713.html> last visited December 30, 2024.

[24] See Nintendo Game Content Guidelines for Online Video & Image Sharing Platforms (November 29, 2018), <https://www.nintendo.co.jp/networkservice_guideline/en/index.html?n> last visited December 30, 2024.

others from entering that market (Zhu, 2017). For example, Tencent states clearly that "live game streaming by an individual must obtain the authorization from the Tencent company."[25] Moreover, almost all game developers in China view promoting live game streaming as an important part of marketing new games. However, the US Court of Appeals for the Second Circuit stated in the *Bill Graham Archives* case, "[i]n a case such as this, a copyright holder cannot prevent others from entering fair use markets merely 'by developing or licensing a market for parody, news reporting, educational or other transformative uses of its own creative work'" (Bill Graham Archives v. Dorling Kindersley Ltd., 2006). This logic was also adopted by the Ninth Circuit Court of Appeals in *Perfect 10 v. Amazon*. In this case, the plaintiff's images were created for the purposes of art and entertainment, while the defendant, Google, used them as a pointer directing users to a source of information. Although the plaintiff began marketing thumbnails of its images for download to cell phones after filing its lawsuit, the court still refused to consider the plaintiff's cell phone market as a potential market that the plaintiff would reasonably enter, even in fact it was a market that the plaintiff had already entered. In its holding, it stated that "Google's display of thumbnail images is fair use, because such use is highly transformative and socially beneficial despite possible harm to the plaintiff's potential market for licensing thumbnails" (Perfect 10, Inc. v. Amazon, Inc., 2007). These two cases show the diminished scope and force of the fourth factor of the fair use test, as well as the fact that transformative uses are not considered to be part of the potential market of the original work. Furthermore, even if the copyright owner may enter or has already entered a licensing market for transformative uses of the work or if it is shown that he would be willing to license the use in question, he cannot prevent others from making such use.

### 6.4.5 Other Considerations

Although the transformative use doctrine presents a relatively straightforward standard for approaching fair use cases, a number of doctrinal issues remain open. First, while a transformative purpose is almost universally viewed as a sufficient condition for fair use, transformative use is not a necessary condition for fair use (Sarl Louis Feraud Int'l v. Viewfinder Inc., 2008). Yet, courts have not provided guidance as to when non-transformative use qualifies as fair use. Second, as courts have almost universally defined "transformative use" as using the copyrighted work for a fundamentally different expressive purpose, it remains uncertain "when and whether a defendant's highly creative incorporation of portions of a copyrighted work for the same general expressive purpose—art or entertainment—can qualify as fair use" (Netanel, 2011). Several cases have addressed instances of incorporating portions of

[25] See 'A Big Test for Live Game Streaming: Tencent Released the Live Game Streaming Code of Conduct[游戏直播迎来大考, 腾讯发布游戏直播行为规范] (February 2019) <http://m.sohu.com/a/296205188_120099897> last visited December 30, 2024.

copyrighted work, albeit with varying results. In the *Elvis Presley* case, the defendant was found to have used multiple short video clips of Elvis Presley's television appearances as raw materials and added narrative voice-overs and interviews to make a 16-h documentary about Presley (Elvis Presley Enterprises v. Passport Video, 2003). Although the Ninth Circuit referenced the transformative use doctrine, stating that works are transformative when they "use copyrighted materials for purposes distinct from the purpose of the original material," it characterized the use in question as "not consistently transformative" and found that the defendant had sought to "profit at least in part from the inherent entertainment value of Elvis appearances" on popular television shows (Elvis Presley Enterprises v. Passport Video, 2003). However, the Second Circuit in *Carious v. Prince* held that the appropriation artist Richard Prince's alteration of Patrick Cariou's copyrighted photographs in some of Prince's paintings and collages was transformative fair use (Carious v. Prince, 2013). The court reasoned that the new works "have a different character, give Cariou's photographs a new expression, and employ new aesthetics with creative and communicative results distinct from Cariou's." This ruling is particularly controversial, as the defendant's expressive purpose was avowedly the same as the plaintiff's —to create an artistic work—and Prince expressly disavowed any intention to criticize or comment on Cariou's work. Furthermore, the court gave little guidance as to how distinct a defendant's "new aesthetics" must be to qualify as transformative use.

Likewise, live game streaming is a means of self-expression from a streamer's perspective, and streamers and streaming platform operators use original game images as raw materials for commentary or jokes to attract and entertain viewers. However, the commentary generally focuses not on the game itself but on the player's or players' skills and strategies or on something else entirely. More broadly, game images are incorporated into the live streaming process by streamers for the same general expressive purposes as the original game, namely art and entertainment. Construing transformative use more narrowly, as the Ninth Circuit did in the *Elvis Presley* case, live game streaming may fail to qualify as transformative use, while under a broader interpretation, as applied by the Second Circuit in the *Cariou* case, it may be considered transformative.

## 6.5 Statutory Licensing Model as an Alternative: Turning Infringement into Profit

Transformative fair use thus is not a reliable defense for streamers or streaming platform operators against infringement claims. Even if live game streaming passes the transformative use test, there are several loopholes in this doctrine that may lead to unpredictable court outcomes. The market correction goal of the fair use doctrine may alternatively be addressed by a regulatory solution such as a statutory licensing or compulsory licensing scheme (Gordon, 1982; Netanel, 2008).[26] In situations where it is necessary to use a work but the finding of fair use may unfairly neglect the copyright owner's efforts, a licensing regulation allows for unauthorized public use of the work with compensation to the copyright holder (PRC Copyright Law art.25). I believe that such a mechanism can be established for licensing games for use in live game streaming. For one thing, providing game developers with strong exclusive rights to control the act of live streaming their games would be overly restrictive of gamers' freedom of expression, and the need to negotiate licenses would result in high transaction costs. Such exclusive rights could also result in monopolies in the live game streaming industry and thus restrict competition, which would be conducive neither to free competition nor to the sustainable development of the industry. It is said that approximately 89% of live game streaming revenue goes into the pocket of game developers (Qiu, 2019). For another, from the perspective of the business model of live game streaming, substantial revenues are mainly obtained from advertising via network flow, as well as from viewers. As game development requires considerable financial investment over a short period, in the interest of fairness, part of the revenue from live game streaming should be distributed to game developers. Such payment would also serve as an incentive for game developers to design games specifically for live streaming, further promoting the industry.

To address the aforementioned concerns of public interest, transaction costs and the potential profits of the live game streaming market, I propose a new statutory licensing mechanism designed specifically for live game streaming. Referencing to the general conditions to establish limitations or exceptions to exclusive rights set forth in Article 13 of the TRIPS Agreement that "(1) confined to certain special cases; (2) do not conflict with normal exploitation of the work; and (3) do not unreasonably prejudice the legitimate interests of the right holder," I outline the proposed statutory licensing scheme for live game streaming below.

### *6.5.1 Proposed Statutory License for Live Game Streaming: Scope and Application*

The TRIPS Agreement criterion that limitations or exceptions to copyrights be confined to certain special cases (art. 13 (1)) requires a statutory license to "be clearly defined" and "to be narrow in a quantitative as well as a qualitative sense" (Chow & Lee, 2012). Thus, my proposed licensing scheme is limited to cases in which a video game work has been published and uploaded to the Internet by the copyright owner independently and directly. This excludes VGs that are distributed only on CD or other hard carriers, as these games are considered more private and improper for

[26] In common law jurisdictions, many countries only adopt the compulsory license without statutory license, or regard compulsory license and statutory license as two types of a system—judicially compulsory licensing and statutory compulsory licensing; while some civil law countries regard the statutory license as a kind of fair use system.

the statutory license. The proposed statutory license would be obtained automatically by an end user's accepting a subscriber agreement with the game developer when downloading or logging a VG published by a game developer on the Internet. The license would grant a gamer the right to transmit the game content to others or perform to the public through online streaming and would impose a duty to pay proper remuneration to the game developer as prescribed in regulations.

### 6.5.2 Remuneration

Generally, streamers bear the responsibility to pay remuneration to game developers (PRC Copyright Law art. 38). Under my proposed licensing scheme, however, streaming platform operators would pay remuneration. There are several reasons for this suggestion. First, it is extremely inconvenient for game publishers to collect remuneration from every streamer, given the large number of streamers. Second, streaming platform operators benefit the most from the game streaming industry. In tournament streaming, the streaming platform operator plays the roles of investor and organizer and is generally responsible for every tournament, investing considerable time and money to build a brand, attract users and negotiate contracts with famous game anchors and players. As for individual streaming, the streaming platform operator also makes agreements with streamers regarding the shared proportion of the revenue. In both tournament and individual streaming, the operator takes a larger share of the revenue than the streamers do. Additionally, the streaming images are fixed on and transmitted through the operator's streaming platforms. Therefore, streaming platform operators' legal status may be compared to that of film producers, as they control the development of the live game streaming industry, whereas game anchors and players are more like actors and have the legal status of performers. Their contractual relationship is comparable to an employer-employee relationship. Thus, the copyrights to any fixed streaming content belong to the streaming platform operators, and as such the streaming platform operators have rights to prevent others from rebroadcasting and transcribing the streaming content without permission. For consistency in rights and obligations, therefore, under my scheme streaming platform operators would be responsible for paying remuneration. This would also greatly reduce transaction costs and improve the efficiency of transmitting.

The PRC Copyright Law does not provide detailed guidance as to standards for remuneration. However, Article 4(1) of the *Measures for Paying Remuneration for the Use of Written Works* provides that "the remuneration standard of original work shall be 3–10% of sales." Referencing to this standard and the business model of live game streaming industry, my proposed scheme includes the provision that the remuneration shall be 20–30% of streaming income for tournament streaming and 10% for individual streaming, including subscription fees in any form and revenue derived from advertising associated with the particular live game stream on the game streaming website. This remuneration would be collected from the streaming platform operator directly on a weekly or monthly basis. As Chow (2012) noted, "prejudice to the legitimate interests of right holders reaches an unreasonable level if an exception or limitation causes or has the potential to cause an unreasonable loss of income to the copyright owner." The proposed remuneration standard would ensure game developers' right to remuneration and the proposed licensing scheme would facilitate advertising of their games, both promoting the legitimate interests of the game developers as copyright holders.

### 6.5.3 *Right of Cancellation for Game Developers*

In some circumstances, live game streaming can damage the reputation of the streamed games. I thus include a right of cancellation in the proposed scheme, permitting game developers to prohibit undesirable streaming of their games to protect their economic interests. Under the scheme, the streaming platform operator would have three days following notice from the game developer in which to transfer that notice to the streamer and shut down the undesirable streaming. By involving streaming platform operators and setting limits on streamers' behavior, the right of cancellation would further protect the interests of the copyright owners and increase game developers' acceptance of licensing. Indeed, streaming promotes game developers' interests by serving as a form of advertising, attracting potential purchasers without conflicting with the normal exploitation of the game by selling the "right to play the game" or peripheral products. Any potential harm caused by live game streaming to the original game market could be addressed by the right of cancellation. However, the cancellation right would only be permitted to avoid such economic harms to the game developers, as unrestricted rights to cancellation would potentially harm streaming platform operators. Therefore, the cancellation right further respects the stakeholders' legitimate interests and would not conflict with the normal exploitation of the games.

### 6.5.4 *Further Considerations*

Traditionally, Chinese law has given copyright owners the power to opt out of statutory licensing. Under Article 23 of the PRC Copyright Law (2021), statutory licensing shall not be applied in cases where the copyright owner "has declared in advance that the exploitation is not permitted." Copyright owners' power to opt out is meant to address the fact that the statutory licensing ignores their willingness to grant licenses and makes them surrender their rights (Wang, 2011). However, a statutory license is a form of compulsory license stipulated by law for the sake of public interest, specifically to solve the problem of market failure resulting from high transaction costs. In this sense, neither statutory licenses nor compulsory licenses in general are optional from a theoretical perspective, as granting absolute power to opt out renders such licensing powerless to protect the public interest. This is why most countries do not permit opting out of compulsory or statutory licensing mechanisms (Guan, 2015). China's "statutory license + opt-out" mechanism has existed for more than 20 years without any effective outcomes (Liang, 2010). Given these facts, the amended PRC Copyright Law (2021) does not allow copyright owners to opt out of statutory licensing (art. 25). Similarly, I do not include an opt-out system in my proposed statutory licensing scheme for live game streaming.

Another consideration concerns the rights of VG streamers or players. As described above, the legal status of streamers and players is similar to that of performers. In general, streaming platform operators sign contracts with streamers, agreeing to pay them a certain amount of remuneration or to give them a specified portion of the revenue from their streaming. In these contracts, performers grant a license or transfer their rights or have their rights sub-licensed to other parties for exploitation in exchange for remuneration. However, streamers are in a relatively weak position when signing such contracts, and their "contractual freedom" is mainly symbolic. There is thus a need to protect these performers' interests. The Directive on Copyright in the Digital Singles Market (also known as "EU Copyright Directive") approved by the European Parliament offers an example of such protections.[27] First, under this directive, performers are entitled to receive appropriate and proportionate remuneration equivalent to the actual or potential economic value of the licensed or transferred rights. The amount of remuneration can be calculated by taking into account the performer's contribution to the overall work and other factors, such as market practices or the actual exploitation of the work. When implementing this principle, parties should be free to use different mechanisms, such as collective bargaining, and should promote contractual freedom as well as balance the rights and interests of the parties (EU Copyright Directive art. 18). Second, as performers tend to be in a relatively weak contractual position, they should be entitled to request relevant information to accurately assess the continued economic value of their rights (EU Copyright Directive art. 19). In the context of live game streaming, streaming platform operators should provide streamers with information on all modes of exploitation and on all relevant revenues worldwide with a regularity appropriate to the relevant sector, and at least annually, for as long as the exploitation of the streaming content is ongoing. This information should be provided in a manner that is comprehensible to streamers and allows for the effective assessment of the economic value of their rights. It should be noted that these concerns do not arise when a streamer enters into an employment contract with a streaming platform operator.

[27] The Directive on Copyright in the Digital Singles Market (also known as "EU Copyright Directive") was approved by the European Parliament on March 26, 2019.

## 6.6 Conclusion

Live game streaming has become immensely popular over the last few years. However, as most streaming content is based on original game images used without authorization, the industry risks incurring copyright infringement claims based on the right of performance or the derivative right held by game developers. When sued for infringement, most streamers seek to apply the fair use doctrine as a defense, especially from the transformative use perspective. An in-depth exploration of this doctrine as applied in the live game streaming context reveals that the doctrine does not offer reliable protection, although live game streaming slightly passes the dual-standard test to be considered transformative use. To protect public interest, lower transaction costs and fairly distribute the considerable profits of live game streaming, I propose a new statutory licensing mechanism specifically for live game streaming. Under this mechanism, streamers would be allowed to stream games without permission and remuneration would be paid to game developers. The proposed scheme would grant streaming platform operators copyrights to any streaming content, providing them with the exclusive rights to prevent others from rebroadcasting or transcribing the streaming content. As such, the streaming platform operators would bear the obligation to remunerate game developers. The licensing scheme would equip game developers with the right of cancellation to prohibit streaming that threatens to harm the game developers' interests. The proposed scheme would extend the scope of statutory licensing to cover the network environment, effectively reducing transaction costs and improving licensing efficiency compared with traditional "one-to-one" licensing. Besides, it would protect the live game streaming industry by legitimizing it while also respecting and promoting the rights and economic interests of game developers. Thus, my proposed statutory licensing scheme would achieve a mutually beneficial balance between game developers, streamers and streaming platform operators.

## References


Adams, E., & Rollings, A. (2003). *Andrew Rollings and Ernest Adams on Game Design* (pp. 20, 22–25). New Riders Publishing.

Beebe, B. (2008). An Empirical Study of U.S. Copyright Fair Use Opinions, 1978–2005. *University of Pennsylvania Law Review, 156*, 549, 582–586, 621.

Bi, Y. [毕颜彬]. (2015). Live Game Streaming: Next 10 Billion Market?[游戏直播,下一个百亿市场?]. *Journal of Publishers [出版人]*, (5), 64–65.

Butterfield, T. (2018). Moving Beyond Transformativeness: How Courts Evaluate the Purpose and Character of Secondary Uses. *Journal of Copyright Society of the U.S.A., 65*, 147, 159.

Chow, D. C. K., & Lee, E. (2012). *International Intellectual Property Problems, Cases, and Materials* (2nd ed., pp. 184, 194). Thomson Reuters.

Eliot, T. S. (1960). Philip Massinger. *The Sacred Wood: Essays on Poetry and Criticism* (Vol. 123, p. 125). Methuen & Co.

Feng, X. [冯晓青]. (2017). Study on the Copyright Attribute of Online Game Live Streaming Images and the Related Copyright Issues[网络游戏直播画面的作品属性及其相关著作权问题研究]. *Intellectual Property[知识产权]*, (1), 11, 12.

Fu, G. [傅钢]. (2017). Discussion on Fair Use in Live Streaming by Professional Live Game Platforms[专业网游直播平台直播中"合理使用"问题的探讨]. *Zhichanli[知产力]*.

Gee, L. L. S., Dolah, J., & Pangayan, V. B. (2019). Visual Preferences for Educational Game Designs Through the Graphic Style Approaches. *Journal Gendang Alam*. https://doi.org/10.51200/ga.vi.2181.

Geeter, D. (2019). Twitch Created a Business around Watching Video Games—Here's How Amazon Has Changed The Service Since Buying IT In 2014. CNBC. Available at: https://www.cnbc.com/2019/02/26/history-of-twitch-gaming-livestreaming-and-youtube.html. Accessed 30 December 2024.

Good, O. S. (2015). Bigtime YouTuber Says Enough is Enough; He Won't Do any More Nintendo Videos. Available at: https://www.polygon.com/2015/4/4/8344341/angry-joe-nintendo-takedown-mario-party. Accessed 30 December 2024.

Gordon, W. J. (1982). Fair Use as Market Failure: A Structural and Economic Analysis of the Betamax Case and Its Predecessors. *Columbia Law Review, 82*, 1600, 1601, 1613, 1614, 1615, 1616, 1620, 1627.

Graziano, D. (2014). The Complete Guide to Streaming Games on Twitch. Available at: https://www.cnet.com/how-to/the-complete-guide-to-streaming-games-on-twitch/. Accessed 30 December 2024.

Guan, Y. [管育鹰]. (2015). Reflection and Reconstruction of Copyright Statutory License System in China [我国著作权法定许可制度的反思与重构]. *Journal of East China University of Political Science and Law[华东政法大学学报]*, (2), 22.

Gutelle, S. (2017). Nintendo Bars Its YouTube Partners From Monetizing Their Live Streams. Available at: https://www.tubefilter.com/2017/10/02/nintendo-youtube-creator-program-live-stream/. Accessed 30 December 2024.

Heymann, L. A. (2008). Everything is Transformative: Fair Use and Reader Response. *Columbia Journal of Law & Arts, 31*, 445, 449, 447.

Iqbal, M. (2020). Twitch Revenue and Usage Statistics. Available at: https://www.businessofapps.com/data/twitch-statistics/. Accessed 30 December 2024.

Jewell, C. (2012). Video Games: 21st Century Art. *WIPO Magazine*. Available at: http://www.wipo.int/wipo_magazine/en/2012/04/article_0003.html. Accessed 30 December 2024.

Jiang, Y. [蒋一可]. (2019). Research on Copyright Issues of Online Game Live Streaming—Taking the Legal Identity of the Anchor and the Rationality of Live Streaming Behavior as the Object [网络游戏直播著作权问题研究—以主播法律身份与直播行为之合理性为对象]. *Law Science Magazine*[法学杂志], (7), 131–133.

Joo, J. (2011). Public Video Gaming as Copyright Infringement. *American Intellectual Property Law Association Quarterly Journal, 39*, 563.

Jungar, E. (2016). Streaming Video Games: Copyright Infringement or Protected Speech? *Press Start, 3*(2), 23, 24, 38.

Landes, W. M. (2003). *The Economic Structure of Intellectual Property Law* (pp. 137–148). Harvard University Press.

Levith, M. J. (2006). *Shakespeare in China* (pp. 4–16). Continuum.

Liang, Z. [梁志文]. (2010). The "Opt-Out" System in Copyright Law and Its Legitimacy[版权法上的"选择退出"制度及其合法性问题]. *The Science of Law [法学]*, (6), 25.

Li, Y. [李扬]. (2017). Copyright Issues Surrounding Live Streaming of Online Games[网络游戏直播中的著作权问题]. *Intellectual Property[知识产权]*, (1).

Liu, Y. [刘银良]. (2019). Miscellaneous Provision of Copyright [著作权兜底条款的是非与选择]. *Science of Law[法学], 11*, 127–128, 134.

Liu, Y. [刘银良]. (2020). Analysis of the Legal Relationship of Online Game Live Streaming[网络游戏直播的法律关系解析]. *Intellectual Property [知识产权]*, (3), 24.

Matsui, S. (2016). Does it Have to Be a Copyright Infringement: Live Game Streaming and Copyright. *Texas Intellectual Property Law Journal, 24*, 215, 231, 244.

Netanel, N. W. (2008). *Copyright's Paradox* (p. 198). Oxford University Press.

Netanel, N. (2011). Making Sense of Fair Use. *Lewis & Clark Law Review, 15*(3), 715, 734, 744, 736, 742, 745, 748, 749–750.

Ou, X. [欧修平], Sun, M. [孙明飞], & Wu, D. [吴东亮]. (2015). Research on the First Case of Live Game Streaming in China: Attribute of Rights and Distribution of Responsibility[庖解中国网络游戏直播第一案:权利属性及责任归属]. *Zhichanli[知产力]*. Available at: http://news.zhichanli.cn/article/1431.html. Accessed 30 December 2024.

Picozzi, B. (2017). What's Wrong with Intentionalism? Transformative Use, Copyright Law, and Authorship. *The Yale Law Journal, 126*, 1408, 1451.

Posner, R. (1977). *Economic Analysis of Law* (2d ed., pp. 3–12).

Puddington, J. (2015). Fair Play: Economic Justifications for Applying Fair Use to the Online Streaming of Video games. *Boston University Journal of Science & Technology Law, 21*, 413.

Qiu, Y. (2017). A Cure for Twitch: Compulsory License Promoting Video Game Live-Streaming. *Marquette Intellectual Property Law Review, 21*, 31, 39.

Qiu, Z. (2019). Evolution of E-sports Industrial Chain: 90% of Revenue Taken by Game Companies. Available at: https://www.yicai.com/news/100251147.html. Accessed 30 December 2024.

Rapoza, K. (2019). Global Esports Popularity Give Gamer Companies Reason to Be Bullish. Available at: https://www.forbes.com/sites/kenrapoza/2019/05/29/global-esports-popularity-give-gamer-companies-reason-to-be-bullish/#1c12a3181bde. Accessed 30 December 2024.

Reese, A. (2008). Transformativeness and the Derivative Work Right. *Columbia Journal of Law & the Arts, 31*(4), 467, 485.

Rogers, J. (2012). Crafting an Industry: An Analysis of Korean StarCraft and Intellectual Properties Law. *Harvard Journal of Law and Technology Digest*. Available at: https://jolt.law.harvard.edu/digest/crafting-an-industry-an-analysis-of-korean-starcraft-and-intellectual-properties-law. Accessed 20 November 2019.

Sag, M. (2015). Copyright Trolling: An Empirical Study. *Iowa Law Review, 100*, 1105, 1122, 1116.

Stim, R. (2023). Fair Use: The Four Factors Courts Consider in a Copyright Infringement Case. Available at: https://www.nolo.com/legal-encyclopedia/fair-use-the-four-factors.html. Accessed 30 December 2024.

Tryndamere. (2015). Spectate Faker—What We Learned and What We'll Do. Available at: https://na.leagueoflegends.com/en/news/riot-games/announcements/spectatefaker-what-we-learned-and-what-well-do. Accessed 30 December 2024.

Wang, Q. [王迁]. (2011). Study on "Statutory License for Making Sound Recordings" and Its Reconstruction in Chinese Copyright Law[论"制作录音制品法定许可"及在我国著作权法中的重构]. *Oriental Law[东方法学]*, (6).

Wang, Q. [王迁]. (2016). Study on the Copyright Issues of Live Streaming of Video Game [电子游戏直播的著作权问题研究]. *Electronics Intellectual Property[电子知识产权]*, (2).

WIPO. (1981 [reprinted 1999]). *Guide to the Rome Convention and to the Phonograms Convention*. WIPO Publication No. 617 (E), para 3.1.

Xie, L. [谢琳]. (2017). Study on the Copyright Fair Use of Live Streaming of video Games[网络游戏直播的著作权合理使用研究]. *Intellectual Property[知识产权]*, (1).

Xiong, W. [熊文聪]. (2018). "Fair Use" Defense in Live Game Straming[网游直播"合理使用"辩]. *Zhichanli[知产力]*. See Zhu Jianjun[祝建军](n 50), p. 25.

Zhu, J. [祝建军]. (2017). Study on the Copyright Issues Surrounding Live Streaming of Online Games[网络游戏直播的著作权问题研究]. *Intellectual Property[知识产权]*, (1).

## Legislations

Beijing Treaty on Audiovisual Performances (BJTAP)

Berne Convention for the Protection of Literary and Artistic Works (1886)
Directive on Copyright in the Digital Singles Market (EU Copyright Directive)
Intellectual Property Code of France
Measures for Paying Remuneration for the Use of Written Works (2014)
PRC Civil Code (2021)
PRC Copyright Law (2021)
Regulation for the Implementation of the PRC Copyright Law (2013 Revision)
Rome Convention
TRIPS Agreement
US Constitution
US Copyright Act
WIPO Copyright Treaty (WCT)
WIPO Performances and Phonograms Treaty (WPPT)

## *Cases*

Allen v. Academic Games League of Am., Inc., 89 F. 3d 614, 616 (9th Cir. 1996).
Authors Guild Inc. v. Google Inc., 721 F. 3d 132, (2nd Cir. 2013).
Authors Guild Inc. v. Google Inc., 954 F. Supp. 2d 282, 289–291(S.D.Y.2013).
Authors Guild Inc. v. Hathi Trust, 902 F. Supp. 2d 445 (S.D.N.Y. 2012) (No. 11 Civ. 6351).
Bill Graham Archives v. Dorling Kindersley Ltd., 448 F.3d 605, 614–615 (2d Cir. 2006)
Blanch v. Koons, 467 F. 3d 247, 253 (2d Cir. 2006).
Bourne Co. v. Twentieth Century Fox Film Corp., 602 f. Supp. 2d 499, 507–508 (S.D.N.Y.2009).
Calkins v. Playboy, 561 F. Supp. 2d 1136 (2008).
Campbell v. Acuff-Rose Music, Inc., 510 U.S. 569, 579 (1994).
Campbell v. Acuff-Rose Music, Inc., 510 U.S. 569, 591 (1994).
Cariou v. Prince, 714 F. 3d 694, 698–99 (2d Cir. 2013).
Carious v. Prince, 714 F. 3d 694 (2nd Cir. 2013).
Divided Court, 420 U.S. 376 (1975) (per curiam).
Elvis Presley Enterprises v. Passport Video, 349 F. 3d 622 (9th Cir. 2003).
Harper & Row, Publishers, Inc. v. National Enterprises, 471 U.S. 539, 566, 568 (1985).
House Report Rep. No.1476, 94th Cong., 2d Sess. 65 (1976) reprinted in 1976 U.S. Code Cong. & Ad. News at 5679.
Litchfield v. Spielberg, 736 F. 2d 1352, 1356 (9th Cir. 1984).
Lyons P'ship, L.P. v. Morris Costumes, Inc., 243 E. 3d 789, 801 (4th Cir. 2000).
NetEase v. Guangzhou Huaduo, [2015] Yue Zhi Fa Zhu Civil Verdict No. 16 [(2015) 粤知法著民初字第16号民事判决书]; [2018] Yue Civil Final No. 137 [(2018) 粤民终137号].
Perfect 10, Inc. v. Amazon, Inc., 508 F. 3d 1146 (9th Cir. 2007).
Pleasant Grove City v. Summum, 555 U.S. 460, 477 (2009).
Red Baron-Franklin Park v. Taito, 883 F. 2d 275 (4th Cir.1989).
Salinger v. Colting (Salinger II), 607 F. 3d 68, 72–73 (2d Cir. 2010).
Salinger v. Random House, 811 F. 2d 90 (2d Cir. 1987).
Sarl Louis Feraud Int'l v. Viewfinder Inc., 627 F. Supp. 2d 123, 128 (S.D.N.Y.2008).
Shanghai Fine Arts Film Studio[上海美术电影制片厂] v. Zhejiang New Film Age Culture Communication Co., Ltd and others[浙江新影年代文化传播有限公司等], [2015] Shanghai IP Court Civil Final No. 730[沪知民终字第730号].
Shanghai Yaoyu Culture Media Co. v. Guangzhou Douyu Network Technology Co., [2015] Civil Verdict No.191 (IP) People's Court of Pudong New Area of Shanghai[上海市浦东新区人民法院(2015)浦民三(知)初字第191号民事判决书]; [2015] Shanghai (IP) Civil Verdict (Final) No. 641[(2015) 沪知民终字第641号].

Shanghai Zhuangyou Information Technology Co. v. Guangzhou Shuoxing Information Technology Co. and others, [2015] Civil Verdict No.529 (IP) People's Court of Pudong New Area of Shanghai [上海市浦东新区人民法院 (2015) 浦民三(知)初字第529号民事判决书].
Sony Corp. of America v. Universal City Studios, Inc.464 U.S. 417 (1984).
Sony Corporation of America v. Universal City Studios, Inc.464 U.S. 451, 417 (1984).
Wang Xin[王莘] v. Google Co., Ltd. and others[谷歌公司等], [2011]1st Intermediate People's Court of Beijing Civil Verdict No. 1321[一中民初第1321号].
Williams & Wilkins Co. v. United States, 487 F.2d 1345, 1359 (Ct. Cl. 1973), aff'd by an equally.

# Chapter 7
# Balancing Creative Expression and Societal Well-Being: A Comprehensive Regulatory Framework for the Chinese Video Game Industry

**Abstract** This chapter presents a comprehensive regulatory framework aimed at balancing creative expression and societal well-being. It first provides a historical overview of the administrative regulation mechanism for copyrighted works, including the origins of governmental censorship and copyright, the historical debate on governmental censorship of copyrighted works and the history of the legal basis for China's copyright administrative regulatory system. Next, it explores the inadequacy of the current administrative regulation mechanism for VGs in China, including the content censorship system and the quasi-content rating system, from both theoretical and practical perspectives. The chapter proceeds to examine the regulation mechanisms for VGs in other jurisdictions—those in North America, the EU, Germany, Japan and South Korea. It then proposes a new administrative regulation mechanism for the VG industry in China in three parts: establishing a new rating system, improving the censorship system and enacting a new gaming law. Implementing this new regulation mechanism would help resolve the conflict between incentivizing creation and protecting public interests to promote the sustainable development of the VG industry.

**Keywords** Addictive potential · Creative expression · Societal well-being · Content censorship system · Administrative regulatory framework

## 7.1 Introduction

Creative industries represent one of the most rapidly expanding sectors worldwide. One such industry, the video game (VG) industry, showcases and supports traditional knowledge and culture while generating innovation as well as wealth for society. IP rights, particularly copyrights, are critical to the development of the VG industry, as they promote the creation of and public access to content while returning value to creators. However, administrative regulatory policy also plays a crucial role in the development of the VG industry. Although increasingly popular, VGs are also controversial due to provocative and objectionable content, such as graphic violence,



Z. Deng, *Constructing an Eco-Balanced Copyright Regime for the Video Game Industry in China*, https://doi.org/10.1007/978-981-96-6056-8_7

virtual sex, nudity and portrayal of criminal activity, as well as links between VGs and addiction and aggression.[1] VG Advocators argue for their protection under laws governing free speech, emphasizing their use as an expressive medium or educational tool, while dissenters assert that VGs are harmful and therefore should be subject to legislative oversight and restrictions. Research has examined the links between VGs and addiction, aggression, violence, social development and a variety of stereotyping and sexual morality problems. The development of problematic VG use is a complex process with many contributing factors (Kuss & Griffiths, 2012). There is no consensus on exactly how problematic VGs are; however, many scholars have claimed that video gaming has a high addictive potential and may thus cause serious harm to minors (King et al., 2010, 2011). Indeed, to encourage repeated play, game developers rely on psychological mechanisms that promote player investment on a long-term basis when designing games (Charlton & Danforth, 2007), as the objective of this profit-oriented industry is to create games that are played by as many gamers as possible for as long as possible. In China, VG opponents have called for the complete prohibition of VGs, arguing that gaming distracts players from learning and results in poor academic performance (Lee, 2017). In June 2018, "gaming disorder" was added to the ICD by the WHO (Scutti, 2018).

The tension between promoting the industry and limiting its negative influence on society urgently requires attention as VGs become increasingly popular (King, 2010). However, gaming addiction has risen over several years with no decisive action taken by Chinese society or legislators. Many Chinese scholars have suggested remedies, but their views have more or less coincided with the perspectives of critics, addressing this issue from the perspectives of the family and school (Zhang et al., 2020; Lin et al., 2021; Sun, 2020; Zhou, 2020), or calling for stronger governmental supervision and improved legislation in the concluding remarks without providing specific and feasible countermeasures (Gong Yuhua, 2020; Chang Yajie, 2019). Some policymakers have recognized the importance of administrative regulatory measures to safeguard the sustainable development of copyrighted works; however, they have tended to rely on the current content censorship system rather than introduce reforms to address problems with gaming (Kang, 2019a, 2019b). Therefore, in this chapter I articulate the need for a new administrative regulation mechanism to help balance the public interest with incentivizing creation in the VG industry. Section 6.2 provides a historical overview of the administrative regulation mechanism for copyrighted works. Section 6.3 explains the inadequacy of the current administrative regulation mechanism for VGs in China—the content censorship system and the quasi-content rating system—from theoretical and practical perspectives. Section 6.4 explores the regulation mechanisms for VGs in other jurisdictions: North America, the EU, Germany, Japan and South Korea. Section 6.5 concludes with some suggestions for a new administrative regulation mechanism for the VG industry in China.

[1] See 'Video Game Content Rating System' <https://en.wikipedia.org/wiki/Video_game_content_rating_system> last visited December 30, 2024.

## 7.2 Administrative Regulation of Copyrighted Works: A Historical Overview

### *7.2.1 Origins of Government Censorship and Copyright*

Government censorship existed long before the emergence of copyright. Governments are entrusted by the public to carry out certain responsibilities and to act in the public's interest, or at least in accordance with a selection of the public's demands (Roberts, 2018). Governments thus have an incentive to promote particular type of information to their constituents and to control or prevent the consumption of other information, especially information revealing the government's shortcomings. Thus, "censorship could be seen as a signal that the political entity has something to hide and is not in fact acting as an agent for citizens" (Roberts, 2018).

Before the advent of print in England, ideas were primarily disseminated orally and via script. As copies of ecclesiastical literature were created by church scribes, the church and the state to which it was closely allied fully controlled manuscripts and their content (Ghosh, 2013). There was no sense of individual ownership of these manuscripts; the scribes and writers were granted only limited compensation for their efforts. By the sixteenth century, the growth of education and the demand for cheaper books had given rise to the printing industry. Like other manufacturers, printers sought to avoid competition and maximize profit from their capital investment; they thus demanded a law to protect the act of book publishing. Printers' guilds' demand for monopolies over the books they printed, combined with continued church and state control over potentially seditious materials, resulted in the earliest forms of copyright legislation (Ghosh, 2013).

The idea of "copyright" thus first emerged as a system to balance the need to incentivize printers to bring literature to the public domain against the need to control the content of such literature. The 1709 Statute of Anne, entitled "An Act for the Encouragement of Learning, by vesting the Copies of Printed Books in the Authors or purchasers of such Copies," recognized that making information accessible to the public encouraged the creation of further works. The law restricted the copyright period to 14 years and permitted the establishment of Circulating Public Libraries, recognizing both the need for free access to information and the need to incentivize the act of bringing information and knowledge into the public domain. Initially, local councils held the power to grant copyright protection, and the conditions for protection often varied substantially, even within jurisdictions. It was not until 1886 that the first move to develop an international standard of copyright was undertaken in the Berne Convention. Followed the establishment of the World Intellectual Property Organization (WIPO) in 1967, the TRIPS Agreement was enacted in 1995 as the most uniform charter to establish an international copyright regime. Copyright laws have grown in scope and severity over time, coming to encompass almost all forms of creative expression. What initially was only the right to copy is now extended to the right to control the usage of a work in any form. Under the TRIPS Agreement, the copyright period was extended to 50 years after the death of the author (Ghosh, 2013).

### *7.2.2 History of US Government Censorship of Copyrighted Works*

As governments may have an interest in controlling the flow of information, government censorship can be regarded as "the restriction of the public expression of or public access to information by authority when the information is thought to have capacity to undermine the authority by making it accountable to the public" (Roberts, 2018). Although censorship is a well-established tradition, its threat to free speech has long been debated, especially in the US. In the Progressive Era, when moving picture technology allowed the mass dissemination of lifelike moving images for the first time, it spawned the so-called "moral panic" (Wittern-Keller, 2008). At that time, censorship carried positive connotations for many, who felt that it "would benefit society by keeping profit-driven movie producers from eroding the proper division between the private realm and the public world, destroying young or impressionable minds in the process and demeaning intimate personal relationships." Censorship of motion pictures thus reflected the willingness of many Americans to restrain seemingly dangerous or threatening ideas for the public good, and it was not considered as a free speech issue at the time. Furthermore, following the English practice of denying copyright protection to illicit works, US courts initially also denied the copyrightability of offending works. In particular, the "clean hands doctrine" was borrowed by early US courts to refuse claims for injunction. This doctrine, as applied to copyrights, states that "illicit content of the work as unclear hands disqualifies its copyright owner from the injunction remedy at equity court" (Zhang & Li, 2015). Later, under the Copyright Clause of the US Constitution (art. I, §8, cl. 8), the illegal or immoral content of works was considered not to promote "the progress of science and useful arts," and thus offending works were not considered copyrightable (Martinetti v. Maguire, 1867; Barnes v. Miner, 1903).

Nevertheless, public awareness of fascisms during World War II and evolving jurisprudence over the meaning of the First Amendment caused a change in attitude toward censorship (Wittern-Keller, 2008). Having witnessed the repressive nature of totalitarianism, liberals began to move away from the communitarian ideals of the Progressive Era toward the veneration of individual rights, or "the concern for personal freedom" (Wittern-Keller, 2008). A society once based on control shifted gradually to a society based on "expressive individualism," or, as some have argued, "excessive individualism" (Wittern-Keller, 2008). As Justice Brennan noted, "[i]f there is a bedrock principle underlying the First Amendment, it is that the government may not prohibit the expression of an idea simply because society finds the idea itself offensive or disagreeable" (Texas v. Johnson, 1989). Today, generally only "obscenity, libel, and words that carry an immediate, direct incitement to violence" are beyond the free speech protections of the First Amendment (Wittern-Keller, 2008). However, notwithstanding that censorship carries connotations of repression, authoritarianism and intolerance, the belief in the special ability of movies to negatively influence society has been so pervasive and tenacious that the US Supreme Court has never abandoned movie censorship. Seventy-five years after instituting its content-regulating Production Code, the Motion Picture Association of America (MPAA) still adopts a rating scheme to classify movies for content suitability. Although movies are rated rather than censored, it has been argued that the rating system is content regulation by another name. Because an NC-17 (formerly X) rating would drastically reduce the number of theaters available and thus reduce profits, producers and directors usually edit their films to conform to the less controversial R ratings (Zhang & Li, 2015).

The changes in attitude toward government censorship reflect the complexity of this issue. Many people sincerely believed that "control of movie producers and directors was necessary to protect women, children and society in general." As explained by Tsesis (2016), "the commitment to safeguarding free speech as an essential value for individuals to pursue happiness, engage in deliberative democracy, and seek truth must be balanced against the needs of society to prevent violence, defamation, child pornography, and other communications harmful to communities of dignified equals. That is the first order constitutional theory of free speech." This balancing theory was developed by courts over the course of the twentieth century. For example, in the *Ferber* case, the court differentiated juvenile from adult pornography, stating that regulation of the former reflects "a government objective of surpassing importance": to prevent the "sexual exploitation and abuse of children." In its reasoning, the court carefully assessed the harm to child victims, the government's *parens patriae* power to safeguard the "well-being of its youth" and the need to "codify a solution to combat a social evil." The court found that "the state's interest in preventing the exploitation of children was of greater value than the creation and distribution of ordinary pornography." Also, in *Hustler Magazine, Inc. v. Falwell*, the court argued that "under ordinary circumstances the state interest in preventing emotional harm will outweigh the speaker's desire to communicate emotional harm." Nonetheless, some courts have ignored this principle of balancing the prevention of harm against the freedom of speech. For instance, in *Brown v. Entertainment Merchants Ass'n*, the court called the state's proposed "'simple balancing test' that weighs the value of a particular category of speech against its social costs" a "startling and dangerous" proposition, and it held unconstitutional a California law that "prohibited the sale and rental of violent VGs to minors."

Copyright protection plays a significant role in societal progress and the public good. Therefore, the constitutional principles of justice, progress, equality and liberty are indispensable in matters of copyright, as "everyone is to be included; none should be excluded; the common welfare and progress are the foci; and although the individual should be able to benefit from his or her own creation, societal advancement is the paramount goal" (Mtima & Jamar, 2010). Thus, a comprehensive theory of copyright and free speech should balance individual and public interests in the expression of ideas against exclusive ownership of copyrighted works while considering the exercise of free speech (Tsesis, 2016).

### *7.2.3 History of the Legal Basis for a Copyright Administrative Regulatory System in China*

China has always used a dual system of judicial and administrative supervision to protect copyrighted works. Judicial supervision is designed to protect the legitimate rights and interests of the copyright holder through the court system, whereas administrative supervision is mainly implemented by the State Copyright Bureau and local copyright administrative departments, who are responsible for the administrative management and enforcement of copyrights to protect the legitimate interests of the rights holders while safeguarding the public interest (Li, 2015). China is well-known for its strict censorship of cultural goods; although copyrighted works follow the principle of automatic protection, the administrative regulatory system plays an important role in maintaining the orderly operation of copyrights. This administrative system has established specialized agencies to register works and to supervise and manage the publication and dissemination of works. Administrative copyright enforcement combats piracy and other illegal behaviors that "are suspected of copyright infringement but also damage the public interest" (PRC Copyright Law art. 48).

Article 1 of the PRC Copyright Law 2011 explicitly states the legislative purpose, that "[t]his Law is enacted, in accordance with the Constitution, for the purpose of protecting the copyright of authors in their literary, artistic and scientific works and the rights and interests related to copyright, encouraging the creation and dissemination of works conducive to the building of a socialist society that is advanced ethically and materially, and promoting the progress and flourishing of socialist culture and sciences." Contrary to this stated legislative purpose, the principle of automatic protection grants a creator of a work the copyright to the work once it is completed (PRC Copyright Law art. 2 (1)); "the enjoyment and the exercise of these rights shall not be subject to any formality" (Berne Convention art. 5(2)), regardless of whether the content of the work supports the stated goal of building of a socialist society that is both ethically and materially advanced. To address this discrepancy, Article 4 of the Copyright Law stipulates that "[c]opyright holders shall not violate the Constitution or laws or jeopardize public interests when exercising their copyright. The State shall supervise and administrate the publication and dissemination of works in accordance with the law" (PRC Copyright Law art. 4). This provision provides the legal basis for China's copyright administrative regulatory system.

Nonetheless, Article 4 of the PRC Copyright Law 2011 has undergone a tortuous process of amendment. Tracing back to history, Article 4(1) of the PRC Copyright Law 1991 stated that "works the publication and/or dissemination of which are prohibited by law shall not be protected by this law."[2] Professor Zheng (1994) clarified the legislative purpose of this clause, pointing out that "it is in nature nothing else but the complete exclusion of works with illicit content from copyrightability, and the formulation of 'not protected by this Law' is only to make it easier to be accepted." Despite wide criticism of this provision on the grounds that it does not conform to the automatic protection principle of the Berne Convention (Wei, 1997; Fu, 1988), legislators balked at revising it for a number of reasons. Offending works were few in number, and authors of such works would be unlikely to request copyright protection from the courts or administrative departments in cases of infringement. Furthermore, Article 4(2) of the Copyright Law 1991 stipulated that "[c]opyright owners, in exercising their copyright, shall not violate the Constitution or laws or prejudice the public interest." Given that "works the publication and/or dissemination of which are prohibited by law" by definition are those works consisting of unconstitutional or illegal content, even if such works are copyrightable, they would be reduced or even denied remedies by Chinese courts in making copyright claim judgements on the basis of Article 4(2) of the Copyright Law 1991.

In 2009, the US government challenged the first clause of Article 4 of the PRC Copyright Law of 2001[3] for being inconsistent with Chinese obligations under Article 5(1) of the Berne Convention and Article 41.1 of the TRIPS Agreement (WTO, 2009), despite the fact that denying copyright protection to offending works on grounds of public policy was commonly accepted by common law jurisdictions, including the US (Martinetti v. Maguire, 1867; Barnes v. Miner, 1903). The WTO Panel ruled in favor of the US government, and China was obliged to revise the legislation. Nevertheless, the deletion of the first clause of Article 4 of the PRC Copyright Law 2001 in the 2010 revision of the Copyright Law does not affect governmental censorship in China, as the revised statute also addresses Chinese public policy concerns. As stressed by the WTO Panel (2009), "The United States' claim did not challenge China's right to conduct content review," and "the Panel's findings do not affect China's right to conduct content review." Specifically, the first clause of Article 4 of the Copyright Law 2010 still imposes restrictions on the exercise and enforcement of the copyright of offending works, and the second clause of this Article grants the administrative regulation mechanism the power to manage the publication and dissemination of literary and artistic works to ensure that their content complies with the Constitution, laws and public interest.

Today, a relatively strict administrative content censorship system is widely taken by the Chinese government to prevent and prohibit the circulation of works with prohibited content. As explicitly stated by the relevant administrative regulations, the aim of this measure is to "promote the socialist spiritual civilization and material civilization"(*Regulations on the Administration of Publications 2011* art. 1; *Regulations on the Administration of Audiovisual Products 2011* art. 1) by ensuring that

[2] Article 4(1) of the PRC Copyright Law 1991 was identical with Article 4(1) of the PRC Copyright Law 2001.

[3] Article 4(1) of the PRC Copyright Law 1991 was identical with Article 4(1) of the PRC Copyright Law 2001.

publishers and distributors of these works "shall give primacy to the social benefits" (*Regulations on the Administration of Publications 2011* art. 4) and "disseminate ideas, morals and scientific, technical and cultural knowledge beneficial to economic development and social progress"(*Regulations on the Administration of Audiovisual Products 2011* art. 3 §1). Accordingly, materials that "propagate obscenity, gambling or violence or instigate crimes" (*Regulations on the Administration of Publications 2011 art. 25(7); Regulations on the Administration of Audiovisual Products 2011 art.* 3§2(7)), among other forbidden content, are prohibited from circulation. Also, "[p]ublications catering to minors shall not include any content enticing minors to imitate the acts in violation of public ethics or illegal or criminal acts, nor shall they include such contents harming the physical and mental health of minors as terror, cruelty, etc." (*Regulations on the Administration of Publications 2011 art. 26*).

The content review system applies to traditional literary and artistic works, such as books and films, as well as to newly emerging works, such as VGs. However, China's VG industry has developed at such a rapid pace, with sales revenue reaching 230.88 billion yuan in 2019 and year-on-year growth of 7.7%,[4] that the corresponding regulatory system lags behind. On the one hand, this regulatory system fails to prevent minors from accessing age-inappropriate game content, leading to increasingly serious social problems among minors, such as violence and gaming addiction. On the other hand, this regulatory model also unduly restricts the games industry, which cannot cater to adult players while complying with the requirement to protect minors. As one scholar noted, "the market access of online games in China is a government-oriented model, which is overseen by relevant governmental departments and self-disciplined by industry associations. Due to the lag of this government censorship system and the indifference of the government to the online game industry, the games industry is confronted with the problem of restraint of development and cannot meet the rapid changing market demand" (Yan, 2018). Hence the regulatory model must be adjusted to align with the characteristics of the era and the real demands of the games industry. Apart from content censorship system, the content rating system is another common measure used in other jurisdictions to regulate some copyrighted works, such as films and VGs. However, this relatively advanced form of regulatory system has not been effectively implemented in Chinese legislation, despite attempts to do so. In the following sections, I examine the legislative and practical concerns associated with these two administrative regulatory models—content censorship system and quasi-content rating system—for VGs in China. I also refer to judicial practice in other jurisdictions before proposing a feasible solution for China.

[4] See the China's Game Industry Report 2019 <http://www.cgigc.com.cn/gamedata/21649.html> last visited December 30, 2024.

## 7.3 Inadequate Administrative Regulation Mechanism for VGs in China: Content Censorship System and Quasi-Content Rating System Divided

### *7.3.1 Inadequacy of Content Censorship System for Regulating VGs*

A VG is an electronic game that involves interaction with a user interface to generate visual feedback on a video display device. VGs' narrative and story elements can be expressed through characters, props and other media in conjunction with specific values and world views. Thus, as with other literary and artistic works, such as films, the audiovisual outputs of VGs may incite pornography, gambling, violence or crime, that are harmful to the physiological and psychological development of young gamers as well as hindrance to the construction of a spiritually and materially advanced socialist society under Chinese law. The content censorship system, a governmental supervision model for traditional copyrighted works, is thus generally used to regulate VGs. However, in contrast with other literary and artistic works, VGs are a type of social medias with a significant interactive element that allows gamers to actively participate in the gameplay rather than passively watch it. The confrontational plots and "win–lose" settings of online games give users emotional and cognitive rewards and stimulation, rendering the gameplay compelling. This introduces the potential for addiction. Many psychiatric studies on gaming addiction have shown that VGs can cause serious harm to minors (Griffiths, 2000, 2008; Stetina et al., 2011). Thus, it is urgently necessary to determine how to avoid gaming addiction in this copyright industry. Notwithstanding that the content review system plays a certain role in regulating pornographic and violent games, it plays little to no role in reducing the number of game addicts. I explore this issue from theoretical and practical perspectives in the following subsections.

#### 7.3.1.1 Theoretical Possibility of Content Review for VGs

Content censorship is the most common method of regulating copyrighted works. Generally, there are two parallel systems: pre-censorship and post-censorship. Pre-censorship is applied to works before they are put on the market; works that failed to pass the requisite content review tests would be prohibited from circulation under administrative regulations. Post-censorship is applied to works already on the market; if their content is found to be illicit, they would be prohibited from publication and dissemination by the relevant administrative department (Zhang & Li, 2015). Pre-censorship is a prerequisite for VGs to be marketed. If pirated VGs or VGs with offending contents are not discovered prior to publication, administrative enforcement departments are also empowered to investigate infringers and crack down on illicit works in circulation (He, 2017).

Article 17 of the Berne Convention serves as the international legislative authority for Chinese government censorship. Pursuant to Article 17 of the Convention, "[t]he provisions of this Convention cannot in any way affect the right of the Government of each country of the Union to permit, to control, or to prohibit by legislation or regulation, the circulation, presentation, or exhibition of any work or production in regard to which the competent authority may find it necessary to exercise that right." This provision acknowledges member countries' sovereign right to take necessary steps (e.g. national legislation or government censorship) to maintain public order (von Lewinski, 2008; WIPO, 1971). Accordingly, certain restrictions on the exercise of and remedies for copyright relating to works of illicit content are justified (Dreier, 2006), and "authors may exercise their rights only if that exercise does not conflict with public order" (WIPO, 1971). This provision, echoed by Article 4 of the PRC Copyright Law of 2010, justifies the Chinese administrative regulations prohibiting the publication and distribution of certain types of content (e.g. those "propagating obscenity, gambling, violence or instigate crimes"(*Regulations on the Administration of Publications 2011* art. 25(7); *Regulations on the Administration of Audiovisual Products 2011* art. 3§2(7)) as well as those requiring pre- or post-censorship of VG content in the interest of China's national public policy.

Notably, freedom of speech is protected by the First Amendment of the US Constitution,[5] and US courts have at times prioritized the right of free speech over other constitutional values (Brown v. Entertainment Merchants Ass'n, 2011; United States v. Alvarez, 2012; McCutcheon v. FEC, 2014). In contrast, free speech is not valued over other basic rights listed in the Constitution of the People's Republic of China. Whereas Article 13 of the PRC Constitution states that "citizens' lawful private property is inviolable," no such clause provides that freedom of speech is inviolable. Thus, when freedom of speech and property rights collide, the latter will probably prevail. For example, if private property is deemed "unlawful," such as a paid-for but private copy or a legally purchased work on illicit topics which was published elsewhere, it is not then "inviolable" (He, 2017). Furthermore, the Chinese government justifies its control of content as necessary to protect cultural industries through copyright and by allowing a degree of free expression in the creative process. The vague phrases of "socialist society that is advanced ethically and materially" and "socialist culture and sciences" are open to interpretation, granting considerable leeway for such censorship when the content of copyrighted works is deemed detrimental to the achievement of such a society. Although the US has managed to initiate disputes with China through the WTO regarding some of the abovementioned problems, apparently it has not substantially influenced China's censorship system, as it is within a country's autonomy to set censorship, as long as it is non-discriminative (WTO, 2009).

[5] The US Constitution Amendment I stipulates that "Congress shall make no law respecting an establishment of religion, or prohibiting the free exercise thereof; or abridging the freedom of speech, or of the press; or the right of the people peaceably to assemble, and to petition the government for a redress of grievances."

Nevertheless, in no way does Article 17 of the Berne Convention authorize the complete denial of copyright or total withdrawal of copyright protection for any works, even those with prohibited content. Under the Berne Convention, copyright in a work "vests immediately and automatically upon creation without any formalities, if the substantive requirements of copyright are fulfilled" (art. 5(2)). That means a work's copyrightability would not be diminished by illicit content or by its distribution having been prohibited by the government. Consequently, offending works should be copyrightable in spite of illegal or immoral content. With respect to VGs, the relevant copyright administrative departments are empowered to review the content of games prior to their dissemination, and the administrative enforcement departments have power to inspect the content of games after their circulation. Under the Chinese tradition, VGs containing content "propagating obscenity, gambling, violence or instigate crimes" (*Regulations on the Administration of Publications 2011* art. 25(7); *Regulations on the Administration of Audiovisual Products 2011* art. 3§2(7)) or including content "harming the physical and mental health of minors" (*Regulations on the Administration of Publications 2011* art. 26) would be restricted for publication and dissemination, but this must not affect their copyrightability. In other words, offending VGs should be copyrightable under the PRC Copyright Law despite of their prohibited content.

#### 7.3.1.2 Practical Inadequacy of Content Review for VGs

In general, the development of China's pre-censorship system can be divided into three major stages: multi-department supervision, function-divided supervision and function integration (Zhang & Lin, 2019). In the early stages of VG development, VGs were subject to multi-department supervision, based on their being cultural products, electronic publications and audiovisual products with a network attribute.[6] The respective functions and powers of each supervisory department were not clearly defined, and their administrative responsibilities overlapped (*Interim Provisions on*

[6] From the perspective of cultural products, the responsibility to administrate cultural market and cultural place belongs to the Ministry of Culture; From the attribute of electronic publications, the Propaganda Department of the CPC Central Committee, the Ministry of Culture, and the National Press and Publication Administration all have supervision power; from the perspective of audiovisual products, the Ministry of Culture, the State Administration of Radio, Film and Television, and the National Press and Publication Administration have cross supervision; From the perspective of internet attributes, the Ministry of Industry and Information Technology also have administrative obligation.

*the Administration of Internet Publishing* art. 4(4); *Interim Provisions on the Administration of Internet Culture* art. 2(2)).[7] This, combined with a lack of centralized leadership, caused administrative difficulties and decreased the efficiency of censorship.

In September 2009, the Ministry of Culture (MC) was put in charge of the regulation of online games in conjunction with the State Administration of Press, Publication, Radio, Film and Television (SAPPRFT).[8] Specifically, the SAPPRFT was responsible for prior approval of the publication of online games, and the MC was responsible for reviewing games' specific content (National Press and Publication Administration, 2009). Governmental regulation of the online games industry thus entered the function-divided supervision stage, wherein several regulations were issued. The most important of these was the *Interim Measures for the Administration of Online Games* (hereinafter referred to as *"Interim Measures"*),[9] which strengthened the operability and enforceability of the administrative measures applied to games. Article 9 of the *Interim Measures* states that the content of online games shall not "propagate obscenity, pornography, gambling, violence, instigate crimes, or violate public ethics." Article 16 further states that "[o]nline game operators shall formulate user guidance and warning messages according to the content, function and application population of the game. Online games with contents harmful to their physical and mental health should not be distributed to minors, and technical measures should be provided to prevent addiction." Despite this refinement of VG oversight, certain problems remain, such as complicated procedures and lengthy review times, which negatively impact the development of the online games market. It takes approximately six months on average after applying for approval for an online game to be released on the market. This poses a challenge to game enterprises participating in a fiercely competitive market; many prefer to launch pirated games than to apply for copyright licenses. For example, NetEase's mobile game *Identity V* entered the domestic survival horror mobile games market and enjoyed substantial success by pirating the elements of *Dead by Daylight* before applying for authorization.[10] Similarly, NetEase launched *Knives Out* and *Terminator 2:Judgment Day,* which were based on Tencent's US-licensed sandbox game *PlayerUnknown's Battlegrounds*, during the review period for the authorization of Tencent's games in

[7] For example, in June 2002, the General Administration of Press and Publication (GAPP) and the Ministry of Information Industry jointly issued the *Interim Provisions on the Administration of Internet Publishing*, making it clear that the GAPP "shall carry out the pre-examination and approval procedure for internet publishing institutions"; while in May 2003, the Ministry of Culture also issued the *Interim Provisions on the Administration of Internet Culture*, clarifying that "game products" should be administrated thereof as Internet cultural products.

[8] On March 22, 2013, the State Administration of Press, Publication, Radio, Film and Television was established, and the former General Administration of Press and Publication as well as the State Administration of Radio, Film and Television were no longer existed.

[9] Decree No.49 of the Ministry of Culture, implemented on August 1, 2010.

[10] See 'Cooperation with Netease Games' <http://archive.deadbydaylight.com/posts/2018/cooperation-with-netease-games/> last visited December 30, 2024.

China.[11] NetEase was later sued for copyright infringement to the tune of US$15 million; however, this inadequately addressed Tencent's loss of potential customers during the censoring determination period. Thus, some game enterprises prefer to pay compensation for copyright infringement than to pursue a license and risk losses during the lengthy review period.

In March 2018, the former MC and the National Tourism Administration were combined into the Ministry of Culture and Tourism (MCT), and online game regulation has since entered the function integration stage. In April of the same year, the State Copyright Bureau was established and listed by the Publicity Department of the CPC Central Committee (PDCPCCC) as responsible for supervising and administrating cultural and publishing activities related to VGs, removing this function from the SAPPRFT (Zhang & Lin, 2019). On May 14, 2019, the MCT issued the *Notice of the MCT on Adjusting the Approval Scope of Internet Culture Operation License*, formally removing online games from its jurisdiction.[12] Since then, the PDCPCCC has assumed responsibility for supervising and administrating the online games industry, including pre-examination and approval of VGs. A few months later, the *Interim Measures* were abolished by the MCT, and the VG review procedure was simplified such that online game enterprises no longer need to obtain a network culture operation license, imported games no longer require pre-approval from the MCT and the operation of online games no longer requires filing.[13] By simplifying the cumbersome review procedure and reducing contradictory review outcomes, these changes may greatly improve the efficiency of the review process. Yet, the actual effects of these changes remain to be seen.

The pre-censorship restriction on game content has a more direct impact on the games industry than the lengthy approval process does. Games are reviewed to determine whether their content is harmful to the unification of the state, public order, valued customs, cultural traditions and/or the health of minors. The *Interim Measures* enumerates several types of prohibited content, including certain subjective and controversial items, such as content that "propagates evil cults or superstition" or "propagates obscenity, gambling, violence or instigates crimes," as well as terms of principle that exclude content that may "endanger the unity of the nation" or "undermine the solidarity of the nations."[14] In recent years, censors have confused the "existence" of unsavory elements with the "propaganda" of those elements, expressing the opinion that the existence of the enumerated offending content creates the possibility of minors' imitation. Censors are particularly sensitive to "obscenity" and "pornography," requiring game companies to delete or change such content. For example,

[11] The *Knives Out* and the *Terminator 2: Judgment Day* are similar sandbox games with *Player Unknown's Battlegrounds.*

[12] See news from <http://www.5dianban.net/keji/387066.html> last visited December 30, 2024.

[13] On July 23, 2019, the Ministry of Culture and Tourism officially abolished the *Interim Measures for the Administration of Online Games*, see <http://game.people.com.cn/n1/2019/0821/c40130-31307591.html> last visited December 30, 2024.

[14] Although the *Interim Measures for the Administration of Online Games* has been abolished, the content of online games should still comply with other regulations such as the *Interim Provisions on the Administration of Internet Culture.*

the online game ethics committee ordered the companies behind the games *Kings of Glory* and *Chor Lau Heung* to rectify the excessive nudity of female characters. In another example, the developer of *Justice Online Treacherous Waters* was accused of making a blood splashing effect too real in its promotional video and was forced to change the images to a black and white ink effect. As people of almost all ages play VGs online and juveniles generally lack self-control, it is understandable for censors to be sensitive to VG content that may pose a threat to juveniles' mental health. However, if all VGs were designed for young players, this would negatively impact adults' gaming experience as well as game developers' cultural creation and freedom of speech.

Another deficiency of the pre-censorship system in China is that it lacks a specific examination standard. Although regulations such as the *Interim Measures*, the *Regulations on the Administration of Internet Information Service* and the *Regulations on the Administration of Online Games Publication* include several provisions on the conditions of content review, these are mainly general principles without specific descriptions of requirements, and final judgement is at the sole discretion of the reviewing authority. Additionally, the review process attaches too much importance to the qualification of game enterprises and the content of online games, ignoring the technical side of VGs. This is evident both in the lack of technical standards in legislation and in the lack of guidance from professionals with technical experience in practice, and it leads directly to subjectivity in review results. It is worth noting that censoring pornographic and violent game content does little or nothing to prevent gaming addiction and that VG addiction has yet to be clearly defined and regulated.

When facing massive amounts of nearly untraceable illegal content online, Chinese government tends to rely on ISPs to do part of their jobs. However, as profit-driven enterprises, ISPs are reluctant to accept this responsibility, and the vague criteria for determining illegal content grant them a degree of discretion (He, 2017). As the Internet is rife with pirated games and games with violent, pornographic and other vulgar content, Chinese administrative enforcement departments also address these illegal games through post-censorship (e.g. the "cleanse net" and "sword net" campaigns). However, these campaigns are only partially successful due to the sheer volume and complexity of infractions (Xinhua, 2019).

### *7.3.2 Inadequacy of the Quasi-Content Rating System for Regulating VGs*

Content rating system is another common regulation mechanism for regulating copyrighted works such as films and VGs. A VG content rating system is a system used by a governmental or self-regulatory organization to classify games according to their suitability for certain age groups. Age ratings create restrictions on the marketing and distribution of games and can help consumers make better choices and provide publishers with legal certainty. An ideal content rating system informs consumers about the type and content of a game to facilitate the selection of games appropriate to their age, intelligence and mental health. This helps to prevent minors from playing games that may adversely affect their physical and mental health. There are several VG content rating systems in existence, such as the ESRB system adopted by the US, Canada and Mexico; the CERO system used in Japan; Germany's USK system; and the PEGI system applied in many European countries.[15] To date, China has not established an explicit VG content rating system, although it has made some attempts to do so. I refer to those measures taken by China collectively as the "quasi-content rating system."

#### 7.3.2.1 Legislative Perspective on the Current Quasi-Content Rating System

Legislative attempts to establish a game content rating system in China date back to July 7, 2004, when the China Consumer Association and the Game Software Branch of the China Software Industry Association jointly launched a press conference on the public welfare activity of "creating a healthy online game environment for minors" and announced that China would establish a content rating system for VGs in the near future.[16] In September of the same year, the China Youth Network Association issued the *Recommendation of Green Game Standards*, which was the first standard set for a game content rating system.[17] However, this standard was merely recommended to the industry; it was not compulsory to be implemented in practice. Following the *Recommendation* standard, a large number of online games (most of which were popular at the time, especially those imported from foreign countries) were rated to restrict their release to players aged 18+ years and older. This led to dissatisfaction among numerous gamers and game operators, who questioned the objectivity and purpose of the standard. As a result, the standard was suspended.

In 2010, the MC entrusted the Institute of Cultural Industry of Peking University and Central China Normal University with conducting a joint study to develop a rating standard for online games. The proposed standard, *5A ~ 20 Latitude Online Game Rating Evaluation Table*, suggests online games for three age levels (0+, 12+ and 18+) based on 5 evaluation indexes and 20 game modules.[18] However, the MC later announced that the standard was for research purposes only; it was not implemented

[15] See 'Video Game Content Rating System' <https://en.wikipedia.org/wiki/Video_game_content_rating_system> last visited December 30, 2024.

[16] See 'Creating A Healthy Environment for Minors, China Will Rate Game Software [为未成年人营造健康环境 中国将对游戏软件分级]', <http://www.chinanews.com/news/2004year/2004-07-07/26/457064.shtml> last visited December 30, 2024.

[17] See 'China Youth Network Association issued the Recommendation of Green Game Standards [中国青少年网络协会绿色游戏推荐标准]' <http://www.360doc.com/content/06/0114/17/1712_58332.shtml> last visited December 30, 2024.

[18] See 'Online Game Rating Standard Initially Established, Three Levels of Age Ratings [网游分级标准初步形成，按受众年龄分三级别]' <https://tech.qq.com/a/20100114/000119.htm> last visited December 30, 2024.

in the MC's working schedule. In pilot programs in Beijing and Shanghai, labels (i.e. "encourage," "prohibit" and "limit") were attached to certain online games based on the standard. No further actions were taken based on this study and rating system.

On June 26, 2019, People's Daily Online, in conjunction with certain notable game enterprises, introduced a pilot content rating system, the *Draft on the Online Game Age-Appropriateness Warning* (hereinafter referred to as "*Draft*") to provide guidance for underage consumers.[19] The *Draft* uses a "negative list" to determine the appropriateness of games based on their content, ultimately classifying games according to four age groups (18+, 16+, 12+ and 6+ ). It is recommended that children under 6 years of age cannot play VGs alone, as this is a critical age for vision development. Besides, any content inappropriate for ages 18+ constitutes illegal publication. The *Draft* standard was based on the psychological and physiological characteristics of gamers; however, it posed major problems. For instance, the *Draft* required that no "blood splashing effect, skeleton sign, brothel, casino scenes, insulting words or sentences or works of 'murder' or 'killing' and scenes describing or suggestive of sexual love" appear in games for consumers aged 18 and older.

These restrictions for adult players reflect the conservative nature of the Chinese public rather than research-based considerations. Violent content is potentially detrimental to the health of minors; however, this content should be restricted to adult players rather than prohibited altogether. I suggest that denying production of these games is an infringement upon the right of free speech, as VGs are a form of expression for game developers. The expression of violent content should be properly restricted to protect minors; however, the outright prohibition of problematic words such as "killing" or casino scenes, for example, affects the intended communication of VGs. The prohibition of violent and sexual content in VGs indicates the continuation of content censorship rather than a more progressive system of age-appropriate ratings. This "one-size-fit-all" rating standard is effectively the same as the censorship system; neither takes into account the diverse needs of adults and juveniles or their physical and mental differences. As mentioned, it violates the right to freedom of speech and conflicts with the legislative purpose of copyright to incentivize creation. In addition, the effectiveness of all of these standards—the *Recommendation of Green Game Standards,* the *5A ~ 20 Latitude Online Game Rating Evaluation Table* and the *Draft*—is questionable, as they are not enforced by the government but only serve as reference documents.

#### 7.3.2.2 Practical Perspective on the Current Quasi-Content Rating System

Due to the call for both a game content rating system and network protection for minors, several quasi-rating measures have been implemented in China. In 2007, a real-name authentication scheme was implemented, requiring gamers to register to

[19] See *Draft on the Online Game Age-Appropriateness Warning* <https://baike.baidu.com/item/游戏适龄提示草案/23592170?fr=aladdin> last visited December 30, 2024.

play online games with their real names and identification (ID) numbers. Online game providers were required to monitor their users' playing time, using this identifying information, and discourage underage users from playing for prolonged periods to combat game addiction and fatigue.[20] Some methods entailed forced termination after a certain period of gameplay; however, the so-called "fatigue system" was more nuanced and reduced the rewards offered in games (experience value and item drop rate) after a certain duration of gameplay. Once an underage gamer reached a cumulative three hours of play, the game's rewards were reduced by 50%, and after five hours of play, the game stopped providing rewards and warned the player via a repeated message that he had been gaming for an unhealthy amount of time and should stop immediately.[21] The fatigue system was unsuccessful and was ultimately discarded.

In 2014, the SAPPRFT issued the *Notice on Further Carrying Out the Real-Name Authentication System of Online Game Anti-Addiction*, setting the implementation of an online game anti-addiction system as a long-term goal. Due to technological limitations, this system was not a requirement for mobile games. To further standardize online game services and prioritize social benefits in VGs, in 2016 China passed the *Regulations on the Protection of Minors Online (Draft for Deliberation)*, which included restrictions on nighttime gaming and duration of gaming sessions for minors, required online gaming service providers to change rules to reduce addiction, provided guidance for minors and required manufacturers to install technical measures for the protection of minors. For the same purpose, the General Administration of Press and Publication issued the *Notice on Preventing Minors from Indulging in Online Games* in November 2019. This document required online game enterprises to establish a real-name registration system and required every user to use a unique ID number to register game accounts before playing. It also applied a strict time-control system that prohibited game services from being supplied to minors between 10 PM and 8 AM and restricted gameplay to 3 h per day on legal holidays and 1.5 h per day on other days. Furthermore, the *Notice* recommended an age-appropriateness warning system wherein online game enterprises would comprehensively evaluate game content and function, the intensity of confrontation, the potential for cognitive confusion, the degree to which dangerous activity was imitated and the consumption level of gamers and issue warnings to gamers based on this evaluation. This warning system resembled standards set by game enterprises themselves, such as that of Tencent's *Tianya Mingyue Dao,* in which gamers were issued warnings such as "Gamers aged 6 to 16 should play under the supervision of parents" and "Gamers aged 13 to 18 should play moderately."[22]

---

[20] See 'First Exposure of Developing Standard of Online Game Anti-Addiction System and the Real-Name Scheme[网游防沉迷系统开发标准及实名方案首次曝光]' <http://tech.sina.com.cn/i/2007-04-11/18491460776.shtml> last visited December 30, 2024.

[21] See 'Online Game Anti-Addiction System and Real-Name Authentication Service Protocol[网络游戏防沉迷系统及实名认证服务协议]' <https://store.steampowered.com/eula/2214430_eula_1> last visited December 30, 2024.

[22] Warning messages showing on the Tencent's online game *Tianya Mingyue Dao*.

I present the example of Tencent Holdings to further illustrate Chinese game enterprises' efforts to combat gaming addiction under China's quasi-content rating system. Tencent Holdings is China's largest gaming and social media company, and it has continuously improved its system to protect minors playing its online games. In 2017, Tencent developed the "Growth Guard Platform" [成长守护平台] to allow parents to monitor their children's game account activity for both PC and mobile games and to set limits on their gaming time and game consumption (Wang, 2020; Yang, 2018). In the same year, the company implemented anti-addiction and real-name registration systems, prohibiting underage players from logging into games from 9 PM to 8 AM and limiting gameplay time (one hour per day for children under 12 and two hours per day for those between 13 and 18). Those exceeding the time limit were forced offline and denied access to the game for one day. The company updated its anti-addiction system after it had been in use for one year, linking it to a public security database, real-name authentication system and the face recognition system. In this sophisticated system, gamers' ages were automatically detected by the real-name authentication system when they logged in with their ID numbers. Underage gamers were then subject to the time limitations of the anti-addiction system. When a gamer who was identified as an adult displaying gaming behaviors associated with minors, the face recognition system was engaged to detect the gamer's approximate age. This expanded anti-addiction system has been described as the most stringent anti-addiction measure in history. Since June 17, 2020, Tencent has used the face recognition technology more widely to screen minors who have used their parents' ID numbers instead of their own (Wang, 2020). In a keynote speech in December 2020, Tencent's vice-president stated that "in the past month, every day about 10.49 million minors' accounts were kicked off … due to the login time exceeding 1.5 h, and every day … an average of 3.51 million suspected minors' accounts triggered the face recognition" (Cui, 2020).

Despite such strategies to safeguard the health of underage online gamers, certain major problems remain in China. President Yang (2018) noted, "the *Notice on the Protection of Minor's Physical and Mental Health and the Implementation of Online Game Anti-Addiction System* was issued in 2007 yet so far, few game enterprises have truly implemented it. This is because the goal of enterprises is to make profits, while implementing these anti-addiction measures requires significant time and money… Hence, the willingness of game enterprises to bear those costs is questionable." Other major obstacles to protecting minors online cited by scholars include pirated online games, which do not abide by anti-addiction regulations (Liu et al., 2015), as well as a "lack of network technology innovation and the corresponding legal system and governance measures" (Kang, 2019a, 2019b). Tencent's face recognition system is not universal, and teenagers can avoid the existing preventive measures by changing accounts, crossing network terminals or counterfeiting or purchasing adults' ID numbers for login. Furthermore, as the content rating system and its corresponding measures have yet to be fully established, China must rely on the content censorship system, which is inadequate to fully protect minors. According to Wang Xixin (2018), a professor at Peking University, the difficulty of protecting minors lies not in the inadequate "expression of rules or the concept of protection, but in the implementing … of these legislative rules in practice…, leading to a huge gap between the expression of rules and the practice of rules."[23] He described the problem of "symbolic governance," wherein many rules are announced but their implementation is very limited. Therefore, he proposed that "it is vital to reconsider the coordination between the expression of rules and the practice of rules, and to tackle four relationships appropriately—supervision versus technology, revenue versus cost, government versus society, and control versus guidance."

## 7.4 Regulation Mechanisms for VGs in Other Jurisdictions

To address the growing public health concern of problematic VG use, governments have issued regulations and gaming companies have imposed their own policies in numerous countries. These efforts have targeted gaming content (i.e. rating systems) as well as accessibility to games. I conduct a comparative analysis of three well-established VG rating systems in the two most important economic regions for VGs, the US and the Europe: the Entertainment Software Rating Board (ESRB) rating system, the Pan European Game Information (PEGI) rating system and the *Unterhaltungssoftware Selbstkontrolle* or Entertainment Software Self-Regulation (USK) rating system. These systems range from pure industry self-regulation (the ESRB) to government co-regulation (the USK). I also investigate regulation mechanisms for VGs in Japan and South Korea, two of the most prosperous Asian countries in the games industry, whose gaming cultures are very distinct from those of the US and Europe. This allows me to explore cultural factors that affect regulation mechanisms.

### *7.4.1 North America*

The ESRB, a self-regulatory organization, was established in the US in 1994, in response to criticism of controversial VGs with excessively violent or sexual content.[24] The board assigns ratings to games based on their content, using six age-based levels intended to aid consumers in determining a game's suitability, particularly for children, and provides "content descriptors" detailing specific types of content (see Table 7.1). The ratings are assigned by a panel of reviewers based on the results of questionnaires and video footage, both provided by games' publishers. The ESRB maintains a code of ethics for the advertising and promotion of VGs based on their ratings to ensure that marketing materials for games are targeted toward appropriate audiences.

---

[23] Statement from Wang Xixin in the 7th Peking-Stanford University Internet Law and Public Policy Conference 2018.

[24] See 'Entertainment software Rating Board' <https://en.wikipedia.org/wiki/Entertainment_Software_Rating_Board> last visited December 30, 2024.

**Table 7.1** ERSB rating system in North America

| | |
|---|---|
| Age Categories | Early Childhood (EC,3+), Everyone (E, 6+ and 10+), Teen (T, 13+), Mature (M, 17+), Adults Only (AO, 18+) |
| Icons | AGE 3+ AGE 6+ AGE 10+ AGE 13+ AGE 17+ AGE 18+ |
| Content descriptors | The system includes over 30 content descriptors, including categories describing levels of violence; language; sexual content; nudity; use of alcoholic beverages, tobacco products and drugs; crude and mature humor; and gambling |
| Rating process/raters | The organization considers game developer's online questionnaire detailing pertinent content (all content, context, rewards systems and player control) as well as a DVD showing all pertinent content, game play, missions, cut scenes, extreme instances of content and all content that is not playable but exists in the game code. The panel comprises a minimum of three raters with experience with children |

The ESRB rating system is primarily enforced on a self-regulatory basis by the US games and retail industries. In markets where it is used, retailers typically require proof of age in the form of photo ID from those who wish to purchase games with a "Mature" (M) rating. They refuse to stock unrated VGs or those rated "Adults Only" (AO) (Chalk, 2007). There have been attempts at both the state and federal levels to introduce laws forcing retailers to comply with the ESRB ratings system, triggering debate on balancing the freedom of speech against the protection of minors. For example, in 2004, California Assemblyman Leland Yee sponsored a state bill requiring retailers to stock M-rated games on shelves at least 5 feet from the ground to restrict young children's access to violent VGs. Before the bill was passed into law, it was modified to require only that retailers raise awareness of the ESRB rating system among their customers (Jenkins & Carless, 2004). The following year, California passed a second bill sponsored by Yee that banned the sale of violent VGs to minors. In a legal case regarding the constitutionality of the law, the games industry argued that the state's ban on VG sales and rentals violated the First Amendment right to free speech and asked for the law to be declared unconstitutional (Brown v. Entertainment Merchants Association, 2011). In 2011, the Supreme Court ruled that the law was unconstitutional, as VGs are a protected form of expression. The court further explained: "like the protected books, plays, and movies that preceded them, VGs communicate ideas—and even social messages—through many familiar literary devices and through features distinctive to the medium. That suffices to confer First Amendment protection." At the federal level, H.R. 287—the Video Games Ratings Enforcement Act—was introduced to require all US retailers to place "clear and conspicuous" ESRB rating labels on all games sold and to give customers information on what those ratings meant (Orland, 2013). As most major retailers already refused to carry games unrated by the ESRB, this clause would have had little practical effect on the games market. However, the law would have mandated the use of the ESRB rating system and criminalized noncompliance. The Video Games Ratings Enforcement Act was also designed to forbid retailers from selling AO-rated games to buyers under 18 and M-rated games to buyers under 17, as suggested by the ESRB, a requirement with which most retailers were already in voluntary compliance. This part of the bill appeared to directly contradict the landmark 2011 Supreme Court ruling, and the bill failed to pass due to likely First Amendment violations.

The ESRB system was praised by the Federal Trade Commission for being the "strongest self-regulatory system" in the entertainment sector; it is generally considered effective due to consumers' and retailers' awareness of the rating system and the organization's efforts to ensure that retailers and publishers comply with the rating system and the marketing code, respectively.[25] Notably, the US government established a preferential tax policy to incentivize game enterprises to take the social

[25] See 'Our History: ESRB Ratings", <https://www.esrb.org/history/> last visited December 30, 2024.

responsibility of protecting minors (Kang, 2019a, 2019b). Despite its positive reception, however, the ESRB has faced criticism for the structure of its operations, particularly in the wake of a 2005 incident surrounding the organization's handling of "hidden" objectionable content in *Grand Theft Auto: San Andreas* that could be accessed using a user-created modification.

## 7.4.2 *Europe/Germany*

In Europe, most countries use the PEGI rating system, which helps parents make informed decisions when buying computer games for their children. Established in 2003, this system is now used in more than 30 countries and is based on a code of conduct and comprises a set of rules to which every publisher using the PEGI system is contractually committed. The PEGI system is composed of five age categories and nine content descriptors that advise on the suitability and content of a game for certain age ranges (see Table 7.2).[26] Some jurisdictions use modified versions of the PEGI rating system.

In 1994, Germany established the USK, a self-regulated body responsible for VG ratings.[27] The USK system takes a different approach from the PEGI and the ESRB and is incompatible with the PEGI system used elsewhere in Europe. The "potential to impair" the development or education of minors is the essential criterion for age classification under the USK system, rather than the nature of the content. Game publishers must submit a market-ready version of the game with all relevant materials (e.g. packaging and manuals) to USK. In an approach unique to Germany, USK game testers play through the entire game and then present the game to a classification committee for review and recommendation. A board comprising raters with different religious, political and professional backgrounds renders a decision on the rating, which must then be ratified by an elected, federal official (the Director for the Protection of Minors), who then issues a formal authorization to affix the relevant rating symbol to the game (Dogruel & Joeckel, 2013). The USK system is an example of third-party rating by an external, non-industry board.

Under Garman constitutional law, freedom of speech must be restricted to measures to protect minors from harmful content (German Youth Protection Act art. 5 §2). The German Youth Protection Act (JuSchG), enacted in 2003 under this precept, requires that games considered harmful to minors be denied classification. Deferral authorities can enter these games on a "list of youth-endangering media," which results in severe restrictions on distribution This applies mainly to games

[26] See 'Pan European Game Information' <https://en.wikipedia.org/wiki/Pan_European_Game_Information#:~:text=Pan%20European%20Game%20Information%20(PEGI,age%20recommendations%20and%20content%20descriptors> last visited December 30, 2024.

[27] See 'Unterhaltungssoftware Selbstkontrolle' <https://en.wikipedia.org/wiki/Unterhaltungssoftware_Selbstkontrolle#:~:text=Advertisement%20of%20games%20rated%20USK,as%20the%20%22Index%22)> last visited December 30, 2024.

**Table 7.2** Comparison of Europe's PEGI and Germany's USK rating systems

| | PEGI rating system | UKS rating system |
|---|---|---|
| Age categories | 3+*, 7+*, 12+, 16+ and 18+ (* In Portugal, 3+ was changed to 4+ and 7+ was changed to 6+.) | 0+ ("without age restriction"), 6+, 12+, 16+ and 18+ |
| Icons |  |  |
| Content descriptors | Violence; bad language; fear/horror; gambling; sex; drugs; discrimination; online; and in-game purchases | Content descriptors and age categories closely linked (e.g. the 16 category allows "acts of violence" in games featuring armed combat) |
| Rating process/ raters | Publishers submit the game with supporting materials and complete a content declaration. The administrator evaluates the game and documents and determines the appropriate PEGI rating level | Publishers submit a market-ready version of the game accompanying with all relevant materials (e.g. packaging, manuals). USK game testers play through the game and present the game to the Classification Committee, which reviews it and recommends a rating. The Director for the Protection of Minors (elected federal official) issues the formal authorization to affix the relevant rating symbol |

including graphic violence, explicit sexual content or references to Nazism. Approximately 600 games have been added to the list to date. The number of games rated AO by the ESRB, in contrast, is relatively small and consists mostly of adult games with strong sexual content.

The JuSchG decree that VGs not be made accessible to minors without a state-issued age-rating effectively mandated USK ratings (Hilgert & Summermann, 2016). This greatly increased the importance of the USK for the regulation of VGs in Germany, as it specified the set-up of the USK as a regulatory body through federal law. Regulation on enforceability has also been introduced in the UK, which requires a rating for games only suitable for age 12 or higher and prohibits the sale of such games without a rating. In the Netherlands, the sale or rental of games rated for players 16 or older to younger persons constitutes a criminal offence.[28]

[28] See Artikel 240a Wetboek van Strafrecht. <https://maxius.nl/wetboek-van-strafrecht/artikel240a> last visited December 30, 2024.

### *7.4.3 Japan*

The Computer Entertainment Rating Organization (CERO) in Japan rates the content of console games to inform customers of their nature and what age group they are suitable for.[29] Established in June 2002 as a branch of the Computer Entertainment Supplier's Association, CERO became an officially recognized non-profit organization in December 2003. The CERO rating system comprises five age categories and nine content descriptors. VGs released for PC and mobile devices are rated by the Ethics Organization of Computer Software (EOCS), which was founded in 1992. The EOCS rating system has three levels of ratings and aims to promote a sense of ethical responsibility with respect to the production, distribution and use of computer software.[30] Local governments refer to these ratings, and the Ordinance Regarding the Healthy Development of Youths prohibits retailers from supplying 18+ rated games to persons under 18.[31] Content rating is not required by law, but most commercial game publishers accept the ratings provided by the industry's rating organizations.

Additionally, distributors must obtain the approval of Japan Contents Review Center (JCRC) for PC and mobile games (mostly dating sims, visual novels and *eroge*, or erotic VGs). The JCRC is a Japanese video and game rating organization established to ensure content adherence to Japanese obscenity laws, which prohibit any display of genitals.[32] While Article 21 of the Japanese Constitution guarantees freedom of expression and prohibits formal censorship,[33] effective censorship of pornographic content is justified by Article 175 of the Penal Code of Japan, which states that "[a] person who distributes, sells or displays in public an obscene document, drawing or other objects shall be punished by imprisonment with work for not more than 2 years, a fine of not more than 2,500,000 yen or a petty fine. The same shall apply to a person who possesses the same for the purpose of sale."[34] This article was amended in 2011 to include "recording media containing obscene electronic or

[29] 'Computer Entertainment Rating Organization' <https://en.wikipedia.org/wiki/Computer_Entertainment_Rating_Organization> last visited December 30, 2024.

[30] 'Ethics Organization of Computer Software' <https://gamicus.gamepedia.com/Ethics_Organization_of_Computer_Software> last visited December 30, 2024.

[31] '有害図書類の指定に係る審査団体の指定について' 2020–01-07 < http://www.pref.hokkaido.lg.jp/ks/dms/ss/dantaishitei.htm > last visited January 16, 2021. See also '都道府県の青少年保護育成条例における有害図書類等の指定等に関する規定について' <https://www.mext.go.jp/b_menu/shingi/chukyo/chukyo0/toushin/07020115/021.htm> last visited December 30, 2024.

[32] See 'Japan contents Review Center' https://en.wikipedia.org/wiki/Japan_contents_Review_Center last visited December 30, 2024.

[33] Article 21 of the Constitution of Japan states that, "Freedom of assembly and association as well as speech, press and all other forms of expression are guaranteed. No censorship shall e maintained, nor shall the secrecy of any means of communication be violated." See <https://japan.kantei.go.jp/constitution_and_government_of_japan/constitution_e.html#:~:text=The%20State%20and%20its%20organs,means%20of%20communication%20be%20violated> last visited December 30, 2024.

[34] See Article 175 of the Penal Code (2007), <http://www.japaneselawtranslation.go.jp/law/detail/?id=1960&re=02&vm=04> last visited December 30, 2024.

magnetic records" as well as "materials distributed by electronic means."[35] Thus, although doujin games[36] would not be restricted by the EOCS, the distribution of such games including obscene materials can be punished under the Article 175 of the Penal Code.[37]

However, the law does not provide a definition of "obscenity," leaving the term to be defined in a series of judicial decisions. In the 1957 *Chatterley* case, the Supreme Court of Japan cited a three-part test for obscenity previously established by the Supreme Court of Judicature in 1928. Under this test, a work is considered obscene if it "arouses and stimulates sexual desire, offends a common sense of modesty or shame, and violates proper concepts of sexual morality."[38] This test was applied in a case in which the defendants had been prosecuted under Article 175 for producing and distributing the hentai manga anthology *Misshitsu*. The defendant argued that the law violated Article 21 of the Constitution of Japan and its protection of freedom of expression.[39] In its 2007 decision, the court upheld the guilty verdict, concluding that *Misshitsu* satisfied the three-part obscenity test and was therefore subject to restriction. This case has had a chilling effect; the majority of pornography produced in Japan has since been censored by its publishers. The primary means of such censorship are digital mosaic or pixelization, an editing technique to blur an image or video by displaying part or all of it at a markedly lower resolution,[40] and censor bars placed over genitalia.[41]

CERO has been criticized for being much stricter than other rating boards on VG content. A recent example is the game *The Last of Us 2*. Despite receiving a Z rating (for ages 18+ only), the maximum rating in the CERO system, the game was still censored due to the game's sexual content (Cooper, 2020) (Table 7.3).

---

[35] See 'Censorship in Japan' <https://en.wikipedia.org/wiki/Censorship_in_Japan> last visited December 30, 2024.

[36] Video games created by Japanese hobbyists or hobbyist groups, more for fun than for profit; essentially, the Japanese equivalent of independent video games or fangames.

[37] See Article 175 of the Penal Code (2007), "A person who distributes, sells or displays in public an obscene document, drawing or other objects shall be punished by imprisonment with work for not more than 2 years, a fine of not more than 2,500,000 yen or a petty fine. The same shall apply to a person who possesses the same for the purpose of sale". <http://www.japaneselawtranslation.go.jp/law/detail/?id=1960&re=02&vm=04> last visited December 30, 2024.

[38] See "Judgement of the Supreme Court" 1953(A)1713, <https://www.courts.go.jp/app/hanrei_en/detail?id=11> last visited December 30, 2024.

[39] See 'Erotic Manga Publisher to Take Case to Supreme Court' <https://web.archive.org/web/20081123050856/http://www.japantoday.com/jp/kuchikomi/366> last visited December 30, 2024.

[40] See 'Pixelization' at <https://en.wikipedia.org/wiki/Pixelization#:~:text=Pixelization%20(British%20English%2C%20pixelisation),is%20primarily%20used%20for%20censorship> last visited December 30, 2024..

[41] See 'Censorship in Japan' <https://en.wikipedia.org/wiki/Censorship_in_Japan> last visited December 30, 2024.

**Table 7.3** CERO & EOCS rating systems in Japan

| | CERO rating system | EOCS rating system |
|---|---|---|
| Age categories | 0+, 12+, 15+, 17+ and 18+<br>Using a lettering/color scheme: A and black (all ages), B and green (12+ years), C and blue (15+ years), D and orange (17+ years) and Z and red (18+) | 0+, 15+ and 18+ |
| Rating marks | | —General (suitable for everyone)<br>—Restricted (suitable for ages 15+)<br>—18+ (suitable for 18+) |
| Content icons and descriptors | love; sexual content; violence; horror; drinking/smoking; gambling; crime; drugs; language. | |
| Rating process/raters | CERO receives an ethics reviewing request. A group of assessors comprising five people unaffiliated with the games industry evaluates the game based on 30 types of expression, each with an upper limit. If any limits are exceeded, the expressions are banned. CERO decides the final rating based upon the evaluation results. The publisher labels the product with the appropriate mark | Rating for general is advisory. restricted and 18+ ratings are enforced |

### 7.4.4 South Korea

VGs are extremely popular in South Korea; gaming contributed more than 13 trillion won (US$11.2 billion) to the country's economy in 2018, according to the Korea Creative Content Agency (Lee, 2019). In contrast with its counterparts in most Western countries, the Game Rating and Administration Committee (GRAC) of South Korea is a governmental organization. The system evaluates games using four age ratings and seven content descriptors.[42] South Korea has one of the "freest media environments" in Asia, ranking ahead of Japan, China and Singapore in the Press Freedom Index.[43] South Korea's laws providing for freedom of speech and

[42] See 'Game Rating and Administration Committee' <https://en.wikipedia.org/wiki/Game_Rating_and_Administration_Committee> last visited December 30, 2024.

[43] See 'Press Freedom Index' <https://en.wikipedia.org/wiki/Press_Freedom_Index> last visited December 30, 2024.

of the press limit censorship, which the government generally respects in practice. Under the National Security Act, the government may only "limit the expression of ideas that praise or incite the activities of anti-state individuals or groups."[44] This limits the rating system's role in preventing minors from accessing to harmful information and gaming addiction; the ratings mainly serve as warning messages.

Nevertheless, the widespread use of information technologies and highly developed online games industry in this country have led to concerns about problematic gaming. A government survey revealed that up to 16% of the country's teens are at risk of developing some form of gaming addiction. In response to these concerns, Article 16 of the Game Industry Promotion Act Enforcement Ordinance was introduced in 2007 to prohibit minors' late-night access to Internet cafés. Internet cafés operators cannot provide services to minors under the age of 18 years outside the legally permitted hours (from 9 AM to 10 PM) unless the minors are accompanied by a legal guardian, otherwise the providers will be financially penalized (about US$900 for a first time offense, with penalties doubling for subsequent offenses and suspension of service after three violations). Thus, Internet cafés can ask players to present their ID cards for age verification, and the cafés are monitored by local authorities and fined for not abiding by the regulation.

In 2012, the Youth Protection Revision Act, commonly known as the Shutdown Law or Cinderella Law, was introduced to ban children under 16 from playing online VGs between 12 and 6 AM (Fingas, 2014). The implementation of the Shutdown Law is rather simple. Gamers must register their online gaming accounts using unique Korean social insurance numbers. At midnight, the underage gamers are forced out of the games. Violation of this law may result in up to two years of imprisonment or a fine of approximately US$9000 (Kiraly et al., 2017). Before the Shutdown Law was enacted, a regulation called the "selective shutdown policy" existed in the Game Industry Promotion Act §12.3 to limit the access of minors to online gaming upon request. Under this policy, those under 18 years of age or their legal guardians could request that gaming service providers prevent their access to gaming for preset hours of their choice, and the game providers were required to comply. In practice, this selective shutdown policy was rarely used. Therefore, to give parents more control over their children's gaming addiction, the South Korean government mandated the "Selection System of Games Availability Period" in 2012. The new regulation gave legal guardians the ability to set the game availability period for their children under 18 years old (Andronicus, 2014). This regulation worked on top of the Shutdown Law, and it required any game company with an annual revenue of at least US$27 million and more than 300 employees to implement this system in their games. It also allowed parents to check the duration of their children's gaming via a website, GameCheck.org. In 2013, two new bills were proposed to curb gaming addiction. The first bill called for the creation of an Internet Game Addiction Center to treat online game addicts, to be funded by a contribution by gaming companies of 1% of their annual sales revenue. The second bill categorized game addiction as one of

[44] See 'Censorship in South Korea' <https://en.wikipedia.org/wiki/Censorship_in_South_Korea#cite_note-:0-1> last visited December 30, 2024.

the four major sources of addiction (also including alcohol, drugs and gambling) and requested that strict government regulations be imposed on gaming companies. However, both bills were suspended due to protest from the gaming community (Andronicus, 2014).

Notably, prior to its enactment in November 2011, the Shutdown Law was challenged by a group of Korean game manufacturers and a cultural organization on the basis of the constitutional rights of freedom and equality for youth. Specifically, the group claimed that parts of the law infringed on the freedom of young people, the freedom of the game provider's occupation, the general freedom of action possessed by youths and the rights of parents (Lee, 2019). On April 24, 2014, the Constitutional Court of Korea rejected the complaint and ruled that the Shutdown Law was constitutional. The court conceded that young people had the right to play VGs but stated that the Shutdown Law did not infringe on their rights or liberty because game addiction was detrimental to their health. In the court's opinion, the rights of parents were not absolute, and the government could exercise control on families in dangerous situations. The court further stated that the Shutdown Law did not unfairly targeted online game providers, as online games were more addictive than other types of games. The ruling was criticized by those citing a 2011 US Supreme Court decision finding Californian laws that restricted sales and rentals of violent VGs to minors unconstitutional (Park, 2012).

The Korea Economic Research Institute (KERI) studied the effectiveness of shutdown policy. According to a 2015 report from the KERI, the Shutdown Law caused the Korean gaming market to shrink by roughly 1.16 trillion won (US$1.09 billion). The KERI report concluded that the law would ultimately save 37 billion won in societal costs; however, it estimated that these savings would be five times larger if the shutdown were not applied unilaterally but rather enforced only when a parent requested it (Sohn, 2018). Moreover, approximately 30% of gamers aged 16 and below used their parents' IDs with their full permission to continue gaming at night. These concerns led to a reform of this law on September 2, 2014, whereby parents or guardians could request that their children be exempted from the law (Andronicus, 2014). This reform returned the responsibility for child management to parents (Table 7.4).

### *7.4.5 Comparison and Conclusion*

The above discussion shows that most countries have adopted a content rating system as a strategy to regulate VGs. Compared with Asian countries, Western ones rely more on the rating systems to evaluate content and age-appropriateness than other measures to prevent overindulgence in gaming. As shown, there are major distinctions between the three major rating systems (ERSB, PEGI and USK), such as the type of age ratings, the use of content icons and descriptors and the rating procedure. Furthermore, each rating system seems to regulate a particular type of content more strictly than others. For instance, the USK seems to be very sensitive with regard to violence

**Table 7.4** GRAC rating system in South Korea

| | |
|---|---|
| Age categories | 0+, 12+, 15+, 18+ and T for testing |
| Age rating symbol |  |
| Content icons and descriptors | Sexuality; Violence; Fear/Horror/Threatening;<br>Language; Alcohol/Tobacco/Drugs; ar/Horror/<br>Crime/Anti-societal Messages/Anti-governmental Messages; Gambling.<br>Threatening; |
| Rating process/ raters | Stage 1: Online application<br>Stage 2: Documents checked<br>Stage 3: In-depth review/technical test and game examination by tester/reviewer<br>Stage 4: Rating/content descriptor determination<br>Stage 5: three options: rating pending, rating decision or provisional rating declined<br>Stage 6: Rating issued with a certificate<br>Rating may be appealed |

and may even deny a rating for certain violent games, and the ESRB has a stricter approach to sexual content than the two European systems. This may be explained by cultural and legislative traditions: a free-market approach with the banning of sexual content in the US and a cooperative mode with a stronger focus on violence in the case of Germany (Gibbons & Humphreys, 2011). Another major difference between the three regulatory systems exists in the level of government involvement. More specifically, the German USK system follows a government co-regulation approach involving instruments of German legislation, a strong focus on rating VGs independently from the industry and a close connection to state regulatory bodies. In contrast, the American ESRB system created by an independent self-regulatory organization is based on pure industry self-regulation. The PEGI takes the middle ground: self-regulation with a close relationship with semi-governmental bodies. Despite the fact that both the ESRB and PEGI systems are primarily enforced on a voluntary basis in the absence of federal or state laws, game developers, publishers and retailers tend to strongly adhere to them. For example, many US retailers refuse to sell VGs without ESRB ratings, which encourages game publishers to obtain ratings for their games. Research shows that systems with strong state involvement are no more effective than pure self-regulation systems in restricting access to potentially harmful VG content (Dogruel & Joeckel, 2013). The ESRB's rating system may even be more restrictive and provide more information for a particular age group (children 12 or younger).

In terms of Asian countries, Japan allows the industry to self-regulate with regard to most commercial VGs; however, PC and mobile games involving dating sims, visual novels and *eroge* must be approved by the JCRC. In Japan, the Ordinance Regarding the Healthy Development of Youths prohibits retailers from supplying 18+ rated games to persons under 18, and Article 175 of the Penal Code of Japan justifies the effective censorship of pornographic content. In contrast, the GRAC rating system in South Korea is operated by a governmental organization; however, censorship in this country is limited by laws protecting free speech. The impacts of the fast development of the VG industry and the high prevalence of problematic gaming in South Korea have forced the country to take the lead in formulating polices to prevent and reduce negative consequences associated with excessive gaming. Both the Shutdown Law, which limits minors' gaming to specific times of the day, and the "Selection System of Games Availability Period," which allows parents or legal guardians to track game-play activity when using the device, are examples of such policies. Nonetheless, the conflicting values between protecting youth from addiction and promoting industrial development have triggered the dilemma in policymaking process of shutdown legislation. A similar debate has occurred in the US concerning a proposed ban on sales and rentals of violent VGs to minors, which was found to conflict with the constitutional right to freedom of expression. The distinct results of these two disputes reflect the contrasting political systems in these two countries. While in Asian countries where government control is strong, many of these actions could be implemented, in the Western world, most of these policy actions invite criticism and protest as attacks on civil liberty (Kiraly et al., 2017). Thus, political and cultural factors must be taken into account when establishing policy, to overcome such conflicts and overlapping roles.

On an international level, a group of rating organizations including the ESRB, PEGI and USK has formed the International Age Rating Coalition (IARC), aimed at streamlining the rating of digitally distributed games and apps by providing a single online system that produces age ratings for all participating regions.[45] The IARC system takes into account the various legal and cultural backgrounds of users worldwide and automates the classification process based on the results of a questionnaire filled out by the game publisher; the system is able to produce a set of localized ratings for apps available in the participating stores. On December 19, 2017, the Japanese GRAC became a participating authority of the IARC.

[45] 'International Age Rating Coalition' <https://en.wikipedia.org/wiki/International_Age_Rating_Coalition> last visited December 30, 2024.

## 7.5 A Comprehensive Regulatory Framework for VGs in China

Clearly, the negative externalities of VGs have drawn the attention of policymakers across the world, and cultural differences have resulted in a variety of approaches to the same problem. Although early copyright law grew out of press licensing statutes enacted in part to allow government control of seditious publications, the threats posed by copyright censorship to free speech have always been hotly debated, especially in the US, where freedom of speech is protected by the First Amendment of the Constitution. In China, content censorship has always been the main approach to regulating copyrighted works and to helping guarantee the legislative purpose of copyright to encourage the creation and dissemination of cultural works conducive to the building of a socialist society. Article 4 of the Copyright Law provides a legal basis for this administrative regulatory system. Despite the simplification of the review procedures and the clarification of departments' responsibilities, certain problems remain, such as the time-consuming nature of the review procedure and the lack of practicability of its examination standard. Furthermore, although China has made some attempts to legislate a content rating system, none has been effectively implemented as yet.

Even with an effective rating system, the goal to protect minors from overuse is difficult to guarantee without the involvement of technology. Some notable game enterprises have voluntarily pioneered this undertaking. For example, Tencent has introduced health management technology into many of its popular games, including limits on gaming duration, a real-name authentication system, an ID authentication system linking to the public security database and face recognition technology. However, as these technical measures are not mandatory and have not been implemented universally, underage gamers are able to circumvent them. Besides, higher technological standards entail higher development costs, which would be a huge burden for small game enterprises. These game enterprises may require government-issued financial incentives and reward policies to develop and implement new technologies. Thus, a cooperative relationship is needed between government and society. Governmental departments should take measures to strengthen the copyright protection of online games and crack down on piracy to make anti-addiction measures meaningful. Moreover, a governmental department to supervise and enforce a rating system would make the system more effective. To address the above concerns while considering cultural factors, in the following section I propose a workable scheme to regulate VGs in China.

### 7.5.1 *Establishing a New Rating System for VGs*

#### 7.5.1.1 With a Clear Rating Purpose in Mind

The continuous development of the VG industry necessitates an effective content rating system. China's failed attempts to establish such a system in the last decade seem to stem from its reliance on the traditional censorship system and policy-makers' confusing of the propaganda of illicit elements with the existence of those elements. VGs propagating evil cults or superstition, those propagating obscenity, gambling or violence, and those instigating crimes should be prohibited from distribution and dissemination based on the current laws and regulations. However, VGs merely containing words or scenes related to these elements, without the intention to propagate or instigate like behaviors, should be made available to adult gamers. For example, in scenario where two guys preset by the game developer are violently fighting with each other, and players acting as other characters like policies and they help to resolve this violence. Then such a VG should not be prohibited. Game developers should be permitted to design VGs with diverse contents to provide a satisfying game experience for adults with normal emotional and cognitive needs; their creative freedom and expression should not be restricted. The protection of minors from such content, which is indeed inappropriate for younger players, may be achieved by restricting their access to these games. Furthermore, potential conflicts with the legislative purpose of copyright law to incentivize creation may be avoided without risking harm to underage players. Herein lies the significance of the proposed content rating system.

#### 7.5.1.2 Appointing a Government-Regulated Rating Institution

Rating systems across jurisdictions all have an established organization (either self-regulated by the industry or government-regulated) to set and implement the rating standard for VGs. This is one of the most important elements of an effective rating system. I propose that a government-regulated organization is best suited to China, based primarily on cultural considerations. Although the ESRB system is primarily enforced on a voluntary basis, its success relies on retailers; refusal to sell VGs without ESRB ratings. In China, experience has shown that a rating system without government supervision or enforcement has little social impact, as Chinese retailers are unwilling to take such actions without the compulsion of the government. Thus, I suggest that a government-regulated rating institution should be established to set and administer the rating standard for VGs.

#### 7.5.1.3 Developing Risk Categories to Depict the Addictive Potential of VGs

Age-based ratings for VGs are an accepted custom, though there are some minor differences between jurisdictions. My proposal for China is to take the educational level and the physical and psychological characteristics of gamers into consideration, while making reference to age for purposes of criminal responsibility before developing a criterion. This can be achieved by making reference to the age distribution at different stages of educations in China and by consulting with psychologists. I also suggest that the rating system should be extended to incorporate risk categories to reflect the addictive potential of VGs. Accessing a VG's addictive potential is much more difficult than rating its content; violent and mature game elements can be quantified relatively easily, whereas addictive potential is a more abstract attribute. Few scholars have proposed such an endeavor. A research survey conducted by Tencent found that different groups have different demands regarding the characteristics of online games.[46] Based on this research, some scholars have emphasized the necessity of paying attention to the network characteristics of VGs when formulating a rating system, namely interactivity, collaborative-ness, equality, addictiveness and consumptiveness (Ma & Liu, 2012). Though this research put forward a new perspective to formulate rating system for VGs, I suggest that this list is incomplete without risk categories pertaining to addictiveness.

One possible way to evaluate the addictive quality of games is to consider their structural characteristics, which are quantifiable to a certain extent. Research has generally found that certain games and game genres are potentially more addictive than others.[47] For instance, massively multiplayer online games such as *World of Warcraft* and first-person shooter games such as *Call of Duty* tend to be more addictive than games that belong to other genres, such as racing and casual games. Also, research has suggested that more addictive games often incorporate well-established psychological principles into gameplay to encourage longer and more frequent gaming sessions (King, 2010). In general, the most addictive VGs are those "with no end," "encouraging online social interactions with other players," "based on a variable ratio interval reward schedule" and "frequently rewarding the player for minimal effort in the early stages of gameplay and then gradually increasing the amount of time and effort that is necessary to receive a reward as the game progresses." However, simply quantifying the addictive game elements may not be a consistently reliable method of rating the addictiveness of VGs, as a given combination of elements or the introduction of an element by chance can also affect addictiveness in a way that would not necessarily be caught by risk assessment software. As an alternative, some have proposed the use of professional gaming reviews to assess potential addictiveness (Kiraly et al., 2017). Gaming reviews by professional

[46] See iREsearch & Tencent, 'White Paper on Online Game Crowd in China' <https://ishare.iask.sina.com.cn/f/12900213.html> last visited December 30, 2024.

[47] 'What makes Video Games Addictive?' <http://www.techaddiction.ca/video-game-addiction.html> last visited December 30, 2024.

journalists can sometimes influence the sales of such games. The "Metacritic score," which summarizes a large number of reviews from different online gaming magazines, can reflect the general success of a VG, which is usually closely related to a VG's addictive potential. Consequently, the Metacritic score could be combined with an evaluation of the structural game elements to assess the addictive potential of VGs. The risk categories of addictive potential could then be used as a basis for rating institution to rate the addictive level of each game. On this basis, a compulsory duty should be imposed on game developers to label the addictive level of each VG on the screen before this game is released on the market.

#### 7.5.1.4 Linking the Chinese Rating System to the IARC

Research has shown that many people are confused by media rating systems and concerned about their accuracy; thus, a universal rating system has been proposed by both scholars and industry professionals (Brekke, 2006). The Henry J. Kaiser Family Foundation (2003) reported general support for the creation of a single rating system for all media to eliminate confusion. Some scholars have also supported this idea, asserting that a worldwide classification system would facilitate greater understanding and ease of use, which in turn would help implement games for rehabilitation use (Marston & Smith, 2013). As mentioned, a number of regional organizations have cooperated to establish the online IARC system, a ground-breaking global rating and age classification system for digitally delivered games and apps that provides tailored age ratings reflecting the unique cultural differences of participating nations and regions. I propose that China join the IARC once a new rating system is established in this country. This would not only simplify the rating process and thus facilitate game circulation locally but also help promote the international cooperation of game enterprises.

### *7.5.2 Improving the Censorship System for VGs*

#### 7.5.2.1 Simplifying Review Procedure and Shortening Review Time

As mentioned, China uses a pre-censorship approach for VGs, although administrative enforcement departments also have the power to address pirated VGs or VGs with illicit content under the post-censorship system. Among the drawbacks of the pre-censorship system are the complexity of its procedures and the overlapping responsibilities of the several departments involved. The PDCPCCC was put in charge of supervising and administrating the online game industry, and it also conducts pre-examinations and processes approvals. This administrative reform avoids the contradictory review outcomes brought by overlapping departments, thereby improving review efficiency. However, although the VG review procedure has been simplified, review times remain lengthy, which contributes to the problem of pirated games.

Therefore, I suggest that censors should take measures to shorten review times, especially as the number of reviews to be processed is likely to rise in the future.

#### 7.5.2.2 Adding Anti-addiction Measures as Compulsory Review Items

The lack of practicability of its examination standard has always been another major defect of the censorship system in China. This was mainly due to the overlapping responsibilities of the administrative departments involved and the lack of a specific review standard; however, the formation of the PDCPCCC and clarification of its duties addressed the problem of overlapping responsibilities. Thus, the next step toward a more practicable system is to set a specific review standard to avoid the subjective influence of censors. Furthermore, to make the review standard more valuable and reliable, I recommend that anti-addiction measures be added as compulsory review items. As copyright in a VG vests immediately and automatically upon creation without any required formalities, it follows that censors cannot legally deny a VG's copyright based on offending content. It is also unfeasible to prohibit the circulation of some VGs based solely on their addictiveness, as addictive potential is too abstract to be defined. However, current technologies permit the relatively easy and reliable review of the anti-gaming addiction measures integrated in games. Some of these measures that could be imposed by state authorities are as follows. Firstly, a real-name authentication system should be employed by using C recognition, lip language live detection and big data technologies to deter fake identity attempts. Secondly, a shutdown system should be applied to prevent minors from gaming between 10 PM and 8 AM (Law of the People's Republic of China on the Protection of Minors, 2021) art. 48) and ensure that the services provided do not exceed 3 h per day on holidays and 1.5 h on other days (Notice on Preventing Minors from Indulging in Online Games, 2019). Thirdly, a parental control system should be adopted in each game. Game designers should provide parents or legal guardians the option to specify the maximum hours their underage children can play the game as well as an option to receive reports on the amount of time they spend playing the game and the amount of money they spend on in-game purchases. Fourthly, a unified VG supervision platform should be established by the National Network Information Department to identify underage gamers and to cross-check their accounts to prevent teenagers from evading the shutdown system by logging into different accounts or switching from one manufacturer's terminal to another. Last but not least, an age-appropriateness warning system should be used to raise gamers' awareness on the possible detrimental consequences of excessive gaming. One useful way is to post educational in-game warning messages related to the risks of excessive game playing, such as the loading screen tips in *World of Warcraft* (e.g. "Remember to take all things in moderation (even World of Warcraft)!"). Another type of warning messages could be customized for gamers who play a game for several hours in a row. For instance, players could be advised to take a break after a predetermined time (e.g. two hours).

#### 7.5.2.3 Strengthening the Post-Censorship System to Fight Against Pirated Games

Historically, China was notorious for rampant piracy. Although the government has recently launched initiatives such as the "seedling protection" and "sword net" campaigns to curtail pirated works, VG piracy continues to be a problem. One of the main factors leading to piracy is the lack of normalization and standardization of law enforcement. Another factor is the overlapping responsibilities of departments,[48] as a result of which no department takes full responsibility for the problem. In some districts, piracy has created a unique interest group, with the local government protecting the software piracy industry; corruption is the most significant obstacle to the fight against piracy. Thus, it is vital to clarify the respective responsibilities of administrative enforcement departments and to normalize the post-censorship. This would encourage game enterprises to implement the pre-review items and ultimately promote the legitimate development of the VG industry.

### *7.5.3 Enacting a New Gaming Law to Regulate VGs*

South Korea's Game Industry Promotion Act and the Game Industry Promotion Act Enforcement Ordinance, enacted to regulate the games market, have yet to be evaluated in terms of effectiveness. However, it is assumed that state regulation is far more effective than self-regulation by game enterprises, given that these enterprises focus more on commercial than social interests. The *Law of the* PRC on the Protection of Minors Online (2021) has imposed on ISPs certain responsibilities regarding the protection of minors, but these entail general administrative obligations, with little deterrent effect (Chapter 5). Moreover, pursuant to the *Regulations on the Protection of Minors Online (Draft for Deliberation)*, the maximum fine for game enterprises that illegally provide online game services to minors is 500,000 RMB (art. 27), which is a trivial amount compared with the over 100 million RMB that many game companies make annually. This mild punishment is a major reason why some enterprises prefer to break the law than to comply with it. Therefore, I suggest that a new gaming law should be enacted to regulate VGs in China, as described below.

First, the new gaming law should clearly define game publishers' and game service providers' distinct respective legal obligations to protect minors, e.g., game publishers have a legal obligation to obtain ratings for their games and game service providers have a legal duty to integrate anti-addiction measures into their gaming products. Second, the law should provide a set of clear and harsh penalties for game enterprises violating the law, such as a substantial fine and the duty to correct the violation within a set time. Third, the law should offer some incentives for game enterprises

[48] As far as administrative enforcement is concerned, the IP Office, the State Copyright Bureau, the Industry and Commerce Bureau and other departments have undertaken part of the functions of IP protection.

to protect minors, such as a preferential tax policy. Also, a special subsidy policy can be used to encourage game developers to increase their investment in educational games for the social good. Furthermore, the new gaming law should stipulate a reward system for the reporting of game enterprises violating the law. Optimizing the existing reporting channels and establishing a unified reporting platform would facilitate this element of the law.

Granted, other proactive interventions in the form of treatment programs could also be included in this legislation; however, such considerations are beyond the scope of this thesis. At the policy level, it is assumed that effective prevention schemes should be prioritized, as they can both address the problem of gaming addiction at an early stage and reach the widest audience. Nonetheless, the thesis believes that creating a cohesive and comprehensive regulation mechanism comprising the aforementioned multiple policy responses would most effectively address the problems posed by minors' access to VGs while promoting creation, thus achieving an "eco-balance" for this copyright industry.

## References

Andronicus. (2014). Understand Game Addiction Law in South Korea in 5 Minutes. Available at: http://treeofsaviorgame.com/general/313/understand-game-addiction-law-in-south-korea-in-5-minutes/. Accessed 30 December 2024.

Brekke, A. D. (2006). Video Game Ratings: Does the System Work for Parents? Dissertation: Unijversity of Tennessee, Knoxvilles, p. 23.

Chalk, A. (2007). Inappropriate Content: A Brief History of Videogame Ratings and the ESRB. THE NEEDLES. Available at: https://v1.escapistmagazine.com/articles/view/video-games/columns/the-needles/1300-Inappropriate-Content-A-Brief-History-of-Videogame-Ratings-and-t. Accessed 30 December 2024.

Chang Yajie [苌雅洁] (2019). Study on the Legal Proection Mechanism to Prevent Minors from Indulging in Online Games [防范未成年人沉迷网络游戏的法律保障机制研究]. 5 Changjiang Forum [长江论坛].

JP Charlton IDW Danforth 2007 Distinguishing Addiction and High Engagement in the Context of Online Game Playing Computers in Human Behavior 23 3 1531 1548

Cooper, D. (2020). The Last of Us 2 Censors Abby Scene in Japan. Available at: https://gamerant.com/last-of-us-2-abby-censor-japan/#:~:text=The%20reason%20why%20The%20Last,scene%20was%20out%20of%20bounds. Accessed 30 December 2024.

Cui, X. (2020). Juvenile Protection is the Top Priority of the Tencent Games. Available at: https://baijiahao.baidu.com/s?id=1686223006260913587&wfr=spider&for=pc. Accessed 30 December 2024.

Dogruel, L., & Joeckel, S. (2013). Video Game Rating Systems in the US and Europe: Comparing their Outcomes. *International Communication Gazette*, p. 675.

Dreier, T. (2006). Berne Convention for the Protection of Literary and Artistic Works. In T. Dreier & P. Bernt Hugenholtz (Eds.), *Concise European Copyright Law*, 2nd Edition (p. 69), Kluwer Law International.

Fingas, J. (2014). South Korea Debates the Wisdom of A Video Game Addiction Law. Available at: https://www.engadget.com/2014/06/23/korea-debates-game-addiction-law/. Accessed 30 December 2024.

Fu, D. [傅鼎生]. (1988). Copyright Protects the Expression of Works. *Law Science [法学]*, Issue 1, pp. 34–36.

Ghosh, A. (2013). Censorship through Copyright: From Print to Digital Media. *Social Scientist, 41*(1/2), 51, 52, 54–56.

T Gibbons P Humphreys 2011 Audiovisual Regulation Under Pressure: Comparative Cases from North America and Europe Routledge

Gong Yuhua [龚玉花]. (2020). Study on the Legal Mechanism of Correcting Minors' Gaming Addiction [未成年人网络游戏沉迷矫正法律机制浅 析]. 8 Children's Study [少年儿童研究].

MD Griffiths 2000 Does Internet and Computer "Addiction" Exist? Some Case Study Evidence Cyber Psychology and Behavior 3 211

MD Griffiths 2008 Videogame Addiction: Further Thoughts and Observations International Journal of Mental Health Addiction 6 182

He, T. (2017). Control or Promote: China's Cultural Censorship System and Its Influence on copyright Protection. *Queen Mary Journal of Intellectual Property* (7), 74, 86, 94, 96.

Hilgert, F., & Summermann, P. (2016). Video Game Age Ratings in Europe. Part 1 of 3: The Basics. Available at: https://gameslaw.org/video-game-age-ratings-in-europe-part-1-of-3-the-basics/. Accessed 30 December 2024.

Jenkins, D., & Carless, S. (2004). Schwarzenegger Signs California Video Games Bill. Available at: https://www.gamasutra.com/php-bin/news_index.php?story=4324. Accessed 30 December 2024.

Kang, Y. [康亚通]. (2019). The Governance of Teenagers' Internet Addiction [青少年网络沉迷问题的治理]. *Education and Protection [教育和保护]*, Issue 5, p. 40.

Kang, Y. [康亚通]. (2019). A Review of the Research on Teenagers' Internet Addiction [青少年网络沉迷研究综述]. *Social Science of Chinese Youth [中国青年社会科学]*, Issue 6, p. 132.

ST King 2010 A Study on the Legislative Direction for Prevention and Solution of Internet Addiction Journal of Hongik Law Review 11 3 1 39

King, D. L., Delfabbro, P. H., & Griffiths, M. D. (2010). Video game structural characteristics: A new psychological taxonomy. *International Journal of Mental Health and Addiction, 8*(1), 90–106.

DL King PH Delfabbro MD Griffiths 2011 The Role of Structural Characteristics in Problematic Video Game Play: An Empirical Study International Journal of Mental Health and Addiction 9 3 320 333

Kiraly, O., et al. (2017). Policy Responses to Problematic Video Game Use: A Systematic Review of Current Measures and Future Possibilities. *Journal of Behavioral Addictions*, 4.

DJ Kuss MD Griffiths 2012 Internet Gaming Addiction: A Systematic Review of Empirical Research International Journal of Mental Health and Addiction 10 2 278 296

Lee, A. (2017). A Chinese Smartphone Game Called a "Poison" by the Government has 200 Million Players-Here's Why. South China Morning Post. Available at: https://www.businessinsider.com/a-chinese-poison-smartphone-game-has-200-million-players-2017-7. Accessed 15 August 2018.

Lee, D. D. (2019). Video Game Powerhouse South Korea Braces for WHO Gaming Addiction Classification. THIS WEEK IN ASIA. Available at: https://www.scmp.com/week-asia/society/article/3017913/video-game-powerhouse-south-korea-braces-who-gaming-addiction. Accessed 30 December 2024.

Li, S. [李顺德]. (2015). Thoughts on Strengthening the Copyright Administrative Law Enforcement [对加强著作权行政执法的思考]. *Intellectual Property [知识产权]*, Volume 11. Available at: http://www.iolaw.org.cn/showArticle.aspx?id=4597. Accessed 30 December 2024.

Lin, Y. [林悦], Liu, Q. [刘勤学] & others. (2021). Study on the Relationship between Parental Neglection and Adolescents' Gaming Addiction: The Mediating Role of Hope and the Moderating Role of Gender [父母忽视与青少年网络游戏成瘾的关系:希望的中介作用和性别的调节作用]. *Psychological Development and Education [心理发展与教育]*, 37(01).

Liu, Y., Ye, Z., & Xu, H. (2015). Improving Online Game Rating System in China From the Perspective of Comparative Study [比较研究视角下我国网络游戏分级制度的完善]. *Journal of Jilin Business and Technology College [吉林工商学院学报], 31*(6), 83.

Ma, X. [马小强] & Liu H. [刘怀恩]. (2012). Analysis of Online Game Rating from Educational Perspective [基于教育视角的网络游戏分级探析]. *Research on Audiovisual Education [电化教育研究]*, Vol. 10, pp. 69, 72–73.

Marston, H. R., & Smith, S. T. (2013). Understanding the Digital Game Classification System: A Review of the Current Classification System and Its Implications for Use within Games for Health. In A. Holzinger, M. Ziefle, M. Hitz, & M. Debevc (Eds.), *Human Factors in Computing and Informatics*. SouthCHI.

Mtima, L., & Jamar, S. D. (2010). Fulfilling the Copyright Social Justice Promise: Digitizing Textual Information. *New York Law School Law Review*, pp. 77, 86.

Orland, K. (2013). House Bill Wants $5,000 Fine For Video Games Without ESRB Rating. Available at: https://arstechnica.com/gaming/2013/01/house-bill-wants-5000-fine-for-video-games-without-esrb-rating/. Accessed 30 December 2024.

J-E Park 2012 Comparative Study: Restriction on Video Game to Minors in the US and its Unconstitutionality, Its Estimation and Suggestion Lawyers Association Journal 61 8 223 273

Roberts, M. E. (2018). *Censored: Distraction and Diversion Inside China's Great Firewall*. Princeton University Press, pp. 21, 23, 37.

Scutti, S. (2018). WHO Classifies "Gaming Disorder" as Mental Health Condition. CNN News. Available at: https://edition.cnn.com/2018/06/18/health/video-game-disorder-who/index.html. Accessed 28 June 2018.

Sohn, J.-Y. (2018). WHO's Labeling of Gaming Addiction as a Disorder Sparks Concern in Korea. Available at: http://www.thejakartapost.com/life/2018/01/04/whos-labeling-of-gaming-addiction-as-a-disorder-sparks-concern-in-korea.html. Accessed 30 December 2024.

BU Stetina 2011 Beyond the Fascination of Online-Games: Probing Addictive Behavior and Depression in the World of Online-Gaming Computers in Human Behavior 27 473

Sun, Q. [孙秋梅]. (2020). Study on the Prevention of Gaming Addiction of Higher Vocational College Students by School Cooperation [学校联合构建预防高职大学生网络游戏成瘾屏障研究]. *Journal of Vocational College [职大学报]* (3).

The Henry J. Kaiser Family Foundation. (2003). Available at: http://www2.kff.org/content/2003/3353/ParentsandMedia.FINAL.pdf. Accessed 30 December 2024.

Tsesis, A. (2016). Balancing Free Speech. *Boston University Law Review*, *96*(1), 33, 53.

von Lewinski, S. (2008). *International Copyright Law and Policy* (pp. 170–171). Oxford University Press.

Wang, B. (2020). Open Cognition and Discover the Infinite Possibility of Game. Available at: https://new.qq.com/omn/20200731/20200731A0LCMK00.html. Accessed 30 December 2024.

Wang Xixin. (2018). Statement from Wang Xinxi in the 7th Peking-Stanford University Internet Law and Public Policy Conference.

WIPO. (1971). *Guide to the Berne Convention for the Protection of Literary and Artistic Works*. Paris Act, at [17.2], p. 99.

Wittern-Keller, L. (2008). *Freedom of the Screen*. The University Press of Kentucky, pp. 4–5, 7, 11, 13, 18.

WTO. (2009). China-Measures Affecting the Protection and Enforcement of Intellectual Property Rights: Report of the Panel. WT/ DS362/R. [hereinafter as "WTO Panel Report"]. Available at: https://www.wto.org/english/tratop_e/dispu_e/362r_e.pdf. Accessed 30 December 2024.

Xinhua, H. [韩新华]. (2019). Online Game Rating and Minors' Protection [网络游戏分级与未成年人保护]. *China Radio [中国广播]*, Issue 3, p. 64.

Yan, Y. [严玉莹], *Research on the Legal System of Online Game Market Access* (Dissertation: Chang'An University 2018).

Yang, L. (2018). Online Protection for Minors—Three Perspectives. In The 7th Peking-Stanford University Internet Law and Public Policy Conference 2018.

Zhang, Y. [张永欣], Zhang, H. [张惠雯] & others. (2020). Study on the Relationship between Psychological Resistance, Parental Online Supervision and Junior High School Students' Gaming Addiction [心理阻抗、父母网络监管与初中生网络游戏成瘾的关系]. *China Journal of Clinical Psychology [中国临床心理学杂志]*, *28*(04).

Zhang, W., & Li, Y. (2015). Content Review and Copyright Protection in China after the 2009 U.S. v. China WTO Panel Ruling. *Journal of the Copyright Society of the U.S.A.*, *62*, 437, 439–440, 446.

Zhang, C., & Lin, L. (2019). The Interim Measures for the Administration of Online Games Has Been Abolished, Can Game Enterprises Run Naked? Available at: https://zhuanlan.zhihu.com/p/78981436. Accessed 30 December 2024.

Zhou, Y. [周瑛]. (2020). *Study on the Relationship between Parentage Communication, School Belonging, Basic Psychological Needs and Adolescents' Gaming Addiction [亲子沟通、学校归属感、基本心理需求与青少年网络游戏成瘾的关系]*. Mphil These: Central China Normal University [华中师范大学].

## *Legislations*

Berne Convention for the Protection of Literary and Artistic Works (1886)
Constitution of Japan
Game Industry Promotion Act Enforcement Ordinance
Game Industry Promotion Act
German Youth Protection Act
Interim Measures for the Administration of Online Games
Interim Provisions on the Administration of Internet Culture
Interim Provisions on the Administration of Internet Publishing
Interim Provisions on the Administration of Network Culture
Law of the People's Republic of China on the Protection of Minors (2021)
National Press and Publication Administration, Notice of the State Administration of Press, Publication, Radio, Film and Television on Further Carrying Out the Real-Name Authentication System of Online Game Anti-Addiction
National Press and Publication Administration, Notice on Implementing the "Three Regulations" of the State Council and the Relevant Explanations of the Central Editorial Office, Further Strengthening the Pre-Examination and Approval of Online Games and the Examination and Approval Administration of Imported Online Games
Notice on Further Carrying Out the Real-Name Authentication System of Online Game Anti-Addiction
Notice on Preventing Minors from Indulging in Online Games (2019)
Penal Code of Japan
PRC Constitution 2004
PRC Copyright Law
PRC on the Protection of Minors Online (2021)
Regulations on the Administration of Audiovisual Products 2011
Regulations on the Administration of Internet Information Service
Regulations on the Administration of Online Games Publication
Regulations on the Administration of Publications 2011
Regulations on the Protection of Minors Online (Draft for Deliberation)
Statute of Anne 1709
The First Amendment of the US Constitution
TRIPS Agreement
US Constitution
Youth Protection Revision Act

## *Cases*

Barnes v. Miner, 122 F. 480, 489–93 (C.C.S.D.N.Y. 1903).
Brown v. Entertainment Merchants Ass'n, 131 S. Ct. 2729 (2011).
Brown v. Entertainment Merchants Association, 564 U.S. 786 (2011).
Hustler Magazine, Inc. v. Falwell, 485 U.S. 46, 53 (1988).
Martinetti v. Maguire, 16 F. Cas. 920, 922–23 (C.C. Cal. 1867) (No. 9173).
McCutcheon v. FEC, 134 S. Ct. 1434, 1449 (2014).
New York v. Ferber, 458 U.S. 747 (1982).
Texas v. Johnson, 491 U.S. 397 (1989).
United States v. Alvarez, 132 S. Ct. 2537 (2012).

# Chapter 8
# Conclusion

## 8.1 Main Findings

Technological advancement raises new questions regarding copyrights allocation and the preservation of balance between exclusive copyrights and social utility (Mtima & Jamar, 2010). The creation of new digital works, such as VGs, is a typical example of innovation that challenges and reshapes copyright law by pressing it into service in areas not previously addressed. VGs constitute a cultural industry as well as a core copyright industry (WIPO, 2015); the imagined worlds created in them offer richly textured emotional and social experiences that cross the boundary from entertainment to culture and art (Jewell, 2012). As part of literary works (i.e. the underlying software) and part of audiovisual works (i.e. the dynamic game images), VGs are unsuited to traditional forms of copyright protection. This is further complicated by their interactive nature, which allows for the extensive intervention and creative expression of gamers, breaking the traditional boundary between authors and users. Additionally, new technologies have introduced new means of exploiting expressive content (e.g. re-skinning and modding) and disseminating information (e.g. live game streaming), which have triggered concerns regarding game developers' right to control the exploitation of their original games. Furthermore, VGs display much stronger negative externalities than traditional forms of media due to their potentially addictive nature, triggering criticism and attempts to ban their use. Thus, administrative regulatory measures are required to avert gaming addiction so as to ensure sustainable development of this cultural industry.

Policymakers have taken different approaches to tackling these issues, based on the diverse cultural backgrounds of their jurisdictions. Nevertheless, Copyright law is the product not only of governmental policymaking but also of negotiations with interest groups (Litman, 1996). In the copyright ecosystem of VGs, game developers represent the interests of the industry; they invest time and money in the creation of new VGs. Thus, there is a strong interest in affording them adequate protection of their copyright property interests. However, the granting of a VG copyright should not be

 
Z. Deng, *Constructing an Eco-Balanced Copyright Regime for the Video Game Industry in China*, https://doi.org/10.1007/978-981-96-6056-8_8

unlimited; rather, it should cease when appropriate access to works is at risk and future creation is jeopardized (Golan v. Holder, 2012). Besides, copyright, as "the engine of free speech" (Eldred v. Ashcroft, 2003), should also be restricted in the interest of preventing minors from the threats posed by violent, pornographic and other harmful contents of cultural works (Tsesis, 2016). At present, the copyright system in China as applied to VGs fails to achieve an eco-balance between incentivizing innovation and reconciling public interest, due to its failure to include all interested parties at the negotiation table. The omission of certain key parties, such as gamers and game streamers, may threaten copyright social utility balance, as it heightens "the risk that certain socio-economic empowerment interests will not be fully considered or addressed in relevant legislation" (Mtima & Jamar, 2010).

Theoretically, an optimal copyright system should favor neither the authors nor the subsequent users of cultural works but rather hold paramount the interests of society in developing a thriving, vibrant culture. Thus, to ensure the sustainable development of the VG industry, copyright protection must grant game developers the opportunity to reap the fruits of their work while also allowing the public to productively use game materials for innovation and reducing or eliminating the conflict between the granting of rights and the protection of minors.

## 8.2 Contributions of the Research

a. Designing a New Copyright Protection Model for VGs

In this book, I argue that VGs should be classified as a new type of copyrighted work distinguished from the computer program or the audiovisual work and afforded a hybrid protection model. This proposal is based on the belief that the multimedia nature of VGs and their significance to the prosperity of culture and innovative art allow them to stand out as a unique category of work deserving of special treatment.

First of all, I believe that VGs should initially be classified as a new type of copyrighted work in an international treaty or an amendment of an international convention; eventually, this principle will be incorporated into Chinese copyright law. Once such legislation is in place, copyright registration of VGs in China should be limited to the newly established category of VGs to eliminate the present dual registration problem, whereby VGs are registered either as audiovisual works or as literary works (to protect the computer program). As the transfer of moral rights differs between audiovisual works and computer programs under some domestic laws, including China's, it is advisable to establish a fixed term within which moral rights to VGs cannot be transferred, to eliminate uncertainty.

Secondly, when comparing works to determine copyright infringement under the proposed law, both the test for audiovisual works and that for computer programs should be applied. Neither model alone is adequate to protect rights to VGs, due to the aforementioned complex nature of such games. As piracy is increasingly rampant in the games industry (Dean, 2016; Meyer, 2010), a hybrid protection model for VGs would be ideal to protect their audiovisual output and prevent reverse engineering of the underlying software. Under this model, the audiovisual images of a VG would receive a level of protection similar to that of an audiovisual work, and the underlying software would be protected as literary works are. The "total concept and feel" test would be used to determine game copyright infringement (Brashears Macatee, 1993), emphasizing both the significance of the audiovisual output and the intrinsic interactive experience operated by the computer program.

Thirdly, it is better to be specified by law that the copyright ownership of a VG should be attributed to the investors, that is, the game developers hold the copyright of the VG as a whole. This is primarily considered from the economic theory of incentives, which aims to maximize the public good by examining the transaction cost associated with the transfer of resources from one economic unit to another. Above all, there are many contributors to the production of a VG, rendering it difficult if not impossible to determine the relative value of the contributions. Granting IP ownership of a VG to its creators is also likely to delay dissemination and increase transaction costs by allowing multiple individual creators to claim ownership. Besides, any additional transaction costs that game developers must bear ultimately pass to consumers. Thus, when determining copyright ownership, one must consider the incentives of contributing creators; the incentives of game developers, who initiate and oversee the production and distribution of VGs; and the interests of the general public, who embrace VGs as an indispensable part of modern culture. Given the complexity of the issue, it is best to avoid confusion by attributing copyright ownership of VGs to the investors—that is, the game developers—by law.

Finally, I suggest that a shorter copyright protection term should be applied to VGs based on the empirical observation. Due to rapid technological advancement and the quickly evolving market, a given VG becomes outdated very quickly, a phenomenon exacerbated by fierce competition in the games market. This is evident from the short life cycle of a modern VG, with the average life cycle of a VG in China no more than 12 months. Thus, these products are marketed immediately upon completion, and the investment is either recouped or lost within a short period. Copyright protection over the long term is thus of little concern to a VG's creators and exploiters; their main concern with copyright is only with respect to their ability to quickly recoup their investment. Long-term copyright protection is therefore an unnecessary and unjustified restriction on competition (Bard & Kurlantzick, 1999). Besides, empirical evidence suggests that copyright terms should depend on the type of copyrighted work (Yuan, 2009). Therefore, a reasonable protection term should be reset for VGs based on the empirical data and market observation.

b. Amending the Game Adaptation Infringement Test

My input for the amendment of game adaptation infringement test is to revise the current three-step test by a more balanced approach: determination of the facts of copying, interlayer analysis and infringement value judgement. This suggestion is based on the fact that current copyright regime fails to acknowledge the core role of the right of adaptation in copyright theory, providing a thin protection for VGs and thus rewarding clone developers at the expense of bona fide innovators. If strictly implemented, this test would avoid unduly restraining competition and follow-on innovation and interfering with the reasonable interests of the original creators.

The first step, determining the facts of copying, comprises a two-part inquiry: regarding "access" and "probative similarity." The plaintiff must prove that the defendant had access to the plaintiff's game and show that the two games are similar enough to support a reasonable inference of copying (Positive Black Talk Inc. v. Cash Money Records Inc., 2004). The possibility of access is proven by evidence and not by speculation (Li, 2014), and the "probative similarity" refers to a "striking similarity" between the two works, which can provide evidence of access (Arnstein v. Porter, 1946). To determine probative similarity, courts can hear from expert witnesses, technical investigators or other technical experts who are able to compare the similarities and differences between the two games. The court should take into consideration both the protected expression and the unprotected ideas or facts in this analysis. The plaintiff bears the burden of proving factual copying. The burden then shifts to the defendant to prove exclusion or independent creation.

The second step, interlayer analysis, is a key link in determining game adaptation infringement, constituting the "substantial similarity" investigation together with the third step of the "infringement value judgement." In this step, it is important to first isolate original elements of the plaintiff's and the defendant's works by identifying and eliminating ideas as distinguished from expression in the games. Next, the court must filter out unprotected habitual expression through the merger and scènes à faire doctrines. In this process, the court should be especially careful not to filter out the inner expression of a game, such as its constitutive rules and elements of game mechanics. Moreover, it should restrict the application of the merger and scènes à faire doctrines and instead evaluate whether there are other ways to express the rules or concepts in the VG context, taking technological advancement into consideration. Once the uncopyrightable elements have been set aside, the court must identify the homologous comprehensive expression (inner form of expression) of the two works. To observe the similarities in the structure of comprehensive expression, the court must screen out the irrelevant expression elements resulting from the special characteristics of the two works, such as type or genre, and then extract the homologous comprehensive expression. If it is difficult to identify a similar structure of comprehensive expression between the two works, then there is no comparative basis for the adaptation infringement value judgement. In such a case, even if there is factual copying between the two works, the plaintiff's work should be regarded as a source of the defendant's inspiration or material for reasonable reference, not an infringing adaptation.

The third step is the infringement value judgement. In this step, I propose that courts should apply the "decomposition" test or the "total concept and feeling" test to comprehensively examine the similarity of expression between the two works from qualitative and quantitative perspectives. In general, the decomposition test should be applied in cases involving derivative works with little originality, such as novels and story-driven games, to comprehensively itemize the specific forms of expression for comparison (Brashears Macatee, 1993). On the contrary, the "total concept and feeling" test should be applied in cases involving works with significant originality, such as open world games, and this approach emphasizes the similarities between the two works in terms of users' perceptions and appreciation, using the "ordinary, reasonable observer" standard (Litchfield v. Spielberg, 1984; Lyons P'ship, L.P. v. Morris Costumes, 2000). In some cases, including those involving cloned games, courts must apply both of these tests to compare the external and internal expression of the works. In such cases, the "total concept and feeling" test can be used to determine the copying of internal expression (Meyer, 2010). If substantial similarity is found between the two works in terms of both external and internal expression, reproduction infringement is established. However, if substantial similarity is found only in terms of the internal expression, this constitutes adaptation infringement. Moreover, the "infringement value judgement" step evaluates not only the proportion of comprehensive expression in the defendant's work that is homologous to that in the plaintiff's work, but also the value of that expression in the defendant's work. When the homologous comprehensive expression bears a new artistic value or achieves a different function from that in the original work, the defendant's work is considered as a transformative use rather than adaptation infringement.

c. Proposing a Scheme for Regulating Game Mods

In response to the modding problem facing by the current copyright system, I propose a two-pronged solution. The first prong concerns the social benefit of game Mods, aiming to change the copyright regime from being exclusive to becoming non-exclusive. The new regime would confer on gamers the legal right to modify VGs without permission but oblige them to remunerate the original developers for commercial use of those Mods. Under the proposed scheme, both the right to modify and the obligation to pay remuneration would pass to the future users of a given Mod. Specifically, the main features of the proposed modding right scheme are summarized as follows:

(i) in creating game Mods, players can modify a VG without asking for permission from the game developer, provided that (a) such use does not affect the normal exploitation of the work and does not unreasonably prejudice the legitimate interests of the game developer, and (b) the game developer has not used TPMs to prevent such modification;
(ii) a game Mod can be used for commercial or non-commercial purposes; in the case of commercial use, reasonable remuneration should be paid to the game developer. Remuneration, which may be made through e-payment, should be apportioned using a pre-determined method set by the game developer, with the modder taking no less than 50%; and
(iii) a game Mod can be used by subsequent modders without permission from either the original modder or the game developer of the underlying game; however, remuneration must be offered to both the original modder and the game developer under the remuneration scheme set forth in Clause (ii) in the case of commercial use, and such use must not undermine the reasonable exploitation of the Mod or the underlying game.

The second prong pertains to the social harm of game Mods and proposes a community-based approach. Under the new scheme, game operators are imposed a common law duty to monitor infringement and to ensure the fair implementation of game developers' TOS. To be more specific, game operators should assume a common-law duty of indirect infringement on the basis of "cooperative operation/direct financial benefit + know or should have known the infringing activity" for presumption of fault. If the law were to impose on game operators such a duty to monitor rather than just passively obey takedown notices, game operators would no longer turn a blind eye to Mods that may infringe third parties' IP rights.

Additionally, the TOS should incorporate certain legal standards and principles to ensure that they be fairly implemented. First, the copyright preemption principle should apply. In other words, TOS should not conflict with copyright law; any such conflict should invalidate the TOS. Under the scheme I propose, TOS that irrationally limit the modding right of gamers would be invalid. Second, unfairness would be prohibited; in other words, TOS would not be permitted to impose unreasonable duties on one party in terms of procedures or content. Third, the abuse of rights would be prohibited under the proposed scheme. This would prevent rights holders from illegally expanding their rights in violation of the basic objectives of copyright law (Lasercomb America, Inc. v. Reynolds, 1990). Finally, I propose that the public policy principle should apply. According to this principle, if the terms of a contract violate basic public policy, they are invalid. Applying this principle would make game operators responsible for policing socially problematic PCC such as overtly sexualized Mods. I argue that courts should rely on this principle when weighing the rights and obligations of game operators and gamers. The public policy principle could also be used by administrative bodies to supervise game operators, thus forming an interactive legal-administrative supervision mechanism. Game operators failing to monitor game Mods that violate social morals would be held both legally and administratively accountable.

d. Constructing a Statutory Licensing Model for Live Game Streaming

Given the concerns of public interest, transaction costs and potential profits of the live game streaming market, I propose a new statutory licensing mechanism designed specifically for live game streaming. The proposed statutory licensing scheme for live game streaming is outlined below.

First, my proposed licensing scheme is limited to cases in which a VG work has been published and uploaded to the Internet by the copyright owner independently and directly. This excludes VGs that are distributed only on CD or other hard carriers, as these games are considered more private and improper for the statutory license. The proposed statutory license would be obtained automatically by an end user's accepting a subscriber agreement with the game developer when downloading or logging a VG published by a game developer on the Internet. The license would grant a gamer the right to transmit the game content to others or perform to the public through online streaming and would impose a duty to pay proper remuneration to the game developer as prescribed in regulations.

Second, under my proposed licensing scheme, streaming platform operators bear the responsibility to pay remuneration to game developers. It is found that streaming platform operators' legal status may be compared to that of film producers, as they control the development of the live game streaming industry, whereas game anchors and players are more like actors and have the legal status of performers. Their contractual relationship is comparable to an employer-employee relationship. Thus, the copyrights to any fixed streaming content belong to the streaming platform operators, and as such the streaming platform operators have rights to prevent others from rebroadcasting and transcribing the streaming content without permission. For consistency in rights and obligations, therefore, under my scheme streaming platform operators would be responsible for paying remuneration. This would also greatly reduce transaction costs and improve the efficiency of transmitting. As for the standard of remuneration, it is advised that the remuneration shall be 20%–30% of streaming income for tournament streaming and 10% for individual streaming, including subscription fees in any form and revenue derived from advertising associated with the particular live game stream on the game streaming website. This remuneration would be collected from the streaming platform operator directly on a weekly or monthly basis.

Third, a right of cancellation is introduced in the proposed scheme, permitting game developers to prohibit undesirable streaming of their games to protect their economic interests. Under the scheme, the streaming platform operator would have three days following notice from the game developer in which to transfer that notice to the streamer and shut down the undesirable streaming. By involving streaming platform operators and setting limits on streamers' behavior, the right of cancellation would further protect the interests of the copyright owners and increase game developers' acceptance of licensing. However, the cancellation right would only be permitted to avoid such economic harms to the game developers, as unrestricted rights to cancellation would potentially harm streaming platform operators.

e. Establishing a Comprehensive Regulatory Framework to Address Gaming Addiction

To address the potential threats posed by gaming addiction while considering cultural differences, I propose a workable administrative regulation mechanism to regulate VGs in China, including establishing a new rating system, improving the censorship system and enacting a new gaming law.

First, policymakers must abandon the shackles of the traditional censorship system, with a clear rating purpose in mind. Regarding this, I advise that the propaganda of illicit elements should be distinguished from the existence of those elements; VGs merely containing words or scenes related to illicit elements, without the intention to propagate or instigate like behaviors, should be made available to adult gamers. I also suggest that a government-regulated rating institution should be established to set and administer the rating standard for VGs. Additionally, the Metacritic score could be combined with an evaluation of the structural game elements to assess the addictive potential of VGs, and the risk categories of addictive potential could then be used as a basis to implement anti-addiction measures. Furthermore, I propose that China join the IARC once a new rating system is established in this country. This would not only simplify the rating process and thus facilitate game circulation locally but also help promote the international cooperation of game enterprises.

Second, censors should pay attention to review efficiency and take measures to shorten review times, especially as the number of reviews to be processed is likely to rise in the future. Moreover, I recommend that a specific review standard be set to avoid the subjective influence of censors and anti-addiction measures be added as compulsory review items to make the review standard more valuable and reliable. This includes employing an advanced real-name authentication system, applying a shutdown system, adopting a parental control system, establishing a unified VG supervision platform and using an age-appropriateness warning system. Furthermore, it is vital to clarify the respective responsibilities of administrative enforcement departments and to normalize the post-censorship. This would encourage game enterprises to implement the pre-review items and ultimately promote the legitimate development of the VG industry.

Third, a new gaming law should be enacted to regulate VGs in China. Above all, the new gaming law should clearly define game publishers' and game service providers' distinct respective legal obligations to protect minors, e.g., game publishers have a legal obligation to obtain ratings for their games and game service providers have a legal duty to integrate anti-addiction measures into their gaming products. Secondly, the law should provide a set of clear and harsh penalties for game enterprises violating the law, such as a substantial fine and the duty to correct the violation within a set time. Thirdly, the law should offer some incentives for game enterprises to protect minors, such as a preferential tax policy. Also, a special subsidy policy can be used to encourage game developers to increase their investment in educational games for the social good. Finally, the new gaming law should stipulate a reward system for the reporting of game enterprises violating the law. Optimizing the existing reporting channels and establishing a unified reporting platform would facilitate this element of the law. It is believed that creating a cohesive and comprehensive regulation mechanism comprising the aforementioned multiple policy responses would most effectively address the problems posed by minors' access to VGs while promoting creation, thus achieving an "eco-balance" for this copyright industry.

## 8.3 Significance of the Research

This book is, to the best of my knowledge, the first attempt to construct an eco-balanced copyright regime for the VG industry in China. My analysis, which integrates doctrinal, empirical, interdisciplinary and comparative approaches, thereby has both theoretical and practical significance, offering insights for scholars, policymakers, game enterprises and other interested parties.

Firstly, this book places the copyright protection of VGs in an ecosystem context and contributes important insights for the advancement of the copyright system in China. Although copyright protection for VGs has been a topic of discussion for a decade, especially in Western countries, it must be reconsidered in the modern context, as VGs have become much more diverse and complex and their business models have consequently changed. VGs also pose a challenge to the existing copyright system due to their relatively recent emergence, especially in developing countries such as China. By focusing on China to clarify its particular copyright problems as applied to VGs and to identify deficiencies in China's regulations for judicial practice, this book adds significantly to knowledge of the VG industry. Moreover, it offers a comparative analysis of relevant provisions and judicial practices in other jurisdictions, which can inform copyright reform in China. Furthermore, this book treats the copyright protection of VGs as an ecosystem, taking into account both internal and external factors. Based on the empirical analysis of the functioning of this copyright industry, it offers recommendations to prevent copyright reform from occurring in an "evidence-free-zone" (Boyle, 2008).

Secondly, this book provides a new perspective to study the copyright protection of VGs that may both support the sustainable development of the VG industry and improve social welfare. The treatment of VG copyrights suggested in this thesis focuses on the public interest. However, whereas many literatures have argued that the public interest is always best served by attempting to eliminate or reduce copyrights (Determann, 2006), this book suggests that an optimal copyright regime must achieve as close as possible to equilibrium among various interests, or the so-called "eco-balance." Furthermore, rather than regarding public interest factor as equivalent in weight to the freedoms of information and expression, the book emphasizes the ultimate aim of copyright law: to promote cultural innovation and social welfare. Culture, information and knowledge are among the most frequently consumed goods that enhance the welfare of modern societies, and copyright laws are put in place to further this broad societal goal. Under this approach, the public interest factor includes consideration of negative externalities of copyrighted works that is detrimental to social welfare. This is particularly important when it comes to VGs, a potentially addictive type of work that can both educate and distract from learning. This book considers gaming addiction to be a public interest consideration and explores how copyright law can better fulfill its societal goals by addressing this problem. Addressing gaming addiction in legislation, as the book proposes, would also promote the sustainable development of the VG industry.

Thirdly, this book helps to promote the efficiency and quality of the respective types of litigations. VG copyrights are a controversial legal issue, and the proper outcomes of related litigation are largely unstandardized. This slows down proceedings, as a lack of clear standards forces courts to spend more time making judgements. With respect to this problem, the proposals provided in this book can do some help. For example, the proposal to classify VGs as a new type of work and afford them a hybrid protection model, as described in Chapter 2, would provide courts with a general idea of "the rights an author has, the scope of protection for those rights, and the way the rights are protected" (Mtima & Jamar, 2010). Additionally, the new three-step test proposed in Chapter 3 to prevent game developers from cloning or re-skinning games at the expense of discouraging innovation would prevent courts from confusing game reproduction infringement with game adaptation infringement. Moreover, the statutory licensing mechanism proposed in Chapter 5 for live game streaming would prevent courts from having to determine whether live game streaming constitutes fair use or transformative use. If implemented, the proposals provided in this book could advance the copyright system in China to provide clearer guidelines for judges, enabling them to handle copyright cases involving VGs more effectively and efficiently.

## References

Bard, R., & Kurlantzick, L. (1999). *Copyright Duration: Duration, Term Extension, the European Union, and the Making of Copyright Policy.* Austin & Winfield, San Francisco, London, Bethesda, p 215.

Brashears Macatee, S. (1993). Total Concept and Feel or Dissection: Approaches to the Misappropriation Test of Substantial Similarity. *Chi-Kent Law Review, 68*, 913, 935.

Boyle, J. (2008). *The Public Domain, Chapter 9.* Yale University Press.

Dean, D. S. (2016). Hitting Reset: Devising a New Video Game Copyright Regime. *University of Pennsylvania Law Review, 164*, 1239.

Determann, L. (2006). Dangerous Liaisons-Software Combinations as Derivative Works? Distribution, Installation, and Execution of Linked Programs under Copyright Law, Commercial Licenses, and the Gpl. *Berkeley Technology Law Journal, 21*, 1421, 1438.

Jewell, C. (2012). Video Games: 21st Century Art. *WIPO Magazine.* Available at: http://www.wipo.int/wipo_magazine/en/2012/04/article_0003.html. Accessed 30 December 2024.

Li, M. [李明德]. (2014). *U.S. Intellectual Property Law [美国知识产权法].* Law Press China, p 358.

Litman, J. (1996). Revising Copyright Law for the Information Age. *Oregon Law Review, 75*, 19.

Meyer, K. R. (2010). Doctrine of the Dead: How Capcom v. MKR Exposes the Decreasing Fit between Modern Copyright Infringement Analysis and Modern Video Games. *Chicago-Kent Journal of Intellectual Property*, (9), 132, 141.

Mtima, L., & Jamar, S. D. (2010). Fulfilling the Copyright Social Justice Promise: Digitizing Textual Information. *New York Law School Law Review, 55*, 77, 80–82, 95, 96, 100.

Tsesis, A. (2016). Balancing Free Speech. *Boston University Law Review, 96*(1), 23, 53.

Yuan, M. (2009). Should Different Information Economies Have the Same Duration of Copyright. *Review of Economic Research, Issue, 6*, 13.

WIPO. (2015). *WIPO Guide on Surveying the Economic Contribution of the Copyright Industries.* Revised Version, pp 51–53.

## *Cases*

Arnstein v. Porter, 154 F. 2d 464, 468 (2d Cir. 1946), *cert. denied*, 330 U.S. 851 (1947).

Eldred v. Ashcroft, 537 U.S. 186 (2003).

Golan v. Holder, 132 S. Ct. 873, 889 (2012).

Lasercomb America, Inc. v. Reynolds, 911 F. 2d 970 (4th Cir. 1990).

Litchfield v. Spielberg, 736 F. 2d 1352, 1356 (9th Cir. 1984);

Lyons P'ship, L.P. v. Morris Costumes, Inc., 243 E. 3d 789, 801 (4th Cir. 2000).

Positive Black Talk Inc. v. Cash Money Records Inc., 394 F.3d 357, 368 (5th Cir. 2004).

# Appendix 1
# Questionnaire Report on Gamers' View on Playing Video Games and Watching Live Game Streaming

–个人基本情况

第1题 您的性别: [单选题]

| 选项 | 小计 | 比例 |
| --- | --- | --- |
| 男 | 643 | 54.63% |
| 女 | 534 | 45.37% |
| 本题有效填写人次 | 1177 | |

第2题 您的年龄是: [单选题]

| 选项 | 小计 | 比例 |
| --- | --- | --- |
| 18岁以下 | 938 | 79.69% |
| 18 ~ 24岁 | 126 | 10.71% |
| 25 ~ 30岁 | 113 | 9.6% |
| 31岁以上 | 0 | 0% |
| 本题有效填写人次 | 1177 | |



Z. Deng, *Constructing an Eco-Balanced Copyright Regime for the Video Game Industry in China*, https://doi.org/10.1007/978-981-96-6056-8

二、选择及排序题

第3题 你玩过网络游戏吗? [单选题]

| 选项 | 小计 | 比例 |
|---|---|---|
| 玩过 | 875 | 74.34% |
| 没玩过 | 302 | 25.66% |
| 本题有效填写人次 | 1177 | |

第4题 您玩游戏的主要原因是?【按重要性从1-7排序】 [排序题]

| 选项 | 平均综合得分 |
|---|---|
| 体验故事情节及竞技和游戏操作乐趣 | 5.47 |
| 消磨时间 | 4.06 |
| 开发智力 | 3.12 |
| 社交需要 | 3.01 |
| 逃避现实, 释放压力 | 2.73 |
| 追求胜利, 获得虚荣感 | 1.79 |
| 其他 | 0.16 |

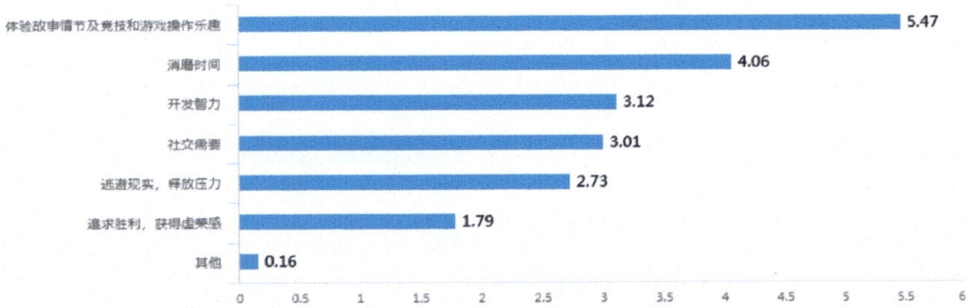


第5题 您玩过"我的世界"之类的沙盒游戏吗? [单选题]

| 选项 | 小计 | 比例 |
|---|---|---|
| 玩过 | 766 | 65.08% |
| 没玩过 | 353 | 29.99% |
| 不知道 | 58 | 4.93% |
| 本题有效填写人次 | 1177 | |

第6题 您听说过"著作权"这个词吗? [单选题]

| 选项 | 小计 | 比例 |
|---|---|---|
| 听说过并理解它的含义 | 666 | 56.58% |
| 听说过但不理解它的含义 | 323 | 27.44% |
| 没听说过 | 188 | 15.97% |
| 本题有效填写人次 | 1177 | |

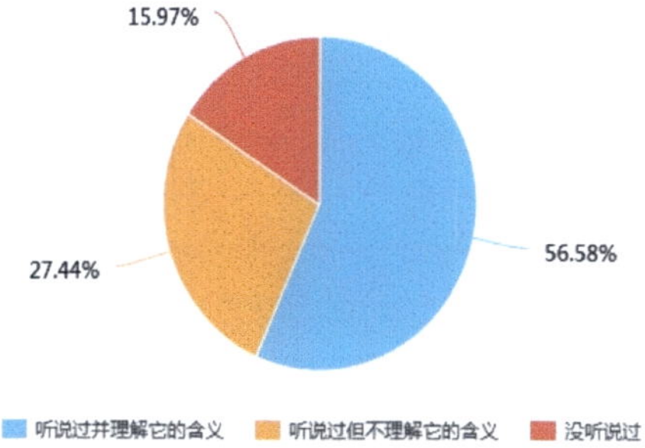


第7题 您玩游戏前,有了解与游戏平台签订的合同条款中的著作权内容吗?[单选题]

| 选项 | 小计 | 比例 |
|---|---|---|
| 不怎么了解 (30%以下) | 531 | 45.11% |
| 部分了解 (30–50%) | 364 | 30.93% |
| 一般了解 (50–70%) | 182 | 15.46% |
| 非常了解 (70–90%) | 63 | 5.35% |
| 完全了解 (90%以上) | 37 | 3.14% |
| 本题有效填写人次 | 1177 | |

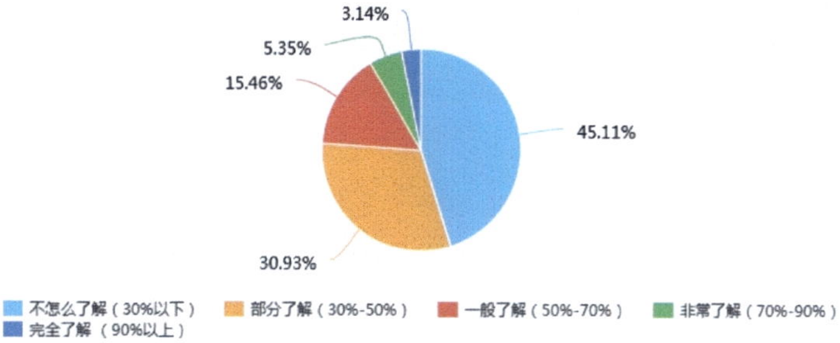


第8题 你看过游戏直播吗? [单选题]

| 选项 | 小计 | 比例 |
|---|---|---|
| 看过 | 978 | 83.09% |
| 没看过 | 199 | 16.91% |
| 本题有效填写人次 | 1177 | |

第9题　您观看游戏直播的主要原因有哪些?【按重要性从1-6排序】　[排序题]

| 选项 | 平均综合得分 |
|---|---|
| 掌握更多玩游戏技巧, 提升技能 | 5.11 |
| 欣赏故事情节 | 3.41 |
| 消磨时间 | 2.54 |
| 与主播互动,帮他撑直播间流量数据 | 2.08 |
| 逃避现实,释放压力 | 1.22 |
| 其他,请说明: | 0.25 |

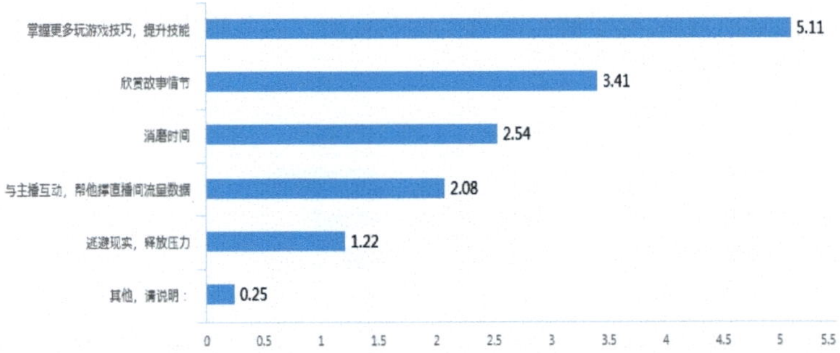


第10题　请选择以下最符合你观看游戏直播后的一种情况。这里没有对错之分, 不要花费太多时间在每一个问题上, 也不要对某个问题留有空白。[矩阵量表题]

该矩阵题平均分:3.66

| 题目\选项:你观看游戏直播后 | 1 = 非常不同意 | 2 = 不同意 | 3 = 中性 | 4 = 同意 | 5 = 非常同意 | 平均分 |
|---|---|---|---|---|---|---|
| (1)会对该游戏产生更大的热衷度 | 5(0.42%) | 21(1.78%) | 343(29.14%) | 704(59.81%) | 104(8.84%) | 3.75 |
| (2)会购买或下载该游戏 | 4(0.34%) | 50(4.25%) | 426(36.19%) | 568(48.26%) | 129(10.96%) | 3.65 |
| (3)会推荐朋友一起玩该游戏 | 4(0.34%) | 58(4.93%) | 426(36.19%) | 557(47.32%) | 132(11.21%) | 3.64 |
| (4)玩该游戏的时间增加了 | 6(0.51%) | 36(3.06%) | 346(29.4%) | 585(49.7%) | 204(17.33%) | 3.8 |
| (5)玩该游戏的次数增加了 | 6(0.51%) | 70(5.95%) | 521(44.27%) | 497(42.23%) | 83(7.05%) | 3.49 |
| (6)觉得玩该游戏更有激情了 | 4(0.34%) | 34(2.89%) | 448(38.06%) | 615(52.25%) | 76(6.46%) | 3.62 |
| 小计 | 29(0.41%) | 269(3.81%) | 2510(35.54%) | 3526(49.93%) | 728(10.31%) | 3.66 |

第11题 从您的经历来看，您觉得观看游戏直播可以替代打游戏吗？[单选题]

| 选项 | 小计 | 比例 |
|---|---|---|
| 可以 | 92 | 7.82% |
| 不可以 | 1085 | 92.18% |
| 本题有效填写人次 | 1177 | |

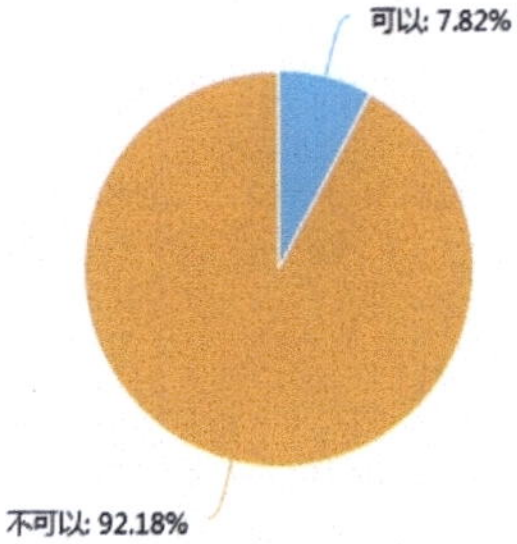

# Appendix 2
# Interview Record 1【Participant 1】

Time: 6:00 pm-6:30 pm, September 13, 2019 [LA Time]
Interviewee: Participant 1, a female gamer aged 26 years old
Interviewer: Deng Zhaoxia
Interview tool: Wechat
Language: Chinese
Deng: 好, 感谢你接受采访! 想问一下你玩过网络游戏吗?
Participant 1: 网络游戏玩过,只是现在比较少玩了。
Deng: 好的。那我想问一下你在玩游戏过程中会使用游戏内编辑器或外部软件对游戏中的关卡、武器等进行修改吗?
Participant 1: 我记得用游戏内的编辑器对游戏中的人物进行修改就试过,其他的就没有。
Deng: 好的。那你修改游戏的目的是什么呢?
Participant 1: 主要是为了好玩吧!而且我一般是把她们修改成我喜欢的样子的,这样当我自己设计出一个新的人物形象时就会特别开心。
Deng: 那你在修改游戏的过程中有遇到什么问题吗?
Participant 1: 这个好像没有。
Deng: 那你平时玩游戏过程中遇到或使用过他人修改的游戏器吗?
Participant 1: 这个没有注意,好像没有。
Deng: 好的。那你觉得在玩游戏过程中,游戏画面对你起着什么作用呢?
Participant 1: 游戏画面的作用,我觉得主要是那个更好的游戏画面肯定会给人更深的一个代入感,或者说游戏中那些打击感中的一些特效的渲染,我觉得是一个好游戏的重要组成部分。
Deng: 那对你而言有什么作用呢?
Participant 1: 对我的作用,我觉得更好的游戏画面可能会让我有进一步玩下去的欲望了。
Deng: 那具体是因为什么让你想继续玩呢?
Participant 1: 就是它的画面很吸引人、情节更生动吧!让人停不下来。
Deng: 哦这样!那不知你看过游戏直播没有?
Participant 1: 看过呀!



Z. Deng, *Constructing an Eco-Balanced Copyright Regime for the Video Game Industry in China*, https://doi.org/10.1007/978-981-96-6056-8

Deng: 那你觉得你作为观众在观看游戏直播过程中,游戏直播画面有什么作用呢?
Participant 1: 通常来说我观看游戏直播是为了和主播互动、聊天,打发时间,所以可以说直播画面就给了我和主播互动的机会吧!
Deng: 那你觉得观看游戏直播是不是可以替代玩游戏呢?
Participant 1: 不完全吧。如果说是像英雄联盟或者王者荣耀之类竞技类的游戏,你偶尔看一下直播,看主播在玩,自己也仿佛跟着玩了。但有时候也不是这样,毕竟你看其他人或主播在玩,你自己可能也会手痒,也会想自己去玩,这样自己玩的感受也不一样。
Deng: 好的,非常感谢你的分享!谢谢!
Participant 1: 嗯嗯,不客气。

# Appendix 3
# Interview Record 2【Participant 2】

Time: 6:00 pm-6:30 pm, September 14, 2019 [LA Time]
Interviewee: Participant 2, a male gamer aged 24 years old
Interviewer: Deng Zhaoxia
Interview tool: Wechat
Language: Chinese
Deng: 感谢你接受采访!请问你玩过网络游戏吗?
Participant 2: 玩过。
Deng: 那我想问一下,你在玩游戏时会使用一些编辑器或外部软件对游戏中的关卡、武器等进行修改吗?
Participant 2: 有时候会。
Deng: 那你修改的目的是什么呢?
Participant 2: 我的话主要是用编辑器对游戏关卡、武器进行提升,因为有时我觉得游戏自带的那些武器不够刺激,我自己制作后玩得更尽兴。
Deng: 那你在修改游戏的过程中有遇到什么问题吗?
Participant 2: 你这问题指的是哪方面?
Deng: 就是说你在修改这个游戏器时有没有遇到阻碍或者说令你担忧或不愉快的事情?
Participant 2: 我觉得问题的话就是有时我自己修改后的游戏组件会莫名其妙被其他游戏玩家删除了。这让我有些苦恼,明明是我自己制作的,却被他人破坏了。
Deng: 好的。那你平时在玩游戏的过程中有遇到或使用过他人修改的游戏器吗?
Participant 2: 有的。有时我会上一些游戏Mod的分享网站去下载其他玩家修改的游戏器。
Deng: 那你觉得那些被修改的游戏器对你玩游戏有什么影响吗?
Participant 2: 大多时候我下载的那些游戏器改变了原来游戏的玩法,感觉更好玩了。不过我也在论坛中看到有一些玩家会自己修改游戏器,然后制作一些加速升级装置或者武器之类的,这样可以更快升级。但我觉得这种做法对其他玩家不公平吧!特别是在竞技类游戏中。
Deng: 好的。那你觉得在玩游戏过程中,游戏画面对你有什么作用呢?



Z. Deng, *Constructing an Eco-Balanced Copyright Regime for the Video Game Industry in China*, https://doi.org/10.1007/978-981-96-6056-8

Participant 2: 游戏画面会影响玩游戏的兴趣。对,我玩游戏的话,其实游戏画面起到了挺大的作用的,如果游戏画面质量不太好,不够美观的话,我可能就不会继续玩下去了。
Deng: 好的。那你看过游戏直播吗?
Participant 2: 看过。
Deng: 那你认为在你观看游戏直播过程中,那些直播画面起到了什么作用呢?
Participant 2: 与原来的游戏画面相比的话,直播画面让我对这个游戏产生了比较直观的了解,比如对一些操作手法,一些操作的动作、技巧的使用的话会有进一步的了解,使我对这个游戏的操作上有帮助。
Deng: 其实你的意思就是说,你观看游戏直播过程中,主要关注的是那些游戏主播的操作技巧是不是?那从你作为观众的角度看,原来的那些游戏画面对你有没有起到很大的作用呢?
Participant 2: 还行,有。因为如果没有原来的游戏画面的话,你只是光看游戏主播的操作手法,你不能很明确的了解他这个时候的操作在游戏当中起到的作用,你只有结合游戏画面、游戏规则说明,才能更理解它的动作、操作手法的作用。这样你也比较能够学到东西。
Deng: 好的了解。那你觉得你观看游戏直播可不可以替代你打游戏?为什么?
Participant 2: 我觉得不能。
Deng: 为什么?
Participant 2: 因为游戏直播更多的是一种感官上的享受,打游戏的话则是有更深的体验感和自我存在感吧!就是将这种在观看过程中学到的一些经验、技巧,用到实践当中去。有时候你看了人家直播你就觉得他这个操作你学会了,但实际上你真正操作起来,可能并没有像游戏主播那样操作得那么流畅,动作有那么快。所以观看游戏直播跟打游戏是两码事。
Deng: 好的。我的采访就到此结束。谢谢!
Participant 2: 好的。

# Appendix 4
# Interview Record 3【Participant 3】

Time: 7:00 pm-7:30 pm, September 14, 2019 [LA Time]
Interviewee: Participant 3, a male gamer aged 21 years old
Interviewer: Deng Zhaoxia
Interview tool: Wechat
Language: Chinese
Deng: 好的,谢谢你能够参加本次的采访。首先我想问一下,你玩过网络游戏没有?
Participant 3: 玩过。
Deng: 好的,那你在玩游戏的时候会使用编辑器或外部软件对游戏的关卡、武器等进行修改吗?
Participant 3: 会的。
Deng: 那你修改游戏的目的是什么呢?
Participant 3: 现在编辑器都很流行了,平时我都会这么玩,可以说这是一种玩游戏的方式吧!而且现在有不少的游戏编辑器分享网站,有时候我们把自己修改的游戏器放到网站和大家一起分享下载玩,也感觉很有自豪感吧!
Deng: 那你在修改游戏的过程中有遇到什么问题吗?
Participant 3: 这个目前好像没有。不过也不是说所有的游戏你都可以修改的,有些游戏中它可能明确规定不能让你修改,那你就不能修改了。
Deng: 那你平时玩游戏过程中遇到或使用过他人修改的游戏器吗?
Participant 3: 这个当然了。刚才我也说了现在有不少游戏编辑器分享网站,很多时候我都会去那边下载别人修改的游戏模组玩。
Deng: 那你觉得那些被修改的游戏模组对你玩游戏有什么影响吗?
Participant 3: 感觉更有意思吧!不同的游戏体验!
Deng: 那有没有什么负面的影响呢?比如这个修改后的游戏器等内容会不会比较令人反感之类的?
Participant 3: 有时候会的。之前我就遇到过一些游戏器内的人物比如说女性人物被改得比较暴露的,有些类似这种的游戏器还会被平台下架的。
Deng: 好的。请问你觉得自己在玩游戏过程中,游戏画面对你有什么作用呢?



Z. Deng, *Constructing an Eco-Balanced Copyright Regime for the Video Game Industry in China*, https://doi.org/10.1007/978-981-96-6056-8

Participant 3: 游戏画面是玩游戏的第一视觉,通过这个游戏画面你就可以知道游戏的好坏,游戏画面比较流畅的话也可以带给别人比较愉悦的感觉,就会让人比较容易喜欢上这个游戏。

Deng: 那你看过游戏直播吗?

Participant 3: 看过。

Deng: 那你认为你在观看游戏直播的过程中,游戏直播画面起到什么作用呢?

Participant 3: 你看游戏直播画面的话,是不是可以让你仿佛自己也身临其中?此时虽然是主播在操作,但你也可以乐享其中,就是仿佛自己也在玩。

Deng: 那么你觉得你观看游戏直播跟自己打游戏,这个游戏画面对你的作用会不会一样呢?

Participant 3: 是不一样的。你看主播直播是既可以娱乐,也可以通过直播学习技巧,然后这跟自己单纯操作是完全不一样的。

Deng: 哪里不一样了?

Participant 3: 就是感受吧!两者的感受很不同的。

Deng: 好的。那你觉得观看了游戏直播之后,可以替代你去玩游戏吗?

Participant 3: 我个人感觉是不可以的,因为看直播的话肯定是和自己操作是有不一样的感觉的。

Deng: 也就是说你观看了游戏直播之后,感觉还不能够阻止你去玩游戏是吧?

Participant 3: 是的。通常我看了游戏直播后,往往会利用其他时间去模仿其他玩家的技巧方法看是不是更厉害,能升级。

Deng: 好的。谢谢!本次采访就到这了。谢谢!

Participant 3: 好的不客气。

# Appendix 5
# Interview Record 4【Participant 4】

Time: 6:00 pm-6:30 pm, September 20, 2019 [LA Time]
Interviewee: Participant 4, a male streamer aged 25 years old
Interviewer: Deng Zhaoxia
Interview tool: Wechat
Language: Chinese
Deng: 好的。请问您当游戏主播多久了?
Participant 4: 差不多半年。
Deng: 那从您经历中,您觉得在游戏直播的过程中,原来的那些游戏画面对您进行直播起到什么样的作用呢?
Participant 4: 我觉得自己主要是利用那些游戏画面来跟粉丝互动吧!因为在直播时总要有话说,可以利用画面来讲解,也可以说些笑话,这样能吸引更多的粉丝。
Deng: 嗯嗯好的,那您觉得直接玩游戏与您进行游戏直播相比,原来的游戏画面的作用有什么变化吗?就您个人而言?
Participant 4: 我自己玩游戏的话,我觉得那些游戏画面就可以引导我去玩咯!就是玩游戏时可以通过画面中的游戏规则知道下一步怎么玩,怎么通关。而我进行直播时,我一般不会太关注画面中的游戏规则,因为我也不是游戏高手,我不是靠讲解技巧来吸引粉丝的,我是在直播中与粉丝聊天、说笑吸引他们。
Deng:好的明白。那您认为网络游戏直播对传统的网络游戏市场有什么影响吗?
Participant 4: 网络游戏直播也是近几年才兴起的,就我个人而言,我觉得以前传统的网络游戏不多,没有什么可挑选的。现在互联网这么发达,再加上有了游戏直播后,玩家就更了解什么游戏好玩什么游戏不好玩,所以从这个角度看我觉得游戏直播也能带动传统的网络游戏发展吧!总的来说应该是利大于弊的。
Deng: 好的。您认为游戏直播的成本、相对于收益来说怎么样?



Z. Deng, *Constructing an Eco-Balanced Copyright Regime for the Video Game Industry in China*, https://doi.org/10.1007/978-981-96-6056-8

Participant 4: 其实我也不是那种专门搞游戏直播的,我只是玩游戏玩了一段时间想换个玩法所以就来做主播了。至于我自己的直播收入,可能有那么一点,但并不高。但我自己也理解,毕竟我玩游戏也不是特别好,也没有产生很大的影响力。

Deng: 如果说法律规定进行游戏直播的时候,游戏主播或者是游戏直播平台需要向原来的那些游戏开发公司支付一定的版权费用,您觉得这样的规定如何?

Participant 4: 如果考虑直播平台的话,其实平台就相当于是第三方或者中介,其实很多时候我们主播本身和原来的游戏厂商是没有直接对接的,除非这款游戏本身就是这个直播平台自己搞的。现在我们主播和平台的模式是这样的:比如说你每个月直播收到的礼物有1000块钱,平台每个月会给你结算一次,就正常来说,他给你结算后你收到的礼物就只有一半了,也就是说你最终只能收到500块钱。但现在这些平台把你收到的礼物扣掉后并没有说明去向。就是你所播的这个游戏内容的生产商有没有向这些平台去收取一些服务费或版权费我就不清楚。但就以我一个主播的身份而言,如果你直播一个游戏,本身只是为了娱乐消遣,也并没有得到多少收益,现在还要向游戏公司支付所谓的版权费的话,我就不会再去直播了。

Deng: 好的,理解您的意思,非常感谢您能够接受采访,我的问题就到此结束,谢谢。

# Appendix 6
# Interview Record 5【Participant 5】

Time: 7:00 pm-8:00 pm, September 20, 2019 [LA Time]
Interviewee: Participant 5, an operation manager of a game company
Interviewer: Deng Zhaoxia
Interview tool: Wechat
Language: Chinese
Deng: 好的,首先非常感谢您接受采访,我们现在就开始了。
Participant 5: 好的,请说。
Deng: 首先请问一下您现在游戏公司担任什么职务?
Participant 5: 运营主管。
Deng: 不知是主管哪个方面的呢?
Participant 5: 我这边主要是负责产品的。以前期上线之前的测试跟调标为主。
Deng: 好的。不知您了解游戏Mod吗?
Participant 5: 那应该是用游戏编辑器修改的一些游戏吧?
Deng: 是的。您觉得游戏玩家在游戏过程中使用那些编辑器或者是外部软件对游戏进行修改的行为对游戏企业来说好不好呢?
Participant 5: 这个要看情况吧!比如有一些游戏Mod就能够带动这款游戏的销售,所以很多游戏厂商也愿意提供编辑器让玩家修改游戏内容。同时这些游戏Mod改变了游戏的玩法,能带给玩家不同的体验,这样他们玩这款游戏的时间也会相对延长,这也可以延长游戏的生命周期吧!不过也有一些游戏Mod是有害的,像一些修改后的游戏器可以更快地升级,能迅速跨越障碍之类的,这也会降低玩家的体验感吧!
Deng: 那您公司一般是如何对待游戏Mod的呢?
Participant 5: 跟其他游戏公司一样,我们近几年推出的很多游戏都会给玩家提供编辑器去让他们自由创作,我们的合同条款也会规定这些创作的条件,一般情况下就是不希望他们在修改编辑中侵犯他人的知识产权。当然,我们也担心这些玩家会要求对这些新的游戏器享有知识产权,这些我们一般也会在合同中规定就是这些权利应该归于我们公司所有,以免产生纠纷。
Deng: 那对于您刚才提到的那些有害的游戏Mod呢?您公司一般如何处理?



Z. Deng, *Constructing an Eco-Balanced Copyright Regime for the Video Game Industry in China*, https://doi.org/10.1007/978-981-96-6056-8

Participant 5: 如果是对我们公司有害的,我们一般都会要求玩家删除或者自行删除的。我们的使用条款也会说明这类游戏Mod是被禁止的。
Deng: 好的。那您觉得游戏公司在设计游戏画面的时候,它的主要目的是干嘛?
Participant 5: 对这游戏画面你是指它的美术表现吗?还是什么?
Deng: 对的。也包括整体的画面,除了美术表现,还有一些比如音效、功能设计、规则玩法这些,就是整个视听效果吧!
Participant 5: 好的,如果说是整个视听画面来说,可能就是玩家操作上会更便利,或者说通过视觉上的体验,让玩家对这个游戏会有更大的吸引力。其次可能说好的一个视觉包装的话,也可以更吸引用户。其实我感觉不同的视觉包装都会体现不同的世界观,或者说不同的题材对用户的体验也会不同,都可能会影响到你在设计游戏时对整个美术包装的考虑。
Deng: 好的。那么您公司有没有运营游戏直播的业务?
Participant 5: 没有,这边其实直播这一块的很少,主要还是以研发产品跟做营销为主。对,主要以做产品发行为主。
Deng: 好的。那您之前的公司有没有做过游戏直播业务呢?
Participant 5: 之前我带过两家公司,其实都没有做过直播这一块的业务。
Deng: 好的。那您作为一个游戏玩家的话,平时接触过游戏直播吗?或者说您在业余时间有没有看过游戏直播?
Participant 5: 这个肯定有的。
Deng: 好的。那以玩家的视角来看,您觉得您在看游戏直播的过程中,这些直播画面起到什么作用?
Participant 5: 看直播的话,我觉得除了看主播的操作之外,更多地可能是希望整个画面有一种观赏性。因为如果你画面本身没有观赏性的话,其实你也很难带入到整个直播中。因为如果直播画面不吸引人,直播观众可能也很难对它产生兴趣。
Deng: 那您觉得看游戏直播跟您自己玩游戏比,这个画面有没有起到不同的作用?
Participant 5: 这个应该说没有太大差别。但可能说当你一个人玩游戏的时候,不一定说画面一定要很好那种,可能是有时候你会更看重一些什么数据体验上的东西,或者说是整个剧情层面上的东西。就是说自己一个人玩游戏的时候,可能说决定他继续玩下去的因素可以很多,但是当你看直播的情况下,可能除了博主给你带来的一种互动体验外,其实就主要是他操作的画面了。
Deng: 好的。现在游戏直播不是很兴盛吗?那您觉得它对传统的网络游戏有没有影响?
Participant 5: 我觉得应该是积极的。其实适合直播的游戏可能说并不是特别多。主要可能还是一些竞技类的产品会更适合做直播,特别是做成直播赛事。总体来说,直播只不过是增加了一种游戏曝光的方式,就是游戏分享或宣传的渠道。
Deng: 那您觉得游戏直播的兴起,对您公司设计一款游戏会有很大的影响吗?
Participant 5: 这要看你是做什么产品的,如果说你做的产品就像我刚才说的不是竞技类的,可能直播能够带来的效益并不多。一般情况下,一个游戏公司也不会说要奔着直播才会去做一款游戏,更多的还是考虑怎么吸引更多玩家去玩才去做一款游戏。就是说直播对设计游戏没有很直接性的影响,但如果说有一些产品适合直播的话,那么可能就会考虑用直播的方式推广了。

Deng: 好的。那站在您的角度看,您觉得规定直播平台在进行游戏直播时应该向原来的游戏开发公司支付一定的版权费用,您觉得这个规定怎么样?

Participant 5: 我觉得还算是合理的。虽然可能说有点垄断意味,但毕竟这也算是知识产品、产权方面范畴的东西。如果说你自己公司做了一些产品不希望其他竞争平台去直播,你就可以按照正常的法律途径去保护自己的权利。但大部分情况下这都是大厂之间的博弈。对于一些中小型公司来说,其实他们更希望有更多的直播平台去推广他们的游戏,所以是否能收版权费对这些中小型公司来说可能并没有太在意。

Deng: 那也就是说您觉得直播平台还是应该要支付版权费给原来的游戏开发公司是吧?

Participant 5: 对,但这个就看原来的游戏公司是否有这样的要求了。比如像腾讯,现在它网站条款里面就有不允许其他人未经允许做直播的要求。如果说他要求支付版权费才能直播,我觉得也还是挺合理的。但也要看不同公司的态度,对大部分厂商来说可能不会要求这些直播平台支付版权费的。

Deng: 好的。非常感谢您分享自己的观点。

# Appendix 7
# Interview Record 6【Participant 6】

Time: 6:30 pm-7:30 pm, September 21, 2019 [LA Time]
Interviewee: Participant 6, a staff in the marketing department of a game company
Interviewer: Deng Zhaoxia
Interview tool: Wechat
Language: Chinese
Deng: 好的,首先非常感谢您能接受我的采访。接下来的问题您就按自己的实际情况回答就可以了,好吗?
Participant 6: 没问题,好的。
Deng: 您目前在游戏公司担任什么职务?
Participant 6: 我现在做的是属于市场营销那一块,属于市场推广。
Deng: 好的。不知您了解游戏Mod吗?
Participant 6: 游戏Mod是不是游戏的修改器之类的?
Deng: 差不多吧!就是玩家在游戏中使用编辑器或软件对游戏进行修改后的游戏器。
Participant 6: 嗯嗯了解一些。
Deng: 那您觉得游戏玩家在游戏过程中使用那些编辑器或外部软件对游戏进行修改的行为对游戏企业来说是好还是坏呢?
Participant 6: 我所了解的一般是正面作用的!据我所知现在的很多开放类游戏比如《我的世界》就会提供编辑器给玩家编辑修改。这能激发玩家的创作热情吧!而且我听说游戏公司也会利用那些游戏Mod进行重新开发,这样可以节省不少开发成本。
Deng: 那不知有没啥坏处呢?
Participant 6: 这个暂时不清楚。
Deng: 好的。那您公司一般是如何对待游戏Mod的?
Participant 6: 我们一般都支持吧!就是那些用户条款中都会规定的。
Deng: 那具体怎么规定您了解吗?
Participant 6: 这个还真不是太了解。
Deng: 好的。那您觉得游戏公司设计游戏画面的目的是什么?



Z. Deng, *Constructing an Eco-Balanced Copyright Regime for the Video Game Industry in China*, https://doi.org/10.1007/978-981-96-6056-8

Participant 6: 我觉得设计画面的目的,其实更多的是想要去看一下它的题材和美术风格契不契合市场。当然可能也会因游戏类型而异,因为我弄的主要是手游类的,像端游类的或者页游类的那些情况可能会有所不同。
Deng: 那依您看也就是说设计画面是为了吸引玩家是吧?
Participant 6: 对,就是让画面更精美之类的,看看它的题材和玩法这些在市场上有多大的空间?基于这种目的去设计。比如会参考某些IP,想要去看看这部分的用户有多少。
Deng: 好的。那么我想问一下您公司目前有没有运营游戏直播的业务?
Participant 6:没有,因为我们走的都是信息流广告,就直播类的没有,几乎很少接触。
Deng: 那您在业余时间有没有看过游戏直播?
Participant 6: 有。因为现在游戏直播是很新奇的,所以平时的话肯定都会去看看。
Deng:好的,那么我就想问一下您以玩家的视角来看的话,您觉得直播画面起到什么作用呢?
Participant 6: 就我个人而言,我觉得我一般在直播中会看看这个游戏在整个社会或者说在整个行业顶尖的玩法是怎样的。如果没有游戏直播的话,以前我就可能要自己去搜索,很麻烦,甚至有可能会落伍。
Deng: 好的,那您觉得有时候自己会不会玩一下游戏?
Participant 6: 会,偶尔玩一下。
Deng:那你觉得自己在玩游戏的时候,跟自己直接看直播的时候比,这个游戏画面会不会有什么区别? 或者说游戏画面对你的来说会不会起到不同的作用?
Participant 6: 基本上现在的游戏直播跟我自己去玩是一样的。因为主播是直接展示,他也几乎做不了假,所以体验感还是契合的。
Deng: 你的意思是说,现在的直播就是直接把原来的游戏画面完全的重复过来,没有什么改变对吧?
Participant 6: 对,现在兴起的游戏直播都是直接玩游戏,然后教你怎么玩,或者告诉你更高端的玩法是怎样的。如果说是一种新游戏,比方说是属于市面上还没法找到的,他想要推广这种游戏,就会利用这种游戏直播,把游戏规则玩法那些直接展现出来,这样观众看了之后以后就可以亲自去体验一下。
Deng: 好的。那么您觉得现在网络游戏直播的兴起,对原来那种传统的网络游戏有什么影响吗?是积极、消极还是没什么影响?
Participant 6: 我觉得如果从行业的角度看,还是比较积极的。因为它能够带动一些玩家对该款游戏的兴趣。比如说给那些以前不知道怎么玩该款游戏、但有兴趣想要充钱去玩的玩家提供了一种平台。因为它可以很及时的提供某款新游戏的资讯,也可以实现玩家们的交流互动。所以对原来的游戏行业还是有促进作用的。
Deng: 那您觉得如果规定直播平台在对游戏进行直播时,需要向原来的游戏开发公司支付一定的报酬,您觉得这种做法如何?
Participant 6: 你说的这种支付报酬怎么理解?
Deng: 就是说授权费。比如近年来不是经常有直播平台和原来的游戏厂商打官司,说那些直播公司没有经过原来的游戏厂商的同意,将他们的游戏进行直播了,但却没有支付他一定的版权费用。您怎么看待这个问题?您觉得直播平台支付版权费合理吗?

Participant 6: 我觉得规定版权费这个问题更多的是针对那些比较大型的游戏而言才是相对比较合理的。因为像一些小众类的游戏,直播平台帮它直播了,反而给它带来了一定的品牌或者口碑,其实换句话说就是帮它在推广宣传了。而且如果你开发的游戏不是很大型的话,其实不太可能损害它的利益,也可以不用给,这样还更自由一点。
Deng: 好的,我的问题就到这里了。感谢您的信息。
Participant 6: 不客气。

# Appendix 8
# Interview Record 7【Participant 7】

Time: 6:00 pm-6:30 pm, September 27, 2019 [LA Time]
Interviewee: Participant 7, a male gamer aged 28 years old
Interviewer: Deng Zhaoxia
Interview tool: Wechat
Language: Chinese
Deng: 好的,首先感谢你能够接受我的采访。这些问题没有对错之分,你就按自己的实际情况回答就可以了,好吧?
Participant 7: 好的。
Deng: 请问你平时玩过网络游戏没有?
Participant 7: 玩过一些。
Deng: 那我想了解一下,你在玩游戏的过程中会不会使用一些编辑器或外部软件对游戏的关卡、武器等进行修改?
Participant 7: 不会吧!我现在比较少玩游戏了。
Deng: 好的。那不知你平时玩游戏时遇到或使用过他人修改的游戏器吗?
Participant 7: 这个好像也没遇到过。
Deng: 好的。那请问你觉得在玩游戏的过程中,那些游戏画面对你有什么作用?
Participant 7: 游戏画面越好的话,当然感觉也越好吧。体验也更好一点。
Deng: 就有这方面的作用是吗?
Participant 7: 对。
Deng: 好的,那你之前看过游戏直播吗?
Participant 7: 也有看一点。
Deng: 那么你觉得在观看游戏直播的过程中这些直播画面有什么作用?
Participant 7: 可以更好地看清楚那些主播是怎么操作的,直播画面越好的话,看到的细节就越多。
Deng: 那你觉得,你玩游戏和看直播的过程中,这两者的游戏画面对你的作用一样吗?
Participant 7: 当然是大部分玩家都是希望画质越好,看得到的那一些方面就更好了,体验也是更好的。



Z. Deng, *Constructing an Eco-Balanced Copyright Regime for the Video Game Industry in China*, https://doi.org/10.1007/978-981-96-6056-8

Deng: 那不知你自己亲自玩游戏的时候和你作为直播观众看主播玩的时候,你觉得那些游戏画面对你来说有什么不同的感受或作用吗?
Participant 7: 基本没什么不同吧。
Deng: 那下一个问题,你觉得观看游戏直播可以替代你玩游戏吗?为什么?
Participant 7: 这个要看个人的需求,如果说你只是想先了解一下这个游戏,你可以先看一下直播,如果你真的是想去体验的话,当然还是要自己去玩的。
Deng: 那你觉得他们两者有没有替代作用还是说没有影响?
Participant 7: 影响应该不大,对大部分人来说都是看直播去学习一下那些游戏操作的,之后他们也一般会自己去实际操作的。
Deng: 好的,感谢你的回答,我的采访就到这里了。
Participant 7: 好的。

# Appendix 9
# Interview Record 8【Participant 8】

Time: 7:00 pm-7:30 pm, September 27, 2019 [LA Time]
Interviewee: Participant 8, a male gamer aged 28 years old
Interviewer: Deng Zhaoxia
Interview tool: Wechat
Language: Chinese

Deng: 首先感谢你能接受我的采访。这些题目你就按自己的实际情况回答就可以了好吧?

Participant 8: 好的。

Deng: 那我们就进入第1个问题,请问你平时玩过网络游戏吗?

Participant 8: 玩过,经常玩。

Deng: 那你在玩游戏时会使用一些编辑器或外部软件对游戏的关卡、武器等进行修改吗?

Participant 8: 会的,现在比较高级的玩法都是要自己去编辑后再玩的。

Deng: 那你编辑游戏的目的是什么呢?

Participant 8: 当然是为了更好玩吧!自己修改的游戏也会更刺激。

Deng: 那你修改那些游戏有没有说是为了提升自己的编辑技能或者说是为了以后的职业发展这方面的考虑呢?

Participant 8: 这个倒没有。因为我自己也只是一个业务爱好者,我就为了好玩,也没打算以后做游戏开发人员是吧?就那些以后想往这方面发展的人来说可能会有这种考虑吧。

Deng: 好的。那你在修改游戏的过程中有遇到什么问题吗?

Participant 8: 修改中没有,不过分享的时候就有时会发现以后自己想去分享网站再下载自己编辑的游戏器就找不到了。其实我们在修改游戏器时也是付出了大部分心血的对吧?所以说如果能有明确的规定谁编辑的谁就拥有权利就可能更好,这样就不会乱套。

Deng: 嗯嗯很有道理。那你平时在玩游戏的过程中遇到或使用过他人修改的游戏器吗?

Participant 8: 用过。

Deng: 那你觉得那些被修改的游戏器对你玩游戏有什么影响吗?

Participant 8: 就是换一种玩法,更新鲜有趣。



Z. Deng, *Constructing an Eco-Balanced Copyright Regime for the Video Game Industry in China*, https://doi.org/10.1007/978-981-96-6056-8

Deng: 没有遇到不好的情况吗?比如内容让人反感之类的?或者有没有一些作弊的游戏器出现?
Participant 8: 有的。现在一些作弊的游戏器也是很常见的,不过我自己倒没遇到过。就那些游戏贴吧上也经常可以看到有人吐槽这一类的事情,就是让人感觉不诚信吧!
Deng: 好的。那你觉得在玩游戏的过程中,那些游戏画面对你有什么作用呢?
Participant 8: 游戏画面是很重要的,因为一个游戏的好坏首先就是从它的游戏画面体现出来的,如果你画面能足够吸引人的话,就会让人有欲望去玩,就有欲望去消费。
Deng: 好的,那么不知道你曾经看过游戏直播没有?
Participant 8: 看过。现在都很流行。
Deng: 那么你以一个直播观众的角度来看,你觉得你在观看游戏直播过程中,这些直播画面对你起到什么作用呢?
Participant 8: 如果只是观看直播的话,这些游戏画面的影响程度或作用程度就会小很多。因为如果你自己玩游戏的话,你肯定会去玩那些热门的、当下流行的、画面比较好的游戏,像一些比较古老的就是20多年前的那些游戏,游戏画面都很一般或者粗糙,跟现在的社会风格也不入。如果你自己去玩的话,对这一类的游戏就会很排斥的。但如果你看直播的话,因为是游戏主播玩而不是你自己去玩,你就会更想了解游戏的剧情,还有游戏里面的内容。此时这个画面的影响程度作用程度就会小很多。
Deng: 也就是说,与自己玩相比,你更侧重于看游戏主播的技巧是吧?
Participant 8: 对,还有整个游戏的剧情了。
Deng: 那么你觉得观看游戏直播可以替代你去打游戏吗?为什么?
Participant 8: 这要分情况去讨论。首先,如果你对某一类游戏特别感兴趣的话,你肯定是即使看了之后还是会去玩的是吧?但对于其他一些你不是太敢玩但又想去了解的游戏的话,就好比恐怖类游戏,一般人都不爱去玩了,但你又想了解恐怖游戏里面它到底发生了什么?它的恐怖点在哪里?这时候如果有游戏主播去玩的话,你就会去看,自己就不会去玩了。 除了恐怖游戏以外,像其他一些偏向剧情类的游戏,你看主播玩过一次之后,也几乎不会再去玩第二遍了,因为你对剧情都了解了,再玩的话就会很无聊,就像你看电视剧一样,你被剧透了之后也不会再看第二遍了。所以总的来说,除非是自己特别喜欢的游戏外,一般看了游戏直播后,基本上就可以替代你去玩了,因为我们自身的空闲时间也是有限的。
Deng: 好的,那你对竞技类游戏有什么看法?那些体育赛事之类的游戏。
Participant 8: 竞技类游戏的话就像是一场场比赛,比如说英雄联盟,是以正式比赛的形式来进行的,就跟那些一般剧情类的游戏不一样了。因为每一局比赛你会遇到不同的人,你每一局发生的结果都是是不一样的,所以这个是基本上是不会替代的。那些观众之所以看英雄联盟这一类的游戏直播的话,主要是想提高自己的技术。这类游戏的话就不可能被替代了。
Deng: 好的,谢谢你的分享。我的采访问题就这些了,谢谢!
Participant 8: 好的。

# Appendix 10
# Interview Record 9【Participant 9】

Time: 6:30 pm-7:30 pm, September 28, 2019 [LA Time]
Interviewee: Participant 9, a game designer of a big game corporation in China
Interviewer: Deng Zhaoxia
Interview tool: Wechat
Language: Chinese
Deng: 好的,首先非常感谢您能够接受我的采访,我们现在就进入采访题目中。首先我想问一下您在游戏公司是担任什么职务呢?
Participant 9: 运维方面的,你可以理解为技术那一类。
Deng: 好的。那不知您了解游戏Mod吗?
Participant 9: 还行。
Deng: 那您觉得游戏玩家在游戏过程中使用那些编辑器或外部软件对游戏进行修改的行为对游戏企业来说是好还是坏呢?
Participant 9: 这要分情况讨论了。很多时候我们游戏公司也会鼓励玩家去修改自创新玩法,这在我们游戏中也会提供一些编辑器。其实玩家创作的这些游戏Mod也给了我们开发游戏的灵感,像现在我们一般也会比较关注玩家论坛或贴吧中分享的那些游戏器,看看玩家的喜好怎样,这样也方便我们下一步开发。当然,也有一些游戏Mod我们是不鼓励的,像一些玩家修改后的Mod只是为了用在竞技比赛中获胜,就类似于我们的作弊工具吧!这类我们就不提倡。
Deng: 好的,那您公司一般是如何对待游戏Mod的?
Participant 9: 这也分情况讨论了。像那些对我们有用的Mod我们就会鼓励玩家去修改创作,对我们有害的就会禁止了!
Deng: 那一般也是通过用户使用协议或合同进行规定的吧?
Participant 9: 没错。
Deng: 那合同中对一些涉知识产权条款或者一些有损社会风气的不良内容的条款您怎么看?
Participant 9: 知识产权方面的,我想一方面主要是怕玩家修改那些游戏器会损害其他人的利益,而他人一般又难以追究玩家的责任,所以最终可能会追诉到我们游戏公司头上,有了这些条款就不用担心这方面的问题。同时也有一些玩家可能也会认为自己对修改过的游戏器拥有知识产权,这样的话如



Z. Deng, *Constructing an Eco-Balanced Copyright Regime for the Video Game Industry in China*, https://doi.org/10.1007/978-981-96-6056-8

果我们后期还想利用那些游戏器可能就会很麻烦,如果合同明确规定那些游戏器的所有权属于我们公司,就可以避免这些纠纷。

Deng: 好的,那对于一些包含不良内容的条款呢,您怎么看?

Participant 9: 那些条款主要是针对一些涉色情或赌博、暴力之类的吧!像现在有些玩家也会特别修改游戏器使得里面的人物着装特别暴露,这些都是不允许的。

Deng: 那如果有玩家上传之类的游戏Mod会怎么样?

Participant 9: 那就会被平台直接下架了!

Deng: 好的,您从技术角度看觉得游戏公司设计游戏画面的目的主要是什么呢?

Participant 9: 主要还是为了吸引玩家。因为游戏画面、风格、剧情都会影响玩家的喜好,所以需要不同的风格去设计。而游戏画面精美的话,就更能提高玩家的游戏体验。

Deng: 好的,那么您公司现在有运营游戏直播的业务吗?

Participant 9: 好像是有一个叫cc直播平台的。

Deng: 有专门的直播平台对吧?您平时应该也看过游戏直播吧?

Participant 9: 对。

Deng: 那么您觉得在游戏直播的过程中,这些直播画面起到什么作用?

Participant 9: 直播画面的作用其实对于那些还没玩过这款游戏的人来说,就是能让他知道这款游戏大概是什么类型的,然后它的主要内容是什么?就有类似于宣传的作用吧!此外我觉得直播画面也有传授一下经验技巧之类的作用。那些主播很多都是游戏高手,很多玩家就想向他们学习。另外一点就是现在游戏职业化之后,那些主播相当于游戏明星,就相当于体育明星那样。直播的话这些游戏明星就能跟他的粉丝之间有一个互动。

Deng: 好的。那从您的角度来看,您觉得现在兴起的游戏直播对传统的网络游戏有没有影响?是消极还是积极还是没什么影响?

Participant 9: 我觉得是有积极的影响。游戏直播平台是一个平台,他一般是要让主播直播一些比较大流量的比较多人玩的那些游戏。这对游戏公司来说刚好起到宣传游戏的效果。如果按照以往的传统的话了,一个网络游戏的宣传要么是通过官网,要么是通过其他一些APP下载平台,这样的宣传效果不是太好,因为官网宣传只是一个画面,还有一些游戏的文字简介,而 APP下载平台的话也只是一些文字的简单描述。如果有了直播平台,它可以更生动形象的去宣传游戏。对于用户来说,通过直播可以很清晰、很深入地去了解这款游戏玩起来到底如何,有没有吸引力之类的。

Deng: 好的。那您觉得游戏直播它的成本相对于收益来说怎么样?

Participant 9: 这个没怎么关注。

Deng: 我知道您可能对这个没怎么关注。那么您觉得如果规定直播平台对某个游戏进行直播的时候需要向原来的游戏开发公司支付一定的版权费用,就是说直播平台需要先获得游戏公司的授权才可以直播,这样的规定合不合理呢?

Participant 9: 我觉得需要授权,因为毕竟你是在直播别人的游戏。虽然直播游戏有宣传效应,但并不是所有的直播平台都去宣传你的游戏,他直播平台直播游戏的目的也不是为了宣传游戏,而是为了赚钱。而且有时候直播也会给游戏带来负面影响,导致其他玩家不想玩了。同时我觉得,即使直播平台向游戏公司支付版权费,由于他直播过程中还能再额外收取广告费之类的,他也还是有盈利的。
Deng: 好的,谢谢您的分享。我的采访就到此结束。谢谢!
Participant 9: 好的。

# Appendix 11
# Interview Record 10【Participant 10】

Time: 9:30 pm-10:30 pm, September 28, 2019 [LA Time]
Interviewee: Participant 10, a marketing planning staff of a big game corporation in China
Interviewer: Deng Zhaoxia
Interview tool: Wechat
Language: Chinese
Deng: 好的。首先感谢您能接受我的采访。这些问题您只需根据自己的实际情况回答就可以了,没有对错之分的,好吧?
Participant 10: 行。
Deng: 好的。首先问一下您在游戏公司是担任什么职务呢?
Participant 10: 营销策划这方面的。
Deng: 好的。不知您了解游戏Mod吗?
Participant 10: 了解一些。
Deng: 那您觉得游戏玩家在游戏过程中使用那些编辑器或外部软件对游戏进行修改的行为对游戏企业来说是好还是坏呢?
Participant 10: 这如果是游戏本身提供的编辑器进行修改,那当然是好的。但如果是游戏本身没提供编辑器的情况下去修改编辑,就不一定了。像一些外挂程序,也可以说是作弊的游戏器吧!玩家在使用了那类游戏器感觉被不公平对待了,自然也不会喜欢我们的游戏。还有一部分游戏Mod的质量太差,也会损害我们公司的名声!
Deng: 那您公司一般是如何对待游戏Mod的呢?
Participant 10: 对于一些能够被修改的游戏,我们一般会提供编辑器让玩家修改,也会在合同中规定哪些Mod能制作哪些不能制作。当然也有一些游戏我们强调是不能被编辑修改的,这类游戏我们可能会运用一些技术措施来保护。
Deng: 好的。以您的经验,您觉得游戏公司它设计游戏画面的主要目的是什么呢?



Z. Deng, *Constructing an Eco-Balanced Copyright Regime for the Video Game Industry in China*, https://doi.org/10.1007/978-981-96-6056-8

Participant 10: 以前游戏对于大部分人来说还是比较陌生的,很多玩家都不会太追求画面或操作或玩法之类的。但现在游戏越来越多的情况下,整个游戏市场的竞争也加剧了。因此精品化无论从玩法、画面,还是从你的人物美术,还有剧情等,都需要进行精品化,就是打造一个有竞争力的游戏。例如现在国内有几款二次元的游戏就会对画面要求非常高。像王者荣耀的话,它去年也把美术人物模型全部进行了更新。这其实就是为了迎合我们整个游戏玩家群体,就画面来说其实就是要符合整个时代的审美,不然整个游戏就要被淘汰了。

Deng: 好的。也就是说主要是提高市场的竞争力,然后吸引更多玩家,对吧?

Participant 10: 是的。

Deng: 好的。那么我想问一下您公司现在有没有运营游戏直播业务?

Participant 10: 我现在的工作就主要是这两块,一个是直播,一个就是电竞。

Deng: 哦好的。那您能否简单介绍一下直播这方面的业务?

Participant 10: 嗯嗯好。就直播这一块的话,像腾讯、网易这样的大厂,他们都会有自己的直播平台。比如腾讯的企鹅、网易的CC,它们其实主要还是为自己的游戏去服务。这对一个游戏的生态很重要,因为其实大厂之间都会相互牵制的。比如说网易开发的一款新游戏,很多时候腾讯是不会播的,甚至会封杀,这个都是很正常的业内现象。你的游戏要活下去,你的直播一定要做起来,不然的话你的游戏很难推广出去。同时直播平台的社交也是很重要的一个作用,除非你的游戏特别火能维持玩家的社交,其实普通的游戏都特别难做到社交化。玩家总有一天会玩腻,所以现在游戏直播的作用就是能维系玩家粉丝,活跃玩家,这是特别重要的,像其他主流直播平台比如斗鱼、a站、b站,都是很清晰的例子。

Deng: 好的。那您觉得直播画面还有其他作用吗?

Participant 10: 其他的话主要就是可观赏性了吧!就是看主播玩游戏将整个剧情呈现出来,就像看电影一样了。

Deng: 那您觉得现在兴起的游戏直播对传统的网络游戏有没有影响?

Participant 10: 我觉得任何事情都有两面性,但总体来说游戏直播对游戏来说正面价值是大于负面的。其实在直播没有出来之前,一个游戏的正常生命周期大概就在两年左右,两年已经算非常不错了,之后你的这款游戏可能就凉了。而游戏直播出来后,现在你的游戏甚至可以发展为电竞,比如像王者荣耀或者吃鸡类的游戏。对于电竞来说它可观看的内容就越来越多,就算你不玩这个游戏你也会看一下,这样其实是把整个游戏的生命周期拉长了。然后,其实以往我们游戏推广的形式非常有限,在最早的这种端游时期来说,我们最有效的媒介就是网吧或者电视广告,而到现在的话我们推出一款新游戏就一定要做直播。现在任何跟游戏有关的比赛或者新版本发布,或者新的玩法,它一定都跟直播有关系,因为直播能够带动粉丝经济,你的核心玩家都在这里。所以整体来说直播对游戏的作用还是非常正向的。

Deng: 好的。那么您觉得,游戏直播的兴起对您公司设计一款游戏有没有影响?

Participant 10: 有的。无论从玩法设计,还是从画面还是从社交等角度,我们都会考虑更有利于直播的方向进行设计。我们很看重直播业务,认为游戏和直播是需要打通的。比如说送礼物会触发什么效果,或者是他在游戏画面中欣赏性如何?这些都要考虑到。然后还有一些游戏可能在玩法上会跟直播有电挂钩,比如说它是一个卡牌类的游戏,要考虑对这个游戏进行直播的适配,它的观看性是不是要加入某些东西以利于更长期的直播下去。

Deng: 那么您觉得游戏直播的成本相对于它的收益来说怎么样?如果规定直播平台进行游戏直播的时候,需要向原来的游戏公司支付一定的版权费用,您的意见如何?

Participant 10: 游戏直播其实是很烧钱的,因为一个顶级主播,他的签约费可能都上亿。不管他年薪有没上亿,至少都有5500万,就正常的一线主播都在1000万以上。就收益来说,其实直播平台主要靠圈流量来赚钱。所以要先有流量才有收益。一般情况下,直播对于游戏产品来说只是一个内容的输出方,给玩家观看。直播平台在直播时需要帮该款游戏设立专区,还要有策划活动,这些成本都是很高的。而如果一款游戏本身知名度不高,粉丝流量也不多的话,也意味着直播平台很难圈流量赚钱。但有些游戏比如去年的英雄联盟赛事,他一个独家版权可能就要几个亿,甚至有人要买他的转播权,这转播权可能就要几千万上亿,这些都是很赚钱的。

Deng: 那您觉得直播平台支付版权费合理吗?

Participant 10: 合理啊!其实这样规定对直播平台也好。因为游戏随便播的话它的商业价值就会降得非常低。而且你支付版权费之后,也可以有转播权,可以防止他人转播。如果你制作的直播非常成功,也可以赚得不少!这是我的理解。

Deng: 好的,谢谢!我的采访就到此结束。

# Appendix 12
# Interview Record 11【Participant 11】

Time: 7:00 pm-8:00 pm, October 2, 2019 [LA Time]
Interviewee: Participant 11, a female streamer aged 22 years old
Interviewer: Deng Zhaoxia
Interview tool: Wechat
Language: Chinese
Deng: 您好!请问您当游戏主播多久了?
Participant 11: 有两年了。
Deng: 好的。从您的经历中,您觉得游戏直播时原来的那些游戏画面对您进行直播有什么样的作用呢?
Participant 11: 游戏画面的话我觉得主要是要进行操作游戏吧!因为我一般是播竞技类的游戏,所以我一般都是边操作边和粉丝互动的。
Deng: 哦好的。那您觉得自己直接玩游戏和您进行游戏直播相比,原来的游戏画面有什么不同的作用吗?
Participant 11: 这游戏画面对我来说作用应该是差不多的。因为我自己玩游戏的话就是跟着这个游戏规则、机制玩,而我在直播时也是需要这么操作的。不过直播的时候我的目的有所不同,我主要是呈现自己的技巧玩法给粉丝,方便与他们互动。
Deng:那您觉得网络游戏直播对传统的网络游戏市场有什么影响吗?
Participant 11: 这主要是能进一步推动游戏的发展吧!据我所知,很多粉丝看了我的直播后自己也会去尝试操作的,他们会不断的升级自己的系统、装备,或者提升技能以便升级。这样的话直播其实也是可以延长游戏的生命周期了,不然很多游戏一般玩几个月就腻了。
Deng: 好的。那您觉得游戏直播的成本相对于收益来说怎么样?
Participant 11: 就我个人而言,我觉得直播的成本主要就是时间和精力了。因为现在直播就相当于我的工作一样,我也是像大家上班一样挣钱的。而靠直播赚钱的话,一部分是来自直播平台的签约费用,一部分是来自粉丝的礼物打赏。不过像我们这样的签约主播,粉丝的礼物打赏很大一部分都是被平台拿去的。签约费用也是有高有低,高的很高,低的也很低吧!我的话就处于中等水平,还没有达到中等吧!就是收入能维持生活水平咯!



Z. Deng, *Constructing an Eco-Balanced Copyright Regime for the Video Game Industry in China*, https://doi.org/10.1007/978-981-96-6056-8

Deng: 好的。那如果说法律规定进行游戏直播的时候,游戏主播或者是直播平台需要向原来的游戏开发公司支付一定的版权费用,您觉得这样的规定如何?
Participant 11: 其实我觉得我们主播的收入参差不齐,如果要我们小主播再交版权费用的话我们应该就不会再去直播这个游戏了。如果是要直播平台交费的话,我觉得还比较合理。毕竟平台有这个实力,比如一些大直播平台它赚的直播流量也是很大的,兑现也就相对多了。所以这对他们来说应该没什么问题。
Deng: 好的,感谢您的分享。我的问题就到此结束,谢谢。
Participant 11: 好的,不客气。

# Appendix 13
# Interview Record 12【Participant 12】

Time: 10:00 pm-11:00 pm, October 3, 2019 [LA Time]
Interviewee: Participant 12, a female streamer aged 24 years old
Interviewer: Deng Zhaoxia
Interview tool: Wechat
Language: Chinese
Deng: 好的。请问您当游戏主播多久了?
Participant 12: 有两年半年了吧。
Deng: 那从您的经历中,您觉得游戏直播时原来的那些游戏画面对您进行直播有什么样的作用呢?
Participant 12: 这个游戏画面的作用就是供粉丝观看,当然也包括我自己。直播的话主要就是要吸引粉丝,我会对游戏画面进行讲解,粉丝也就会跟着进来看了。
Deng: 哦那就是主要是为了吸引粉丝看是吗?
Participant 12: 是的。另外我也可以利用画面与他们互动。如果没有画面的话,我也不知道说什么好。当然也不是说我完全是靠那些游戏画面吸引他们,因为他们会当我的粉丝肯定与我本人也有关,比如可能喜欢我的直播风格,我的幽默个性等。
Deng: 好的。那您觉得自己一个人玩游戏和您进行游戏直播相比,原来的游戏画面有什么不同的作用吗?
Participant 12: 其实除了直播外我自己是比较少玩游戏的。因为我直播玩游戏是为了好玩,为了扩大粉丝量,或者更直接地说是为了赚钱。其实我的游戏技术并不高,所以粉丝们也并不是完全要靠我的技术能力。
Deng: 那您觉得游戏画面在自己玩游戏与直播时比有什么不同的作用吗?
Participant 12: 这个游戏画面的话我觉得直播时多了一些窗口,因此直播时可能会更关注原来游戏画面之外的东西,比如与粉丝的对话、还有一些广告的出现!其他的话应该没什么很大差别。
Deng:好的。那您觉得游戏直播对传统的网络游戏市场有什么影响吗?
Participant 12: 这个从我个人经历看主要是能提高游戏的知名度。因为我本人以前也不怎么玩游戏的,现在都对很多游戏的名称耳熟能详了。
Deng: 那您觉得游戏直播的成本相对于收益来说怎么样?


Z. Deng, *Constructing an Eco-Balanced Copyright Regime for the Video Game Industry in China*, https://doi.org/10.1007/978-981-96-6056-8

Participant 12: 我觉得这要看个人吧!我自己的话感觉还行。有些知名主播他们的收入就不得了了。
Deng: 那如果说法律规定进行游戏直播的时候,游戏主播或者是直播平台需要向原来的游戏公司支付一定的版权费用,您觉得这样的规定如何?
Participant 12: 我觉得这也不是每次游戏直播都能有很大的收入,这收入是不固定的。你粉丝打赏得多收入就高,打赏不多收入也就不高了。如果要交版权费的话也太不合理了,而且也很麻烦!如果是要直播平台去交,那应该还行。我们直播打赏收入也被平台分去了一大部分,而且有那么多主播直播,他们收入肯定就很高了。
Deng: 好的,我的问题就这些,谢谢您的分享!
Participant 12: 嗯嗯不客气。

# Appendix 14
# Interview Record 13【Participant 13】

Time: 6:30 pm-7:30 pm, October 5, 2019 [LA Time]
Interviewee: Participant 13, a game designer of a big game corporation in China
Interviewer: Deng Zhaoxia
Interview tool: Wechat
Language: Chinese
Deng: 好的,感谢您接受我的采访。首先我想问一下您在游戏公司担任什么职务?
Participant 13: 我主要是负责游戏开发的。
Deng: 好的,不知您了解游戏Mod吗?
Participant 13: 您是指玩家制作的那些游戏模组吗?
Deng: 是的,大概就是那个意思。不知您觉得那些玩家在游戏过程中使用编辑器或者是外部软件对游戏进行修改的行为对游戏企业来说是好还是坏呢?
Participant 13: 这有利有弊吧!说实话现在这种游戏编辑修改还是很流行的。我是负责游戏开发的,平时也会去借鉴那些玩家制作的模组进行创新完善。不瞒您说,有时我们也会直接将一些好的游戏模组用在我们的新游戏中了。我觉得大多数玩家还是比较喜欢这种模式的吧!但有时我们也担心那些玩家制作的模组会侵犯别的商家的知识产权,这时可能我们也会面临侵权风险。
Deng: 那不知你们公司承认那些玩家享有这些游戏Mod的知识产权或者说版权吗?
Participant 13: 一般我们都不会承认的。我们的合同会严格规定他们在游戏中制作的这些模组就是属于我们游戏公司的。不过我也发现有些公司为了鼓励玩家玩,的确会承认玩家也可以和游戏公司一起享有权利,但那些权利一般也是受公司制约的。
Deng: 那你们公司有提供一些付费的游戏Mod吗?您是怎么看的?
Participant 13: 我们公司自己会研发一些游戏模组供玩家替换玩,那些模组大多数是要付费的。但我们还没有提供玩家上传的模组是付费的。现在有一些模组分享网站上的应该也是免费的,付费的应该还比较少。
Deng: 那您觉得玩家制作的游戏Mod付费合理吗?



Z. Deng, *Constructing an Eco-Balanced Copyright Regime for the Video Game Industry in China*, https://doi.org/10.1007/978-981-96-6056-8

Participant 13: 这个从我个人的角度还是合理的,毕竟像我们这些开发人员去制作这些模组时也是花费了大量时间和精力的,相较来说那些玩家也是付出了劳动的。
Deng: 好的,那除了用合同规定外,您公司还会采取什么措施来制止一些不好的Mod吗?比如说一些作弊的模组?
Participant 13: 对于那些作弊组件我们都会启用严格的技术保护措施的。如果他们越过了那些措施,那只能走法律程序了。
Deng: 好的。那从您的角度看,您觉得游戏公司设计游戏画面的目的主要是什么呢?
Participant 13: 我设计这个游戏画面的话,主要是要让这画面具有足够的可玩性。这要考虑的有很多,比如画面的美术、游戏题材、规则玩法呀,都需要综合考虑的。只有这样才能提高玩家的体验感,吸引更多玩家。
Deng: 嗯嗯。那您公司现在有运营游戏直播的业务吗?
Participant 13: 有的。这也是我们公司的主要业务之一。
Deng: 那您平时应该也看过游戏直播吧?
Participant 13: 是的。
Deng: 那您觉得在游戏直播时这些游戏直播画面有什么作用呢?
Participant 13: 在我们公司直播的话主要是直播一些竞技类的游戏,因为这类游戏一般是可以对战的,就像体育赛事一样具有观赏性,人们会很期待双方对战的场面情况。当然也有一些直播窗口是专门用来直播一些新游戏的,这一般会起到宣传的作用吧!现在我们也推出了直播平台供一般的游戏玩家直播,这类直播的画面就丰富多彩了,很多玩家都会互动成为好友。
Deng: 那您觉得您自己设计的原游戏画面被用在直播中的时候作用有变化吗?
Participant 13: 我觉得这个还是原来的游戏画面,可能用在直播中就有不同的作用,就像我刚才说的那些。
Deng: 好的。那从您的角度来看,您觉得游戏直播对传统的网络游戏有没有影响呢?
Participant 13: 这是肯定的。像以前我们开发游戏一般都是考虑怎么让剧情、人物画面更吸引玩家,现在的话往往会多考虑一下怎么跟直播连结。而且我们在开发竞技类游戏时,上级都是要求将来把它们纳入直播范围的,所以我们就需要更精心设计研发。
Deng: 您的意思是说游戏直播对您开发游戏也多了个考量因素是吧?
Participant 13: 是的没错。
Deng: 好的。那您觉得游戏直播的成本相对于收益来说怎么样?
Participant 13: 对我们公司来说游戏直播的成本就包括一些像游戏开发的成本、主播签约费用、直播平台的设计、以及其他一些费用。而收益就主要是靠广告费、流量兑现以及粉丝给主播的礼物打赏。具体的收入能达到多少这公司也不会透露,所以我也不是太清楚。但总的来说直播业务还是很赚钱的,不然我们公司也不会很重视这一块。
Deng: 嗯嗯明白。其实你们公司一般是直播自己开发的游戏的对吧?但如果说你们直播平台要直播其他公司开发的游戏,或者说其他直播平台直播你们开发的游戏,然后法律规定在这种情况下直播平台需要向原来的游戏开发公司支付一定的版权费用,或者说直播平台需要先获得游戏开发公司的授权才可以直播,这样的规定合不合理呢?

Participant 13: 这个问题如果从我作为游戏开发者的角度看当然是支持的。就比如说这款游戏原本是你开发的,那你肯定拥有这款游戏的知识产权或者版权,如果我拿这款游戏去直播赚钱却不支付版权费用给你的话,你心里当然也不乐意,这样是不是会导致很多人不愿意去开发游戏而直接去直播游戏了呢?不过如果从公司的角度出发,对于大型的电竞赛事,现在像我们这样的大厂一般都是直播自己的游戏而不会去直播别的公司开发的游戏的,这是因为直播能起到宣传效果,这也是我们自己要发展直播业务的原因之一。如果从这个角度看的话,直播是不是对原来的游戏起到了推广作用?那为什么还要去支付费用给游戏开发商呢?而且据说起初一些自己没有直播业务的游戏公司还要花钱让直播平台帮忙直播宣传!这样的话再谈所谓的版权费用以及授权的问题是不是有点多余?如果每直播一款游戏都需要经过原开发商授权,问题会不会搞得更复杂?同时需要注意的是现在都是主播在直播,除了名气大的主播会与直播平台签约,很多小主播都是自己直播的,这样的话你说他们怎么去支付版权费用给原游戏开发商?这一系列问题你都是需要考虑的。

Deng: 好的,非常感谢您的意见。我的采访就到此结束。谢谢!

Participant 13: 好的。不客气!

The manufacturer's authorised representative in the EU is Springer Nature Customer Service Centre GmbH, Europaplatz 3, 69115 Heidelberg, Germany. If you have any concerns regarding our products, please contact ProductSafety@springernature.com

Printed and bound by CPI Group (UK) Ltd, Croydon, CR0 4YY

01/10/2026

02225923-0007